JOACHIM JERE

THE EUCHARISTIC WOR

JOACHIM JEREMIAS

THE EUCHARISTIC
WORDS OF JESUS

SCM PRESS LTD

BLOOMSBURY STREET LONDON

Translated by Norman Perrin from the German,
Die Abendmahlsworte Jesu
3rd edition published 1960 by Vandenhoeck & Ruprecht, Göttingen
with the author's revisions to July 1964

334 00414 4
FIRST PUBLISHED 1966
SECOND IMPRESSION 1973
© JOACHIM JEREMIAS 1966
PRINTED IN GREAT BRITAIN BY
REDWOOD PRESS LIMITED
TROWBRIDGE, WILTSHIRE

CONTENTS

PREFACE TO THE NEW ENGLISH EDITION

THIS IS A fresh translation based on the third German edition (*Die Abendmahlsworte Jesu*[3], Göttingen, 1960), which, in contrast with the second edition (1949) upon which the original English translation (Oxford, 1955) was based, has been thoroughly revised and much enlarged. In addition to what had been written on the Eucharistic Words since the second edition, the Qumran Scrolls and recent research on the Passover of the Quartodecimanians called for special consideration. The section on 'The Contribution of Astronomy' was reworked (p. 36ff.). A study on 'The Influence of Worship upon the Transmission of the Eucharistic Texts' was added as chapter III (pp. 106ff.). In chapter IV ('The Oldest Text of the Eucharistic Words of Jesus'), which is devoted to recovering the oldest form of the eucharistic tradition, the section dealing with the semitisms has been enlarged (pp. 173ff.). Although their number has been increased in treating the Markan account, I no longer consider this account as the oldest form of the tradition; rather I should prefer to think that in the earliest times we have to reckon with quite a number of parallel versions behind which the *Urform* lies hidden. Whether this was Aramaic or Hebrew must remain an open question; we shall have to be content to state that the text was probably passed on in both idioms (pp. 196ff.). Linguistic evidence points to a pre-liturgical historical account as the oldest stage of tradition (pp. 191ff.). The final chapter V ('The Meaning of the Eucharistic Words of Jesus') was the one most affected by revision. Jesus' avowal of abstinence is given a fresh interpretation by means of the Quartodecimanian texts (pp. 207ff.). The *anamnesis* problem is approached on the basis of a comprehensive collection of the relevant materials (pp. 237ff.). Finally, guided by the Late Jewish exegesis of Ps. 118.25ff. referring to the antiphonal choir which was to greet the Messiah at his *parousia*, it is shown that the Lord's Supper was from the very beginning an anticipation—or more precisely an 'antedonation'—of the final consummation (pp. 255ff.).

My aim has been to present the historical evidence as the basis for a careful exegesis of the Eucharistic Words. Studies in the Lord's Supper not infrequently leave the reader with the uneasy feeling that the author has unconsciously read into the text what he would like to find. Must we not all learn better to listen to the text alone? To do this, research into Jesus' environment provides an indispensable help. The endeavour to re-create the world in which Jesus lived and which lent him its language will give us many fresh insights. No doubt it will also confront us with unexpected and bewildering questions which, however, will eventually deepen our understanding, if we do not attempt to evade them. Exegesis is, after all, a matter of obedience.

My warmest thanks are due to Dr N. Perrin of the University of Chicago Divinity School, who spared no time and pains to present this book in an exact and readable translation. I thank him especially for translating the Greek and Semitic material into English, and for changing book references to their English translations, if such were available. I am also indebted to Dr C. Burchard and Dr B. Schaller who helped to prepare the manuscript and see it through the press.

May this study not only serve to promote further research, but also to help those who carry on the ministry of the Word.

Göttingen   JOACHIM JEREMIAS
July 1964

TRANSLATOR'S NOTE

PROFESSOR Jeremias' work is, by its nature, rich in quotations from foreign languages, ancient and modern, and in the German edition these are always given in the original. For this English edition, however, an attempt has been made to render them all into English, except where the quotation was short and the meaning self-evident, or where the words of the original were necessary to the argument. Further, where books are quoted in languages other than English, the vast majority of the instances, an attempt was made to locate an English translation or edition and, where such was found, to quote or refer to it. Lastly, the references to the New Testament, always quoted by Professor Jeremias in Greek, have been either given in English or are accompanied by an English translation, depending upon whether the Greek was necessary to the argument. This has proven to be an immensely complicated task and the translator begs indulgence for the inconsistencies that have resulted; he felt it was necessary to take every possible step to render the book into as widely available and readily understandable a form as was possible, even at the necessary risk of inconsistency.

The translator wishes to thank Dr H. H. Oliver of Boston University for preparing a first draft of the translation of Chapter IV and for help at various other parts of the work.

ABBREVIATIONS

APOT	R. H. Charles (ed.), *The Apocrypha and Pseudepigrapha of the Old Testament in English*, Oxford, 1913; reissued 1963
ATR	*Anglican Theological Review*, Evanston, Ill.
Bauer: A. and G.	W. F. Arndt and F. W. Gingrich, *A Greek-English Lexicon of the New Testament and Other Early Christian Literature*, Cambridge and Chicago, 1957 (adapted ET of W. Bauer, *Griechisch-Deutsches Wörterbuch zu den Schriften des N.T. und der übrigen urchristlichen Literatur*[4], Berlin, 1952)
BFChTh	Beiträge zur Förderung christlicher Theologie, Gütersloh
Billerbeck	H. L. Strack–P. Billerbeck, *Kommentar zum Neuen Testament aus Talmud und Midrasch*, Munich, I 1922, II 1924, III 1926, IV 1928, J. Jeremias–K. Adolph, V 1956, VI 1961
Blass-Debrunner	F. Blass–A. Debrunner, *A Greek Grammar of the New Testament and Other Early Christian Literature*. A translation and revision of the ninth-tenth German edition by R. W. Funk, Cambridge and Chicago, 1961
BWANT	Beiträge zur Wissenschaft vom Alten und Neuen Testament, Stuttgart
BZAW	Beihefte zur *Zeitschrift für die Alttestamentliche Wissenschaft*, Giessen, Berlin
BZNW	Beihefte zur *Zeitschrift für die Neutestamentliche Wissenschaft*, Giessen, Berlin
CSEL	Corpus Scriptorum Ecclesiasticorum Latinorum, Vienna, Prague, Leipzig
ET	English translation
EvTh	*Evangelische Theologie*, Munich
FRLANT	Forschungen zur Religion und Literatur des Alten und Neuen Testaments, Göttingen

GCS	Die Griechischen Christlichen Schriftsteller der ersten Jahrhunderte, Leipzig, Berlin
HUCA	Hebrew Union College Annual, Cincinnati, Ohio
JBL	Journal of Biblical Literature, Philadelphia, Pa.
JQR	The Jewish Quarterly Review, Philadelphia, Pa.
JTS	The Journal of Theological Studies, Oxford
KlT	Kleine Texte für Vorlesungen und Übungen, Bonn, Berlin
MGWJ	Monatsschrift für Geschichte und Wissenschaft des Judentums, Frankfurt a. M.
MPG	J.-P. Migne (ed.), Patrologiae cursus completus (Series Graeca), Paris
MPL	J.-P. Migne (ed.), Patrologiae cursus completus (Series Latina), Paris
N.F.	Neue Folge
NTA	Neutestamentliche Abhandlungen, Münster
NTD	Das Neue Testament Deutsch, Göttingen
NTS	New Testament Studies, Cambridge
RAC	Reallexikon für Antike und Christentum, Stuttgart, 1950 ff.
RGG	Die Religion in Geschichte und Gegenwart, Tübingen, [1]1909–1913; [2]1927–1932; [3]1957 ff.
RHPhR	Revue d'Histoire et de Philosophie Religieuses, Paris
RSV	Revised Standard Version
SBT	Studies in Biblical Theology, London
ThBl	Theologische Blätter, Leipzig
ThLBl	Theologisches Literaturblatt, Leipzig
ThLZ	Theologische Literaturzeitung, Leipzig, Berlin
ThR	Theologische Rundschau, Tübingen
ThSt	Theologische Studien, Zollikon-Zürich
ThStKr	Theologische Studien und Kritiken, Leipzig
ThZ	Theologische Zeitschrift, Basel
TU	Texte und Untersuchungen, Leipzig, Berlin
TWNT	G. Kittel (ed.), Theologisches Wörterbuch zum Neuen Testament, Stuttgart, 1933ff.
UNT	Untersuchungen zum Neuen Testament, Leipzig
ZAW	Zeitschrift für die alttestamentliche Wissenschaft, Giessen, Berlin
ZDPV	Zeitschrift des Deutschen Palästina-Vereins, Leipzig, Wiesbaden

ZKTh	*Zeitschrift für katholische Theologie*, Vienna
ZNW	*Zeitschrift für die neutestamentliche Wissenschaft*, Giessen, Berlin
ZThK	*Zeitschrift für Theologie und Kirche*, Tübingen
ZWTh	*Zeitschrift für wissenschaftliche Theologie*, Leipzig, Frankfurt a. M.

When quoting the Tosephta I have added page and line of the edition by M. S. Zuckermandel, *Tosefta nach den Erfurter und Wiener Handschriften*, Pasewalk, 1877–88; reprint Jerusalem, 1963.

I

WAS THE LAST SUPPER A PASSOVER
MEAL?[1]

ALL FOUR GOSPELS agree that the day of Jesus' death was a Friday (Mark 15.42; Matt. 27.62; Luke 23.54; John 19.31, 42). Since at the time of Jesus the day was reckoned from sunset to sunset,[2] *this Friday* (from 6 p.m. on Maundy Thursday to

[1] [German *'Passamahl'*. Transl.] The *spelling* 'Passah' with final 'h' is wrong because it is derived from the Hebrew *pesaḥ* whereas 'Passa' is an Aramaic *status emphaticus*.

With regard to the *pronunciation* of the word the following points can be established: (1) In Palestinian Aramaic at the time of Jesus the consonant *p* (except in the case of some foreign loan words) was uniformly pronounced as an aspirate, 'ph', even at the beginning of a syllable (G. Dalman, *Grammatik des jüdisch-palä-stinischen Aramäisch*[2], Leipzig, 1905 [= *Grammatik*], 67f.; W. Gesenius–E. Kautzsch –G. Bergsträsser, *Hebräische Grammatik* I[29], Leipzig, 1918, 39f.; H. Laible, 'Die drei Sprachen Jesu' [I], *ThLBl* 44 [1923], cols. 115f.). We know this especially because of the way in which *p* is regularly represented by φ 'ph' in the second column of the Hexapla (P. E. Kahle, *The Cairo Geniza*[2], Oxford, 1959, 180), from the explicit testimony of Jerome (C. Siegfried, 'Die Aussprache des Hebräischen bei Hieronymus', *ZAW* 4 [1884], 63f.), and by the way in which *p* is pronounced as 'f' among the Samaritans (F. Diening, *Das Hebräische bei den Samaritanern* [Bonner Orientalistische Studien 24], Stuttgart, 1938, 15). Corresponding to this, the Hebrew *pesaḥ* is uniformly transcribed in the Greek texts with an initial aspirate (φ): φασέκ/φασέχ (LXX eighteen times in II Chron. 30, 35; Jer. 38[31]. 8; Philo, *Leg. all.* 3.94; Aq. Josh. 5.10; Sy. Ex. 12.11, 27; Num. 9.2; Josh. 5.10) or φεσέ (Aq. Deut. 16.1) or *phase* (Vulg.). (2) Surprisingly, in the case of the Aramaic *pasḥa* we find a difference in that the Greek representation of this varies between a usual πάσχα (LXX, Philo, NT, Josephus, Aquila, Symmachus, Theodotion) and an occasional φάσκα (Josephus, *Ant.* 5.20; 9.271; 14.21 *v. l.*; 17.213; *Bell.* 2.10 *v. l.*). The pronunciation of *pasḥa* with an initial 'p' is not an irregularity due to the influence of the Greek πάσχειν 'to suffer' (so Dalman, *Grammatik*, 138), but rather the common Greek dissimilation from φ–χ to π–χ which is attested elsewhere (Blass-Debrunner, § 39.2). (3) The vocalization with 'i' (*pisḥa*) in Targum Onḳelos, Jerusalem Talmud and Midrash is late, witness the concurrence of LXX, Philo, NT and Josephus (Laible, *ThLBl* 45, 115f.); this transition from *a* to *i* in a closed syllable can be observed in all dialects of Palestinian Aramaic.

The correct pronunciation of the word is therefore *phasḥa*.

[2] In all that follows it is to be noted that among the Jews at the time of Jesus it

6 p.m. on Good Friday) includes the whole of the Passion in its narrower sense: the Last Supper, Gethsemane, arrest and trial, crucifixion and burial (Mark 14.17–15.47; Matt. 26.20–27.61; Luke 22.14–23.56a; John 13.2–19.42); all the four evangelists agree also on this point.

In view of this agreement, it is all the more surprising that the evangelists apparently differ from one another in a further question, in the question as to *whether this Friday was the first day of the passover festival*, i.e. as to whether or not the Last Supper was a passover meal. The solution of this problem is not only important for the chronology of the life of Jesus, but still more—and here lies the interest theology and the Church have in the question—for the understanding of the eucharistic words of Jesus and for an appreciation of the *heilsgeschichtliche* connections in which the Eucharist stands.[1]

THE PROBLEM

The *synoptic evangelists* hold the view that the Last Supper was a passover meal,[2] and therefore took place in the night of Nisan 14/15.[3]

---

was the uniform practice to have the day begin at sunset—more exactly: with the first appearance of the stars after sunset (b. Ber. 2a, b Bar.). Instructive in this respect is the determining of the boundary between the days in the tradition of the Samaritans. It lay midway between the sun's becoming golden before its setting and the disappearance of the evening red after sunset. So Finḥas ibn Isḥak, *Kitab el-ḥulf ben es-samira wel-yahud* (*c.* 1885), manuscript in my possession, 85 (cf. G. Dalman, 'Das samaritanische Passah im Verhältnis zum jüdischen', *Palästinajahrbuch* 8 [1913, correctly 1912], 123; J. Jeremias, *Die Passahfeier der Samaritaner* [BZAW 59], Giessen, 1932 [= *Passahfeier*], 80). Finḥas adds that the end of the day is therefore some two minutes after sunset.

The fact that in late Judaism the day was reckoned from the evening is shown most clearly in that the Sabbath was 'sanctified' after sunset, and twenty-four hours later at sunset was 'dismissed' (see below, p. 26).

[1] S. Schöffel, 'Offenbarung Gottes im hl. Abendmahl', *Luthertum* 48 (1937), 340–6, 353–72; 49 (1938), 33–54; M. Barth, *Das Abendmahl. Passamahl, Bundesmahl und Messiasmahl* (ThSt 18), Zollikon-Zürich, 1945 [= *Abendmahl*].

[2] Mark 14.12, 14, 16 (par. Matt. 26.17, 18, 19; Luke 22.7, 8, 11, 13); Luke 22.15; also Gospel of the Ebionites in Epiphanius, *Haer.* 30.22.4 (K. Holl, *Epiphanius* I [GCS 25], Leipzig, 1915, 363.4–6).

[3] Again and again we find dilettantes maintaining that at the time of Jesus the passover meal was eaten in the night of Nisan 13/14 (e.g. G. Amadon, 'Ancient Jewish Calendation', *JBL* 61 [1942], 245; 'The Johannine Synoptic Argument', *ATR* 26 [1944], 110f.; 'Important Passover Texts in Josephus and Philo', *ATR* 27 [1945], 115); it is even maintained that this is still today the practice of the Samaritans. All this is fable, cf. Jeremias, *Passahfeier*, 78.

It is true that when Mark 14.12 has (with reference to the previous day ending at sunset): 'and on the first day of Unleavened Bread, when they sacrificed the passover lamb', there is a contradiction between the first half of this time reference and the second. According to the usual reckoning Nisan 15 is the first day of the feast of the Unleavened Bread[1] (only very sporadically in learned discussion is the day of Preparation, Nisan 14, designated the first day of the feast).[2] But the second part of the reference to time ('when they sacrificed the passover lamb') so clearly indicates Nisan 14[3] that only this day can be meant. Mark 14.12 is one instance of a rule which often applies in this gospel: when two time references are given, in what looks like a pleonasm, the second is intended to determine more exactly the first. Examples of this are: 1.32, 'that evening—after sunset' ('evening' can indicate the time both *before* and *after* sunset: the second time reference shows that here the time *after* sunset is meant; sick people could only be carried after the end of the sabbath); 15.42, 'and when evening had come—since it was the day of Preparation, that is, the day before the sabbath' (the second time reference shows that here 'evening' refers to the time before the beginning of the sabbath, i.e. *before* sunset); 1.35, 'and in the morning —a great while before day' ('morning' can be the time both *before* and *after* sunrise; the second phrase shows that the time *before* is

---

[1] LXX (Lev. 23.11), Philo (*De spec. leg.* 2. 155–7), Josephus (*Ant.* 3.250), Targum (Jer. I Lev. 23.11; Num. 28.18) all agree on this. D. Chwolson, *Das letzte Passamahl Christi und der Tag seines Todes*, Leipzig, 1892, ²1908 [= *Passamahl*], has vigorously defended this point.

[2] Billerbeck II, 812–15; J. Mann, 'Rabbinic Studies in the Synoptic Gospels', *HUCA* I (1924), 344f. But Mann offers no evidence: the appeal to eight festival days in Josephus, *Ant.* 2.317 is incorrect, since the eighth day is not Nisan 14 but Nisan 22, which was included by the Jews of the Dispersion. From the evidence offered by Billerbeck both Mek. Ex. 12.15 and b. Pes. 36a are to be eliminated; both of these passages certainly mean by 'the first day of the feast' Nisan 15 and not 14. There remain, as witnesses for the designation of Nisan 14 as the first day of the feast, only: b. Pes. 5a (school of R. Ishmael, died AD 135), j. Pes. 1.27c.43f. (R. Judah, *c.* 150), j. Pes. 1.27a.30 (anonymous), i.e. only limited evidence. The concern is with the exegesis of two scriptural texts. Ex. 12.15 prescribes: 'on the first day (= Nisan 15) you shall put away leaven out of your houses'; but at the time of Jesus the established custom was to put away this leaven already on Nisan 14 (Pes. 1.1ff.), and so there arose a contradiction between the prescribed law and the established custom, unless it were possible to read the 'first day' in Ex. 12.15 as a reference to Nisan 14. In this context 'day' was wrongly supplied to *barišon* in Ex. 12.18 ('month' should have been supplied) so that in this text Nisan 14 was designated the 'first day'.

[3] The slaughter of the passover animals took place in the afternoon of Nisan 14. I gave the evidence for this in *Passahfeier*, 78–80.

meant); 16.2, 'and very early in the morning of the first day of the week they went to the tomb—when the sun had risen' (the second time reference shows that here 'morning' means *after* sunrise); 14.30, 'today—this very night' ('today' comprises the whole twenty-four-hour day beginning after sunset, both night and day, the second time reference shows that the actual concern is with the hours immediately following); 4.35, 'on that day—when evening had come'; 10.30, 'now—in this time'; 13.24, 'in those days—after that tribulation'; 14.43, 'and immediately—while he was still speaking'. The same is true in Mark 14.12: the time reference 'on the first day of Unleavened Bread', which is most probably due to a translation error,[1] is unambiguously determined by the further 'when they sacrificed the passover lamb', so that the preparation of the upper room for Jesus and his disciples took place on Nisan 14, the day of Preparation.[2] According to Mark 14.17 par., the celebration of the Lord's Supper then followed that evening, i.e. during the night Nisan 14/15, and *was therefore a passover meal*. This is borne out by Mark 14.14 par. ('where I am to eat the Passover with my disciples') and 14.16 par. ('and they prepared the Passover'). Now, all of these verses come from the passage, Mark 14.12–16, which we must regard as an expansion of the original passion narrative.[3] It is therefore important that another text which represents an early, independent, separate tradition,[4] Luke 22.15 ('I have earnestly desired to eat this Passover[5]

[1] That has been recognized by Chwolson, *Passamahl*, 180. However, his suggested *bywm' ḳmy dpsḥ'* is open to correction because he, without any justification, represents ἄζυμα by *psḥ'* to support his chronological theory (on which see below, pp. 22f.). We should read: *bywm' ḳmy dpṭyry'*, which can have two meanings: (1) *on the day before the* ἄζυμα = πρὸ μιᾶς τῶν ἀζύμων (see following note), i.e. Nisan 14, which is the original meaning of Mark 14.12; (2) *on the first day of the* ἄζυμα = τῇ πρώτῃ ἡμέρᾳ τῶν ἀζύμων, which is the translation error we read in Mark 14.12.

[2] So Luke 22.7 has understood the Markan text: 'Then came the day of Unleavened Bread (= the day on which at 11 a.m. all leavened food was burnt = Nisan 14) on which the passover lamb had to be sacrificed' (= Nisan 14).

[3] See below, pp. 92f.

[4] See below, pp. 160–2.

[5] L. von Sybel, 'Das letzte Mahl Jesu', *ThStKr* 95 (1923/24), 119, suggests that Luke 22.15–18 is a free transformation of the eucharistic formula by Luke, who substituted 'passover' for 'bread'. He is followed by R. Bultmann, *The History of the Synoptic Tradition*, Oxford, 1963 [= *Tradition*], 266f., who, with a certain reserve, raises the question whether in Luke 22.15 bread was originally mentioned instead of passover. The same suggestion is made more confidently by A. Loisy, 'Les origines de la cène eucharistique' in *Congrès d'histoire du Christianisme* (A. Loisy Festschrift) I (*Annales d'histoire du Christianisme* I), Paris, 1928, 80. This violent emendation of the text is against all probability: the tradition tends (as, e.g., the

with you') witnesses to the paschal character of the Last Supper, for
the 'this' permits linguistically (however the rest of the verse may be
understood) scarcely any other reference than to a lamb actually
present before Jesus,[1] as, in fact, the Lukan source had already understood it.[2] We can add to this New Testament testimony the witness
of the Quartodecimanians ('On the 14th the Lord ate the lamb with
the disciples, on the great day of Unleavened Bread [Nisan 15] he
suffered')[3] which is especially weighty because the Quartodecimanian
passover celebration represents, as we know today,[4] the direct
continuation of the primitive Christian passover.[5]

In *John* it is different. It is true that the statements of the fourth
evangelist about the time of the Last Supper are not unanimous, as
we shall see,[6] but there is at least *one* place where he differs from the
synoptic dating: John 18.28. The Jewish accusers of Jesus 'did not
enter the *praetorium*, so that they might not be defiled, but might eat
the Passover'. Since, according to John 18.28 (cf. 19.14), at the time
of Jesus' accusation before Pilate the passover lambs had not yet been
eaten, the crucifixion of Jesus occurred, according to John, on Nisan
14, the day of Preparation. The Last Supper was therefore not a
passover meal (John, in fact, nowhere maintains that it was), but
rather took place twenty-four hours earlier. The same dating is to be
found in the Gospel of Peter,[7] perhaps in dependence upon John.[8]

---

feeding stories show) to be modified towards conformity to the eucharistic formula,
not away from it.

[1] C. K. Barrett, 'Luke XXII.15: To Eat the Passover', *JTS* 9 (1958), 305–7.
[2] We shall see that the tradition preserved in Luke has seen in the Last Supper,
as described in Luke 22.15–20, the prototype of the Christian passover celebration.
It has therefore certainly conceived the Last Supper as a passover meal (cf.
below, pp. 123f.).
[3] *Chronicon paschale* (L. Dindorf, *Chronicon Paschale* I [Corpus Scriptorum Historiae
Byzantinae 16], Bonn, 1832, 14.1–3). Further evidence below, pp. 83f.
[4] See below, p. 122 n. 3.
[5] Concerning the Quartodecimanian passover tradition and passover festival
see below, pp. 122–4, and above all pp. 216f.
[6] See below, pp. 79–82.
[7] 2.5 (M. R. James, *The Apocryphal New Testament*, Oxford, 1924, 91): Jesus'
trial and crucifixion took place 'before the first day of Unleavened Bread' (=
Nisan 14). On the other hand, as G. Dalman, *Jesus-Jeschua*, London and New
York, 1922 (ET of *Jesus-Jeschua*, Leipzig, 1922), 89, rightly supposed, the often
quoted passage b. Sanh. 43a (Bar.): 'on the day of preparation Jeshu was hanged'
does not refer to Jesus but to a namesake, a disciple of R. Joshua b. Peraḥiah
(*c.* 100 BC), cf. b. Sanh. 107b (Bar.) par. b. Soṭ. 47a.
[8] E. Schwartz, 'Osterbetrachtungen', *ZNW* 7 (1906), 26 n. 2.

This brings us to the *problem* with which we shall be concerned in the first part of our work: John locates the Passion in its narrower sense, i.e. all the events from the Last Supper to the Burial, during the night of Nisan 13/14 and Nisan 14, the synoptics during the night of Nisan 14/15 and Nisan 15. To put it differently: according to John all the events occurred on the day of Preparation; according to the synoptics on the day which began with the eating of the passover meal, the first day of the passover festival. According to John it was a day the sanctification of which through cessation of work varied very much from place to place;[1] according to the synoptics a high festival day. According to John the Last Supper was an ordinary evening meal; according to the synoptics a passover meal with its solemn ritual. Who is right?

Attempts at harmonization, which seek to bring the synoptic and Johannine datings into agreement, are possible, and have been attempted, in three ways.

1. *The synoptics are right and John should be interpreted accordingly* (the view of the medieval Latin Church, which accordingly used unleavened bread at Holy Communion, and of the Reformers). Those who follow this course have to interpret the word 'passover' in John 18.28 so that it does not denote the paschal lamb. In this case 'to eat the passover' must either be interpreted in the light of II Chron. 30.22 as 'to celebrate the (seven day) feast of Unleavened Bread',[2] or in the light of such Talmudic sayings as 'to eat the paschal sacrifices'.[3] As the reading of II Chron. 30.22 is uncertain (cf. LXX), only the second possibility is admissible. It is true that the paschal sacrifices (*ḥagigah*) which were eaten during the seven days of the feast (Nisan

---

[1] Pes. 4.1 distinguishes between places where work went on until noon on the day of Preparation, and places where men did not work (as long as that). Pes. 4.5: in Judaea they work until noon; in Galilee the Shammaites demand that work should be stopped completely, whereas the Hillelites prohibit it from sunrise only. Pes. 4.6: tailors, hairdressers and fullers may work on the day of Preparation, and according to R. Jose b. Judah shoemakers as well.

[2] So, e.g., Th. Zahn, *Das Evangelium des Johannes*[5, 6], Leipzig-Erlangen, 1921, 631–3, cf. *Einleitung in das Neue Testament* II[3], Leipzig, 1907, 523, 534–6; cf. C. C. Torrey, 'The Date of the Crucifixion according to the Fourth Gospel', *JBL* 50 (1931), 239f.

[3] So already J. Lightfoot, *Hebrew and Talmudical Exercitations* on John 18.28 (in *The Whole Works of the Rev. John Lightfoot* [ed. J. R. Pitman] XII, London, 1823, 404f.); Chr. Schoettgen, *Horae hebraicae et talmudicae* [I], Dresden-Leipzig, 1733, 400f.; C. C. Torrey, *op. cit.*, 237–9; 'In the Fourth Gospel the Last Supper Was the Paschal Meal', *JQR* 42 (1951–2), 244, and many others.

15–21) sometimes are called *pesaḥ*[1] in accordance with Deut. 16.2 and II Chron. 35.7, so that John 18.28 could be referred to Nisan 15. The meaning then would be that the members of the Sanhedrin did not enter the *praetorium* lest they be defiled and so prevented from eating the paschal sacrifices (*ḥagigah*). The dating of John would then agree with that of the synoptics. But it is extremely questionable whether the Gentile Christians for whom John wrote would be able to understand such a linguistic subtlety.[2] They would be bound to understand the phrase 'but they might eat the passover' of John 18.28 in its normal sense, as, e.g., in Luke 22.15, as referring to the eating of the paschal lamb, i.e. to understand John's report as implying that Jesus was already buried when the paschal lamb was eaten in the houses of Jerusalem.

2. *John is right and the synoptics should be interpreted accordingly* (the view of the Greek Church, which consequently uses leavened bread at Holy Communion). Those who follow this course have to assume that Jesus on his own authority anticipated the passover meal[3] and, perhaps because he foresaw that at the regular time of the passover meal he would be already dead, celebrated it one day earlier than the people, i.e. very early on Nisan 14 (which began at sunset). But this point of view breaks down in view of the wording of Mark 14.12 par., and also because a private, anticipatory celebration of the passover was an impossibility.[4]

3. *Both the synoptics and John are right* (a widely held view in post-Reformation times). Those who follow this course have to assume that the contemporaries of Jesus *celebrated the passover meal on two*

---

[1] Billerbeck II, 837f.

[2] Dalman, *Jesus-Jeshua*, 87f.; Billerbeck II, 839f.

[3] So, e.g., L. J. Rückert, *Das Abendmahl*, Leipzig, 1856, 45; Franz Delitzsch, 'Passah', in E. C. A. Riehm, *Handwörterbuch des Biblischen Altertums* II, Bielefeld-Leipzig, 1884, 1143; A. Merx, *Das Evangelium Matthaeus* (Die vier kanonischen Evangelien nach ihrem ältesten bekannten Texte II. 1), Berlin, 1902 [= *Matthaeus*], 377–82; H. E. D. Blakiston, 'The Lukan Account of the Institution of the Lord's Supper', *JTS* 4 (1902–3), 548–55; P. Joüon, *L'Évangile de Notre-Seigneur Jésus-Christ* (Verbum salutis V), Paris, 1930, 432; J. Schniewind, *Das Evangelium nach Markus* (NTD 1)[10], Göttingen, 1963 [= *Markus*], 179f.; K. H. Rengstorf, *Das Evangelium nach Lukas* (NTD 3)[9], Göttingen, 1962 [= *Lukas*], 241; O. Procksch, 'Passa und Abendmahl', in H. Sasse, *Vom Sakrament des Altars*, Leipzig, 1941, 19–25, and others.

[4] Billerbeck II, 844f., and IV, 49, who rightly refers to Zeb. 1.3; Tos. Pes. 3.8 (162.2). It should be noted that such a private, anticipatory celebration of the passover would have been a serious breach of the Mosaic law. G. Dalman, *The Words of Jesus*, Edinburgh, 1909 (ET in revised form of *Die Worte Jesu*[1], Leipzig, 1898) [= *Words*], 48; *Jesus-Jeshua*, 88f., sharply denies this attempt at harmonization.

consecutive days in the year of his death. This view has been taken on the one hand by D. Chwolson,[1] followed by J. Klausner,[2] I. Zolli[3] and, with an insignificant modification, M.-J. Lagrange,[4] and on the other by J. Lichtenstein,[5] followed by H. L. Strack[6] and P. Billerbeck.[7] Chwolson assumes that at the time of Jesus the passover lambs were still slaughtered in the twilight of the evening of Nisan 14/15 in accordance with the rule of Ex. 12.6; Lev. 23.5; Num. 9.3, 5, cf. 11f. Since in the year of Jesus' death Nisan 15 fell on a Sabbath, with the consequent coincidence of Sabbath and the slaughter of the passover lambs, the lambs were slaughtered in this year one day earlier, i.e. at dusk Nisan 13/14. The Pharisaic section of the people, including Jesus and his disciples, celebrated the passover meal immediately after the slaughter, i.e. in the night Nisan 13/14; the Sadducean section,[8] however, at the usual time, i.e. in the night Nisan 14/15. So both the synoptics and John are right; the former in describing the Last Supper as a passover meal, the latter in saying that on the day of the crucifixion the passover meal had yet to take place. This ingenious conjecture breaks down in the face of three difficulties: (a) it is true that down to the second century BC the passover lambs were slaughtered in the evening twilight so that the coincidence of passover and Sabbath, which Chwolson assumes for the year of Jesus' death, could occur, if Nisan 15 was a Sabbath. In that event, however, the slaughter would not be brought forward a whole twenty-four hours[9] but only four to six hours, to the afternoon of Nisan 14, as is shown by, among other things, the ancient practice of the Samaritans, which is still valid today.[10] (b) But such an exceptional bringing for-

---

[1] Chwolson, *Passamahl*.

[2] J. Klausner, *Jesus of Nazareth*, London, 1925 (many subsequent reprints), 326–8.

[3] I. Zolli, *Il Nazareno*, Udine, 1938, 207–9, with insignificant modifications.

[4] M.-J. Lagrange, *L'Évangile de Jésus-Christ* (Études bibliques), Paris, 1928 [= *Évangile*], 495–7.

[5] N. N., *Aus J. Lichtenstein's hebräischem Kommentar zum Neuen Testament* (Schriften des Institutum Judaicum zu Leipzig 43), 1895, 24–29; J. Lichtenstein, *Commentary on St Matthew* (in Hebrew)[2], Leipzig, 1913, 122ff. on Matt. 26.18.

[6] H. L. Strack, *Pᵉsaḥim*, Leipzig, 1911, 10*.

[7] Billerbeck II, 847–53.

[8] According to Lagrange (*Évangile*, 497), the Galileans.

[9] Chwolson, *Passamahl*, 43: 'When the 14th fell on a Friday there was no other solution than to bring forward the slaughter of the sacrificial lamb to the preceding day, i.e. Thursday the 13th.' Chwolson's error is contained in the words: 'there was no other solution'.

[10] Jeremias, *Passahfeier*, 1f., 83–86, especially 83. I have myself witnessed in 1931 such a bringing forward of the passover slaughter because of the Sabbath. In that

ward of the slaughter is quite out of the question for the year of Jesus' death; after the second century BC the general practice was not to slaughter the passover lambs in the evening twilight of Nisan 14/15, but in the afternoon of Nisan 14, after 2 p.m.[1] So there could be no collision of passover and Sabbath even if Nisan 15 fell on a Sabbath in the year of Jesus' death.[2] (c) It is out of the question that the Sadducees should have slaughtered the passover lamb in the evening twilight of Nisan 13/14 and then not have eaten it for twenty-four hours, because Ex. 12.10 forbids anything to be left over until the next morning. This consideration completely invalidates Chwolson's theory.

Lichtenstein, Strack and Billerbeck assume that in the year of Jesus' death the Sadducees and the Pharisees dated differently the beginning of the month of Nisan, which was determined by the first sighting of the new light.[3] Their argument runs as follows: The difference was connected with the stubborn conflict between these two groups concerning the dating of Pentecost, which arose out of different interpretations of Lev. 23.11. The Pharisees had determined Nisan 1, and therefore also the day of the passover meal (Nisan 15), one day earlier than the Sadducees, and the two parties had compromised by making an exception and having two consecutive days for the passover slaughter and the following passover meal in that year; the Pharisaic party, and with them Jesus and his disciples, held both one day earlier than the Sadducees. The synoptics are following the Pharisaic reckoning of the days of the month, John the Sadducaic, and this explains the differences in dating between the synoptic gospels and John. This theory has been so thoroughly and carefully argued, especially by Billerbeck,[4] that its possibility has to be admitted. Its weakness is that it is wholly conjectural; there is no evidence that the passover lambs were ever slaughtered on two

---

year Nisan 15 fell, according to the Samaritan reckoning, on a Sabbath (May 2, 1931) and the slaughter took place on Nisan 14—at 12.30 p.m. This Samaritan practice is not the only evidence for the fact that the slaughter was brought forward only four to six hours; it can be confirmed by the generally accepted practice among the Jews at the time of Jesus, as I have shown op. cit., 84.

[1] Jub. 49.10, 19: from 'the third part of the day' onwards; Philo, De spec. leg. 2.145: 'beginning at noon'; further evidence in Passahfeier, 79, cf. 83–85.
[2] In such a case the slaughter took place one hour earlier than usual in view of the Sabbath (Pes. 5.1).
[3] See below, pp. 36f.
[4] Billerbeck II, 847–53.

consecutive days in the Temple, and it seems most unlikely that such a thing ever could have happened.[1]

J. Pickl[2] has a simpler solution: the great number of passover participants made it impossible for all of them to slaughter their lambs on Nisan 14 and then celebrate the ritual meal, as there was not sufficient room in the houses. So the custom developed that the Galileans slaughtered their lambs on Nisan 13 (hence the rest day in Galilee on Nisan 14: Pes. 4.5, see above, p. 20 n. 1), and the Judeans theirs on Nisan 14. However, when Pickl adduces as evidence for this a comparison between Josephus, *Ant.* 3.249, seven-day ἄζυμα, and 2.317, eight-day ἄζυμα, he is incorrect—the second passage refers to the practice of the Dispersion where the Jews celebrated all festivals one day longer than in Palestine. There is therefore no evidence for Pickl's thesis; it, too, remains pure conjecture.

Lastly, an ingenious attempt to harmonize the synoptics and John has been made by A. Jaubert.[3] The authoress takes her point of departure from an altogether remarkable chronology of the passion week which is to be found in the *Syriac Didascalia* 21 (first half of the third century AD), in Victorinus of Pettau (died 304),[4] and in a letter of Epiphanius of Salamis (367/72).[5] According to this chronology Jesus celebrated the Last Supper with his disciples on the Tuesday evening of passion week, and the arrest followed during the subsequent night, Tuesday/Wednesday. The authoress combines this dating with observations concerning a solar calendar which is known to us (unfortunately only in its general principle) from the book of Jubilees and from the Qumran texts. According to this calendar the year comprises 364 days, divided into four quarters of 91 days, with each quarter beginning on a Wednesday, so that the yearly festivals always fell on the same day of the week. There are a good many details concerning this calendar about which we are completely in the dark, e.g. the procedure of intercalation. (The solar year has $365\frac{1}{4}$ days. How the annual excess of $1\frac{1}{4}$ days, 35 days or 5 weeks in the course of 28

---

[1] Further objections were raised by J. Krengel in his review of Billerbeck I in *MGWJ* 70 (1926), 421f.; S. Zeitlin, 'The Date of the Crucifixion according to the Fourth Gospel', *JBL* 51 (1932), 263–8. Already in 1898 G. Dalman (*Words*, 48) had raised strong objections to Lichtenstein's theory.

[2] J. Pickl, *Messiaskönig Jesus*, Munich, 1935, 247f.

[3] A. Jaubert, *La date de la Cène. Calendrier biblique et liturgie chrétienne* (Études bibliques), Paris, 1957.

[4] Victorinus of Pettau, *De fabrica mundi* 3 (J. Haussleiter, *Victorini episcopi Petavionensis opera* [CSEL 49], Vienna-Leipzig, 1916, 4.17–22).

[5] K. Holl, 'Ein Bruchstück aus einem bisher unbekannten Brief des Epiphanius', in *Gesammelte Aufsätze zur Kirchengeschichte* II, Tübingen, 1928, 204–24.

years, was fitted into this calendar we have no idea.) This solar calendar, according to which the passover meal always fell on Tuesday evening, is, in A. Jaubert's view, the basis for the passion week chronology which we find first in the Didascalia. The authoress ventures to declare this passion chronology authentic. Jesus actually celebrated the passover meal with his disciples on Tuesday evening (thereby observing the Essene calendar!) and was arrested during the night Tuesday/Wednesday. The synoptics assume this dating of the passover according to the solar calendar, whereas John follows the official lunar calendar in assuming that in that year the passover meal was celebrated in the evening immediately after Jesus' crucifixion. This gives us the following picture: 'Jesus celebrated the passover meal *on Tuesday evening, the time of the passover meal* according to the ancient sacerdotal calendar. Arrested in the night Tuesday/Wednesday, Jesus died on *Friday Nisan 14, the time of the passover meal* according to the *official* calendar.'[1]

I can only regard this as unfounded. Without going into detailed objections, the decisive observation is that the strange passion week chronology first found in the *Didascalia* is a secondary development out of the fasting practice of the Church, as K. Holl has recognized.[2] As is well known, the Didache already prescribes that Christians should not fast, as did the Pharisees, on Monday and Thursday, but, in order to differentiate themselves from them, on Wednesday and Friday (8.1). But the fasting of the Early Church was, as we shall see in discussing the Christian passover fasting,[3] pre-eminently vicarious fasting for Israel.[4] Thus the new fast days, Wednesday and Friday, were each given a basis by saying, The weekly Wednesday fast is a vicarious fasting for the sin of the Jews in arresting Jesus, the weekly Friday fast for that of crucifixion. It is questionable whether there were any chronological considerations at all in this establishment of, and giving of meaning to, the weekly Wednesday fast. If one wants to find such considerations then one should recall that according to Mark 14.1 par. Matt. 26.2 the arrangements for the betrayal were made with Judas on a Wednesday. Only secondarily, in the third or possibly late second century, was the meaning given to the Wednesday fast made the basis for a new fanciful division of passion week which was linked with an equally fanciful new reckoning of the three days and three nights between the death and resurrection, quite regardless of the contradiction with the statements in the gospels which they involved. These constructions certainly have no historical worth.

[1] Jaubert, *La date de la Cène*, 107.
[2] Holl, *ibid.*
[3] See below, pp. 216f.
[4] The evidence is given by B. Lohse, *Das Passafest der Quartadecimaner* (BFChTh II 54), Gütersloh, 1953 [= *Passafest*]. Miss Jaubert has overlooked this important work.

None of these attempts at harmonization therefore is convincing; the situation still is quite simply that the synoptic and Johannine datings of the Last Supper sharply contradict one another, and that means that the question remains an open one: Was the Last Supper of Jesus a passover meal or not?

THE LAST SUPPER—KIDDUŠ MEAL? ḤABURAH MEAL? ESSENE MEAL?

(a) *Kidduš Meal?*

At the end of the last century a wholly new element was introduced into the discussion: the *kidduš* meal. It was thought that the question —passover meal or not?—could be solved by saying that the Last Supper was neither a passover meal nor an ordinary meal but a *kidduš* meal.

In the realm of exegesis there is scarcely a matter about which so much has been written in error—this must be said quite openly—as about the *kidduš*; so it is necessary next to say something about it.[1]

1. *What is a kidduš?*[2] *kidduš* means sanctification. The *kidduš* is a blessing which was pronounced at the beginning of each Sabbath or feast day. It was quite simple: 'R. Eleazar b. Zadok (born between AD 35 and 40 in Jerusalem)[3] said: My father . . . used to say over the cup, "(blessed be) he who has sanctified the Sabbath day". He did not add a closing benediction.'[4] This blessing marks the separation of the sacred period from the profane at its beginning, just as the *habdalah* ('separation blessing' at the close of Sabbaths and feast days) does at the end. A separation of the *kidduš* or *habdalah* from the sacred day is absolutely unthinkable and without example.

---

[1] I. Elbogen, 'Kiddush', *Jewish Encyclopedia* VII, 483f.; A. Berliner, *Randbemerkungen zum täglichen Gebetbuch* I, 1909, 43, 73ff.; I. Elbogen, 'Eingang und Ausgang des Sabbats nach talmudischen Quellen', in *Festschrift zu Israel Lewy's 70. Geburtstag*, Breslau, 1911, 173–87; *Der jüdische Gottesdienst in seiner geschichtlichen Entwicklung*[2], Frankfurt a. M., 1924 [= *Gottesdienst*], 107–12; G. F. Moore, *Judaism in the First Centuries of the Christian Era* II, Cambridge (Mass.), 1927 [= *Judaism*], 36; J. Jarecki, 'Kiddusch', *Jüdisches Lexikon* III (1929), cols. 685f.; J. Singer, 'Kiddush', *The Universal Jewish Encyclopedia* VI (1942 = 1948), 379f.

[2] Or *keduššah* (fem.).

[3] Cf. A. Schlatter, *Die Tage Trajans und Hadrians* (BFChTh 1.3), Gütersloh, 1897, 8of.

[4] Tos. Ber. 3.7 (6.22). Another, somewhat longer wording of the Sabbath *kidduš* is to be found in b. Ber. 49a, which also gives the feast-day *kidduš*.

2. *How is the ḳidduš performed?* When the first stars appear after sunset[1] the head of the household (on the Sabbath: after lighting the Sabbath candle) says the blessing[2] at table over a cup of wine,[3] in the midst of his family and guests. Then he himself drinks and after him the other people present. In the case that the Friday afternoon meal lasted until the beginning of the Sabbath, or on into the Sabbath itself, the meal was ended[4] and then the *ḳidduš* was inserted into the grace after the meal.[5] In the case of the passover meal, which was the only meal of the year which began after sunset,[6] the sanctification of the feast took place at the beginning of the meal. *The ḳidduš is therefore neither a meal,[7] nor a sacrifice,[8] nor does it have sacrificial significance,[9] but it is just a simple blessing.* 'Ḳidduš meals' (the term is a modern inven-

[1] Cf. above, p. 15 n. 2.

[2] The taking of the wine calls for a further blessing of the wine. The sequence of two blessings (*ḳidduš* and the blessing of the wine) was a matter of dispute between the schools of Shammai and Hillel, i.e. in the first century AD, which shows that the rite was not stereotyped at that time: Ber. 8.1; Pes. 10.2; in more detail Tos. Ber. 6.1 (13.6); Tos. Pes. 10.2 (172.14); cf. b. Pes. 114a; Mek. Ex. 20.8.

[3] The cup is first mentioned *c.* AD 50 (R. Zadoḳ), Tos. Ber. 3.7 (6.24f.); cf. the passage quoted above, p. 26.

[4] So R. Jose (*c.* 150) who certainly in this matter, as often, represents the older tradition: Tos. Ber. 5.2 (11.23) par. b. Pes. 100a (Bar.); 102a, b (Bar.); j. Pes. 10.37b. 37; further Tos. Ber. 5.3f. (11.29).

[5] For the evidence see below, p. 45 n. 4. So R. Eliezer (*c.* 90), the consistent representative of the early tradition, b. Ber. 48b (Bar.). As later (according to Elbogen, *Gottesdienst*, 107, 263, in the time of the Amoraim) the custom arose, first in Babylon and then also in Palestine, of holding a service at the beginning of Sabbaths and feast days, then the meal was interrupted in order to attend the service (Tos. Ber. 5.6 [11.28], said to be the opinion of R. Judah [*c.* 150]), and at a still later period it was postponed until after sunset (Tos. Ber. 5.1 [11.22], also said to be the view of R. Judah), so that the *ḳidduš* was now said at the beginning of the meal. This is still the practice today.

[6] See below, p. 46.

[7] M. Dibelius, *Jesus*, Philadelphia, 1949 = London, 1963 (ET of *Jesus*, Berlin, 1939), 123. M. D. Maxwell, *An Outline of Christian Worship*, London, 1936, 5f., even says that the *ḳidduš* was a custom particularly followed in Messianic circles (!) and actually describes the ritual of a *ḳidduš* meal: first there were religious discussions and then followed a simple meal 'of common bread and wine mixed with water' (!)—all without any kind of support in the sources!

[8] K. G. Goetz, 'Abendmahl und Messopfer' in *Schweizerische Theologische Zeitschrift* 35 (1918), 15–24: the Lord's Supper is a *ḳidduš* and therefore a sacrifice, 'because *ḳidduš* means nothing other than sanctification, dedication: that is to say, sacrifice' (p. 16)!!

[9] I. M. Nielen, *Gebet und Gottesdienst im Neuen Testament*, Freiburg i. Br., 1937, 264: 'In view of the uncertainty not only of the sacrificial significance of the *ḳidduš* as such (!!), but also of its equation (!) with the Last Supper, this alone (!) cannot be regarded as sufficient proof for the sacrificial character of the δεῖπνον κυριακόν of primitive Christianity.'

tion) *have never existed, if anything more is meant by them than meals at which a special blessing was inserted into the normal grace because of the fact that a Sabbath or feast day had begun during, or before, the meal.*

F. Spitta,[1] P. Drews,[2] J. Foxley,[3] G. H. Box,[4] P. Batiffol,[5] and R. Otto[6] have maintained that the Last Supper is to be identified with the Sabbath-*kidduš* rite, i.e. the ritual 'sanctification' of the Sabbath. There has been a strong tendency to accept this identification because today at the Sabbath-*kidduš* the blessing of the wine is followed by the breaking of bread which begins the meal. But this combination of blessing the wine and breaking the bread arose only in the late Tannaitic, or perhaps early Amoraic, period as we saw,[7] as a consequence of the development of a Friday evening service in Babylon. It does not go back to the time of Jesus. Above all, however, the sanctification of the Sabbath took place on Friday evening after sunset, whereas the Last Supper, according to the unanimous testimony of all four gospels, was held on Thursday evening. How should Jesus have arrived at the idea of celebrating the Sabbath rite on a Thursday evening?[8] W. O. E. Oesterley[9] has therefore explained

[1] F. Spitta, *Zur Geschichte und Litteratur des Urchristentums* I, Göttingen, 1893, 247.

[2] P. Drews, 'Eucharistie', *Realencyclopädie für protestantische Theologie und Kirche*[3] V (1898), 563.

[3] J. Foxley, *Contemporary Review*, February 1899.

[4] G. H. Box, 'The Jewish Antecedents of the Eucharist', *JTS* 3 (1901–2), 357–69: 'I venture to suggest, then, that the real Jewish antecedent of the Lord's Supper was the weekly *Kiddûsh*' (p. 363).

[5] P. Batiffol, *L'Eucharistie*[1], Paris, 1905. Batiffol says in the first editions of his book ([1,2]1905, [3]1906) that the Last Supper exhibits similarities to the Jewish meal on Sabbath-eve (*kidduš*); in the later editions (from [5] 1913) he is more cautious. Cf. *Études d'histoire et de théologie positive* II. *L'Eucharistie. La présence réelle et la transsubstantiation*[8], Paris, 1920 [= *Études* II. *L'Eucharistie*], 136.

[6] R. Otto, 'Vom Abendmahl Christi', *Die Christliche Welt* 31 (1917), col. 246. Independently of the scholars previously mentioned Otto, while taking part in a Jewish sanctification of the Sabbath, reached the conclusion that 'Jesus prayed the *kiddush* with his disciples and at the same time interpreted it so as to give it a particular new meaning' (col. 246). Later Otto realized that this theory was untenable (*Kingdom of God and Son of Man*[2], London, 1943 = Boston, 1957 [ET of a revised edition of *Reich Gottes und Menschensohn*, Munich, 1934], 283f.), but did not want to give it up completely. So he derived the Lord's Supper from rites similar to the *kidduš* 'which had long been known and familiar at certain meals' (*op. cit.*, 284) to which Jesus gave a new meaning. These rites similar to the *kidduš*, for the existence of which not an iota of proof is offered, are Otto's own invention.

[7] See above, p. 27 n. 5.

[8] That the Sabbath *kidduš*, under the influence of the high spiritual ideas of Jesus, was severed 'from its formal connexion with the weekly sabbath' (Box, *op. cit.*, 363) is an entirely unfounded assumption.

[9] W. O. E. Oesterley, *The Jewish Background of the Christian Liturgy*, Oxford, 1925, 167–79, especially 175.

the Last Supper as a passover *kidduš*, a ritual 'sanctification' of the feast, which is supposed to have taken place on the evening before the feast[1] (i.e. twenty-four hours before its beginning), and G. H. C. Macgregor,[2] H. Huber,[3] F. Gavin,[4] T. H. W. Maxfield[5] and M. Dibelius[6] have followed him without realizing that the idea of a passover *kidduš* which takes place twenty-four hours before the beginning of the feast is *pure fantasy*; not one shred of evidence can be adduced for it.[7] It should have sufficed that already in 1916 F. C. Burkitt had clearly demonstrated that '*Kiddūsh* immediately precedes the actual celebration of the day, e.g., *Kiddūsh* for Sabbath is done on what we call Friday evening, not twenty-four hours earlier':[8] the passover *kidduš* accordingly is the opening of the passover meal and was spoken over the first of the four passover cups. When will this wholly illusory passover *kidduš* on the eve of the feast finally vanish from the discussion?

(b) *Ḥaburah Meal?*

Another way of explaining the external circumstances of the Last Supper has been suggested by H. Lietzmann, who is followed by K. G. Goetz,[9] R. Otto,[10] and G. Dix.[11] These scholars, in seeking to

---

[1] A similar view was held before Oesterley by K. Bornhäuser, *Zeiten und Stunden in der Leidens- und Auferstehungsgeschichte* (BFChTh 26.4), Gütersloh, 1921, 8–13: The Last Supper was an 'opening meal' which took place on the day before the slaughter of the passover lambs. But the support for this quoted by Bornhäuser, p. 8, Mek. Ex. 12.16 ('Honour it [the first day] with eating, drinking and a clean robe'; older text: Siphre Num. 147 on 28.18) certainly refers not to Nisan 14 but to Nisan 15, cf. K. G. Kuhn, *Sifre zu Numeri* (Rabbinische Texte II. Tannaitische Midraschim 3), Stuttgart, 1959, 597f.

[2] G. H. C. Macgregor, *Eucharistic Origins*, London, 1928, 37–39.

[3] H. Huber, *Das Herrenmahl im Neuen Testament* (Diss. Bern), Leipzig, 1929, 21, 70.

[4] F. Gavin, *The Jewish Antecedents of the Christian Sacraments*[2], London, 1933, 65f.

[5] T. H. W. Maxfield, *The Words of Institution*, Cambridge, 1933, 22ff.

[6] M. Dibelius, *Jesus*, 123.

[7] W. O. E. Oesterley's contention that the passover *kidduš* in the year of Jesus' death was an anticipatory Sabbath *kidduš* (p. 175) is a conjecture which piles one impossibility upon another: (1) it is unthinkable that the 'sanctification' of the Sabbath should be moved forward, and (2) it is impossible that the Passover should be 'sanctified' twenty-four hours before it began.

[8] F. C. Burkitt, 'The Last Supper and the Paschal Meal', *JTS* 17 (1915-16), 294.

[9] K. G. Goetz, *Der Ursprung des kirchlichen Abendmahls blosse Mahlgemeinschaft von Jesus und seinen Jüngern oder eine besondere Handlung und Worte von Jesus?*, Basel, 1929, 27. Goetz here refers to his book *Die (²heutige) Abendmahlsfrage in ihrer geschichtlichen Entwicklung*, Leipzig, 1904, ²1907, 243ff., where on p. 245 he quotes a tractate 'Joanith 2.5' [*sic*!] (he means Taanith 2.5, although this passage says nothing about the Amen after grace at meals, but only mentions the Amen in the

understand the Last Supper, refer to 'the Jewish meals, invested with religious solemnity, which might be held by a company of friends, ḥbwrh, whenever they felt the need'.[1] Unfortunately it must be said concerning this suggestion that here again we have an *ad hoc* conjecture for which there is absolutely no evidence. Every meal had 'religious solemnity' because of the grace that was always said, irrespective of whether it was taken alone or in company, or of whether it was a mere snack or a formal meal with which wine was taken. Certainly 'fellowships' are occasionally mentioned in connection with ritual meals, but these 'fellowships' were *ḥaburot miṣwah*, i.e. 'fellowships for the observance of a commandment',[2] and the *ḥaburah* meals in which they took part, and to the cost of which they subscribed, were exclusively[3] *duty* meals, such as those connected with betrothals, weddings, circumcisions, funerals,[4] in which participation as a paying guest was considered meritorious. That these fellowships, which, moreover, were of a charitable nature,[5] or other

---

Synagogue service!), and on pp. 245f. he maintains that it was the practice at Jewish meals to save pieces of the 'consecrated' [*sic*!] bread for the poor, quoting as support for this Sanh. 11 which, however, is a discussion of the crimes punishable by strangulation!! Cf. J. Jeremias, 'Das paulinische Abendmahl—eine Opferdarbringung?', *ThStKr* 108 (1937–8), 124–41.

[10] R. Otto in his valuable study of the Last Supper in *Kingdom of God and Son of Man*, 278–80. Otto sees the Last Supper as belonging to the category 'of the religious festive meal of a *ḥeber* or *ḥaburah*, with sacramental character [*sic*!] and with ritualistic peculiarities' (p. 278). He quotes *verbatim* a sentence from A. Geiger, *Urschrift und Übersetzungen der Bibel*, Breslau, 1857, 123: 'All meals which were held in fellowship were meritorious, and consecrated by a religious character' (p. 278 n. 1), but this statement is erroneous, for Sanh. 8.2—the passage adduced by Geiger—is concerned with a *ḥaburat miṣwah* (cf. what follows in the text above) and not with meals in general. With this erroneous statement the consequences which Otto draws from it also fall to the ground; cf. also above, p. 28 n. 6.

[11] G. Dix, *The Shape of the Liturgy*, Westminster, 1945, 50–70.

[1] H. Lietzmann, *Mass and Lord's Supper*, Leiden, 1953ff., 170f., 185. Lietzmann follows G. Loeschcke, 'Zur Frage nach der Einsetzung und Herkunft der Eucharistie', *ZWTh* 54 [19] (1912), 202, who found evidence for 'semi-cultic meals' in b. R. H. 29a and b. Ber. 46a. Actually both of these passages are concerned with the grace said over the bread at every meal.

[2] Sanh. 8.2; b. Pes. 113b.

[3] K. G. Kuhn, 'Die Abendmahlsworte', *ThLZ* 75 (1950), col. 401.

[4] Tos. Meg. 4.15 (226.13) par. Semaḥoth 12 (Babylonian Talmud, Frankfurt a. M., 1721, IX, fol. 16b).

[5] Billerbeck IV, 276 under 's'; 607–10; J. Jeremias, *Jerusalem zur Zeit Jesu*[3], Göttingen, 1962 (revised edition of [1]1923–37 =[2]1958) [= *Jerusalem*], 282–4. There I have indicated the reasons which suggest that these charitable fellowships were connected with the Pharisaic fellowships, although this can only be suggested, not proven.

'communities of friends' met at any time 'whenever they felt the need to do so' to hold a ritual meal, let alone a sacramental meal,[1] cannot be proven. 'I cannot . . . satisfy myself' that the Jerusalem lay fellowships 'ever held community meals other than the passover meal', judged a great expert already more than fifty years ago;[2] and with only too much justification C. W. Dugmore warns: 'constant repetition of the Ḥabūrāh theme does not constitute proof'.[3]

(c) Essene Meal?

Finally, K. G. Kuhn,[4] in the context of his important works on Qumran, has, with some reservations, drawn upon the ceremonial meal which the Essenes daily ate together as an aid to understanding the Last Supper.[5] In his view the Essene cultic meal has influenced the Eucharist in two ways: it has determined (1) the form of the early Christian meals, and (2) the reports of the evangelists (except Luke) about the Last Supper, but not what Jesus himself did at the Last Supper.

1. In connection with *the early Christian meals* it is indeed notable that both in Jerusalem and at Qumran we find a community whose members gather themselves together daily for a communal meal. The question of Essene influence upon the Christian practice arises immediately;[6] but, in fact, the external differences between the two are too great for this. The meals for which the monks at Qumran assembled together in their monastery twice daily, at eleven o'clock and in the late afternoon,[7] were an integral part and an expression

[1] So H. Lietzmann, *An die Korinther* I. II³, Tübingen, 1931, 56; Otto, *loc. cit.*

[2] A. Büchler, *Der galiläische 'Am-ha'Areṣ des zweiten Jahrhunderts*, Vienna, 1906, 208 n. 2.

[3] C. W. Dugmore, review of G. Dix, *The Shape of the Liturgy*, *JTS* 47 (1946), 109.

[4] I am grateful to my colleague, Professor Kuhn, for reading the following pages in manuscript, and for his acknowledgment that we are in agreement upon the decisive question, despite the fact that we differ upon some of the individual points.

[5] K. G. Kuhn, 'Über den ursprünglichen Sinn des Abendmahls und sein Verhältnis zu den Gemeinschaftsmahlen der Sektenschrift', *EvTh* 10 (1950–1), 508–27. A revised version of this has appeared in English as: 'The Lord's Supper and the Communal Meal at Qumran' in K. Stendahl (ed.), *The Scrolls and the New Testament*, New York, 1957 = London, 1958, 65–93, 259–65.

[6] Kuhn, *op. cit., passim*; F. M. Cross, Jr, *The Ancient Library of Qumran and Modern Biblical Studies*, New York, 1958 [= *Ancient Library*], 177f. Cross also contends that both the Essene meal and the Lord's Supper were anticipations of the Messianic Banquet, but this is questionable so far as the Essene meal is concerned (see below, pp. 35f.).

[7] Josephus, *Bell.* 2.129–33.

of their monastic community life, whereas from the very beginning women took part in the Christian meals,[1] which were held successively 'in private houses'[2] and probably took place only in the evenings.[3] And in finding 'decisive similarity' in the fact that both the Essenes (according to 1QS 6.4–6) and the early Christians (according to Didache 9) began the meal with the blessing of the bread and the wine, Kuhn himself admits that the order differs:[4] for the Essenes it is bread/*tiroš*, in Didache 9 it is wine/bread—which is enough in itself to render a connection between the two improbable. We must add to this the fact that the early Christian rite differs from the Essene meal not only in the order of the blessings but also in its whole procedure (instruction at the beginning, prayers at the end, see below, pp. 118f.). In the early Christian meals we are not dealing with an imitation of Essene practice but with a continuation of daily table fellowship with Jesus. This Kuhn rightly emphasizes, and one cannot quite understand why he then goes on, in the very next sentence, to refer to the cult meal of the Essenes.[5]

2. Is it not, however, possible, that even if the early Christian meals have not been influenced by the Essene practice, at any rate the *reports of the Last Supper* may have been so influenced? It is well known that these reports differ from one another markedly in that Mark and Matthew have the wine-word immediately following the bread-word, whereas Paul and Luke insert 'after supper' between the bread and the wine. Kuhn finds evidence of Essene influence in the Markan-Matthaean account. He is of the opinion that the immediate sequence of blessings over the bread and the wine in Mark and Matthew 'reflects. . . an earlier pre-Christian usage, namely, that of the Essene cult meal', whereas Paul and Luke have 'no longer understood' 'the distinctive character' of the older liturgical formula in Mark and so have returned to 'the common Jewish usage' and divided the words of blessing by the insertion of the meal.[6] But does not this interpretation read too much into the texts?

So far as texts which portray the Essene meal are concerned, we have at the moment only three, all very laconic in their description of the table rite, but in general agreement with one another. 1QS 6.4–6 tells us only that the priest blessed *the bread and the drink* (*tiroš*, on this

---

[1] So we gather from Acts 6.1 (cf. 1.14; 12.12) and from Matt. 14.21; 15.38.
[2] Acts 2.46.   [3] Acts 20.7–12.
[4] Kuhn, 'Lord's Supper', 73, cf. 260 n. 25.
[5] Kuhn, *op. cit.*, 86.   [6] Kuhn, *op. cit.*, 73.

word see below, pp. 51f.) *before* the meal;[1] this is also the ritual
according to 1QSa 2.17–21.[2] According to Josephus, *Bell.* 2.131, the
priest said a prayer *both before and after the meal*.[3] More details can be
added only if one is prepared, with K. G. Kuhn (I am myself sceptical
at this point), to derive the work *Joseph and Asenath* from Therapeutic-
Essene circles and so make use of the five passages in this work in
which reference is made to the bread of life and the cup of blessing,[4]
for in three of these five passages there appears as a third element
beside the bread and wine: the oil of incorruptibility.[5] But in the

[1] 1QS 6.4–6: 'And when they arrange the table for eating, or (*'w*) the *tiroš* for
drinking, each time the priest shall first stretch out his hand to the first part of the
bread or the *tiroš* so that the blessing may be spoken.'

[2] 1QSa 2.17–21 (D. Barthélemy–J. T. Milik, *Qumran Cave I* [Discoveries in the
Judaean Desert I], Oxford, 1955, 111): 'And [when] they gather to the community
tab[le], [or to drink the *t*]*iroš*, and the table of the community is arranged and
[the] *tiroš* [mixed] for drinking, (then) shall [no] one [stretch out] his hand to the
first part of the bread and [of the *tiroš*] before the priest for [he b]lesses the first
part of the bread and the *tiro*[*š* and stretches out] his hand to the bread before
them and after[wards] the anointed (King) of Israel [shall str]etch out his hands
to the bread [. . . ., see below] the whole assembled community, ea[ch according
to] his rank' (continued on p. 35 below). The part missing towards the end
(line 21) has been supplied by Milik (*op. cit.*, 111) [*w'hr ybr*]*kw*: '[and afterwards]
the whole assembled community [shall bl]ess each according to his rank'. But
this reading cannot be maintained, as C.-H. Hunzinger points out ๙ me. Milik
himself remarks that nowhere in the realm of late Judaism do we have any evidence for a practice whereby table companions each say a blessing for themselves
after a blessing had been said 'for all' (*op. cit.*, 118).

[3] Josephus, *Bell.* 2.131: 'The priest prays before the meal, and it is unlawful for
anyone to partake before the prayer. The meal ended, he prays again; thus at the
beginning and at the close they pay homage to God as the bountiful giver of life.'

[4] *Joseph and Asenath* 8.5, 9; 15.5; 16.16; 19.5 (E. W. Brooks, *Joseph and Asenath*
[Translations of Early Documents II. Hellenistic-Jewish Texts 7], London, 1918,
32, 33, 47f., 52, 58. The Greek text is given by P. Batiffol in *Studia Patristica* 1–2,
Paris, 1889–90, 49, 61, 64, 69).

[5] *Joseph and Asenath* 8.5 (Brooks, 32): Joseph refused to kiss the Egyptian
Asenath in greeting: 'It is not meet for a man that worshippeth God, who blesseth
with his mouth the living God, and eateth the blessed bread of life, and drinketh
the blessed cup of immortality, and is anointed with the blessed unction of incorruption, to kiss a strange woman, who blesseth with her mouth dead and deaf
idols and eateth from their table the bread of strangling and drinketh from their
libation the cup of deceit and is anointed with the unction of destruction.' 15.5
(Brooks, 47f.): an angel promises the penitent Asenath, who has destroyed her
idols: 'From this day thou shalt be renewed and refashioned and requickened, and
thou shalt eat the blessed bread of life and drink a cup filled with immortality
and be anointed with the blessed unction of incorruption.' 16.15f. (Brooks, 52):
'Then the divine angel stretched out his right hand and took a small piece from
the (honey)comb and ate, and with his own hand placed what was left in Asenath's
mouth and said to her, "Eat," and she ate. And the angel saith to her: "Lo! now
thou hast eaten the bread of life and hast drunk the cup of immortality and been
anointed with the unction of incorruption." '

Essene texts we find no mention of any such oil; to the contrary, Josephus reports that the Essenes, for ascetic reasons, did not anoint themselves.[1] If we consider these texts as a whole we find in them a great many elements which have no equivalents in the reports of the Last Supper, and which therefore make it unlikely that there is any connection between the two groups of texts: the placing of the bread and wine ritual at the beginning of the meal, the execution of the benedictions by a priest who takes precedence over all others present, and (?) the anointing with oil. To this must be added the fact that, as we shall see,[2] the word *tiroš* has several meanings, so that we cannot be sure that the Essenes drank wine with their meals.

The New Testament texts themselves speak against the possibility that they have been influenced by the meal practice of the Essenes. We must ask: Is it very probable that Mark and Matthew intend the bread-wine sequence to be understood as taking place at the beginning of the meal (only if this is the case do we have a parallel to the Essene practice) when everything we know about the early Christian meals indicates that the eucharistic acts had their place at the end of the meal?[3] Is it at all conceivable that the Markan account reflects a non-Christian usage at variance with the Christian practice? Can we believe that at a very early period, before the time of Paul, the distinctive character of the Markan formula was 'no longer understood', and that because of this the Pauline-Lukan tradition concerning the portrayal of the Last Supper returned to 'the common Jewish usage'?

The remaining arguments that can be adduced for the contention that Mark, Matthew and John portray the Last Supper in the way of an Essene meal are scarcely convincing. Even if John 13.24 may be taken to mean that table rules were strictly enforced (which is not completely certain), such rules were not only to be found among the Essenes, but also among the rabbis.[4] Whether or not the old, pre-Markan tradition assumes that women were excluded from the Last Supper, as they were from Essene meals, will be discussed later.[5] That Jesus is 'not characterized as *paterfamilias*' at the Last Supper (how could he be?) but as 'leader and master of the circle of his twelve disciples'[6] is not only reminiscent of the Essene practice, but also of

---

[1] Josephus, *Bell*, 2.123.   [2] Below, pp. 51f.   [3] See below, pp. 117ff.
[4] An example is to be found in Billerbeck I, 515 under 'y'.   [5] See below, p. 46.
[6] Kuhn, 'Über den ursprünglichen Sinn des Abendmahls', *EvTh* 10, 519; 'Lord's Supper', in *The Scrolls and the New Testament*, 84.

the practice at the passover when this meal was celebrated by a group of pilgrims in Jerusalem, and beyond that of the practice of the rabbis when they held meals with their students, as we know from many examples. Finally, the fact that Jesus offered a blessing not only over the bread but also over the wine corresponds not only to the Essene ritual[1] but also to the general Jewish practice: at the beginning of the festival meal the head of the household offered the blessing 'for all' both over the bread and over the wine,[2] and also at the end of the meal pronounced the benediction over the wine, when no guests were present. In short, the case for Essene influence on the accounts of the Lord's Supper is, in my opinion, not proven.

3. If it is not possible to prove that the Essene meal has influenced either the early Christian Lord's Supper or the accounts of the Last Supper, then there remains for investigation only the possibility that *Jesus himself* was following an Essene pattern as he celebrated the Last Supper. Here one could find a starting-point in that Jesus, according to Luke 22.16, described the passover meal as the type of the passover of the consummation, for it is said that the Essenes saw their meal as an anticipation of the Messianic Banquet.[3] But did they really do this? The only evidence that can be adduced is 1QSa 2.21f., where the description of the order of precedence in which the table companions take their place and help themselves to the food at the future Messianic Banquet (quoted above, p. 33 n. 2) is followed by: 'And they shall proceed according to this rule at every mea[l at which are as]sembled at least ten men.' This sentence is normally read as indicating that every meal of this community is to be regarded as a liturgical anticipation, as a symbolic prior realization of the Messianic meal. But of this the text, which unfortunately breaks off at this point, does not speak. It only says that at every meal where at least ten members of the community are gathered together that ritual and order of precedence of the table companions is to be followed which had been depicted in connection with the Messianic meal. But perhaps even this interpretation reads too much into the text. C.-H. Hunzinger has pointed out to me that it is most improbable that the sentence with which we are concerned had anything at all to do with general, daily meals of the Essenes. Since the whole of the passage

[1] 1QS 6.4–6.

[2] j. Ber. 6.10d.1 par. b. Ber. 43a; the parallel in Tos. Ber. 4.8(9.8), where the words 'and one offers the blessing for all' are missing, is to be interpreted in the same way (with Billerbeck IV, 621).

[3] E.g., Cross, *Ancient Library*, 63–67, 177–9.

which precedes this sentence is concerned with the Messianic time, it is, in fact, most probable that this sentence also has this connection. In the Messianic time the community will be divided into groups (1QSa 1.29–2.1), and the closing sentence says that even the smallest group, the unit of ten, should also follow the depicted ritual, when the Messiah shall have come. If this is correct then 1QSa 2.21f. is not concerned with anticipation of Messianic meals in the present, but with the meals of the Messianic time itself. But even if the Essenes did consider their two daily meals as anticipations of the Messianic meal (for which there is no real evidence, as we have just seen), we must not overlook the fact that the conception and practice of liturgical anticipation was well known to the Jews of the ancient Synagogue. As we shall see, the conclusion of the *Hallel* (Ps. 118.25–29) was recited at the passover meal as liturgical anticipation of the coming of the Messiah,[1] and Jesus knew this interpretation of Ps. 118.25–29.[2] So it is here if anywhere, and not among the Essenes, that we must look for the preformation of the element of anticipation in Luke 22.16.

The results of this investigation are completely negative. An influence of the Essene meal practice upon Jesus has not yet been demonstrated—in this I am completely at one with Kuhn[3]—and unless new texts turn up offering us some unexpected surprises, we can expect no help from the accounts of the Essene meals in understanding the Eucharistic Words of Jesus.

THE CONTRIBUTION OF ASTRONOMY

In recent times various attempts have been made to solve the question of the day of Jesus' death (and with it the question whether or not the Last Supper was a passover meal) with the help of astronomical chronology. At the time of Jesus the beginning of each month was determined empirically by the sighting of the new light. The new moon is, of course, not visible; what is visible is the new light, about one or two days after the new moon, a faintly glowing curved line appearing over the western horizon shortly after[4] sunset.[5]

---

[1] See below, pp. 256ff.: The antiphonal choir at the *parousia*.

[2] See below, pp. 259f.

[3] Kuhn, 'The Lord's Supper' in *The Scrolls and the New Testament*, 84f. Cross also does not maintain that the Last Supper itself was influenced by Essene usage.

[4] If the astronomical new moon comes at nightfall, then shortly before sunset on the second day.

[5] O. Gerhardt, *Der Stern des Messias*, Leipzig-Erlangen, 1922, 119.

In the evening of the twenty-ninth day of each month the priestly calendar commission[1] assembled and waited for witnesses who would testify under oath that the new light had appeared. When at least two trustworthy witnesses appeared before the appearance of the stars[2] the new month was proclaimed. Since it is possible today to calculate the astronomical new moon 'to within a few minutes',[3] astronomers are in a position to reconstruct the Jewish calendar at the time of Jesus and to state, with some measure of probability, the days of the week on which Nisan 14 and 15 fell in the years around AD 30.

There remain, however, two uncertain factors. (1) The *actual visibility* of the new light. If astronomical calculation shows that the new light *could* be seen, it does not necessarily follow that it actually *was* seen, because its actual visibility would depend upon factors which cannot now be reconstructed (whether the atmosphere was clear or misty, the horizon clear or clouded, the dusk light or dark). (2) *Leap-months.* In the course of nineteen years no less than seven leap-months have to be added to even out the difference between the lunar and the solar year. We possess, however, no historical reports as to the proclamation of leap-months in the years between AD 27 and 33.

But these two uncertain factors are greatly reduced in importance by certain established rules of the calendar; the second by the rule that the passover must fall after the spring equinox[4] in order that the first-fruits might be ripe for presentation on Nisan 16,[5] and the first by the rule that no month may have less than twenty-nine or more than thirty days—*thus the possible difference amounts to one day at the most.*[6]

So the question to be asked of astronomical chronology is this: in any of the years around AD 30 did Nisan 14 or Nisan 15 fall on a Friday? In the first case the Johannine, in the second case the

---

[1] This was the older custom: R. H. 1.7, cf. B. Zuckermann, *Materialien zur Entwicklung der altjüdischen Zeitrechnung im Talmud*, Breslau, 1882, 7; A. Büchler, *Die Priester und der Cultus im letzten Jahrzehnt des jerusalemischen Tempels*, Vienna, 1895, 158 n. 1. After the destruction of the Temple the right of determining the beginning of the months was claimed by the Sanhedrin (R. H. 1.7).

[2] See above, p. 15 n. 2.

[3] P. V. Neugebauer, *Astronomische Chronologie* I, Berlin-Leipzig, 1929, 75, cf. 78.

[4] Anatolius of Alexandria (second half of the third century), *Concerning the Passover* (according to pre-Christian Jewish authorities) in Eusebius, *Hist. Eccl.* 8.32. 16–19. Cf. E. Schürer, *History of the Jewish People in the Time of Jesus Christ*, Edinburgh, 1890, I.2, 371.

[5] Tos. Sanh. 2.6 (417.1). If necessary, a leap-month was inserted.

[6] Cf. Gerhardt, *op. cit.*, 119–24; Schürer, *op. cit.*, 363–77.

synoptic chronology would be correct. The answer is shown in the following table:[1]

Year 27	Nisan 14		Thu., April 10	poss.[2]	Fri., April 11
	Nisan 15		Fri., April 11		Sat., April 12
Year 30	Nisan 14	unlikely[3]	Thu., April 6	prob.[4]	Fri., April 7
	Nisan 15		Fri., April 7		Sat., April 8
Year 31[5]	Nisan 14		Wed., April 25	poss.[6]	Thu., April 26
	Nisan 15		Thu., April 26		Fri., April 27
Year 33[7]	Nisan 14		Fri., April 3	poss.[8]	Sat., April 4
	Nisan 15		Sat., April 4		Sun., April 5
Year 34	Nisan 14		Tue., March 23	or[9]	Thu., April 22
	Nisan 15		Wed., March 24		Fri., April 23

[1] Gerhardt, *op. cit.*, 124–36. Cf. K. Schoch, 'Christi Kreuzigung am 14. Nisan', *Biblica* 9 (1928), 48–56; J. Schaumberger, 'Der 14. Nisan als Kreuzigungstag und die Synoptiker', *ibid.*, 57–77; O. Gerhardt, 'Berichtigung', *ibid.*, 464f.; K. Schoch, 'Entgegnung auf obige "Berichtigung" ', *ibid.*, 466–8; O. Gerhardt, 'Das Datum der Kreuzigung Christi', *Astronomische Nachrichten* 240 (September–December 1930), cols. 137–62; 'Zum Datum der Kreuzigung', *ibid.*, 242 (April–July 1931), cols. 305–10; U. Holzmeister, 'Neuere Arbeiten über das Datum der Kreuzigung Christi', *Biblica* 13 (1932), 93–103; J. K. Fotheringham, 'The Evidence of Astronomy and Technical Chronology for the Date of the Crucifixion', *JTS* 35 (1934), 146–62; G. Ogg, *The Chronology of the Public Ministry of Jesus*, Cambridge, 1940, 203–77. G. Amadon, 'Ancient Jewish Calendation', *JBL* 61 (1942), 227–80, is unfortunately unusable because the authoress is dependent in her comprehensive astronomical calculations upon the assumption which we rejected as untenable above, p. 16 n. 3, that at the time of Jesus the passover meal was celebrated in the night Nisan 13/14 (cf. the diagram *JBL* 61, 245, and 'The Johannine-Synoptic Argument', *ATR* 26 [1944], 110f.; 'Important Passover Texts in Josephus and Philo', *ATR* 27 [1945], 115f.). In fact, it is absolutely indubitable that from ancient times right down to the present the Jewish passover meal has never been celebrated at any other time than the night of Nisan 14/15. It is a matter of the deepest regret that G. Amadon should have rendered her painstaking work quite worthless through this mistake and further mistakes following upon it.

[2] According to the sighting of the new light which marked the beginning of the month, which was astronomically possible (first column), but could have been hindered by atmospheric conditions so that the sanctification of the month was delayed for a day (second column).

[3] See below, pp. 39f.

[4] See above, n. 2.

[5] Only in the case of a leap-month.

[6] See above, n. 2.

[7] A leap-month was possible in this year, but unlikely. If there was one, Nisan 14 = Saturday, May 2, or Sunday, May 3; Nisan 15 = Sunday, May 3, or Monday, May 4.

[8] See above, n. 2.

[9] If there was a leap-month, which in this year was very probably the case in view of the nearness of March 23 to the equinox (March 22).

This table shows that *Nisan 15* probably fell on a Friday in the year 27, and possibly in the years 30, 31, and 34; these years, then, are suited to the synoptic chronology. *Nisan 14* probably fell on a Friday in the years 30 and 33, and possibly in the year 27; these years, then, would agree with the Johannine chronology. Now, however, the years 27 and 34 are certainly to be excluded from consideration, because they cannot be fitted into the context of the general New Testament chronology as years of the death of Jesus, and the year 33, although not completely impossible, is improbable.[1] Consequently the problem is concentrated in the question: What was the situation in the years 30 and 31?

Turning first to the *year 30*—the reader is asked to consult the table —the question is: Did Friday, April 7, fall on Nisan 14 or 15? O. Gerhardt, in 1922, had maintained on the basis of observations of the new light made in Palestine during the First World War, and of an extensive study of the rabbinical rules for the proclamation of the new month, that it is most probable that April 7, 30, fell on Nisan 15 (= synoptic chronology);[2] the identification April 7, 30, with Nisan 14 (= Johannine chronology) he regarded as possible, but astronomically less probable.[3] In 1928 K. Schoch (*Astronomisches Recheninstitut* in Berlin-Dahlem), who had specialized in observations of the modern new light and the checking of hundreds of Babylonian reports of new light observations, questioned Gerhardt's results and argued strongly for the identification of Friday, April 7, 30, with Nisan 14.[4] Schoch died soon after this. O. Gerhardt was so kind as to inform me, some little time before his own death on February 2, 1946, about the further course of the debate (letter dated May 21, 1944): 'At first Schoch repeatedly wrote to me expressing his agreement

---

[1] According to Luke 3.1 John the Baptist first appeared in the fifteenth year of Tiberius, which according to the Syrian calendar is the period from October 1, 27, to September 30, 28; this rules out Passover of the year 27 as a date for the death of Jesus. The inscription of Gallio and the chronology of the Sabbath years (J. Jeremias, 'Sabbathjahr und neutestamentliche Chronologie', *ZNW* 27 [1928], 98–103) date the Apostolic Council in the year 48; according to Gal. 1.18; 2.1 the conversion of Paul took place seventeen years earlier (or, if the first and last years are counted as full years: fifteen years plus the months of the first and last years), i.e. in 31 or 32 (hardly 33). The year of Paul's conversion is the latest possible year for the death of Jesus; 34 is therefore impossible as the year of the crucifixion. Fotheringham, *op. cit.*, 161, pronounced himself in favour of April 3, 33, also Ogg, *op. cit.*

[2] O. Gerhardt, *Der Stern des Messias*, 129–31.

[3] Gerhardt, *op. cit.*, 134f. under a–f, 139.

[4] K. Schoch, 'Christi Kreuzigung am 14. Nisan', *Biblica* 9 (1928), 48–56.

with my conclusion: April 7, 30 = Nisan 15, which he still did when the calculations in question had been effected several times. One day Fotheringham of Oxford read of this somewhere and wrote to him that there was a mistake somewhere in this matter, as by the formulae April 7, 30, must be Nisan 14. Schoch examined his calculation, found a mistake of $1\frac{1}{2}$ hours, and published all this in *Biblica* in 1928. Later both Schoch and Fotheringham, on the basis of a new light observation made by many people in Kubebe, were compelled to admit that their formula was not accurate. Neugebauer, who was much more of an expert than Schoch, made an extensive calculation in my presence showing that the identification April 7, 30 = Nisan 15 is correct. And finally Fotheringham has publicly taken my side: "on March 23 in the year 30 the sickle of the moon stood a good deal closer to the sun than Prof. Gerhardt requires"—and it was visible, so that April 7 = Nisan 15.' Concerning these last sentences, it must be critically remarked that Gerhardt, who was not a professional astronomer, although he had a good knowledge of the subject, had fallen into some errors of memory which had coloured the picture he was presenting. In fact, Schoch did not give up the identification of April 7, 30, with Nisan 14, and J. K. Fotheringham had expressed himself in 1934 with much more reserve than one would gather from Gerhardt's account. Fotheringham did admit that Gerhardt's identification of April 7, 30, with Nisan 15 was not absolutely impossible,[1] but himself remained convinced that the true identification was April 7, 30 = Nisan 14.[2] In the second German edition, and accordingly the first English edition, of this book I depended mainly upon Gerhardt's letter of May 21, 1944, although I did express myself more cautiously than he and only said that the astronomical calculations 'lend a certain limited probability' to the synoptic chronology. The establishment of the fact that Gerhardt's account of the debate has to be corrected at one important point leads me to an even more cautious formulation in the summary with which I shall end this section.

[1] Fotheringham, *op. cit.*, 159: 'In all the naked-eye observations that have come to my notice or Schoch's there was only one evening when the moon was seen nearer to the sun than Schoch's formula permits, in fact a good deal nearer than Professor Gerhardt requires. That was in 1916, May 2, when two maids looking for Zeppelins at Scarborough, and two ladies looking for Zeppelins at Heighington, succeeded in observing the lunar crescent. It is well known to astronomers that there are rare occasions of abnormal atmospheric transparency. Apart from these Schoch's formula will not admit of so large an exception.'

[2] Fotheringham, *op. cit.*, 162.

So far as *the year 31* is concerned, in that year Friday, April 27, could fall on Nisan 15 granted two presuppositions: (1) that 31 was a leap-year, and (2) that the sighting of the new light at the beginning of the month had been delayed by one day because of cloudiness, so that Nisan 1 fell on April 13.[1]

We may summarize this discussion as follows: astronomical chronology leads unfortunately to no certain result. It establishes the probability that *Friday, April 7, 30*, and *Friday, April 3, 33*, fell on Nisan 14, which would correspond to the Johannine chronology.[2] But it does not completely exclude the possibility that *Friday, April 27, 31* (or, as a considerably weaker possibility, Friday, April 7, 30), fell on Nisan 15, which would agree with the synoptic chronology. The only certain result which astronomy gives us is that in AD 29 and 32— irrespective of whether these years were leap-years or not, and irrespective of what the conditions were for sighting the new light at the beginning of the month of Nisan—neither Nisan 14 nor Nisan 15 could have fallen on a Friday; both of these years therefore must be excluded from consideration as possible years for the crucifixion.

THE LAST SUPPER–A PASSOVER MEAL!

Under these circumstances our only hope for further progress is some new material. The following discussion seeks to provide it by the establishment of a series of points previously not, or not sufficiently, taken into account,[3] but which in my opinion permit a definite conclusion as to whether or not the Last Supper was a passover meal. The fact that the features of the gospel narratives to which we shall be calling attention in what follows are for the most part of no material significance, and are apparently only mentioned in passing without serving any particular purpose, adds very considerably to their value as evidence.

[1] Fotheringham, *op. cit.*, 159f.

[2] The objection that April 7 was an unlucky day (*dies nefastus*) to the Romans, a day on which certain judicial actions were avoided, is scarcely of any weight. In the first place governmental measures for the punishment of mischief-makers and evil-doers were excepted (J. Schaumberger, 'Der 14. Nisan als Kreuzigungstag und die Synoptiker', *Biblica* 9 [1928], 61f.), and in the second we do not know whether this 'metropolitan superstition' of the city of Rome was also taken into account in the provinces (U. Holzmeister, 'Neuere Arbeiten über das Datum der Kreuzigung Christi', *Biblica* 13 [1932], 99f.).

[3] A typical example is the judgment of M. Goguel, *Life of Jesus*, London, 1933, 430: 'In the account (of the Last Supper) given by Mark and Matthew there is not a single feature which refers to the ritual of the Passover.'

1. According to the unanimous testimony of the synoptics (Mark 14.13 par.; 14.26 par.) and of John (18.1) *the Last Supper took place in Jerusalem.* This is by no means a matter of course! In the days before the passover, and still more during the festival itself, Jerusalem was filled to overflowing with pilgrims. As I have attempted to show elsewhere,[1] our knowledge of the topography of the Temple area (together with rabbinical reports about the space taken up in the Temple area for the slaughter of the passover lambs) permits us to estimate within broad limits their numbers during the period before the destruction of the Temple. Such an estimate would be of between 85,000 and 125,000 pilgrims,[2] to which must be added the population of Jerusalem, which would number about 25,000–30,000, reckoning on the basis of one person to every 35 square metres.[3] We have therefore to reckon with a number of well over 100,000 celebrants of the festival who were to be found in Jerusalem during passover. How extraordinarily overcrowded Jerusalem was after the arrival of the caravans of passover pilgrims can be shown by a few examples. It was impossible for all the pilgrims to find lodging in Jerusalem; the majority of them had to sleep in tents which were set up all around Jerusalem, and particularly in the plain,[4] i.e. to the north of the city.[5] Further, as early as the first century BC it proved impossible to maintain the cultic practice going back to the Josianic Reform,[6] whereby all the participants in the feast ate the passover sacrifice in the Temple forecourts.[7] For lack of space the place of slaughter had to be separated from the place of eating: from the first century BC only the

---

[1] Jeremias, *Jerusalem*³, 90–98.

[2] For the time of Jesus the lower number is the more probable.

[3] J. Jeremias, 'Die Einwohnerzahl Jerusalems zur Zeit Jesu', *ZDPV* 66 (1943), 24–31. Similarly G. Dalman, verbally: 10,000–20,000, at the most 30,000. (In *Jerusalem*¹,² I, 96, a basis of one person to every 25 square metres was used and the number of 55,000 inhabitants of Jerusalem reached, a number which is probably too high; cf. now *Jerusalem*³, 98.)

[4] Josephus, *Bell.* 2.12.

[5] Josephus, *Ant.* 17.217; cf. *Jerusalem*³, 69f. The *aulizesthai* used of Jesus in Matt. 21.17 ('He went out of the city to Bethany and *lodged* there') and Luke 21.37 ('He went out and *lodged* on the mount called Olivet') should probably be interpreted in this way. It means 'to spend the night (in a courtyard), to bivouac', cf. W. Schmauch, 'Der Ölberg. Exegese zu einer Ortsangabe besonders bei Matthäus und Markus', *ThLZ* 77 (1952), col. 395.

[6] Before 621 BC the Passover had been a domestic festival, after 621 BC it became a cultic festival, cf. Jeremias, *Passahfeier*, 66–72.

[7] Deut. 16.7; II Chron. 35.13f.; Jub. 49.16, 17, 20. The Samaritans have kept up the ancient practice to this day, according to which the place of slaughter and the place of eating is the same, cf. *ibid.*, 99.

slaughter took place in the Temple area; the passover meal was trans-ferred to the houses of Jerusalem.[1] It also proved impossible in prac-tice for all the pilgrims to spend the passover night in Jerusalem, as was demanded by Deut. 16.7 according to contemporary exegesis. Accordingly permission had to be given for the passover night to be spent (but not for the passover meal to be eaten) in the immediate environs of Jerusalem.[2] But all these measures were inadequate. Because of the great number of passover pilgrims the overcrowding on the passover night was such that a great many of the participants were forced to eat the passover meal in the courtyards, indeed, even on the roofs of the holy city,[3] despite the coldness of the season (cf. Mark 14.54!).

This is in keeping with the reports in Mark 11.11 par.; 11.19; Luke 21.37; Mark 14.3 par.; Luke 22.39 that during his last stay in Jerusalem Jesus regularly left the holy city in the evening and went to Bethany (Luke: the Mount of Olives). Why then did he, contrary to this custom, remain in the overcrowded city for the Last Supper? The answer is that *it was laid down that the passover lamb*, which belonged[4] to the category of sacred things of the lower grade,[5] *must be eaten within the gates of Jerusalem*.[6]

---

[1] Pes. 5.10; 7.12f.; 10.1ff., etc.

[2] Law and reality were reconciled by defining a district of Greater Jerusalem which included Bethphage, cf. Jeremias, *Jerusalem*[3], 115f.; Billerbeck I, 839f., 992; II, 833f.; Dalman, *Jesus-Jeshua*, 95; *Orte und Wege Jesu* (BFChTh II 1)[3], Gütersloh, 1924 [= *Orte und Wege*], 338, n. 4, cf. 269f.; *Ergänzungen und Verbesse-rungen zu Jesus-Jeschua*, Leipzig, 1929, 8.

[3] 'Although it is written: "it is to be eaten in one and the same house" (Ex. 12.46), they nevertheless eat it (the passover lamb) in their courtyards and on their roofs' (Tos. Pes. 6.11 [166.2f.]). Taan. 3.8 shows that everywhere in Jerusalem ovens for the baking of the passover lambs were to be found in the open. Further cf. j. Pes. 7.35b. 36, where it is apparently also presupposed that the passover meal was eaten on the roofs of Jerusalem (see below, p. 87 n. 5).

[4] Zeb. 5.8.

[5] *Ḳodašim ḳallim.*

[6] Siphre Num. 69 on 9.10: 'Which is the place where it (the passover lamb) should be eaten? *Within the gates of Jerusalem.*' Num. R. 7.8 on 5.2: 'Holy things of the lower grade (the passover lamb belongs to this category of sacrifices, see above, n. 4) and the second tithe are eaten in Jerusalem.' Pes. 7.9: 'The passover lamb which has been carried out (of Jerusalem) or has become unclean must be burnt immediately.' Makk. 3.3: 'He who eats sacred things of the lower grade outside the (city) wall . . . receives 40 strokes.' Further Kel. 1.8; Tos. Sanh. 3.4 (418.22); Midr. Tann. to Deut. 14.23; 15.20. Cf. Dalman, *Jesus-Jeshua*, 93ff.; *Orte und Wege*, 332f.; *Arbeit und Sitte in Palästina* IV (BFChTh II 27), Gütersloh, 1935, 112. On the exception (b. Pes. 91a) made for prisoners, to whom one might bring the passover flesh in prison if the prison lay within the districts of greater Jerusalem (see above, n. 2), cf. Jeremias, *Jerusalem*[3], 116.

2. Mark 14.13–15 par. presupposes that *the room for the meal* was made available to Jesus and his disciples without ado. This could be connected with the passover customs, because a Baraita (b. Meg. 26a; Tos. M. Sh. 1.12f. [87.9]) comments that since Jerusalem was considered a national possession it was not permissible to let rooms in Jerusalem (to passover pilgrims) for a financial consideration; it was, however, customary for the pilgrims to recompense the householder by letting him have the hide of passover lambs.[1] But the narrative Mark 14.13–15 is too much coloured by legend to form the basis for any certain conclusions.

3. According to I Cor. 11.23 and John 13.30 the Last Supper was held *at night*;[2] in agreement with this Mark 14.17 and Matt. 26.20 report that Jesus came with his disciples 'when the *evening* had come' to celebrate the last supper.[3] Again we must say: this is by no means a matter of course! Nowhere else in the gospels do we hear that an ordinary[4] meal was held at night; only once do we hear that a meal took place in the evening (Matt. 14.15, 'when it was evening'), the feeding of the 5,000, but it is expressly stated in the same verse that 'the time (for a meal) is already past'.[5]

In fact, it was customary to have two meals a day: a very simple[6] breakfast between 10 and 11 a.m.[7] and *the main meal*[8] *in the late after-*

---

[1] Cf. J. Mann, 'Rabbinic Studies in the Synoptic Gospels', *HUCA* 1 (1924), 343 n. 64.

[2] This has been pointed out by A. Oepke, 'Ursprung und ursprünglicher Sinn des Abendmahls im Lichte der neuesten Forschung [III]', *Allgemeine Evangelisch-lutherische Kirchenzeitung* 59 (1926), col. 58: 'So far as I know it has not yet been taken into account that Paul expressly states that the historical Last Supper was held at night (I Cor. 11.23).' It should be noted that I Cor. 11.23 represents the introduction of the liturgical eucharistic formula and is therefore a very early piece of evidence.

[3] The fact that the meal continued into the night also follows from Mark 14.30 (cf. Matt. 26.34; Luke 22.34) 'today, this very night': since the 'today' began at sunset, this must have been spoken during the night. Further, cf. John 18.3, 'with lanterns and torches'.

[4] Matt. 25.1–13 seems to presuppose a wedding feast that began at midnight. Luke 11.5 is concerned with the exceptional case of a traveller who must be cared for at midnight. In Luke 12.37f. an unreal situation is created through intentional exaggeration when it is said that the master, returning from a party at night, will recompense his watchful servants by acting as their host.

[5] Besides, 'evening' here probably refers to the time *before* sunset (see above, p. 17).

[6] Billerbeck II, 204; see below, p. 51.

[7] b. Shab. 10a (Bar.): '. . . . at 4 (i.e. 10 a.m.) is the mealtime for the labourers; at 5 (i.e. 11 a.m.) for all other people' (the parallel in b. Pes. 12b Bar. names the sixth hour [noon] as the general mealtime, but according to Josephus,

noon.[1] Such, for example, was the custom of the Essenes: breakfast between 10 and 11 a.m.,[2] then further work 'until the afternoon', when they had their main meal.[3] Discussions about the words of blessing used to usher in the Sabbath (*ḳidduš*) provide ample evidence that in the early times with which we are dealing the main meal was taken in the *afternoon* (*beminḥah*), both on Friday and on the Sabbath.[4]

Vita 279, this applies only to the Sabbath). 10 a.m. is also assumed as the normal time for breakfast in b. Pes. 107b; Targ. Ḳoh. 10.16f. At 9 a.m., the time of morning prayer, people have not yet had breakfast: Acts 2.15.

[8] δεῖπνον, Heb. *se'uddah*, Aram. *se'uddeta*.

[1] S. Krauss, *Talmudische Archäologie* III, Leipzig, 1912, 29: 'in the hours before evening'; Billerbeck II, 204, 206; IV, 615: in the 'later hours of the afternoon'; Bauer: A. and G., 172 *s.v.* δεῖπνον: 'toward evening'; Mek. Ex. 18.13: 'the mealtime' comes before evening ('*rb*). Shab. 1.2: shortly before the time of the *minḥah* (the afternoon prayer which according to Acts 3.1, cf. 10.3, 30, was at 3 p.m.) one should not sit down at table (so that one does not miss the afternoon prayer). b. Pes. 107b: King Agrippa (I or II) was accustomed to eat at the ninth hour (3 p.m.). The late afternoon is also indicated as the mealtime in Luke 24.29: 'it is toward evening and the day is now far spent' (cf. Dalman, *Orte und Wege*, 244; *Arbeit und Sitte in Palästina* I.2 [BFChTh II 14.2], Gütersloh, 1928, 613f.). It is in this context that the brief report 'for it was about the tenth hour' in John 1.39 becomes intelligible: Jesus admits the two disciples of John the Baptist to his table fellowship.

[2] Josephus, *Bell.* 2.129: they work 'until the fifth hour' (10–11 a.m.) and then assemble for their meal.

[3] Josephus, *Bell.* 2.131f.

[4] FRIDAY: b. Ber. 48b (Bar.) lays down the way in which the Sabbath-*ḳidduš* (see above, p. 26) is to be fitted into the grace after the meal; it is therefore assumed that the meal will be held on Friday in the late afternoon, and may last until sunset. Since R. Eliezer (*c.* AD 90), the thoroughgoing representative of the old tradition, offers an opinion as to the manner in which the *ḳidduš* and the grace after the meal are to be brought together, the custom must be very old. The same case, that the Friday afternoon meal may last until the beginning of the Sabbath, is also found in Tos. Ber. 5.2 (11.23) par., b. Pes. 100a (Bar.) and j. Pes. 10.37b. 37; Tos. Ber. 5.3f. (11.28); b. Pes. 102a, b (Bar.); b. Erub. 73b. Only later, at the earliest in the second century AD and perhaps not until the third (cf. above, p. 27 n. 5), the view is proposed that one should not take a meal on the Friday afternoon, so as to enter the Sabbath with a good appetite: Tos. Ber. 5.1 (11.22); b. Pes. 99b (Bar.); j. Pes. 10.37b. 33.

SABBATH: Tos. Shab. 12.16 (128.15). Ber. 8.5 reports a discussion between the schools of Shammai and Hillel (first century AD) on the question as to how the prayer after the meal was to be combined with the *habdalah* (words of praise spoken at the end of Sabbaths and feast days, after sunset): it is again assumed that the meal began late in the afternoon of the Sabbath and ended at sunset. Cf. I. Elbogen, 'Eingang und Ausgang des Sabbats nach talmudischen Quellen', in *Festschrift zu Israel Lewy's 70. Geburtstag*, Breslau, 1911, 173–87, especially 179ff., 83; Lietzmann, *Mass and Lord's Supper*, 165f., 167.

Only in the case of special occasions, such as a circumcision[1] or a wedding,[2] is it reported that a meal lasted into the night.

In the light of this it is certain that *the hour of the Last Supper is not in accordance with the general custom*. How does it come about that this meal begins 'in the evening' and lasts 'into the night'? I see only one answer: *from its inception the passover meal was eaten at night*.[3] 'The Passover may only be eaten at night.'[4] The passover meal began after sunset[5] and lasted far into the night.[6] How unusual the night hours of the passover meal were can be seen from the fact that again and again detailed instructions are given as to the measures to be taken to keep the children awake at the passover meal.[7]

4. According to Mark 14.17 (par. Matt. 26.20) Jesus celebrated the Last Supper with the Twelve.[8] It is not possible, however, to assume from this that the women mentioned in Mark 15.40; Luke 23.49, 55 were excluded; in Eastern texts the argument from silence is inadmissible in such cases.[9] Equally, one cannot put any weight on the fact that the group described as being at table together in Mark

[1] Deut. R. 9.1 on 31.14; Midr. Koh. on 3.2.

[2] Ber. 1.1 (cf. H. L. Strack, *Berakhoth*, Leipzig, 1915, 1 *ad loc.*).

[3] So, rightly, A. Oepke, 'Ursprung und ursprünglicher Sinn', *Allgemeine Evangelisch-lutherische Kirchenzeitung* 59 (1926), col. 58, who refers, among other things, to the passover song with its refrain *belailah, belailah* ('in the night, in the night'). But his argument achieves its full force only when one recognizes the fact that the general mealtime was already in the late afternoon.

[4] Zeb. 5.8.

[5] Ex. 12.8; Jub. 49.1, 12; Tos. Pes. 1.34 (158.4); j. Pes. 5.31d.27; Siphre Deut. 133 on 16.6; Mek. Ex. 12.6.

[6] A rule by which it was intended to forestall any breach of Ex. 12.8 ('they shall eat the meat in the same night') forbids the eating of the passover lamb after 2 a.m. (Jub. 49.10, 12), or after midnight (Pes. 10.9; Zeb. 5.8; Tos. Pes. 5.2 [163.17], etc.). Still more instructive is the report of Josephus (*Ant.* 18.29) that on the passover night the gates of the temple were opened at midnight.

[7] Tos. Pes. 10.9 (172.27), see below, p. 84 n. 5; b. Pes. 108b, 109a, etc.

[8] In the apocryphal tradition the circle has widened. The Gospel according to the Hebrews records James the brother of the Lord as a participant, so Jerome, *De viris illustribus* 2 (E. Klostermann, *Apocrypha* II [KlT 8][3], Berlin, 1929, 11; MPL 23 [1865], cols. 643: 'James had sworn that he would not eat bread from that hour in which he had drunk the cup of the Lord . . .' The old Greek translation of *De viris illustribus* (A. Resch, *Agrapha. Aussercanonische Schriftfragmente* [TU II 15.3-4][2], Leipzig, 1906, 248; MPL 23 [1856], col. 644) is different, having: 'James had sworn that he would not eat bread from that hour in which the Lord had drunk the cup . . .' (a dogmatic correction: James did *not* drink).

[9] Cf. Luke 15.20, where the mother's presence cannot be excluded. According to the *Apostolic Church Order* 26f. (A. Hilgenfeld, *Novum Testamentum extra canonem receptum* IV[2], Leipzig, 1884, 118f.) Mary and Martha were present at the Last Supper, but were not allowed to partake of the sacrament because Mary had laughed.

14.17 par. (Jesus and the Twelve) is nowhere else expressly mentioned in the gospels, for this is certainly pure chance. It seems to be a fact, however, that during his preaching ministry Jesus was in the habit of eating with the large circle of his hearers. This is evidenced by the warning given to those who confessed him with their lips only, that it would avail them nothing to appeal to the table fellowship they had shared with him on the occasions when he had preached near their homes (Luke 13.26f.). According to Mark, Jesus was frequently so closely surrounded that he could not even eat (3.20; 6.31). Often, especially on a Sabbath (Mark 1.29–31; Luke 14.1), Jesus was invited to a meal, together with other guests (Mark 14.3; Luke 7.36; 11.37; John 2.1–11); sometimes he entertained his own guests (Luke 15.1f., cf. John 1.39 above, p. 45 n. 1), on one occasion in large numbers (Mark 2.15).[1] The description of Jesus as 'a gluttonous man and a wine-bibber, a friend of publicans and sinners' (Matt. 11.19), supports the assumption that he frequently took his meals in considerable company. On his journeys Jesus often took his meals in the open (Mark 6.32–44; 8.14; John 4.8, 31; 21.12), surrounded by disciples and followers. The size of the circle of his table companions may be gauged with the help of such texts as Luke 8.1–3; 24.33; Acts 1.21–26; on one occasion the caravan of passover pilgrims formed the table fellowship of Jesus (Mark 6.32–44). We also find Jesus at table with his hosts, when he lodged as a traveller (Luke 10.38–42; cf. 10.7f.).

Because of this the limitation of the table companions of Jesus to a narrow circle is striking. *Is it chance that the small group in some ways corresponds to the passover practice?* The passover ḥaburah had to consist of at least ten persons[2] and this was the average number,[3] as it was assumed that a one-year-old lamb would provide sufficient food for about ten people. None the less the number could exceed the minimum,[4] as it does among the Samaritans today.[5]

---

[1] Cf. E. Lohmeyer, *Das Evangelium des Markus*[14], Göttingen, 1957 [= *Markus*], 55f.; J. Jeremias, *The Parables of Jesus*, London and New York, 1963 (ET of *Die Gleichnisse Jesu*[6], Göttingen, 1962) [= *Parables*], 227 n. 92.

[2] Tos. Pes. 4.3 (163.4) par. b. Pes. 64b (Bar.) and Midr. Lam. on 1.1; Josephus, *Bell.* 6.423, 425.

[3] Josephus and the Talmud both witness to this fact.

[4] Pes. 8.3.

[5] According to a communication from C.-H. Hunzinger they have one lamb for each two groups of celebrants. Each of the families celebrating the passover pictured in Jeremias, *Passahfeier*, plates 45–47, has therefore half a lamb before it.

5. A further point on which the synoptics (Mark 14.18; Matt. 26.20; Luke 22.14)[1] and John (13.12, 23!, 25, 28)[2] agree is that Jesus and his disciples *reclined* at table at the Last Supper. This also is not to be taken as a matter of course! For at the time of Jesus the diners *sat* down (Heb. *yašab*, Aram. *yeteb*)[3] as we know from rabbinical sources.[4] Wherever the gospels speak of reclining at meals[5] they mean either a meal in the open (the feeding of the multitudes), or a party (Mark 12.39 par.; 14.3 par.; Luke 7.36, 37, 49; 11.37; 14.15; John 12.2), or a feast (Mark 2.15 par., especially Luke 5.29), or a royal banquet (Mark 6.26 par.), or a wedding feast (Matt. 22.10, 11; Luke 14.8, 10), or the feast of the salvation time (Matt. 8.11; Luke

[1] Further: Mark 14.15; Luke 22.12 ἐστρωμένον, 'furnished with cushions for the meal', cf. Ezek. 23.41, LXX, κλίνη ἐστρωμένη.

[2] Cf. also John 21.20.

[3] G. Dalman, *Arbeit und Sitte* VII (BFChTh II 48), Gütersloh, 1942, 220: 'the term does not exclude squatting (p. 214).'

[4] E.g., j. Ber. 7.11c.48: *yšbw w'klw*; j. Ber. 8.11d.57 (cf. 50): *hyh ywšb w'wkl bšbt*; the same in Aramaic texts b. Sanh. 38a: *ytbw bsᶜdt*; j. Ber. 7.11b. 62 and (verbally identical) 11c.42: *hww ytbyn 'klyn*; further Ber. 6.6; b. Ber. 41b. Cf. Franz Delitzsch, *Ein Tag in Capernaum*², Leipzig, 1873, 152 n. 1: 'At official or ceremonial banquets people reclined at table in the graeco-roman manner. So did Jesus with his disciples at the Last Supper. . . . But the ancient custom of Israel was to sit at table. Such was the case here in the house of the Galilean fisherman'; Billerbeck IV, 617f.: 'At the daily family meal people were seated'; G. Beer, *Pesachim*, Giessen, 1912, 189; S. Krauss, *Talmudische Archäologie* III, Leipzig, 1912, 43f.; H. L. Strack, *Bᵉrakhoth*, Leipzig, 1915, 14 n. f; A. Schlatter, *Der Evangelist Matthäus*, Stuttgart, 1929 [= *Matthäus*], 278: 'The reclining at table denotes this as a ceremonial meal'; C. C. McCown, 'Luke's Translation of Semitic into Hellenistic Custom', *JBL* 58 (1939), 218f.; Dalman, *op. cit.*, 222. In the earliest time the Israelites squatted on the floor for their meals; in later times they sat at table (I Sam. 20.5, 24f.; cf. further Gen. 27.19; Ex. 32.6 [= I Cor. 10.7]; Judg. 19.6; I Kings 13.20; Prov. 23.1; Ecclus 31.12, 18, etc.), cf. Beer, *Pesachim*, 188; I. Benzinger, *Hebräische Archäologie* (Angelos-Lehrbücher 1)³, Leipzig, 1927, 105f. The prophet Amos protested against the custom imported from Mesopotamia whereby the nobles reclined at table (Amos 3.12; 6.4); Ecclus 41.19 is possibly directed against the same custom being taken over from the hellenistic world, but the passage is ambiguous. In everyday life the common people and their families never adopted this foreign custom, but maintained the ancient use of sitting down for an ordinary meal.

[5] ἀνακεῖσθαι, Mark 6.26; 14.18; 16.14; Matt. 9.10; 22.10, 11; 26.7, 20; Luke 22.27; John 12.2; 13.23, 28. συνανακεῖσθαι, Mark 2.15; 6.22; Matt. 9.10; 14.9; Luke 7.49; 14.10, 15. κατακεῖσθαι, Mark 2.15; 14.3; Luke 5.29; 7.37. ἀναπίπτειν, Luke 11.37; 14.10; 17.7; 22.14; John 13.12. ἀνακλίνειν, Luke 12.37; passive Mark 6.39; Matt. 8.11; 14.19; Luke 13.29. κατακλίνειν, Luke 9.14f.; passive Luke 7.36; 14.8; 24.30. πρωτοκλισία, Mark 12.39; Matt. 23.6; Luke 14.7, 8; 20.46. Cf. κόλπος, John 13.23; 1.18; Luke 16.22, 23. Further cf. n.1. However, the possibility is to be noted that these expressions (like the post-biblical Hebrew *heseb*) had lost their original force and had come to mean simply 'to have a meal'. Cf. McCown, *op. cit.*, 219.

13.29, cf. 16.23).[1] There are only two exceptions to this rule: Luke 24.30 and [Mark] 16.14; but the first is a typically Lukan idiom (κατακλίνειν is found only in Luke in the New Testament), and the second belongs to a stratum of tradition too late to serve as evidence for Palestinian table customs at the time of Jesus. It is *absolutely impossible* that Jesus and his disciples should have *reclined* at table for their ordinary meals. How is it then that they recline at table in the case of the Last Supper? There can be only one answer: at the passover meal it was a *ritual duty* to recline at table as a symbol of freedom,[2] also, as it is expressly stated, for 'the poorest man in Israel'.[3]

6. According to John 13.10 the Last Supper was eaten *in a state of levitical purity*: 'He who has bathed ("he who has taken the [Num. 19.19 prescribed] plunge-bath [on the seventh day of the time of cleansing]") does not need to wash, except for his feet.' Levitical purity was not required of the laity for their ordinary meals, but it was for partaking of the passover lamb which, as we saw above, p. 43, belonged to the category of holy things of the lower grade.

7. According to Mark 14.18–21, 22; Matt. 26.21–25, 26, Jesus broke the bread *during the course of the meal*. It is true that the words 'as they were eating' (Mark 14.22 par. Matt. 26.26) are probably a redactional transition to the institution of the Eucharist,[4] but even the redactor, and certainly Mark, who hailed from Jerusalem,[5] must have been conscious of the fact that with the words 'as they were eating' he was describing a sequence quite different from that of an ordinary meal. In addition to this we can see that even without these connecting words Mark 14.18–21 par. Matt. 26.21–25 presupposes that the meal was already in progress before the breaking of the bread. That is remarkable, because the ordinary meals began with the breaking of bread; the only exceptions to this were the festival meals among the upper classes, where, following hellenistic custom, a preliminary course was first served outside the dining-room, and then

---

[1] Luke 22.27 is also not concerned with an ordinary meal, as can be seen from the mention of the servant waiting at table, but with either a party (so most probably) or a meal in a wealthy household. The same is true of Luke 12.37, where the returning master serves his servants. This meal, too, is a banquet.

[2] j. Pes. 10.37b. 53f.: 'R. Levi (*c.* 300) has said: "because slaves eat standing, here (at the passover meal) people should recline to eat, to signify that they have passed from slavery to freedom".' Ex. 12.11 was regarded as a rule that was valid only for the actual exodus itself.

[3] Pes. 10.1; Tos. Pes. 10.1 (172.12).

[4] See below, p. 113.

[5] Acts 12.12.

the meal proper began with the breaking of bread after one had reclined at table in the dining-room.[1] But such a preliminary course served in an anteroom cannot possibly be meant by 'as they were eating',[2] which can only refer to a meal already in progress. But then it is most unusual that Mark 14.22 describes a meal in which the breaking of bread follows the serving of a dish (14.20). How unusual this is can be seen from the following fact. In order literally to fulfil the command of Ex. 12.26f. to explain the passover ritual to the children in answer to their questions, the *paterfamilias*, according to established tradition, introduced his passover devotions in such a way as to stimulate the children to ask about the special aspects of the evening. One of these children's questions introducing the Passover devotion was, 'How is it that on every other evening we dip bread into the dish but on this evening we simply dip (without bread) into the dish?'[3] *This children's question shows conclusively that the passover meal was the only family meal in the year at which the serving of a dish* (Mark 14.20) *preceded the breaking of bread* (Mark 14.22).[4]

8. Jesus and his disciples drink wine at the Last Supper (Mark 14.23, 25 par.).[5] This also is not to be taken as a matter of course.[6] Wine was drunk only on festive occasions.[7] First and foremost at family celebrations: when entertaining guests,[8] celebrating a circumcision,[9] engagement,[10] or marriage.[11] It was also customary to serve wine in the house of the bereaved during the seven days of mourning.[12] Secondly the annual festivals provided an occasion for the drinking of wine,[13] especially the three pilgrimage festivals (Passover, Pentecost, Tabernacles); the drinking of wine was prescribed as part of the

[1] Billerbeck IV, 616.
[2] Because such a preliminary course was taken sitting (Billerbeck IV, 616) whereas Jesus and his disciples were already reclining at table from Mark 14.18.
[3] j. Pes. 10.37d. 4f.
[4] Cf. below, p. 85 (A. Preliminary Course).
[5] V. Zapletal, *Der Wein in der Bibel* (Biblische Studien 20.1), Freiburg i. Br., 1920; G. Dalman, *Arbeit und Sitte in Palästina* IV (BFChTh II 33), Gütersloh, 1935, 291–413; VI (BFChTh II 41), Gütersloh, 1939, 124–9.
[6] Ber. 8.8: 'If wine is brought to them after the meal . . .'
[7] b. Pes. 109a (Bar.).
[8] Billerbeck IV, 613ff. *Mištuta* 'drinking' has therefore come to mean precisely 'festive meal'.
[9] Midr. Ḳoh. on 3.2, and often.
[10] Billerbeck II, 394.
[11] John 2.1–10. Billerbeck I, 514 under 'u'; 517 under 'ee'.
[12] Krauss, *Talmudische Archäologie* II, 70; Billerbeck IV, 594, 600, 602ff.; Dalman, *op. cit.*, IV, 396. Cf. already Jer. 16.7: 'the cup of consolation'.
[13] b. Pes. 109a (Bar.).

ritual of Passover[1] and Purim,[2] and was customary at the meals for the 'sanctification' and the 'dismissal' of the Sabbath.[3] Otherwise wine was generally used in everyday life only for medicinal purposes; it was regarded as an excellent medicine.[4]

In everyday life water was drunk. The daily breakfast consisted of 'bread with salt, and a tankard of water',[5] and even at the main meal bread and water were the chief ingredients,[6] not only for the poor, who even in the evening had to do without further additions to their diet and be satisfied with bread and salt.[7] The scribes especially were expected to lead a Spartan existence: 'This is the way (to gain knowledge) of the Torah: eat bread and salt and "drink water by measure" (Ezek. 4.11). Sleep on the ground, lead a life of self-denial and take pains over the Torah.'[8] To give one example: Rabban Gamaliel had two dates and one jug of water brought to his tabernacle.[9]

Whether the *Essenes* were an exception to this and drank wine every day is questionable. Their ceremonial daily meal began with the blessing over the bread and *tiroš*[10] and the question is, what is the meaning of *tiroš*? The word had changed its meaning; in the Old Testament it is the archaic word for 'wine', but in later colloquial speech there is a difference between *yayin* (the normal word for wine) and *tiroš* as we can see from the following regulation: 'He who gives up *tiroš* for the sake of a vow is forbidden every kind of sweet (unfermented)[11] drink, but he is permitted wine.'[12] The Gemara elucidates this saying from the Tosephta as follows: '(This regulation) reflects the opinion that vows are to be interpreted according to the colloquial language; but according to the opinion that vows are to be interpreted in accordance with the language of the Torah (wine must be forbidden), because the Torah calls it (wine) *tiroš* (so Deut. 11.14):

---

[1] According to Pes. 10.1 four cups should be the minimum.

[2] Krauss, *op. cit.*, 243.

[3] Krauss, *op. cit.*, 242.

[4] Cf., e.g., Luke 10.34; I Tim. 5.23. Shab. 19.2, at circumcision; b. Shab. 129a, after blood-letting; Ned. 9.8, old wine is good for the health; b. B. B. 58b, 'where no wine is available, medicines are necessary'. Billerbeck I, 428; III, 654f.; Dalman, *op. cit.*, IV, 261, 263, and especially 398.

[5] b. B. M. 107b (Bar.).

[6] Krauss, *Talmudische Archäologie* III, 29; Dalman, *Arbeit und Sitte in Palästina* VI (BFChTh II 41), Gütersloh, 1939, 123f.

[7] b. Ber. 2b.

[8] P. Ab. 6.4.

[9] Suk. 2.5.

[10] 1QS 6.4–6, cf. 1QSa 2.17–21 (see above, pp. 32f.).

[11] M. Jastrow, *A Dictionary of the Targumim, the Talmud Babli and Yerushalmi, and the Midrashic Literature*, New York–Berlin–London, 1926, 862 *s. v. metika*.

[12] Tos. Ned. 4.3 (279.14f.).

"your *tiroš*, that is wine".[1] We can see that it was well known that the everyday linguistic usage (*tiroš* is *not* considered to be wine) did not correspond with that of the Old Testament (*tiroš* =wine). Since we do not know which linguistic usage is being followed in the Manual of Discipline, the question as to whether or not the Essenes took wine at their daily ritual meals must be left open.

The gospel narratives agree with what we have said. Only twice elsewhere is it reported that Jesus drank wine: Matt. 11.16–19 par., which reflects a practice of Jesus to take part in festive meals arranged for him by grateful followers, and John 2.1–11, in the story of the wedding at Cana. Apart from this it may be assumed, although it is not expressly stated, that Jesus and his disciples drank wine when they were invited to a festal occasion, for example by a Pharisee on the Sabbath (Luke 14.1), and assuredly if this was an invitation to the 'dismissal' of the Sabbath.[2] It is, however, quite out of the question that Jesus and his disciples should have drunk wine with their daily meals. The simplicity of their ordinary meals is shown by Mark 6.38 par., where they have only bread and two fish to be eaten with it.[3] *How is it then that at the Last Supper wine is drunk?* The answer is: at the passover meal it was the duty of every participant to take wine, according to Pes. 10.1 at least four cups, 'even if it is from the pauper's dish [i.e. from charity]'.[4]

[1] j. Ned. 7.40b. 59–61.

[2] See above, p. 26.

[3] An observation by A. Schlatter is instructive with regard to the rarity of the drinking of wine in everyday life. I Cor. 11.25 adds to the commandment to repeat the taking of the cup the limiting phrase 'as often as you drink it' which has no equivalent in the commandment to repeat the taking of the bread. Luke 22.19f. has the commandment of repetition only in the case of the bread. A. Schlatter, *Das Evangelium des Lukas*, Stuttgart, 1931 [= *Lukas*], 422, has observed that both indicate that the cup of wine 'was only seldom on hand at the meals of the congregations'. On the celebrations *sub una* (in one kind, with bread alone), cf. A. Harnack, *Über das gnostische Buch Pistis-Sophia. Brod und Wasser: Die eucharistischen Elemente bei Justin* (TU 7.2), Leipzig, 1891, 115–44; C. Clemen, *Religionsgeschichtliche Erklärung des Neuen Testaments*², Giessen, 1924, 174–7; Lietzmann, *Mass and Lord's Supper*, 195–203; W. Goossens, *Les origines de l'Eucharistie*, Gembloux–Paris, 1931, 161, 164ff.; A. Greiff, 'Brot, Wasser und Mischwein die Elemente der Taufmesse', *Theologische Quartalschrift* 13 (1932), 11–34; A. Arnold, *Der Ursprung des christlichen Abendmahls* (Freiburger Theologische Studien 45), Freiburg i. Br., 1937, 10–53; G. Dix, *The Shape of the Liturgy*, 61; H. J. Schoeps, *Theologie und Geschichte des Judenchristentums*, Tübingen, 1949, 194f.; G. Gentz, 'Aquarii', *RAC* I (1950), cols. 574f.; E. Schweizer, 'Abendmahl I. Im NT', *RGG*³ I (1957), col. 16.

[4] Pes. 10.1 (see on the 'pauper's dish' below, p. 54 n. 2). The taking of wine at the passover meal is an established custom already in the pre-Christian period: Jub. 49.6, 9, where it is treated as an ancient custom.

9. Jesus and his disciples drank *red wine* at the Last Supper. That follows clearly from the comparison between the wine and blood. In Talmudic times there was in Palestine red,[1] white[2] and black[3] wine. That the red wine was the most common[4] is questionable in view of the relative rarity with which it is mentioned.[5] It is therefore the more noteworthy that R. Judah (*c.* AD 150), the consistent representative of the older tradition,[6] laid down the requirement that red wine must be drunk at the passover meal;[7] according to R. Jeremiah (*c.* 320) the use of red wine at the passover was actually *miṣwah*, a binding prescription.[8]

10. According to John 13.29 some of the disciples assume that Jesus had commissioned Judas, who left the table after the meal (v. 26), to make some last-minute *purchases for the festival* ('quickly', v. 27). Such purchasing at night would be completely incomprehensible if the incident occurred on the evening before Nisan 14, because then the whole of the next day, Nisan 14, would be available for this purpose. But the situation would be quite different if the incident occurred on the passover evening, *for then the matter would be urgent, because the next day, Nisan 15, was a high feast day, and the day following that, Nisan 16, a Sabbath.* A purchase on passover evening would not be impossible, for the division between Passover and the feast of Unleavened Bread, which was made[9] in view of the Old Testament,[10] makes it possible that the strict feast-day regulations did not come into force until the morning of Nisan 15.[11] Apart from this, even if the night Nisan 14/15 was governed by the feast-day rules, the purchase of necessities was permissible in cases of emergency.[12]

[1] Krauss, *Talmudische Archäologie* II, 241 no. 18.
[2] *Ibid.*, nos. 14, 16.   [3] *Ibid.*, nos. 15, 17, 19.
[4] So Dalman, *Arbeit und Sitte in Palästina IV*, 370, who, however, can only refer to the situation in Lebanon in support of this contention.
[5] Krauss, *op. cit.*, 241.   [6] Billerbeck I, 931.
[7] R. Judah required that the wine used at the passover meal should have 'the taste and appearance of wine' (Tos. Pes. 10.1 [172.14] Vienna MS.; b. Pes. 108b); the word 'appearance' refers to Prov. 23.31 which speaks of wine as 'red' and 'sparkling in the cup' (so, correctly, Raba, b. Pes. 108b).
[8] j. Pes. 10.37c. 27 par. j. Shab. 8.11a. 31; j. Shek. 3.47b. 61. The evidence here is therefore (cf. the preceding note) not only the teaching of a single rabbi from the fourth century AD, as K. G. Kuhn ('The Lord's Supper' in *The Scrolls and the New Testament*, 82f.) maintains following Billerbeck IV, 61.
[9] Billerbeck I, 987f. under 'c'.
[10] Lev. 23.5f.; Num. 28.16f.; II Chron. 35.17.
[11] P. J. Heawood, 'The Time of the Last Supper', *JQR* 42 (1951–2), 40.
[12] See p. 77 under 'd'.

11. According to John 13.29 some of the disciples assumed that Jesus had commissioned Judas *to give something to the poor*. 'And it was night' (v. 30). That Jesus should have given gifts to those poorer than himself although he himself lived from gifts (Luke 8.3 and often) is quite in accordance with the Palestinian practice of piety: 'Even a poor man who himself lives from alms, should give alms.'[1] It is difficult to imagine that it was Jesus' custom to arrange for the distribution of alms at night; but it must have been a custom, or the disciples would not have interpreted the sudden, nocturnal disappearance of Judas in this way. *It was, however, customary to do something for the poor on the passover night.* Even the poorest had the right to four cups of wine, 'even if it is from the pauper's dish [i.e. from charity]'.[2] An ancient Aramaic passover saying, spoken by the *paterfamilias*,[3] ran: 'Behold, this[4] is the bread of affliction, which our fathers had to eat as they came out of Egypt. Whoever hungers, let him come and eat, and whoever is in need, let him come and keep the passover (with us).'[5] That this invitation to the poor to come to the passover table was not only theoretical can be seen from an incidental remark in the Mishnah, that it was not unusual to 'invite somebody from the street'[6] to the passover meal. So when Billerbeck takes the report of Josephus that the Temple gates were opened at midnight on the passover night[7] and draws from it the conclusion that there would be no lack of beggars around the Temple on that festival night,[8] no one with any knowledge of Palestine conditions can do other than agree.

12. The Last Supper ends, as is mentioned quite incidentally

[1] b. Giṭ. 7b (Mar Zuṭra, died 417). The evidence is late, but the rule itself is old, as can be seen from Mark 12.41–44 par. Luke 21.1–4. Cf. K. H. Rengstorf, ' "Geben ist seliger denn Nehmen". Bemerkungen zu dem ausserevangelischen Herrenwort Apg. 20, 35' in *A. Köberle-Festschrift*, Hamburg, 1958, 23–33, especially 30–32.

[2] 'From the pauper's dish' means from the daily distribution of food, as opposed to 'the box', the weekly distribution of relief in cash (which was given on Fridays).

[3] According to I. Lewy, 'Ein Vortrag über das Ritual des Pesach-Abends', in *Jahresbericht des jüdisch-theologischen Seminars Fraenckel'scher Stiftung*, Breslau, 1904, 11, it was spoken at the open door of the house. But this report is late, coming from a Gaon of Pumbedhitha, *c.* 860, who, however, refers to earlier sources.

[4] The wafers of unleavened bread (*maṣṣah*).

[5] The saying still belongs to the passover ritual today. See further below, p. 57 n. 7. [The modern form of this saying can be found in *The Passover Haggadah*, New York, 1953, 21: 'This is the (lit. 'behold the') bread of poverty which our forefathers ate in the land of Egypt. Let all who are hungry enter and eat; let all who are needy come to our passover feast.' Transl.]

[6] Pes. 9.11.   [7] Josephus, *Ant.* 18.29f.   [8] Billerbeck II, 842f.

(Mark 14.26; Matt. 26.30), with the *singing of a hymn*. Since the '*hallel* at the conclusion of an ordinary meal', mentioned in several modern studies of our subject, is a product of fantasy—the thanksgiving prayer after the meal (Mark 14.23; Matt. 26.27: 'and blessed') cannot possibly be described by 'to sing a hymn'—the reference can only be to the second half[1] of the passover *hallel*,[2] which in the rabbinical literature, as Billerbeck[3] has shown, is sometimes called *himnon*[4] [a loan-word derived from the Greek ὕμνος, 'hymn'. Transl.].

13. After the meal *Jesus did not return to Bethany*, although according to Mark 11.11f.; Matt. 21.17[5] he had spent the preceding nights there. Rather he went to the Mount of Olives (Mark 14.26 par.), into a garden (Mark 14.32 par.) which, according to John 18.1, was situated on the east bank of the brook Kidron. Why? The night of the passover had to be spent in Jerusalem (contemporary exegesis derived this commandment from Deut. 16.7). In order to make it possible to keep this commandment the city district had been enlarged and for the purpose of spending the passover night was held to include Bethphage.[6] *Bethany, however, lay outside this enlarged city district* and therefore must not be entered by Jesus during the night Nisan 14/15, whereas the Kidron valley and the western slope of the Mount of Olives, including therefore Gethsemane, lay within the permitted district of greater Jerusalem.[7]

14. Of absolutely decisive significance is one last observation. The present writer can say that this is for him the convincing argument for the paschal character of the Last Supper. Jesus announces his impend-

---

[1] The first half of the *hallel* (according to the school of Shammai Ps. 113, according to the school of Hillel Pss. 113–14) was sung after the passover *haggadah* (Pes. 10.6; Tos. Pes. 10.9 [173.2]), the second half (Pss. 114–18 or 115–18) after the ending of the meal (Pes. 10.7). Probably in this matter, as often, the school of Shammai represents the older use, for the response with Hallelujah (see below, pp. 255f.) suggests that both parts of the *hallel* began with this word (Ps. 113.1; 113.9 = 113.1 in LXX).

[2] A. Wünsche, *Neue Beiträge zur Erläuterung der Evangelien aus Talmud und Midrasch*, Göttingen, 1878, 334; J. Wellhausen, *Das Evangelium Marci*[2], Berlin, 1909 [= *Evangelium Marci*], 119; Dalman, *Jesus-Jeshua*, 131f.; J. Mann, 'Rabbinic Studies in the Synoptic Gospels', *HUCA* 1 (1924), 341f.; Billerbeck IV, 75f.; Schlatter, *Matthäus*, 745.

[3] Billerbeck IV, 76.

[4] The same in Philo, *De spec. leg.* 2.148: the passover is celebrated 'with prayers and hymns'.

[5] Luke 21.37; 22.39 has 'the Mount of Olives'. John 18.2 (Gethsemane), on the other hand, is not referring to the place where he had stayed at night.

[6] See above, p. 43 n. 2.

[7] Cf. Lohmeyer, *Markus*, 311.

ing passion at the Last Supper by *speaking words of interpretation over the bread and the wine*. What led him to this altogether extraordinary manner of announcing his passion? I can see only one answer to this question: *interpretation of the special elements of the meal is a fixed part of the passover ritual*. This custom, still practised today, developed out of the exegesis of Ex. 12.26f.; 13.8. It took place after the preliminary course and the mixing of the second of the four ritual cups. The interpretation of the special elements of the passover meal was introduced by the son's[1] question about the *peculiarities* of this meal, which the *paterfamilias* answered by telling the story of the Exodus, based on Deut. 26.5–11, and combining with this the interpretation (Pes. 10.4). In this interpretation of the peculiarities of the passover meal three elements of the meal had to be specially mentioned: 'Rabban Gamaliel (almost certainly Gamaliel I, *c.* AD 30)[2] used to say: "Whoever does not mention (in his interpretation) these three things at Passover has not fulfilled his obligation: the passover lamb, the unleavened bread and the bitter herbs (cf. Ex. 12.8)" ' (Pes. 10.5).[3] The form in which the interpretation was couched is shown by the continuation of the same passage. 'The passover lamb (should be interpreted as follows): because God passed over (*pasaḥ*) in mercy the houses of our fathers in Egypt (Ex. 12.27); unleavened bread: because our fathers were redeemed from Egypt; the bitter herbs: because the Egyptians embittered the lives of our fathers in Egypt (Ex. 1.14)' (Pes. 10.5).

Of special interest to us is the interpretation given to the flat loaves of unleavened bread. The one just quoted from Gamaliel I seems to depend upon a word-play (not made explicit) between *maṣṣah* (unleavened bread) and *yaṣa* (to go out), i.e. it interprets the unleavened bread as 'exodus bread'. The official passover *haggadah* interprets with the help of Ex. 12.34, 39: 'This *maṣṣah* which we eat, what is the reason for it? Because the dough of our fathers had not had time to leaven when the King of all kings revealed himself to them and redeemed them.'[4] This interpretation in terms of the great haste in

---

[1] In case of need, the question was asked by the housewife or by another adult.
[2] So correctly E. Baneth in *Mischnaioth* II, Berlin, 1920, 248 n. 35, and D. Daube, *The New Testament and Rabbinic Judaism* (Jordan Lectures in Comparative Religion 2), London, 1956, 187, because the interpretation of the passover lamb presupposes the act of sacrifice and therefore that the Temple was still standing.
[3] It was customary to elevate the bitter herbs and the *maṣṣot* while interpreting them (b. Pes. 116b).
[4] [Cf. *The Passover Haggadah*, New York, 1953, 49. Transl.]

which the exodus took place is already to be found in the Mekilta on Exodus[1] and in Philo.[2] A related, but different, interpretation is based on Deut. 16.3, where the unleavened bread is called 'the bread of affliction'. Josephus, to explain the custom of eating unleavened bread at the passover, refers to the thirty days after the exodus from Egypt, in which the Israelites passed through the desert and in their need had to eat unleavened bread for lack of other food.[3] 'Therefore, in memory of that misery, we celebrate a feast of eight days, the feast of Unleavened Bread.'[4] Deut. 16.3 is also[5] the basis for the ancient Aramaic formula of interpretation of the *maṣṣot*, already referred to on p. 54, which still today serves to introduce the passover *haggadah*[6] and which is of particular importance because its beginning is related in form to Jesus' words of interpretation: 'Behold, this is the bread of affliction (cf. Deut. 16.3) which our fathers had to eat as they came out of Egypt.'[7]

But the interpretation of the unleavened bread was not necessarily limited to an historical retrospect. In Philo we find no less than four allegorical interpretations.[8] The first: that the unleavened bread is 'unfinished' ($\dot{a}\tau\epsilon\lambda\dot{\eta}s$), and thus reflects nature before harvest-time— the unleavened loaves are intended to raise men's hopes for the gifts of nature.[9] The second: unleavened bread is a gift of nature while leavened bread is an artificial product—the unleavened loaves are intended to exhort men to the life of primitive times, a life without artificial demands or needs.[10] The third: the unleavened loaves are 'bread of affliction' (Deut. 16.3)—they should remind man that a

---

[1] Mek. Ex. 12.39.

[2] Philo, *De spec. leg.* 2.158.

[3] Josephus, *Ant.* 2.316.

[4] *Ibid.*, 2.317.

[5] Cf. also Siphre Deut. 130 on 16.3: 'R. Simeon said: Why is it called the bread of affliction? Because of the affliction they had to endure in Egypt.'

[6] I.e. the ritual of exposition and prayer by the *paterfamilias*, cf. above, p. 56, and below, p. 85.

[7] Following the Yemenite *Siddur* quoted by Dalman, *Jesus-Jeshua*, 139. These words are not a formula of distribution, as is so often alleged; they are not spoken at the breaking of bread by which the main meal is opened (see below, pp. 84ff.), but before this, as an introduction to the interpretation of the elements during the passover *haggadah*.

[8] A source analysis of these interpretations has been given by I. Heinemann, *Philons griechische und jüdische Bildung*, Breslau, 1932 (reprint Darmstadt, 1962), 121–4.

[9] Philo, *De spec. leg.* 2.158.

[10] *Ibid.*, 2.159–61.

great task can only be accomplished by labour and self-denial.[1] The fourth: the unleavened loaves are a warning to turn away from arrogance.[2]

The multiplicity of Philonic allegorical explanations is matched by the multiplicity of interpretations given to 'bread of affliction' (*lehem 'oni*), Deut. 16.3, in Palestine.[3] Alongside the widespread interpretation already mentioned, which refers it to Israel's sufferings in Egypt, or during and after the exodus from Egypt, we find also the following: (1) 'bread of affliction' = simple bread (as distinct from pastry or cake);[4] (2) (reading *lehem 'oni*)[5] = 'bread which (also) may be eaten during mourning;'[6] (3) 'bread over which (at the passover) many words are spoken' ('*onin*);[7] (4) 'bread of the poor' (reading *lehem 'ani*) = fragments of bread,[8] or bread for the baking of which the *paterfamilias* himself has to heat the oven.[9] We can see, then, that in Palestine also the interpretation of the unleavened bread was by no means limited to an historical retrospect. On the contrary, the special elements of the passover meal were interpreted to a large extent *in relationship to the present*, as we can see in the following statement referring to this interpretation: 'In every generation a man must so regard himself as if he himself came forth out of Egypt' (Pes. 10.5).[10]

Although the interpretation of the elements in the ritual of the passover meal was concerned chiefly with the three ingredients mentioned in Ex. 12.8, passover lamb, unleavened bread and bitter herbs, it was by no means limited to these, as we can see from Pes. 10.5.[11] It is

[1] *De congressu eruditionis gratia* 161–7.

[2] *Quaest. in Exodum* 1.15 (J. B. Aucher, *Philonis Judaei Paralipomena Armena*, Venice, 1826, 459f.; R. Marcus, *Philo. Supplement* II. *Questions and Answers on Exodus* [The Loeb Classical Library], London and Cambridge, Mass., 1953, 24f.).

[3] This is one example of the correctness of Billerbeck's remarks about the differences between the allegories of the Alexandrian and of the Palestinian scholars. In the former the letter of Scripture is seen only as the outer shell of its spiritual content, in the latter it retains its full validity (Billerbeck III, 397f.).

[4] Siphre Deut. 130 on 16.3, cf. b. Pes. 36a.

[5] Cf. Deut. 26.14.

[6] b. Pes. 36a (Bar.).

[7] b. Pes. 36a; 115b.

[8] See below, pp. 68f.

[9] b. Pes. 115b, 116a.

[10] This sentence is omitted in the Mishnah codices Kaufmann (now in the possession of the Oriental Library of the Hungarian Academy of Sciences, a facsimile edition was published by G. Beer, Den Haag, 1930), De Rossi (the Parma manuscript), Vatic. Hebr. 109, and Cambridge University Library Add. 470.1 (published in transcription by W. H. Lowe, 1883).

[11] See above, p. 56.

important for our investigation to note that in the Jerusalem Talmud we have evidence of an allegorical interpretation of the four cups: 'R. Johanan (bar Nappaḥa, died 279) said in the name of R. Bannaia (c. 200): (the four cups) correspond to the fourfold description of redemption (in Ex. 6.6f.)[1] . . . R. Joshua b. Levi (c. 250) said: (they) correspond to the four cups of Pharaoh (Gen. 40.11, 13) . . . R. Levi (c. 300) said: (they) correspond to the four world empires. The scholars said: (they) correspond to the four cups of punishment which the Holy One, blessed be he, will one day give to the nations of the world to drink. . . . And similarly the Holy One, blessed be he, will give four cups of comfort[2] to Israel to drink.'[3] This passage is significant, because not only does it bear witness to the allegorical interpretation of the four passover cups, but proves at the same time that these interpretations of the peculiarities of the meal combine a looking back over the history of God's saving activity in the past with a looking forward to the saving event of the Messianic future.[4]

But of particular importance is the fact that there is also to be found an *eschatological interpretation of the unleavened bread*, side by side with the historical interpretation and that which relates it to the present. ' "Go thy way forth to the ends[5] of the flock (of Israel)" (S. of S. 1.8). R. Eliezer (ben Hyrcanus, c. 90) said: Of the ash-cake (the unleavened bread) which Israel took out of Egypt have they eaten for 31 days (Nisan 15-Iyyar 15). . . . From this you may learn[6] what I shall do to them subsequently in the End, and so it is written, "There shall be an abundance of corn in the land" (Ps. 72.16).'[7] So already in the first century AD we can trace the eschatological interpretation of the unleavened bread: on it God had miraculously fed Israel during their journey through the desert, and had thus given a type of the abundance of bread in the Messianic time. It is no accident that in the New Testament the unleavened loaves are also eschatologically interpreted: I Cor. 5.7b–8. This passage (from 'for our passover') is probably based upon an early Christian passover *haggadah*.

---

[1] 'Bring you out', 'deliver you', 'redeem you', 'take you for my people'.
[2] Ps. 16.5; 23.5 and 116.13 (plural = two cups).
[3] j. Pes. 10.37b. 61–37c.10 par. (quoting different authorities) Gen. R. 88.4 on 40.9–11; Midr. Ps. 75, §4 (anonymous).
[4] See below, pp. 206ff.
[5] So the Midrash, instead of 'in the footsteps'.
[6] With A. Wünsche, *Der Midrasch Schir Ha-Schirim*, Leipzig, 1880, 37, and Billerbeck I, 86, we follow the reading of *Mattenot Kehunnah*.
[7] Midr. S. of S. on 1.8.

Evidence for such a supposition is to be found in the interpretation of the passover lamb, the bitter herbs and the unleavened bread, which corresponds to the passover ritual; in the abrupt introduction of the comparison between Jesus and the passover lamb (v. 7b), only found here in Paul; possibly also in the change from the second person (vv. 6–7a) to the first (vv. 7b–8); and above all in the language, which is un-Pauline[1] and Semitic.[2] The theme of this early Christian passover meditation is: on Good Friday the great passover festival has begun. Therefore to be a Christian means: to live in the passover, in the deliverance from the bondage of sin. This theme is developed in the text as follows: the passover lamb is interpreted as the symbol of the Messiah who was sacrificed as the unblemished lamb. The leaven which is removed from all the houses during the night of Nisan 13/14 is the symbol of the evil and wickedness which characterizes the old world. The unleavened loaves are interpreted eschatologically in two ways: as pure dough they represent the purity and truth which characterizes the new world (I Cor. 5.8), and as new dough they symbolize the redeemed community (I Cor. 5.7a).[3]

When we add that Jesus' interpretation of the bread 'this is my body' bears a formal likeness to the ancient Aramaic interpretation of the unleavened bread 'this is the bread of affliction' (*ha lahma ʿanya*) quoted above,[4] we must conclude that *the ritual interpretation of the*

---

[1] Vocabulary: ἑορτάζειν only here in the NT, ἄζυμος only here in Paul, θύειν elsewhere in Paul only at I Cor. 10.20 (twice), ζύμη again in Paul at Gal. 5.9 (a proverb). Style: it is noticeable that in I Cor. 5.7a the adjective comes before the noun (τὴν παλαιὰν ζύμην, νέον φύραμα) as is usually the case in Paul; in 5.8, on the other hand, it follows the noun (ἐν ζύμῃ παλαιᾷ).

[2] The use of ἐν in ἑορτάζειν ἐν ζύμῃ/ἀζύμοις is non-Greek; it reflects *hgg b* (cf. I Sam. 30.16). The positioning of the adjective to follow the noun (see the previous footnote) is the only possibility in Semitic languages. The absence of the article in the genitive constructions ἐν ζύμῃ κακίας/καὶ πονηρίας and ἐν ἀζύμοις εἰλικρινείας καὶ ἀληθείας is a usage which occurs in the NT 'almost only in passages with strong Semitic colouring' (Blass-Debrunner, § 259); it represents a use of the construct state.

[3] An analogous eschatological interpretation of the unleavened bread may underlie the eucharistic prayer in Did. 9.4: the bread, the grains of which were gathered from the mountains, symbolizes the gathering of the scattered community of God at the end of time. I Cor. 10.17 testifies to the antiquity of this eschatological interpretation of the bread when it says 'Because there is one loaf, we who are many are one body'; the one loaf, which is broken and distributed among the participants, symbolizes and realizes the redeemed community. The fact that this is an old tradition follows, as R. Hupfeld, *Die Abendmahlsfeier*, Gütersloh, 1935, 74, has remarked, from the omission of a similar allegory for the wine (the multitude of grapes from which the old wine was produced) both in the Didache and I Corinthians.

[4] See above, pp. 56f.

special elements of the passover meal which we have described was the occasion for the interpretation which Jesus gave to the bread and the wine at the Last Supper. That means: structurally Jesus modelled his sayings upon the ritual of interpreting the passover. Only here is there a ritual pre-formation for speaking words of interpretation. This conclusion is supported by the fact that the annual interpretation of the special elements of the passover meal became a model for other such occasions. In this connection the following tradition may be mentioned, which refers to the meal on the ninth of Ab, the memorial day to the destruction of Jerusalem by the Babylonians and the Romans:[1] 'When Rab (died AD 247) had ended his meal, he took a damaged cake of bread, sprinkled some ashes on it and said (in imitation of the passover usage): "This is the meal of the ninth of Ab." '[2] The difference between the interpretation of the special elements in the passover ritual and Jesus' words of interpretation, that the former are mainly concerned with past salvation events whereas Jesus looks to a salvation event in the present, can be accounted for on the basis of the special situation of the Last Supper, and it is the less surprising because, as we have seen, eschatological interpretations are not lacking in the rabbinical exegesis of the passover, and the prospect of the Messianic future was indissolubly connected with the passover.[3] The further difference, that Jesus did not combine his interpretation with the passover *haggadah* at the end of the preliminary course, but with the saying of grace before and after the main meal, and accordingly limited it to the bread and wine, has probably arisen from his desire to combine his new interpretation with the distribution of the elements.[4]

The fourteen observations that have been made above concern not only the framework of the narrative but also its substance. It cannot be said therefore that only later embellishment has made the Last Supper a passover meal. It is much more the case that the passover character of the last meal of Jesus is unanimously supported by:

(1) the ancient liturgical formula itself: nos. 3, 8, 9, and, above all, 14;

---

[1] Cf. Dalman, *Jesus-Jeshua*, 139.
[2] Midr. Lam. on 3.16.
[3] See below, pp. 205ff.; Dalman, *Jesus-Jeshua*, 183; Billerbeck II, 256. Cf. the text of the present-day passover ritual.
[4] See below, pp. 231ff.

(2) the so-called 'eschatological prospect': Luke 22.15;

(3) the description of the meal: nos. 3–7, 10–13;

(4) the report about the arrangement of the room: nos. 1, 2 and Mark 14.12, 14, 16.

In conclusion it should be noted that the report of the synoptic gospels that the Last Supper was a passover meal *is at variance with the rite of the Early Church*. The Early Church did not celebrate the Lord's Supper according to the passover ritual, nor yet only once a year, but daily or on each Lord's day. The reminiscences of the passover can therefore not have come from the liturgical practice; 'for the liturgy gave no occasion for them'.[1] So when the synoptic gospels nevertheless describe the Last Supper as a passover meal and do not allow this to be lost in the tradition, the reason is obviously that the recollection of the fact was too firmly established to be removed by the influence of the ritual practice.[2] We have here, then, 'the survival of an historical reminiscence'.[3]

OBJECTIONS

We turn now to those considerations which have led to a questioning of the synoptic assertion (Mark 14.12, 14, 16 par.; Luke 22.15) that the Last Supper was a passover meal. The main objections are as follows:[4]

1. Ever since a short study by J. Wellhausen appeared in 1906[5] it has been frequently contended that the Last Supper could not have been a passover meal, because Mark 14.22 par. speaks of 'bread' (ἄρτος) whereas only 'unleavened bread' (ἄζυμα, Heb. *maṣṣah*, Aram.

---

[1] J. Delorme, 'La Cène et la Pâque dans le Nouveau Testament', in 'L'Eucharistie dans le Nouveau Testament', *Lumière et Vie* 31 (February 1957), 36.

[2] K. Völker, *Mysterium und Agape*, Gotha, 1927, 19. Cf. W. Marxsen, *Die Einsetzungsberichte zum Abendmahl* (Diss. Kiel, 1948), 14f.

[3] Delorme, *op. cit.*, 21.

[4] Those objections which are obviously erroneous I shall not discuss, as for instance the contention of M. Goguel, *L'Eucharistie des origines à Justin Martyr* (Diss. Paris), La Roche-sur-Yon, 1910, 62, that the Last Supper could not have been a passover, because the distribution of the bread at the passover took place only 'after the meal proper'. See below, p. 85 nn. 1, 2.

[5] J. Wellhausen, "Ἄρτον ἔκλασεν, Mc 14,22', *ZNW* 7 (1906), 182. The same view had been expressed earlier, e.g., by G. W. Pieritz, *The Gospels from the Rabbinical Point of View*, Oxford–London, 1873, 30, and still earlier in a fragment Περὶ τῶν ἀζύμων (MPG 95, col. 388) ascribed to John of Damascus (died AD 749), most probably falsely (cf. M. Lequien, 'Dissertatio sexta: De azymis, in qua etiam de postremo Domini nostri Jesu Christi Paschate', in MPG 94, cols. 367f.).

paṭṭira)[1] could properly be used in describing a passover meal. Unleavened bread cannot be designated 'bread' (ἄρτος). But not one of the numerous writers[2] who have repeated Wellhausen's thesis has taken the trouble to check it, although as early as 1912 G. Beer[3] had seriously challenged it. As a matter of fact, the contention that unleavened bread cannot be called 'bread' (ἄρτος) is incorrect. Quite apart from the possibility of a mere inaccuracy in the report when Mark 14.22 par. speaks of 'bread' (ἄρτος),[4] or from the fact that the eucharistic practice of the earliest churches which used ordinary leavened bread[5] might have led to some inaccuracy of expression, it has to be stated that the words *leḥem* and ἄρτος could be used of both leavened and unleavened bread.[6] It can further be shown that it was *quite the common practice* to call unleavened bread simply 'bread' (*leḥem* or ἄρτος). Decisive proof of this—in view of the extraordinary abundance of testimony—is the description of the twelve loaves of *shewbread* which were arranged on their special table in the sanctuary of the Temple.[7] We know for certain that the shewbread was unleavened, a fact not mentioned, probably by accident, in the Old Testament, but reported unanimously by Philo,[8] Josephus[9] and the Talmud.[10] Nevertheless the shewbread is *always* called simply 'bread'

---

[1] E.g., Targ. Jer. I Ex. 12.15.
[2] The latest is J. Finegan, *Die Überlieferung der Leidens- und Auferstehungsgeschichte Jesu* (BZNW 15), Giessen, 1934 [= *Überlieferung*], 62.
[3] Beer, *Pesachim*, 96.
[4] Bultmann, *Tradition*, 265 n. 4.
[5] Unleavened bread was hardly at hand in everyday life.
[6] Cf. *leḥem maṣṣot* Ex. 29.2; *leḥem paṭṭir* Targ. Jer. I, Onḳ., Samar. Ex. 29.2; ἄρτος ἄζυμος LXX Ex. 29.2; Lev. 2.4; 8.26; Num. 6. (15), 19; Judg. 6.20A (B: ἄζυμα); Philo, *De spec. leg.* 2.158; *De congressu eruditionis gratia* 168; *De vita contemplativa* 81; Josephus, *Ant.* 3.142. Cf. G. Beer, *Pesachim*, 96; A. Oepke, 'Ursprung und ursprünglicher Sinn des Abendmahls im Lichte der neuesten Forschung [III]', *Allgemeine Evangelisch-lutherische Kirchenzeitung* 59 (1926), col. 58; P. Fiebig, review of J. Klausner, *Jesus von Nazareth*[2], *ThLZ* 59 (1934), col. 416.
[7] Cf. the catalogue of the names given to the shewbread in Billerbeck III, 719, together with the numerous Talmudic testimonies in the quotations concerning the shewbread collected by Billerbeck III, 719–28; I, 618f.
[8] Philo, *De spec. leg.* 2.161; *De congressu* 168; *De vita* 81.
[9] Josephus, *Ant.* 3.142: ἄρτους τε δώδεκα ἀζύμους; 3.255: σῖτος ὀπτὸς ζύμης ἄμοιρος.
[10] Siphra on Lev. 2.11 (*ed. princ.*, Venice, 1545, 7c.15): ' "no cereal offering which you offer unto Jahweh may be made with leaven" (Lev. 2.11). R. Jose the Galilean (about AD 110) said: (that is said) in order to include the shewbread.' According to Men. 5.1, cf. 7.1, all flour offerings were unleavened with the exception of ten of the forty cakes of the salvation thank-offering (cf. on these cakes below, p. 65) and the two loaves of the first-fruits at Pentecost (Lev. 23.16f.); b. Men. 77b.

in the Old Testament and the Mishnah (*lehem*), in the Targum (*lahma*), in the Talmud (*lehem* or *lahma*) and in the Septuagint and Aquila[1] (ἄρτοι). For example, Ex. 25.30, *lehem panim*; Targ. Onk., *lehem appayya*; Targ. Jer. I, *lahma gawwa'ah*; LXX, ἄρτοι ἐνώπιοι; Aq., ἄρτοι προσώπου. The New Testament usage is exactly the same: οἱ ἄρτοι τῆς προθέσεως (Mark 2.26; Matt. 12.4; Luke 6.4), ἡ πρόθεσις τῶν ἄρτων (Heb. 9.2). Most significant is the fact that the shewbread can simply be called *hallehem* (Lev. 24.7; without the article: Ex. 40.23).[2] This simple designation 'bread' without any addition is also to be found in Philo, Josephus and the Mishnah. Philo calls the shewbread (*a*) by its Old Testament names, as, e.g., ἄρτοι τῆς προθέσεως,[3] (*b*) in some places ἄρτοι ἄζυμοι,[4] (*c*) elsewhere simply ἄρτοι;[5] Josephus has ἄρτοι ἄζυμοι,[6] ἄρτοι τοῦ θεοῦ[7] or also simply ἄρτοι;[8] the Mishnah usually uses the Old Testament expression *lehem happanim*,[9] but in one place has the simple *hallehem*,[10] three times repeated. The Old Testament, Philo, Josephus and the Mishnah therefore do not hesitate to describe the unleavened shewbread as *lehem* or ἄρτοι without further qualification.

This description of unleavened bread as *lehem* or ἄρτος without further qualification is by no means restricted to passages concerning the shewbread. According to Ex. 29.31ff.; Lev. 8.31f., a sacrificial meal follows *the consecration of the priests*. The unleavened bread (Ex. 29.2) eaten by the priests on this occasion is called simply 'bread' in the various versions of Ex. 29.32, 34; Lev. 8.31, 32: Heb., *hallehem*; Targ. Onk., Jer. I, *lahma*; LXX, οἱ ἄρτοι.[11] Four kinds of cakes were offered

---

[1] In the fragments of Symmachus and Theodotion we have no texts preserved in which shewbread is mentioned.

[2] The shewbread eaten by David at Nob (I Sam. 21.1–7) is called simply *lehem*, LXX, ἄρτος, in I Sam. 21.7. At a later time this shewbread of the sanctuary at Nob was understood to have been unleavened bread, as can be seen from b. Men. 95b, where the regulations concerning the shewbread of the Jerusalem Temple are applied to I Sam. 21.1–7. Also b. Men. 29a; 96b supports this conclusion.

[3] Philo, *De fuga* 185.

[4] Instances given above, p. 63 n. 6.

[5] Philo, *De spec. leg.* 1.172, 175; *De vita Mos.* 2(3). 104. Cf. *De spec. leg.* 2.161.

[6] Josephus, *Ant.* 3.142.

[7] *Ant.* 8.39.

[8] *Ant.* 3.143; 8.90; *Bell.* 5.217.

[9] E.g., Men. 6.2, 6; 11.7; Tam. 3.3; Mid. 1.6, and elsewhere.

[10] Men. 11.8.

[11] At the consecration of the priests it was also the rule to burn three unleavened loaves, among them, according to Ex. 29.23: 'one loaf of bread (*lehem*) and one cake of bread (*lehem*) with oil'; Targ. Onk. 'one loaf of bread (*lehem*) and one cake of bread (*lehem*) with oil', similarly Targ. Jer. I; LXX (only one loaf instead of these two), καὶ ἄρτον ἕνα ἐξ ἐλαίου. In Lev. 8.26 these two unleavened loaves are

with the *salvation thank-offering*, of which three (loaves, wafers and
cakes of meal mixed with oil) were unleavened (Lev. 7.12) and the
fourth leavened (Lev. 7.13). The unleavened cakes (*hallot maṣṣot*,
Lev. 7.12) are called ἄρτους ἐκ σεμιδάλεως in the Septuagint (LXX,
Lev. 7.12) and *lahmah šel todah* in the Tosephta;[1] the Mishnah includes
all four in the collective term *hallehem*,[2] and the Talmud the three
unleavened kinds in the collective term *lhmy twdh*.[3] Finally, the
Nazirite sacrifice includes the offering of a basket of unleavened cakes
and wafers. The LXX calls the former ἄρτους ἀναπεποιημένους ἐν ἐλαίῳ
(Num. 6.15), while the Mishnah again includes the unleavened cakes
and wafers of this offering in the collective term *lehem* (without
further qualification!).[4]

The evidence already given, which is complete for the Hebrew
OT, the LXX, Philo and the Mishnah, and which could easily be
enlarged by further references from the Tosephta, the Midrashim and
the two Talmuds, proves that it is wrong to maintain that ἄρτος
in Mark 14.22 par. cannot possibly mean unleavened bread. Moreover, there is no lack of direct evidence for the fact that *the unleavened
bread eaten during the feast of the Passover could be described as lehem or
ἄρτος*. In this respect we must recall Deut. 16.3 where the unleavened
bread is called 'bread of affliction' (*lehem 'oni*; Targ. Onk., *lehem
'anni*; Jer. I, *lahma 'anya*; LXX, ἄρτος κακώσεως). Dependent upon
Deut. 16.3 is the ancient Aramaic formula from the passover liturgy
quoted above,[5] in which the unleavened bread is called *lahma
'anya*, and also the comments in b. Pes. 36a, b; 37a; 38a; 115b; 116a,
in which the passover unleavened bread, following Deut. 16.3, is
called *lehem*. But this usage can also be found independently of Deut.

---

called 'one unleavened cake (*maṣṣah*) and one cake of bread (*lehem*) with oil';
Targ. Onk., Jer. I 'one unleavened cake (*paṭṭirta*) and one cake of bread (*dilehem*)
with oil'; LXX, ἄρτον ἕνα ἄζυμον καὶ ἄρτον ἐξ ἐλαίου ἕνα.

In these passages, too, the simple *lehem* or ἄρτος are used without further qualification to designate unleavened bread; only LXX, Lev. 8.26, has the more definite ἄρτος ἄζυμος along with the simple ἄρτος.

[1] Tos. Sheḳ. 1.11 (174.24) puts side by side (*a*) *minhat todah* and (*b*) *lahmah
šel todah*; according to b. Men. 77b, the former is leavened and the latter therefore
unleavened. The '*al* in Lev. 7.13 (meaning 'in addition to') caused the leavened
bread to be regarded as *minhah*, and the unleavened as its complement.
[2] Men. 2.3; 7.3, 4, 5; Tem. 3.2.
[3] b. Pes. 37a; cf. b. Men. 78b.
[4] Meil. 3.2; Naz. 4.4; Zeb. 10.2.
[5] See above, pp. 54, 57.

16.3. Philo calls the passover unleavened bread ἄρτος ἄζυμος (*De spec. leg.* 2.158), and Josephus once describes the unleavened bread which the Israelites ate as they fled from Egypt simply as ἄρτοι (*Ant.* 2.316). Also, in Luke 24.30, 35, ἄρτος must mean unleavened bread: the Emmaus incident took place during passover week. Finally, it is significant that in the passover liturgy the blessing over the unleavened bread begins with the words of the ordinary blessing for bread: 'Blessed art thou, our God, king of the universe, who brings forth bread from the earth.'[1]

Thus, the word ἄρτος in Mark 14.22 par. by no means excludes the possibility that the accounts of the Last Supper are accounts of a passover meal.

2. A second objection can be quickly disposed of, the objection that the daily[2] repetition of the supper in the Early Church speaks against the passover character of the Last Supper. Is it not the case, the argument runs, that if the Last Supper were a passover meal we would expect a yearly repetition? The objection presupposes that the meals of the earliest Church were repetitions of the last meal with Jesus. But that is a mistake. *The meals of the Early Church were not originally repetitions of the last meal which Jesus celebrated with his disciples, but of the daily table fellowship of the disciples with him.*[3] Only gradually, although indeed already in pre-Pauline times, was the early Christian celebration of meals linked with, and influenced by, the remembrance of the Last Supper.

There was, however, one group in the Early Church which did practise a yearly repetition of the Last Supper at passover time: the Jewish Christians. We learn from Epiphanius that the Ebionites used unleavened bread at this yearly festival.[4] This yearly festival is very old, and we have already (above pp. 59f.) called attention to a passover meditation used in connection with it.

3. A further objection is that Mark 14.22–25 par. contains *no*

---

[1] B. Italiener–A. Freimann–A. L. Mayer–A. Schmidt, *Die Darmstädter Pessach-Haggadah, Tafelband*, Leipzig, 1928 [f. 29b]; Maimonides, *Hilkot ḥameṣ umaṣṣah* 8.6, 8 (ed. Berlin, 1862, 103a).

[2] Acts 2.42.

[3] E. Schwartz, 'Osterbetrachtungen', *ZNW* 7 (1906), 1; Wellhausen, *Evangelium Marci*, 117f.; Lietzmann, *Mass and Lord's Supper*, 204f.; Schlatter, *Lukas*, 455.

[4] Epiphanius, *Panarion* 30.16.1 (*GCS* 25.353.10–12): 'Apparently they celebrate the mysteries (i.e. the Eucharist) in imitation of the holy (meals) in the (great) Church, (but) from year to year with unleavened (bread) and the other part of the mystery (i.e. the cup) only with water.' Cf. Jeremias, πάσχα, *TWNT* V (1954), 902 n. 54.

explicit reference to the passover ritual, in particular none to the paschal lamb and the bitter herbs. This is true; but this silence is only surprising so long as we do not take seriously the fact that Mark 14.22–24 is a cultic formula, and as such does not purport to give an historical description of the Last Supper[1] but only of those *moments which were constitutive for the celebration of the primitive Church.* Since this celebration was not originally a repetition of the Last Supper with all its historical accompaniments, but of the daily coming together of the disciples in table fellowship with the Messiah,[2] it is natural that only the rites which continued to be performed by the Church should be mentioned in the liturgical formula. A striking parallel is to be found in the elaborate description of the passover meal in Pes. 10, which only mentions the eating of the paschal lamb (the central act) in an aside: 'and in the time of the temple they used to bring before him the body of the passover offering',[3] although the slaughter and preparation of the paschal lambs had been extensively described in earlier chapters (Pes. 5ff.). The reason for this strange neglect of the paschal lamb is to be found in the fact that Pes. 5ff. describes the passover sacrifices as they were made at a time when the Temple still stood, whereas in Pes. 10 there follows the ritual for the contemporary annual celebration of the feast at which, after the destruction of the Temple, no paschal lamb was eaten. Thus we have in the Mishnah tractate Pesaḥim precisely *the same combination of historical report and cultic ritual* as in the texts describing the Last Supper, and in both cases we can observe the same thing happening: the cultic ritual overshadows the historical facts and concentrates attention upon the continuing rites.[4] All the more important, therefore, is the direct mention of the paschal lamb in Luke 22.15 and the indirect reference to the bitter herbs in Mark 14.20 par. ('dipping').[5]

4. A fourth objection consists in the thesis that *the description of the Last Supper is inconsistent with the passover ritual.* On the one hand it is

[1] It is not a 'protocol' (B. Frischkopf, *Die neuesten Erörterungen über die Abendmahlsfrage* [NTA 9.4–5], Münster, 1921, 16).

[2] See above, p. 66; below, pp. 204f.

[3] Pes. 10.3 end.

[4] 'It is astonishing that so clear a difference in the literary genres seems to escape critics who have made so many correct observations on the relationships between the life of the primitive community and the formulation of gospel pericopae', writes correctly P. Benoit, 'Le récit de la Cène dans Lc. XXII, 15–20', *RB* 48 (1939), 385.

[5] For the possibility that Jesus compared himself to the lamb in the passover meditation see below, p. 222.

held that at the passover—in distinction from the normal usage—*the bread was broken first and the blessing said after this*.[1] Since the reverse sequence is presupposed in Mark 14.22 par. ('having blessed [Luke 'having given thanks'] he broke'), many[2] have drawn the conclusion that because of this difference the Last Supper could not have been a passover meal. On the other hand, it is claimed that by the time of Jesus *individual cups were used* at the passover meal; since, according to Mark 14.23 par., all the people present at the Last Supper drank from the same cup, supposedly this is evidence for the fact that the Last Supper could not have been a passover meal.[3] Finally, it is explained that each participant in the passover meal was supposed to have *his own dish* before him, and this stands in contrast to the eating from the common dish presupposed by Mark 14.20.[4]

(*a*) As regards first the thesis that at the passover meal the bread was broken first and the blessing said after this, I have attempted to show elsewhere[5] that this is simply incorrect. The error has been caused by misunderstanding a saying of Maimonides (died 1204). Maimonides[6] says that in his time a practice was customary, which first appears in b. Pes. 115b, 116a, of saying the blessing at a passover meal over only part of a loaf. This practice was meant to symbolize—following Deut. 16.3, where the unleavened bread is called 'the bread of affliction'—the poverty of the Israelites as they came out of Egypt: the poor man does not have a whole loaf. It was J. Lightfoot, as far as I can see, who first mistook this initial dividing (Maimonides uses *ḥlḳ* 'to divide', not *prs* 'to split') *before* the blessing for the 'breaking of bread' *after* the blessing,[7] and others have followed him in this

[1] So M. Haller, 'Das Heilige Abendmahl und das Passahmahl', *Theologische Studien aus Württemberg* 8 (1887), 68f.; F. Spitta, *Zur Geschichte und Litteratur des Urchristentums* I, Göttingen, 1893, 238; C. Clemen, *Der Ursprung des heiligen Abendmahls*, Leipzig, 1898, 25; K. G. Goetz, *Die heutige Abendmahlsfrage in ihrer geschichtlichen Entwicklung*[2], 132; Batiffol, *Études* II. *L'Eucharistie*, 72; A. Greiff, *Das älteste Pascharituale der Kirche, Did. 1–10, und das Johannesevangelium* (Johanneische Studien I), Paderborn, 1929, 149.

[2] E.g., Haller, Spitta, Goetz.

[3] G. H. Box, 'The Jewish Antecedents of the Eucharist', *JTS* 3 (1901–2), 359; Beer, *Pesachim*, 97–99; K. G. Goetz, *Das Abendmahl, eine Diatheke Jesu oder sein letztes Gleichnis?* (UNT 8), Leipzig, 1920, 18 n. 1; Oesterley, *The Jewish Background of the Christian Liturgy*, 163.

[4] Bultmann, *Tradition*, 264; Finegan, *Überlieferung*, 66.

[5] J. Jeremias, 'Das Brotbrechen beim Passahmahl und Mc 14, 22 par.', *ZNW* 33 (1934), 203f.

[6] Maimonides, *Hilkot ḥameṣ umaṣṣah* 8.6 (ed. Berlin, 1862, 103a).

[7] J. Lightfoot, *Exercitations* on Matt. 26.26 (*Works* XI, 332).

mistake right down to the present. The truth is that at the passover, as at every other meal, the blessing was said *first*, and *then* the unleavened bread was broken and the fragments distributed. The sequence 'blessing—breaking of the bread' (Mark 14.22 par. 'having blessed he broke') is therefore in full accord with the passover ritual.

(*b*) What, then, is the situation with regard to the other contention that at the time of Jesus individual cups were used at the passover meal? The fact is that from the second century AD onwards there were objections on hygienic grounds to the practice of drinking from *one* cup.[1] However, these very protests show that it was not uncommon for several people to drink from one cup. In fact, R. Joshua b. Levi, who lived in the middle of the third century, still allowed for the two possibilities of individual cups and a common cup at communal meals,[2] and on festal occasions it remained the general practice for the cup of blessing to be passed to all the participants after the one who had said the blessing had drunk from it.[3] It is therefore, as Dalman has shown,[4] extremely probable that the *earlier custom* prescribed that the cup over which *grace after the meal* had been said should *be handed round*[5] to let everyone present share in the benediction. This view is supported by the analogous treatment of the bread: the bread over which the blessing had been said was broken so that every guest could share in the blessing by eating a piece.

As regards the passover meal in particular, the words of Pes. 10.2, 4, 7 (10.2: 'the first cup has been mixed *for him*'—for the *paterfamilias*?[6] for each guest?[7]) leave room for some doubt whether the common or individual cup is meant, although the context favours the

---

[1] Tos. Ber. 5.9(12.9); Derek ereş R. 8, cf. Billerbeck IV, 59 under *a*. Evidence dating from a later period in Strack, P*e*saḥim, 11*.

[2] j. Ber. 6. 10a.58, cf. Billerbeck IV, 58f., 62.

[3] Dalman, *Jesus-Jeshua*, 153.

[4] Dalman, *ibid.*; further 'Der Wein des letzten Mahles Jesu', *Allgemeine Evangelisch-lutherische Kirchenzeitung* 64 (1931), col. 798; *Arbeit und Sitte in Palästina* IV (BFChTh II 33), Gütersloh, 1935, 393.

[5] Cf. Ber. 8.8: 'If wine is brought after the meal and there is but that one cup . . .'; according to Billerbeck Tos. Ber. 7.2 (15.2) *kos eḥad* is perhaps to be understood similarly. But the expression 'but that one cup' is ambiguous; it does not necessarily mean that only one drinking-vessel was available, but can also be understood in the sense that the supply of wine was not sufficient to offer it while the meal was still in progress.

[6] Beer, *Pesachim*, 190.

[7] Billerbeck IV, 59, 61; Strack, P*e*saḥim, 32; E. Baneth in *Mischnaioth* II, 238 n. 8; 239 n. 11.

former.[1] However, even if the Mishnah should presuppose the individual cup, its testimony would scarcely be valid for Jesus' time. For the Mishnah describes the celebration of the passover as it was held after AD 70, when it was no longer celebrated by the whole nation in Jerusalem but by individual families in the places where they lived. More significance is to be attached to the fact that b. Pes. 108b reports that in some cases the *paterfamilias* invited his children and other members of the family to drink from his cup; this could be the survival of an earlier custom. For the time of Jesus, however, a simple technical consideration seems to me to be decisive: were there enough eating utensils in that overcrowded holy city for each one of the pilgrims who filled its houses, courtyards and roof-tops in tens of thousands for the passover celebration to have his own cup? Anyone who knows something of oriental households will certainly have to answer in the negative.

It must therefore be regarded as most probable that the *earlier custom* was to share one *common cup* at the passover meal, at least in the case of the cup of blessing, the third of the four passover cups, and that Mark 14.23 therefore reflects the situation of a passover meal at the time of Jesus.

(*c*) Finally, we come to the contention that at a passover meal each participant had his own dish before him, to which Mark 14.20 is contrary. This is derived from a statement by Billerbeck,[2] but his statement refers to the main course only and not to the preliminary course, and is in any case in need of further limitation. It is true that evidence from the Amoraic period shows that each participant in a passover meal had a small table at his side on which stood the side-dishes (fruit purée, unleavened bread and bitter herbs), while the main courses were served on the common table. But conclusive evidence for this custom is forthcoming only for Babylonia, and from there not until the fourth and fifth centuries,[3] although it is possible

---

[1] Pes. 10.2: 'The first cup has been mixed for him; now, according to the Shammaites he pronounces the benediction over the day.' The subject of the second clause is certainly the *paterfamilias*, and therefore he should be the subject of the first, since there is no sign of a change of the subject. Similarly Pes. 10.7: 'The third cup has been mixed for him; now he says the benediction after the meal.' Here also the subject of the second clause is the *paterfamilias*. It seems therefore to be assumed that it is his cup which circulates.

[2] Billerbeck I, 989; IV, 65f., 71f.

[3] b. Pes. 115b: R. Shimi b. Ashi (after 400). It is probable that the incident reported in the same passage as having occurred in the house of Rabbah b. Naḥmani (died 330) is to be understood in this way.

that a remark by Palestinian scholars presupposes it in the third century.[1] But that individual tables should have been in general use in the quite different circumstances of an overcrowded Jerusalem— in part on the roof-tops!—cannot be proven and is altogether improbable.

Thus there is no single point at which a contradiction between the description of the Last Supper and the passover ritual of the earlier period can be demonstrated.

5. A fifth objection is concerned with Mark 14.2. The Sanhedrin attempted to arrest Jesus by a ruse: ἔλεγον γάρ· μὴ ἐν τῇ ἑορτῇ, μήποτε ἔσται θόρυβος τοῦ λαοῦ. The translation 'not during the feast' for μὴ ἐν τῇ ἑορτῇ is usual at this point and the conclusion is often drawn from this that *the decision of the Sanhedrin* not to arrest Jesus 'during the feast' *excludes the synoptic chronology*, according to which Jesus was arrested during the night of the first day of the feast (which began at sunset).[2] But even if we assume this translation to be correct, the conclusion is still left hanging in the air. How do we know that the decision of the Sanhedrin was carried out? It was, after all, reached *before* Judas's offer to play the traitor, which provided an unexpected opportunity to arrest Jesus during the feast.

But quite apart from this, the interpretation of the words μὴ ἐν τῇ ἑορτῇ as a definition of time, which has called forth a whole literature, is untenable because it makes no sense. If they are interpreted, with the majority of scholars, as 'not during the feast, but *before*',[3] they make no sense, because the great mass of pilgrims had already arrived several days before the feast for the performance of the purification rites (John 11.55); a 'tumult' was therefore just as much to

[1] b. Pes. 115b: scholars from the school of R. Jannai, who was active *c.* 220–50.

[2] So, e.g., Wellhausen, *Evangelium Marci*, 108. He is followed by Schwartz, 'Osterbetrachtungen', *ZNW* 7 (1906), 23, who states categorically, 'the earliest report, Mark 14.1–2, which is still free from corrections, says explicitly that he (Jesus) was arrested two days before the passover'; C. G. Montefiore, *The Synoptic Gospels* I², London, 1927, 309; M. Dibelius, *From Tradition to Gospel*, London and New York, 1935, 191; Finegan, *Überlieferung*, 61–63; Th. Preiss, *Life in Christ*, London, 1954, 82.

[3] Spitta, *Zur Geschichte und Litteratur des Urchristentums* I, 223f.; Schwartz, *ibid.*; Wellhausen, *ibid.*; *Einleitung*, 133; K. Bornhäuser, *Das Wirken des Christus durch Taten und Worte* (BFChTh II 2), Gütersloh, 1921, 195; E. Klostermann, *Das Markusevangelium*⁴, Tübingen, 1950, 141; Lietzmann, *Mass and Lord's Supper*, 173; O. Holtzmann, *Das Neue Testament nach dem Stuttgarter griechischen Text* I, Giessen, 1926, 61; Montefiore, *op. cit.*, 309f.; M. Dibelius, 'Das historische Problem der Leidensgeschichte', *ZNW* 30 (1931), 194f.; Goguel, *Life of Jesus*, 436; Finegan, *Überlieferung*, 3; Lagrange, *Évangile*, 495.

be feared on the two days before the feast (Mark 14.1) as during the feast itself. If they are understood as 'not during the feast, but *afterwards*',[1] then this also gives no satisfactory sense, since the return of pilgrims was permissible at any time after the second feast day (Nisan 16),[2] and who could guarantee that Jesus would still be in Jerusalem after the seven days of the feast were over? Lastly, any temporal interpretation of the words μὴ ἐν τῇ ἑορτῇ is excluded by the preceding 'for' (γάρ), which is meant to explain the words 'by stealth' (Mark 14.1). Jesus had to be arrested by a ruse so that no tumult be caused among the crowd—this precaution makes sense only if he is supposed to be arrested *during the feast*.

All these difficulties disappear when it is recognized that ἑορτή in our passage has the meaning 'festal *assembly*, festal *crowd*'.[3] This meaning is found in John 7.11, 'they were looking for him at the feast (ἐν τῇ ἑορτῇ)': the Jews sought Jesus *among the festal crowd*;[4] and further in John 2.23.[5] We may compare this usage with that in LXX, Ps. 73(74).4, '. . . . in the midst of your *festal assembly* (ἑορτῆς)', and 117(118).27, 'bring a *festal procession* (ἑορτήν) together'; and in Plotinus, *Enn.* 6.6.12 we find ὄχλον καὶ ἑορτὴν καὶ στρατὸν καὶ πλῆθος,[6] where ἑορτή is clearly established as meaning the festal crowd by the three co-ordinated nouns.[7]

In Mark 14.2 ἐν τῇ ἑορτῇ is therefore by no means necessarily to be understood as a temporal reference, it may well be *local*, '*in the presence of the festal crowd*'.[8] Only in this way can an intelligible mean-

---

[1] H. J. Holtzmann, *Die Synoptiker*[3], Tübingen-Leipzig, 1901, 171; Th. Zahn, *Das Evangelium des Matthäus*[2], Leipzig, 1905 [= *Matthäus*], 679; Dalman, *Jesus-Jeshua*, 98; A. Schlatter, *Markus. Der Evangelist für die Griechen*, Stuttgart, 1935, 249f.; Lohmeyer, *Markus*, 290f., and others.

[2] Billerbeck II, 147f. According to Luke 24.13ff. two followers of Jesus left Jerusalem on Nisan 17 (cf. p. 79 n. 3); they regarded Jesus as another returning pilgrim (24.18).

[3] Recognized by G. Bertram, *Die Leidensgeschichte Jesu und der Christuskult* (FRLANT 32), Göttingen, 1922, 13; J. Pickl, *Messiaskönig Jesus*, 62f.

[4] So also R. Bultmann, *Das Evangelium des Johannes*, Göttingen, [10]1956 (= [10]1941) [= *Johannes*], 222 n. 2.

[5] A. Loisy, *Les évangiles synoptiques* II, Ceffonds (Haute-Marne), 1908, 491.

[6] *Plotinus* VI (Loeb Classical Library 445).

[7] 'The passage has special weight because it intends to give a definition, and this definition is accounted generally accepted and self-evident' (Bertram, *op. cit.*, 13 n. 2); cf. H. G. Liddell–R. Scott, *A Greek-English Lexicon*, new ed., Oxford, 1925–40, 601b *s. v.* ἑορτή 4: 'assembled multitude at a festival'.

[8] Cf. for this frequent use of ἐν P. Petrie IV 6.15f. (255–54 BC): διωὸν γάρ ἐστιν ἐν ὄχλῳ ἀτιμάζεσθαι, '. . . in the presence of a crowd' (Bauer: A. and G., 258); Ecclus 50.5: ὡς ἐδοξάσθη ἐν περιστροφῇ λαοῦ; cf. 49.2.

ing be given to Mark 14.1f.: Jesus must be arrested secretly by a ruse, for 'they said, not at the feast (i.e. in the presence of the festal crowd), lest there be an uproar of the people'. Μὴ ἐν τῇ ἑορτῇ corresponds exactly in substance to Luke 22.6, ἄτερ ὄχλου ('in the absence of the multitude').[1] If, however, Mark 14.2 contains no time reference, then no conclusion can be drawn from it as to the chronology of the day of Jesus' death or the character of the Last Supper.

6. In favour of the Johannine chronology Pes. 8.6 has been adduced: 'They may slaughter (the passover lamb) . . . for one whom they (the authorities) have promised to release from prison.' This regulation has been referred to the passover amnesty (Mark 15.6 par.; John 18.39),[2] and it has been argued that this amnesty must have come in time for the prisoners to take part in the passover meal. This would support the Johannine chronology, according to which the trial before Pilate took place before the passover evening, against the synoptic chronology, according to which the passover meal had already been held on the previous evening. Although this consideration is one that has to be taken seriously, it does have a weak point: it is by no means certain that Pes. 8.6 refers to the Roman passover amnesty. There is, as already J. Merkel has seen,[3] a fundamental difference between Pes. 8.6 and the passover amnesty referred to in the passion narrative: Pes. 8.6 is concerned with a promise of freedom, the passion narrative refers to an actual and definite release. The *promise* of freedom points to the Jewish authorities, as the matter is understood by the Jerusalem Talmud: 'The saying concerns one who is held prisoner by the Israelites.'[4] This means that Pes. 8.6 presumably refers to the case where a prisoner being held by the Jewish authorities received a promise of temporary release in order that he may participate in the passover festival, i.e. is paroled for the passover evening.[5] If this is correct, then Pes. 8.6 contains nothing relevant to the dating of the passover events.

[1] Cf. in this connection also Mark 11.32, 'they were afraid of the people' par. and Jesus' rebuke, Mark 14.49 par.

[2] Most recently J. Blinzler, *The Trial of Jesus*, Westminster, Md, and Cork, 1959 [= *Trial*], 218–21; 'Qumran-Kalender und Passionschronologie', *ZNW* 49 (1958), 249f.; E. Stauffer, 'Neue Wege der Jesusforschung', *Wissenschaftliche Zeitschrift der Martin-Luther-Universität Halle-Wittenberg, Gesellschafts- und sprachwissenschaftliche Reihe* 7 (1957–8), 464.

[3] J. Merkel, 'Die Begnadigung am Passahfeste', *ZNW* 6 (1905), 306f.

[4] j. Pes. 8.36a. 45f. The Babylonian Talmud differs (b. Pes. 91a), but in such questions is further removed from the Palestinian conditions.

[5] So also E. Baneth in *Mischnaioth* II, 225 n. 40.

7. Occasionally I Cor. 5.7b is adduced as an argument against the passover character of the Last Supper: 'For Christ, our paschal lamb, has been sacrificed.' The passover lambs were slaughtered on the afternoon of Nisan 14.[1] The comparison of Jesus with the paschal lamb presupposes, so runs the argument, that Jesus was crucified at the time of the passover slaughter and therefore before the eating of the passover meal. The question arises, however, as to whether the paschal lamb comparison arose out of the actual time of the crucifixion or, as is much more likely, out of the sayings of Jesus at the Last Supper.[2] If the latter is the case, then I Cor. 5.7b is evidence for the passover character of the Last Supper.

8. Also I Cor. 15.20 (cf. 23), where Christ is designated as ἀπαρχὴ τῶν κεκοιμημένων ('the first-fruits of those who have fallen asleep'), is occasionally introduced as supporting the Johannine chronology. The first-fruits were offered on Nisan 16 and this reference to the resurrected Christ as the 'first-fruits' apparently presupposes, so runs the argument, that Easter Day fell on Nisan 16, which would make Good Friday Nisan 14. But, in I Cor. 15.20 (cf. 23), as in other places where the word is used figuratively, the original meaning of ἀπαρχή (first-fruits) is greatly weakened, so that it becomes almost = πρῶτος (first), as W. Bauer rightly points out.[3] Since this is the case, we may not draw any conclusions as to chronology from I Cor. 15.20.[4]

9. The two most important objections (nos. 9 and 10) still remain to be discussed. The first maintains that *many of the incidents* reported in Mark 14.17–15.47 *could not possibly have taken place on Nisan 15,*

---

[1] Josephus, *Bell.* 6.423, 'from the ninth hour till the eleventh' (from 3 p.m. till 5 p.m.); Pes. 5.1, after 'a half after the eighth hour', i.e. 2.30 p.m. (if a Friday: after 'a half after the seventh hour', i.e. 1.30 p.m.). Without mention of the hour Philo, *De spec. leg.* 2.145, 'from noon till eventide'. Cf. further Jeremias, *Passahfeier*, 78–80.

[2] See below, p. 222.

[3] Bauer: A. and G., 80.

[4] It is just as much a mistake to attempt to argue that I Cor. 11.23, 'the Lord Jesus on the night when he was betrayed . . .', excludes the possibility that the Last Supper was a passover meal. If, so runs this argument, the Last Supper was a passover meal, then Paul would have mentioned this and not have used the colourless chronological reference 'on the night when he was betrayed'. This argument from silence completely overlooks the liturgical character of the text. 'The night when he was betrayed' is no more a chronological reference than the 'not at the feast' in Mark 14.2, but rather these words derived from an older tradition, with their echo of Isa. 53, have a ring of the *Heilsgeschichte* (see on this below, pp. 112f., and cf. E. Lohmeyer, 'Vom urchristlichen Abendmahl [I]', *ThR* 9 [1937], 184f.). In their present context they are intended to remind the Corinthians of that grave earnestness of the meal which they have tended to neglect.

which, as the first day of the feast of Unleavened Bread (at least from dawn onwards),[1] had the character of a feast day and so, to a limited extent, that of a Sabbath.[2] Maintained as irreconcilable with the dating on Nisan 15 are: (1) Jesus' going to Gethsemane in the night of the passover; (2) the bearing of arms by the temple guards and some of the disciples in this night; (3) the meeting of the Sanhedrin and condemnation of Jesus during the night of the feast; (4) the tearing of the robe at the trial; (5) the participation by the Jews in the session of the Roman court on the morning of the feast day; (6) the coming in of Simon of Cyrene ἀπ' ἀγροῦ on the morning of Nisan 15; (7) the execution of Jesus on the high feast day; (8) the purchase of the shroud for the burial on the evening of the feast day; (9) the burial of Jesus with the accompanying removal of the body from the cross and the rolling of the stone; (10) the preparation of spices and ointments. This much-discussed objection was examined simultaneously[3] but independently by G. Dalman in his book *Jesus-Jeshua*, 86–98 (ET, 93–106), and P. Billerbeck in the second volume of his *Kommentar*, 815–34. They brought to the task a sovereign knowledge of the material and they agreed in rejecting the objection.

The ten individual objections mentioned above are not of equal importance, but vary greatly in weight. (*a*) *Some of them rest upon sheer ignorance of the* halakah; *these have no weight at all and should never be mentioned again.* Such are nos. 1, 2, 4, 9 and 10. (1): certainly Jerusalem could not be left during the passover night, but while the passover lamb had to be eaten within its walls the night could be spent anywhere within the greater Jerusalem district. Gethsemane lay within this district (see above, p. 43 n. 2; p. 55, no. 13). (2): according to the earlier *halakah*, which was in force at the time of Jesus (it probably goes back to the battles of the Maccabean period), the bearing of arms was permitted on the Sabbath

---

[1] See above, p. 53.

[2] Ex. 12.16; Lev. 23.7; Num. 28.18: the feast day has the character of a Sabbath. However, according to Ex. 12.16c, the preparation of food was permitted on Nisan 15. Following this the Mishnah says: 'A feast day differs from the Sabbath in naught save in the preparing of needful food' (Beṣ. 5.2; Meg. 1.5). This regulation was understood as permitting on a feast day (except on the day of atonement) slaughter, skinning, lighting a fire, kneading, baking, cooking, and similar acts necessary to the preparation of food. Beyond this it was permitted to carry objects from private to public territory and *vice versa*, even when this work had nothing to do with the preparation of food (E. Baneth in *Mischnaioth* II, 359, 377). Since all of this work was forbidden on a Sabbath one can only speak of a feast day possessing the character of a Sabbath to a limited extent.

[3] Dalman's book was published in 1922, Billerbeck's work was completed in that same year.

(and on a feast day), Shab. 6.4 (according to R. Eliezer b. Hyrcanus, the constant champion of the earlier tradition). Outside of this, it is not completely certain that the night Nisan 14/15 was already subject to the regulations of a feast day.[1] (4): the tearing of the robe at the trial is not a breaking of the regulation: 'If he tore his raiment in his anger or because of his dead . . . he is not culpable' (Shab. 13.3). (9): the express rule of the Torah, Deut. 21.23: 'his body shall not remain all night upon the tree, but you shall bury him the same day', was, of course, also applicable on a feast day. (10): 'They may make ready (on the Sabbath or on a feast day) all that is needful for the dead, and anoint it and wash it, provided they do not move any member of it' (Shab. 23.5). One should notice also that the preparation, or perhaps the laying out, of the spices and ointments on the evening of the burial is reported only in Luke 23.56; according to Mark 16.1 they were first purchased after the Sabbath had ended. (b) *Two of the objections are concerned with matters that lay not in the hands of the Jewish authorities but in the hands of the Roman governor.* No. 5, whereby it should also be noted that the occasion arose out of the popular acclamation following the carrying out of the passover amnesty (Mark 15.6 par.) and it may therefore not have been Pilate's original intention to hold a court hearing, and no. 7:[2] Polycarp of Smyrna is also reported to have been executed by the Romans 167/8[3] 'on the high Sabbath',[4] and the fact that it was a Sabbath did not prevent the Jews from making a notable contribution to the carrying of wood and twigs to the pile.[5] (One also remembers that Luke 4.29 took place on a Sabbath and John 10.22–39 at the feast of the Dedication of the Temple. Cf. also a case from an earlier period: Jose ben Joezer of Zereda suffered martyrdom[6] in 162 [or 88] BC on a Sabbath.[7]) It is arguable that the presence of the crowds at the feast may have seemed to the Romans to provide an opportunity for using the three executions as an impressive deterrent. (c) *One of the objections rests upon arbitrary assumptions.* (6): the report that Simon of Cyrene came ἀπ' ἀγροῦ (Mark 15.21) contradicts the synoptic chronology only on the assumption that he came from *work* in the fields. This, however, is most unlikely so early in the morning (Mark 15.25). We should note that it was quite in order for Simon, on a feast day, to go to his field within the distance permitted on a Sabbath (2,000 cubits, i.e. 880 metres, reckoned from the

---

[1] See above, p. 53.

[2] W. Bauer, *Das Johannesevangelium*[4], Tübingen, 1933, 215.

[3] On the dating of the martyrdom of Polycarp see J. Jeremias, *Infant Baptism in the First Four Centuries*, London, 1960, 60–62.

[4] Mart. Polyc. 21. Cf. 8.1, 'being a high Sabbath'.

[5] Mart. Polyc. 13.1.

[6] Gen. R. 65.18 on 27.27. Text, with variants, published by G. Dalman, *Aramäische Dialektproben*[2], Leipzig, 1927, 35.

[7] So the editions of Constantinople 1512, Venice 1545, and Saloniki 1593.

circumference of the built-up urban district) in order, for instance, to fetch 'from the field' some wood or the parts of a sick or injured animal that had had to be destroyed.[1] But in any case it is by no means certain that the phrase ἔρχεσθαι ἀπ' ἀγροῦ must be translated 'to come from the field'; ἀπ' ἀγροῦ can also mean 'from the country', 'from the village'[2] or 'from outside the city'.[3] Simon may have lived outside the city wall[4] and have been on his way to the 9 a.m. morning prayer (Acts 3.1) in the Temple[5]—that is, if he were a Jew. But was Simon of Cyrene a Jew? This is nowhere stated. Simon was also a common name among Greeks. If he were not a Jew, then the feast day was no concern of his. (d) *Only two objections remain to be taken seriously*: nos. 8 and 3. (8): according to Mark 15.46 Joseph of Arimathea purchased a shroud (ἀγοράσας σινδόνα) on Good Friday. The report, which incidentally is found only in Mark, seems to contradict the rule which forbade buying and selling on the Sabbath. But the necessities of life had led to relaxations of this rule: merchants were allowed to hand out foodstuffs to their customers if nothing was said about measurement, weight and price.[6] The case of passover feast is specifically discussed in Shab. 23.1: 'So, too, in Jerusalem on the eve of passover when it falls on a Sabbath, a man may leave his cloak (as surety with the seller)[7] and eat[8] his passover lamb and make his reckoning with the seller after the feast day'. As well as foodstuffs, a coffin and a shroud might belong to the necessities of life, as Shab. 23.4 explicitly states. This would certainly be the case when, as in the year of Jesus' death, two rest days came together. In the Palestinian climate an early funeral, at the latest on the day following the actual death, was essential. About the coffin and the shroud it is said: 'And he said (on the Sabbath) to him: if you cannot get it at the designated place, fetch it from such and such a place; and if you cannot get it for one mina (100 denarii) then get it for 200 (denarii). R. Jose b. Judah (about AD 180) said: Only he must not mention the exact price.'[9] Adding to this that the rule prohibiting work on the feast day was less stringent than that for the Sabbath immediately

---

[1] Evidence in Billerbeck II, 828f.

[2] Luke 11.6 D. The Emmaus Disciples go εἰς ἀγρόν 'to their village' ([Mark] 16.12).

[3] Evidence in Dalman, *Jesus-Jeshua*, 101.

[4] On the settlement of the immediate neighbourhood of Jerusalem in NT times cf. J. Jeremias, 'Einwohnerzahl', *ZDPV* 66, 28–31. At that time about 20,000 people lived inside the city wall and 5,000–10,000 outside it (pp. 28, 31).

[5] Dalman, *Jesus-Jeshua*, 101.

[6] Evidence in Billerbeck II, 832.

[7] The earlier part of this passage discusses the borrowing of wine, oil and bread.

[8] With the majority of the early manuscripts w'wkl (not wnwṭl) is to be read, cf. the apparatus in H. L. Strack, *Schabbâth* (Schriften des Institutum Judaicum in Berlin 7), Leipzig, 1890, 51.

[9] Tos. Shab. 17.13 (137.14); b. Shab. 151a.

following,[1] and that an express rule of the Torah (Deut. 21.22f.) required the burial of Jesus on the same day as his death (see above, no. 9), then the report about the purchase of a shroud on the first day of the passover cannot be regarded as presenting any difficulty. *The only serious difficulty is* (3): could the sitting of the Sanhedrin and the condemnation of Jesus have taken place on the night of the feast? 'None may sit in judgment . . . on a feast day'; this was a valid law at the time of the Mishnah.[2] (It must be emphasized that this objection applies just as much to the Johannine account as to the synoptic: criminal processes were also not permitted on the day of preparation for a feast.[3] This means that if this objection is held to be valid it does not favour the Johannine dating of Good Friday on Nisan 14 as over against the synoptic dating, as is commonly but erroneously supposed, but rather weighs equally against both the Johannine and synoptic chronology of the death of Jesus.[4]) We do not need to delay to discuss the question as to whether the regulation forbidding legal hearings on a feast day was already in force at the time of Jesus (which is very questionable)[5] but rather we can turn at once to the decisive question. Deut. 17.12 prescribes the death penalty for anyone who opposes the decisions of the priests and judges of the High Court in Jerusalem. As a deterrent such a case was to be made public: 'And all the people shall hear, and fear, and not act presumptuously again' (Deut. 17.13). Since 'all the people' were assembled together in Jerusalem only on the occasions of the three pilgrimage feasts, it follows from Deut. 17.13 and the parallel texts Deut. 21.21; 13.12 that the executions in those cases designated by the Torah as ⁺he most serious offences were—despite the rule against executions on a feast day[6]—to be carried out *baregel*, 'during the feast'. 'The obstinate (against his parents) and intractable son (Deut. 21.18–21), the scribe who rebels against the (supreme) court (Deut. 17.8–13), the seducer (to idolatry, Deut. 13.7–12), he who turns away (a community to idolatry, Deut. 13.13–19), *the false prophet* (Deut. 18.20) and the false witnesses

---

[1] See above, p. 75 n. 2.

[2] Beṣ. 5.2; Tos. Beṣ. 4.4 (207.15); Philo, *De migr. Abr.* 91. Cf. Billerbeck II, 815–20.

[3] Sanh. 4.1; b. Sanh. 35a.

[4] It cannot be argued that John's gospel does not depict a condemnation of Jesus by the Sanhedrin but only a 'purely personal' ruling of Annas and Caiaphas (Dalman, *Jesus-Jeshua*, 99). With Bultmann, *Johannes*, 500f., I am sure that John 18.24, is intended to describe an official hearing at which (cf. Mark 14.53 par.) the High Council is present.

[5] Blinzler, *Trial*, 149–57 (Excursus VI: 'On the question of whether the Mishnic Code was in operation in the time of Jesus'). With regard to one particular regulation Blinzler, 'Die Strafe für Ehebruch in Bibel und Halacha. Zur Auslegung von Joh. VIII. 5', *NTS* 4 (1957–8), 32–47, demonstrates conclusively that the rabbinic-mishnaic criminal law was not yet in force at the time of Jesus.

[6] Evidence in Billerbeck II, 816, 822f.

(Deut. 19.18–21) are not to be executed at once but are to be brought to the Sanhedrin in Jerusalem and kept in prison until the feast, and *the sentence carried out at the feast*; for it is said: "And all the people shall hear it, so that they may fear it and not act presumptuously again" (Deut. 17.13).'[1] Here was such a case. Jesus was regarded by his opponents as a false prophet. This we see most clearly from Mark 14.65 par.: after the condemnation by the High Court a kind of blind man's buff is played with Jesus, by means of which he should show himself a prophet (Mark 14.65; Matt. 26.68; Luke 22.64: 'prophesy'). Since the mockery of the condemned travesties the charge of which he has been accused (so Luke 23.11: the white garment is the native Jewish royal robe; further Mark 15.16–20 par.: the purple cloak is the hellenistic royal robe),[2] the untendentious report of the mockery of Jesus before the High Court is an unassailable witness to the fact that Jesus was condemned as a false prophet. But as a false prophet he had to be sentenced at once so that the commandment of the Torah (breaking all contrary decisions of the *halakah*) Deut. 17.13 might be carried out and the execution take place before 'all the people', i.e. on Nisan 15, because on Nisan 16[3] the passover pilgrims were at liberty to go home.[4]

We can see therefore that *the passion narratives portray no incident which could not have taken place on Nisan 15.*

10. We come now to the chief objection which is raised against the synoptic representation of the Last Supper as a passover meal. *This is the report of the fourth gospel.* We have already seen (p. 19) that the phrase 'to eat the passover' (John 18.28) implies that Jesus was crucified *before* the passover evening. None the less the following has to be borne in mind:

[1] Tos. Sanh. 11.7 (432.1), R. Akiba (died after AD 135). That the tradition is older than Akiba can be seen from the shorter, anonymous parallel b. Sanh. 89a (Bar.); also Luke 13.33 shows that the rule to execute a false prophet in Jerusalem was in force in Jesus' day. One concrete bit of evidence that the prescription that the most serious offenders should be executed at a feast was practised is offered by b. Sanh. 43a (Bar.), see above, p. 19 n. 7: Jeshu, the pupil of R. Joshua b. Perahiah (about 100 BC), was hanged on the day of preparation for the passover (Nisan 14) because he 'practised sorcery (Deut. 18.10) and misled Israel (to idolatry, Deut. 13.7), and enticed them to apostasy (Deut. 13.14)'. The fact that this passage is very old makes it very strong evidence. (In contrast, b. Sanh. 67a is worthless because it has been influenced by 43a.)

[2] R. Delbrueck, 'Antiquarisches zu den Verspottungen Jesu', *ZNW* 41 (1942), 124–45.

[3] If this day fell on a Sabbath: on Nisan 17. So Luke 24.13ff.

[4] See above, p. 72 n. 2. This disproves Lietzmann's suggestion, *Mass and Lord's Supper*, 174 n. 1, that *baregel* Deut. 17.13 might refer to all the subsequent days 'on which "the people" would still be in Jerusalem'. And the preceding days did not yet belong to the feast.

(a) John 13.1, 'before the feast of the Passover' cannot be used in support of this chronology, because the time reference here clearly belongs to 'knew'[1] and simply asserts that Jesus already knew before the Passover that his death was imminent. Also in connection with the phrase 'it was the day of preparation for the Passover' (John 19.14) caution is required in interpretation. The expression 'day of preparation for the passover' (παρασκευὴ τοῦ πάσχα) has not yet been found in the earlier Aramaic literature.[2] But this may be pure chance. Anyway, most probably παρασκευὴ τοῦ πάσχα—undoubtedly an Aramaism—is a rendering of an Aramaic construct form[3] 'arubat pasha, 'day of preparation for the passover'. None the less, as C. C. Torrey[4] in disagreement with P. Billerbeck[5] has shown, the possibility cannot be excluded that the phrase represents an Aramaic genitive, 'arubta di pasha, 'Friday of passover week',[6] since 'arubta, 'Friday', was established linguistic usage in early Aramaic and early Syriac.[7] This is in any case the meaning which παρασκευή has in John 19.31, as is shown by the mention of the Sabbath.[8] John

---

[1] So already the Greek commentators (Zahn, *Johannes*, 531); Bauer, *Johannes-evangelium*, 167; Bultmann, *Johannes*, 352.

[2] While the Hebrew 'ereb pesahim or 'ereb happesah, meaning the day of preparation for the passover, Nisan 14, is already to be found at the time of the Mishnah (e.g. Pes. 10.1 etc.), the corresponding Aramaic construct form 'rwbt psh' is never found in earlier times. The expression is first found in Midr. Ruth 3.4 on 1.17, one of the latest midrashim. In earlier Aramaic the day of preparation for the passover is usually called either m'ly ywm' dpysh' ('beginning of the passover day', Targ. Jer. I Gen. 14.13) or ywm' dmykmy hg' ('the day preceding the feast', Targ. Jer. I Ex. 12.15), as the usage of the Targum shows and as Mark 14.12 bears out, if the retranslation of τῇ πρώτῃ ἡμέρᾳ τῶν ἀζύμων given on p. 18 n. 1 is correct. Cf. also Gospel of Peter 2.5 (p. 19 n. 7): πρὸ μιᾶς τῶν ἀζύμων.

[3] On the analogy of 'rwbt ryš št' (day before the New Year), 'rwbt swm' rb' (day before the Day of Atonement).

[4] Torrey, 'The Date of the Crucifixion according to the Fourth Gospel', *JBL* 50 (1931), 232–7, 241; 'In the Fourth Gospel the Last Supper Was the Paschal Meal', *JQR* 42 (1951–2), 237–50.

[5] Billerbeck II, 834–7.

[6] Cf. šbt bpsh. Siphra Lev. on 23.15 (ed. princ., Venice, 1545, 50d. 51) meaning 'Sabbath of passover week'.

[7] 'rbh 'Friday' is already to be found on Aramaic Egyptian ostraca of the fifth century BC (A. Dupont-Sommer, 'Sabbat et Parascève a Éléphantine d'après des ostraca araméens inédits' in *Extraits des mémoires présentés par divers savants à l'Académie des Inscriptions et Belles-Lettres*, Paris, 1950, 1–22).

[8] The attempt by S. Zeitlin, 'The Date of the Crucifixion according to the Fourth Gospel', *JBL* 51 (1932), 268–70, to refute Torrey's argument is altogether unconvincing because Zeitlin in a most incredible manner pays absolutely no attention to the NT usage in his statements on παρασκευή and πάσχα. Zeitlin's first thesis that παρασκευή is a designation for the eve of Sabbaths or feast days used

19.14 may therefore only be used with reservations as support for the Johannine chronology of the Passion.

(*b*) On the other hand, a trace of the synoptic chronology is to be found in John 19.31, for the 'high Sabbath' which here follows the day of the crucifixion is probably the day of the *sheaf-offering* (Lev. 23.11). According to the pharisaic tradition which determined the practice[1] this was Nisan 16. John 19.31ff. therefore comes 'from a tradition . . . according to which Jesus was already crucified on Nisan 15 as in the synoptics'.[2]

(*c*) There are other traces of the synoptic chronology in the fourth gospel, especially in the account of Jesus' last supper (John 13.2ff.). The fact that John depicts here the same meal as that described in Mark 14.17–25 par. is shown by the betrayal scene (John 13.18–30, cf. Mark 14.18–21 par.) as well as by the ensuing walk to Gethsemane (John 18.1ff., cf. Mark 14.26ff. par.).[3] Some of the remarks made by John presuppose that this was a passover meal. According to John also the Last Supper, as we have seen, took place in Jerusalem despite the overcrowding of the holy city by the passover pilgrims (cf. John 11.55; 12.12, 18, 20).[4] According to John also the Last Supper was held at an unusual hour: it lasted into the night.[5] According to John also Jesus celebrated this meal with the closest circle of his disciples. According to John also the Last Supper was a ceremonial meal: those who took part in it reclined at table.[6] According to John also when the meal was over Jesus did not return to Bethany but went to a garden on the other side of the Kidron valley.[7] In this connection we must also consider John 13.10: the meal was

---

only by non-Jewish writers may be supported by the decree of Augustus in Josephus, *Ant.* 16.163, but is invalidated by John 19.14 (where the reference is not to the evening hours but to the sixth hour, i.e. 11 a.m. to 12 noon) and Did. 8.1 (where παρασκευή is the whole Friday). How untenable nis second thesis is, that πάσχα (or *psḥ, psḥ'*) can only refer to the passover lamb and not to the seven-day feast, would have been made clear to him by one glance at John 2.13; 11.55; 12.1; 18.39; Acts 12.4.

[1] Cf. Billerbeck II, 848.
[2] Bultmann, *Johannes*, 524 n. 5; in this quotation 'rather' should be substituted for 'already'.
[3] Cf. also the announcement of Peter's denial, John 13.36–38; Mark 14.29–31 par.
[4] See above, p. 42.
[5] See above, p. 44.
[6] See above, p. 48.
[7] See above, p. 55.

taken in a state of levitical purity;[1] further 13.29: the supposition of some of the disciples that Judas was either to purchase necessities for the imminent feast or to distribute alms may also indicate that it was passover night.[2]

The Johannine report is therefore not uniform. Rather, alongside the dating of the Last Supper on the eve of the Passover—actually only unambiguously stated in John 18.28—we find traces of a tradition according to which the Last Supper was a passover meal.[3]

(d) The connection between the Passion and the Passover seems to be severed by John's dating of the Last Supper on the eve of the Passover; but in actual fact this serves to emphasize the connection.[4] For (1) dating the events of the Passion twenty-four hours earlier makes the crucifixion of Jesus coincide with the slaughter of the paschal lambs. While hundreds and thousands of paschal lambs were being slaughtered in the temple, the true paschal lamb, of which according to the will of God no bone should be broken (John 19.36, cf. Ex. 12.46; 12.10, LXX; Num. 9.12; Ps.[LXX] 33.21),[5] died unrecognized outside the gates of the city. This comparison of Jesus with the paschal lamb is very early (I Cor. 5.7; I Peter 1.19, cf. Rev. 5.6, 9, 12; 12.11; John 1.29, 36); Paul presupposes it as already known, as is apparent from the way in which he argues in I Cor. 5.7.[6] It was probably an established part not only of the Pauline[7] but also of the early Christian passover *haggadah* in general.[8] It was

---

[1] See above, p. 49.

[2] See above, pp. 53f. under 10 and 11.

[3] '13.21–30. Jesus and his disciples are here still at table, and in fact at the passover meal, i.e. at the Lord's supper of the synoptics; in contradiction to 13.1; 18.28; 19.14—it is idle to shut one's eyes to this contradiction', says J. Wellhausen, *Das Evangelium Johannis*, Berlin, 1908, 60.

[4] A. Oepke, 'Jesus und der Gottesvolkgedanke', *Luthertum* 42 (1942), 61 n. 77; E. Gaugler in G. Deluz–J.-Ph. Ramseyer–E. Gaugler, *La Sainte-Cène*, Neuchâtel-Paris, 1945, 58f.; F. J. Leenhardt, *Le Sacrement de la sainte Cène*, Neuchâtel-Paris, 1948, 11f.; Th. Preiss, 'Was the Last Supper a Paschal Meal?' in *Life in Christ*, 81–99.

[5] The use of hyssop (ὑσσώπῳ) in John 19.29 also belongs here. According to Mark 15.36 par. Matt. 27.48 it was a 'reed' (κάλαμος) upon which the sponge full of vinegar was offered to Jesus. The use of 'hyssop' instead of 'reed' by John presents problems because the stem of the hyssop (*origanum maru*) is much too weak for this purpose (Dalman, *Arbeit und Sitte in Palästina* I. 2 [BFChTh II 14.2], Gütersloh, 1928, 544). How does the tradition come to use 'hyssop'? Because of reminiscence of the expiatory passover rite, Ex. 12.22!

[6] J. Weiss, *Der erste Korintherbrief*, Göttingen, 1910, 135f.

[7] See above, pp. 59f.

[8] See below, pp. 222f.

quite possibly the popularity and vividness of this comparison which affected the recollection of the events of the Passion and caused them to be antedated by twenty-four hours in that branch of the tradition to which the gospels of John and Peter[1] belong. 'The typology' came to be 'understood as chronology'.[2] (2) A second factor has perhaps also to be taken into consideration here. The early practice of the Quartodecimanians, which goes back to the primitive Christian community,[3] was to fast on the passover night, in deliberate contrast to the Jewish festival practice. This shows that in Palestine and in Asia Minor, i.e. in precisely the geographical location of John's gospel and its tradition, there was a strong emphasis upon the difference between the Jewish and the Christian passover: the Jewish passover (the fourth gospel says 'the passover of the Jews', accenting the contrast as strongly as possible[4]) has come to an end with the offering of the true paschal lamb. This anti-passover attitude[5] could have led to a minimizing of the passover character of the Last Supper; one could no longer conceive of Jesus celebrating the passover *more Iudáico*. In any case the antedating of the Last Supper by one day in John's gospel is certainly not a deliberate and careful change, for John 18.28 'has nothing forced, or "constructed". . . . The detail here does not appear to be governed by a theology.'[6]

11. Finally, a newly discovered text has revealed as erroneous the oft-repeated assertion that the Quartodecimanians dated the crucifixion on Nisan 14, therefore representing the Johannine chronology.[7] Actually the Quartodecimanians celebrated the passover each year at the same time as the Jews[8] and toward the close of the second century they were appealing for support in this to the example of Jesus.[9] They therefore represent the synoptic chronology of the

---

[1] See above, p. 19.

[2] J. Betz, *Die Eucharistie in der Zeit der griechischen Väter* I. 1, Freiburg i. Br., 1955, 21 n. 85.

[3] See below, p. 122 n. 3.

[4] John 2.13; 11.55, cf. 6.4.

[5] W. Michaelis in a letter dated July 28, 1949.

[6] J. Delorme, 'La Cène et la Pâque dans le Nouveau Testament', *Lumière et Vie* 31 (February 1957), 31.

[7] See below, pp. 122f.

[8] See below, *ibid.*

[9] This is apparently the meaning of Polycrates of Ephesus when he says in his letter to Victor of Rome (about 190–1) that the Quartodecimanians celebrated their passover on Nisan 14 'according to the gospel' (in Eusebius, *Hist. eccl.* 5.24.6); cf. on this point Lohse, *Passafest*, 91–93.

Passion[1] and they did, in fact, constantly appeal for support to the synoptic gospels, as we can see from the statements of their opponents.[2]

The result of this investigation has been to show that none of the eleven objections are sufficient to refute the synoptic report that the Last Supper was a passover meal.

THE EUCHARISTIC WORDS OF JESUS WITHIN THE FRAME-WORK OF THE PASSOVER MEAL

If, in consequence of what has been said above, we are entitled to regard the Last Supper as a passover meal, then it remains for us to set the words of interpretation spoken by Jesus within the framework of such a meal. The ritual of this meal, which consisted of a preliminary course and a main meal, is known;[3] we can therefore content ourselves with outlining it briefly. It has to be said, however, that the depictions of the passover ritual to be found in the more recent commentaries on Mark's gospel exhibit serious errors; these we shall correct without comment as we proceed.[4] Especially we must emphasize, for it is essential to our purpose, that *no bread was eaten with the preliminary course*,[5] despite the fact that one reads the exact opposite in modern commentaries on Mark.[6] In addition to this it must be noted

---

[1] See above, p. 19.

[2] Lohse, *op. cit.*, 18–20, 93, 123f., 136.

[3] An excellent collection and presentation of the source material is to be found in Billerbeck IV, 41–76. For orientation in connection with the modern Seder rite Strack, *Pesaḥim*, 36–48, is to be recommended. For a history of the rite see B. Italiener, 'Der Ritus der Handschrift' in *Darmstädter Pessach-Haggadah, Textband*, 71–165.

[4] Even the oft-quoted description of the passover celebration by A. Merx, *Die Evangelien des Markus und Lukas* (Die vier kanonischen Evangelien nach ihrem ältesten bekannten Texte II. 2), Berlin, 1905 [= *Markus und Lukas*], 416–49, needs to be corrected at several places, see, e.g., below, p. 85 n. 2.

[5] The clearest evidence for this (j. Pes. 10.37d. 4f.) was quoted above, p. 50 under (7); cf. also the very full discussion by E. Baneth in *Mischnaioth* II, 242–5 n. 27. Another clear proof is found in Tos. Pes. 10.9 (172.27): 'R. Eliezer (about AD 90, representative of the early tradition) says: one breaks in advance (*hoṭephin*, literally: 'to make haste', then 'to do in advance', 'to break bread without benediction', cf. Jastrow, *Dictionary*, 450) a piece of unleavened bread for the small children, lest they fall asleep (during the passover *haggadah*).' The use of the verb 'to break in advance' shows clearly that the adults first ate unleavened bread after the preliminary course (A) and the liturgy (B). The 'breaking in advance' was done without a benediction because the blessing over the bread had its place at the beginning of the main meal (C).

[6] Wellhausen, *Evangelium Marci*, 111, also is mistaken when he says that the

that the custom whereby the *paterfamilias* distributes half of an unleavened loaf among the guests after the meal but before the grace is
of late origin.[1] Any description of the Last Supper which refers to this
custom[2] will therefore be incorrect.

A. Preliminary Course:[3]

Word of dedication (blessing of the feast day [*kidduš*][4] and of
the cup[5]) spoken by the *paterfamilias* over the first cup (the
kidduš cup).
Preliminary dish, consisting among other things of green herbs,
bitter herbs and a sauce made of fruit purée.[6]
The meal proper (see C) is served but not yet eaten; the second
cup is mixed and put in its place but not yet drunk.

B. Passover Liturgy:

Passover *haggadah* by the *paterfamilias* (in Aramaic).
First part of the passover *hallel*[7] (in Hebrew).
Drinking of the second cup (*haggadah* cup).

---

blessing over the bread (Mark 14.22) belongs to the beginning of the whole meal.
Finegan, *Überlieferung*, 67f., goes so far as to claim that Mark 14.22 'in a way that is
impossible according to the Jewish custom' puts 'the breaking of the bread right
in the middle of the meal'. Even more fatal than these false statements themselves
are the drastic literary critical operations on the text of the Passion narrative
which have again and again been based upon them.

[1] It first arose in connection with the late custom, mentioned above, pp. 68f.,
of saying the grace before the meal over a broken piece of unleavened bread.

[2] Merx, *Markus und Lukas*, 424; R. Eisler, 'Das letzte Abendmahl [I]', *ZNW* 24
(1925), 161–92 (devastatingly criticized by H. Lietzmann, 'Jüdische Passahsitten
und der ἀφικόμενος. Kritische Randnoten zu R. Eislers Aufsatz über "Das letzte
Abendmahl" ', *ZNW* 25 [1926], 1–5); P. Fiebig, 'Die Abendmahlsworte Jesu',
Neues Sächsisches Kirchenblatt 42 (1935), col. 376.

[3] The source material for the post-biblical passover tradition has been collected
in my work *Passahfeier*, 54.

[4] Discussed in detail above, pp. 26f.

[5] So the Shammaites. The Hillelites prescribed the reverse order, Pes. 10.2;
Tos. Pes. 10.2 (172.14).

[6] Pes. 10.3; Tos. Pes. 10.9 (173.6), cf. the cry of the Jerusalem spice pedlars,
p. 86. The fruit purée (*haroset*) was a mixture of squeezed and grated fruits (figs,
dates, raisins, apples, almonds), spices and vinegar. The preliminary dish was
intended to stimulate the appetite.

[7] See p. 55 n. 1.

C. Main Meal:

Grace spoken by the *paterfamilias* over the unleavened bread.
Meal, consisting of passover lamb,[1] unleavened bread, bitter
herbs (Ex. 12.8), with fruit purée and wine.
Grace (*birkat hammaṣon*) over the third cup (cup of blessing).

D. Conclusion:

Second part of the passover *hallel*[2] (in Hebrew).
Praise over the fourth cup[3] (*hallel* cup).

The fact that the ritual outlined here was substantially that of the
time of Jesus can be shown with the help of numerous individual
observations. With regard to the *food and drink* mentioned, the eating
of the passover lamb, unleavened bread and bitter herbs was prescribed already in the Old Testament (Ex. 12.8, etc.). That fruit
purée was eaten with them in New Testament times is shown by the
cry of Jerusalem spice pedlars, noted by R. Eleazar b. R. Zadok
(born between AD 35 and 40 in Jerusalem[4]): 'Come and buy ingredients for your religious obligations (of the fruit purée)'.[5] And the
drinking of wine at the passover meal is presupposed as an old custom
in the book of Jubilees[6] written about 120 BC.[7] So far as *the liturgical
rite* is concerned, the sequence of the blessing of the feast day and of
the cup at the initial benediction was already a subject of discussion

---

[1] Before the passover lamb it was permissible to eat a voluntary sacrifice (an
ox, sheep, lamb or goat), Pes. 6.4f.

[2] See p. 55 n. 1.

[3] The earliest witnesses for the four cups are: Pes. 10.1; Tos. Pes. 10.1 (172.13);
b. Pes. 108b (Bar.). Doubts in regard to the age of the fourth cup are expressed by
Merx, *Matthaeus*, 386; *Markus und Lukas*, 151. They arise from Mark 14.25: Jesus
says before the *hallel* that he will drink no more wine on earth. But this argument
has no weight if Mark 14.25, as we believe (see below, pp. 207ff), refers to an
avowal of abstinence on the part of Jesus. Also Dalman, *Die Worte Jesu* I[2], Leipzig,
1930, 402 [This section is not in the English *Words*. Transl.]; 'Der Wein des
letzten Mahles Jesu', *Allgemeine Evangelisch-lutherische Kirchenzeitung* 64 (1931),
col. 797f., expresses doubts whether the rabbinical rule for the drinking of wine at
the passover (four cups of obligation) was generally in force at the time of Jesus.
For our investigation this question is unimportant.

[4] Cf. Schlatter, *Die Tage Trajans und Hadrians*, 80f.

[5] b. Pes. 116a (Billerbeck IV, 65); the same is found anonymously in j. Pes.
10.37d. 9.

[6] Jub. 49.6, 9.

[7] On the date of Jubilees cf. S. Klein, 'Palästinisches im Jubiläenbuch', *ZDPV*
57 (1934), 16–27.

between the Shammaites and Hillelites;[1] Rabban Gamaliel I concerns himself with the passover *haggadah*, which grew out of Ex. 12.26f.; 13.8;[2] and the antiquity of the *hallel* is guaranteed by another discussion between the Shammaites and the Hillelites,[3] by Philo[4] and by a Jerusalem proverb from the time before the destruction of the Temple.[5]

What has been said above makes it clear that, if the Last Supper was a passover meal, Jesus spoke the word of interpretation over the bread in connection with the grace before the beginning of the main meal. Only at this point was a grace said over bread, since no bread was eaten with the preliminary course at a passover meal.[6] So far as the word of interpretation over the wine is concerned, this must have been spoken in connection with the grace (Mark 14.23: 'having given thanks') *after* the main meal, since according to Mark it was said *after* the breaking of bread (14.22) but *before* the passover *hallel* (14.26). This setting of these words is supported by two things to be found in Paul: the very archaic[7] 'after supper' (I Cor. 11.25) and the expression 'the cup of blessing'[8] (I Cor. 10.16). *Jesus, therefore, used the prayers before and after the main course of the passover meal to add his words of interpretation concerning the bread and the wine.*[9] Both prayers of Jesus were preceded by the passover meditation; this is an important observation because it justifies the conclusion that the disciples were thereby prepared for the words of interpretation, in themselves

---

[1] Pes. 10.2, cf. Ber. 8.1, and above, p. 27 n. 2.

[2] Pes. 10.5. See above, p. 56.

[3] Pes. 10.6f. See above, p. 55 n. 1.

[4] *De spec. leg.* 2.148, 'with prayers and hymns'; the word 'hymns' may well refer to the *hallel*, cf. Mark 14.26 par., 'when they had sung the hymn'; see above, p. 55 n. 4.

[5] j. Pes. 7.35b.36: 'the Passa is only like an olive, and yet the *hallel* breaks through the roofs', i.e. although each participant received a piece of meat no bigger than an olive, the jubilation of those holding the meal on the roofs was so great that the roofs collapsed—little strokes fell great oaks. The passover *hallel* is perhaps mentioned already in Isa. 30.29; II Chron. 30.21; Jub. 49.6; Wisd. 18.9 ('songs of praise of the fathers' in the passover night).

[6] See above, pp. 49f.

[7] See below, p. 121 n. 2.

[8] Because *kos šel beraka* (cup of blessing) is an established technical term for the cup of wine over which the grace after the meal was said; the evidence is given by Billerbeck IV, 628, 630f., further 58, 72.

[9] So also Billerbeck IV, 75. The fact, therefore, that the bread word and the wine word occur together in both Mark and Matthew must not lead us to the conclusion that the one was spoken immediately after the other. Rather, this reflects the development of the Christian eucharistic liturgy (see below, pp. 121f).

puzzling. Jesus' vow of abstinence came, as we shall see below, pp. 160f., either at the very beginning of the meal (Luke 22.15f.) or at the taking of the first cup (Luke 22.17f.).

*   *   *

In all of this we are not concerned, as is often claimed, with questions of only archaeological or chronological interest. It is much more a question of the setting of the Last Supper within the context of the *Heilsgeschichte*. The relationship between the old covenant and the new, between promise and fulfilment, are brightly illuminated, if Jesus' last meal was a passover meal. But above all we shall see that *Jesus' avowal of abstinence, the words of interpretation and the command to repetition first become fully understandable when they are set within the context of the passover ritual.* It should also be emphasized, however, that the Last Supper would still be surrounded by the atmosphere of the passover even if it should have occurred on the evening before the feast.

III

THE ACCOUNT OF THE LAST SUPPER
WITHIN THE FRAMEWORK
OF THE PASSION NARRATIVE
AND AS INDEPENDENT TRADITION

THE INVESTIGATION OF the eucharistic words of Jesus themselves is best begun by discussing the *problem of literary criticism*: What is the position of the account of the Last Supper within the framework of the passion narrative as a whole? We start from:

A COMPARISON OF THE MARKAN PASSION NARRATIVE WITH THE JOHANNINE

This comparison, which is intended to provide the standards for a literary-critical judgment of the accounts of the Last Supper, leads to three conclusions of fundamental importance for the literary criticism of the passion narrative.

1. While John's account of the ministry of Jesus shows only infrequent parallels to the synoptic gospels,[1] the picture changes completely with the entry into Jerusalem, i.e. with the beginning of the passion narrative. The material in Mark, from the entry into Jerusalem to the empty tomb (Mark 11.1–16.8), is now found substantially in John, if not in the same words or with the same details,

---

[1] Apart from individual sayings and isolated points of contact in subject-matter, John and the synoptics have no more than four pericopes in common up to the passion narrative: (1) the Baptist and the baptism of Jesus, Mark 1.2–11 par. and John 1.19–34; (2) the miraculous draught of fish, Luke 5.1–11 and John 21.1–11; (3) the centurion at Capernaum, Matt. 8.5–13 par., Luke 7.1–10 and John 4.46–53; (4) the feeding of the multitude and the walking on the water, Mark 6.30–52 par. and John 6.1–21. Close similarities are shown by (5) the healing of the blind man, Mark 8.22–26 and John 9.1–7; and (6) Peter's confession, Mark 8.29 (33) and John 6.69 (70f.).

at any rate with the same general themes. The passion narrative is thus clearly shown to be a very early cycle of tradition.

Mark's gospel itself supports this result. Chapters 1–10 are a secondary structure, not, as is frequently maintained, of individual stories and sayings, but of separate blocks of traditional material (see below, pp. 91f.) loosely connected together, but without a continuous chronological or topographical coherence. Chapter 11 begins a compact, purposeful and coherent narrative (the passion narrative) with precise geographical and temporal references, which as such has only one remote analogy elsewhere in the gospel, in the block of material in Mark 1.16–38. Both this agreement between John and the synoptics from the account of the triumphal entry onwards, doubly surprising after the preceding differences, and also the structure of the Markan passion narrative in comparison with the remainder of the gospel, prove that *the passion narrative constitutes a coherent and very early block of the gospel tradition.*

2. We are led a step farther when we notice which sections within the present Markan passion narrative (11.1–16.8) *have nothing even approximately corresponding to them in John.* Three sections are missing from John's gospel: (a) the cursing of the fig tree (Mark 11.12–14) with its subsequent discussion (11.20–25); (b) the great collection of controversy stories (chapter 12) and the eschatological discourse (chapter 13); (c) the account of the preparation for the passover celebration (14.12–16). The accounts of the Last Supper itself (14.22–25) and of Gethsemane (14.32–42) do not belong here. It is true that they are not found in John, but John 18.1; 12.27; 18.11; 14.31 show that he knew the Gethsemane tradition, and John 6.51c–58 shows that the same is true of the account of the institution of the Last Supper,[1] which he has omitted for special reasons.[2]

It can hardly be an accident that these three sections missing from John can also be clearly recognized as expansions of the original narrative in their Markan setting. In connection with (a), the cursing of the fig tree (Mark 11.12–14) and the subsequent discussion (11.20–25), the different place which Matthew assigns them over against Mark is immediately obvious, although in view of the way in which

[1] Often the story of the feet washing (John 13.1–20) is also regarded as having reference to the Lord's Supper, so recently by O. Cullmann, *Early Christian Worship* (SBT 10), London, 1953, 105–10; E. Lohmeyer, 'Die Fusswaschung', *ZNW* 38 (1939), 90f., even regards the pericope as a substitute for the synoptic report of the institution of the Last Supper.

[2] See below, p. 136.

Matthew frequently changes the order of Markan material this may not be too significant. More important is the fact that both are missing not only from John but also from Luke. Furthermore, literary-critical consideration of the Markan text shows traces of editorial work before the account of the cursing of the fig tree and both before and after the subsequent discussion: Mark 11.11 is a Markan connecting link;[1] Matthew and Luke are right in making the triumphal entry lead directly to the cleansing of the temple. Mark 11.18b–19 shows itself in form[2] and content as one of the many Markan summaries. Finally 11.27a is a connecting link;[3] John 2.18 confirms the original connection between the cleansing of the temple and the question as to Jesus' authority, a connection which first supplies a reference for the twice-repeated ταῦτα (Mark 11.28), which in its present position has no such reference. But the decisive argument against the setting of the cursing of the fig tree and the subsequent discussion in the passion narrative is that these two things separate what clearly belongs together. For the regal entry, the cleansing of the temple and the question of Jesus' authority form an indivisible whole. Not only is it a fact in the East that enthronement and restoration of the cult are closely connected as symbols of the new age and of Messianic authority,[4] but also in this particular situation, where Jesus is proclaimed king on his way to the temple, everything presses towards a conclusion on his arrival at the holy place, which to this day is the goal of all pilgrimages. All these observations lead to one and the same conclusion, that the original sequence—triumphal entry, cleansing of the temple, question about Jesus' authority—has been disturbed at some later date by the insertion of the account of the cursing of the fig tree and of the subsequent discussion as read in Mark.

(b) With regard to chapters 12 and 13, we have to begin from the fact that the whole of Mark's gospel has arisen out of the combination

---

[1] V. 11a is repeated in 15a; περιβλεψάμενος and οἱ δώδεκα (without an accompanying μαθηταί) are favourite Markan words, and the time reference in v. 11b is every bit as redactional as those in vv. 12 and 19 (on v. 19 see the next note). The redactional character of Mark 11.11, 19, 27a does not, of course, exclude the possibility that the remark that Jesus used to leave Jerusalem in the evenings (see p. 55) is a valid historical reminiscence.

[2] Through the two words διδαχή and ἐκπορεύεσθαι, which are favourite words with Mark.

[3] The plural 'they came' (v. 27a) disagrees with the singulars 'he' and 'to him' (twice) in 27b and 28, and πάλιν is another of Mark's favourite words.

[4] J. Jeremias, Jesus als Weltvollender (BFChTh 33.4), Gütersloh, 1930, 35–44.

of blocks of traditional material, a conclusion of fundamental importance for the understanding of its composition.[1] One of these blocks
of traditional material is to be found in the collection of controversy
stories, chapter 12, and another is the collection of eschatological
sayings of Jesus in chapter 13. It is characteristic of all the various
blocks of tradition in Mark that they are only loosely connected to
the whole. In our case the controversy about Jesus' authority, Mark
11.27b–33, clearly attracted the great complex of controversy stories,
12.1–40,[2] to which the apocalyptic discourse, chapter 13, was then
added.[3] The fact that these two blocks did not originally belong to the
passion narrative is borne out by the observation that they interfere
with the close-knit structure of the story, which proceeds immediately
from 11.15–33 to 14.1–2, for it was the cleansing of the temple which
had as its direct consequence the plot to kill Jesus.

(c) In Mark 14.12 the time reference comes as a surprise. Whereas
14.1, 'It was now two days before the Passover (Nisan 14) and the feast
of Unleavened Bread (Nisan 15–21)' is a perfectly correct reference,[4]
the matter is quite different with 14.12, 'and on the first day of Unleavened Bread, when they sacrificed the passover lamb'. Here Nisan
14 is included in the feast of Unleavened Bread (see above, p. 17).

---

[1] If Mark 1.1, like Matt. 1.1, 'The book of the genealogy of Jesus Christ', is a
chapter heading, then the 'of Jesus Christ' is a subjective genitive ('How Jesus
Christ began to preach the Gospel'); this heading would then cover Mark 1.1–15.
The first obvious block of tradition is the day in Capernaum, 1.16–38, which section
is characterized by the constant use of the name Simon, 1.16 (twice), 29, 30, 36.
There follows: the collection of controversy stories, steadily increasing in violence,
2.1–3.7a; the breach with the family, 3.20–35; the parables, 4.1–34; the cycle of
miracle stories connected with the sea shore, 4.35–5.43; the rejection of the Gospel,
6.1–32. In 6.34–7.37 and 8.1–26 there follow two parallel blocks of tradition. The
crisis, 8.27–9.1, has been brought together under the catechetical themes of confession and discipleship in suffering. This is followed by the events on the mount,
9.2–29, and the great collection of sayings linked by catch-words and introduced
by a passion prediction, 9.30–50. 10.1–31 is a catechetical collection of three stories
of Jesus, concerned with the attitude to women, children and possessions. 10.32–45:
suffering and discipleship.
With 10.46 the passion narrative begins, into which two blocks of tradition have
been introduced: 12.1–40, controversy stories; 13, apocalyptic discourse.

[2] 12.41–44 has been added as a pendant to 12.40 because of the references to
'widow' (vv. 40, 42).

[3] The addition of chapter 13 was probably occasioned by the identity of location
(11.27 takes place 'in the temple', 12.35, the same; 12.41, Jesus is seated 'opposite
the treasury'; 13.1 he leaves the sanctuary).

[4] Following the OT usage (Num. 28.16f.; II Chron. 35.17), it was customary to
distinguish between the passover and the feast of Unleavened Bread. Post-canonical
evidence in Billerbeck I, 988 under 'c'.

Even though G. Dalman's verdict, 'No Jew with even a little knowledge of the Tora could have called the eve of the feast "the first day
of the feast" ',[1] is too harsh (in learned discussions of Ex. 12.15, 18 the
designation of Nisan 14 as 'the first day of the feast' is occasionally
found),[2] still he is substantially correct. For these learned discussions
should not be cited in support of Mark 14.12, rather should it be
admitted that here we have either the faulty expression of a non-
Jewish author or, much more probably, a mistranslation.[3] So the
section Mark 14.12–16 is shown by the time reference to belong to a
different stratum of tradition from 14.1, as it also is by the designation
of the disciples: in verses 12, 13, 14, 16 they are called 'the disciples',
as opposed to 'the twelve' in verse 17 (cf. 10, 20). Furthermore, as
'the twelve' shows, verse 17 knows nothing of the despatching of the
two disciples who, as verse 16 suggests, probably had to see to the
slaughter of the lamb, its transport to the house, and its preparation
(otherwise it would have to read 'with the ten').[4]

All this leads us to an important conclusion. Both the comparison
between the Markan and Johannine passion narratives on the one
hand, and the literary criticism of the text of Mark on the other, lead
to the conclusion *that there was a stage in the development of the passion
narrative when it contained in close succession perhaps*[5] *the triumphal entry,
the cleansing of the temple, the question of Jesus' authority, the announcement
of the betrayal, the Last Supper, Gethsemane, the arrest, and so on.* We will
call this account the *long account.*

3. Finally, a careful comparison of the *sequence of events* in the
Markan and Johannine passion narratives leads us to a third conclusion. Up to and including the Gethsemane story the arrangement
of the material varies greatly:

---

[1] Dalman, *Jesus-Jeshua*, 105.
[2] The witnesses are quoted above, p. 17 n. 2.
[3] Above, p. 18 n. 1.
[4] Lohmeyer, *Markus*, 300.
[5] An exact determination, let alone a reconstruction of a written source, is quite
impossible. It is simply a stage in the development of the oral tradition, which
probably showed very marked local differences. An example of this process of
development can be found in the account of the anointing at Bethany (Mark
14.3–9). On the one hand, this belongs to the material which the Markan and
Johannine passion narratives have in common, and is therefore a part of the passion
narrative at a comparatively early stage. On the other hand, it can be shown to be
an accretion, first because it disrupts the connection between Mark 14.1f. and 10f.,
and secondly because its place is not fixed: in Mark it follows the triumphal entry,
whereas in John it precedes it.

Mark 11.	1–10	John 12.12–16
	15–17	2.13–17[1]
	24	14.13f.; 16.23
	28	2.18[1]
14.	1–2, 3–9	11.47–53; 12.1–8
	10–11	cf. 13.2
	18–21	13.21–30
	26–31	18.1a; 16.32; 13.36–38
	32–42	18.1b; 12.27; 18.11b; 14.31

From the arrest of Jesus onwards (Mark 14.43–50; John 18.2–11), by contrast, John agrees with the synoptic gospels in the arrangement of the material. This observation that the arrest of Jesus marks a distinct break in the tradition is supported by other evidence. Whereas up to the arrest of Jesus large portions of the material are not shared by Mark and John, this picture changes after the arrest; apart from some lesser incidents, dialogues, particular episodes and the like, the synoptic and Johannine accounts now run parallel without any larger portions in the one not found in the other. In particular, the fourth gospel keeps its own particular character, defined by the discourses, right up to the high priestly prayer (chapter 17); but from 18.1ff. onwards, i.e. from the arrest of Jesus, there follows a continuous narrative quite in the synoptic manner.

These observations agree in leading to the conclusion *that at a very early stage the passion narrative began with the arrest of Jesus* (the *short account*).[2] We can adduce evidence for the existence of such a short account: the early passion summary which constitutes the so-called third prediction of the passion has as the first of its eight parts the delivering up of Jesus to the chief priests and the scribes.[3] This agrees with the witness of the other early summaries of the passion kerygma. Apart from the betrayal of Jesus they mention: the condemnation of Jesus by the Sanhedrin,[4] the delivering up to Pilate,[5] the trial before

[1] The view advanced in the second edition of this work [ET, p. 66 n. 1. Transl.] that the setting of John 2.13–18 at the beginning of John's gospel may be due to displacement of leaves, is one that I would no longer hold. The technical difficulties in which one becomes involved in the theory of the displacement of leaves in the fourth gospel are much too great for this, cf. Jeremias, ποιμήν κτλ., *TWNT* VI (1959), 494.1–28.

[2] On the basis of quite different considerations Bultmann, *Tradition*, 279, comes to this same conclusion.

[3] Mark 10.33f., cf. 9.31; Matt. 26.2.

[4] Mark 8.31; 10.33; Luke 17.25; Acts 4.11; 13.27.

[5] Mark 10.33; Luke 24.7, 20; Acts 2.23; 3.13; 7.52.

Pilate,[1] the mocking and scourging,[2] the crucifixion[3] and the burial[4] —*in no single instance* does one of these early summaries begin with an event of the passion preceding the betrayal by Judas.[5] Further, it should be noted that the traitor is introduced in Mark 14.43 with the words 'Judas, one of the twelve' as if he were as yet quite unknown to the reader, although he had already been designated in 14.10 as 'Judas Iscariot, who was one of the twelve' (here with reason, since he had been mentioned before only in the list of the apostles, 3.19). In the Lukan passion narrative, which is independent of the Markan,[6] this new introduction of Judas is repeated at the beginning of the story of the betrayal: 'the man called Judas, one of the twelve' (Luke 22.47). The phrase 'the man called' (δ $\lambda\epsilon\gamma\acute{o}\mu\epsilon\nu os$), which is very noticeable in the present context, seems to be the remains of what was once a new beginning 'which was designed to introduce Judas, a person as yet unknown to the reader'.[7] Finally, it is notable that in Mark and Luke the designation of the disciples as 'disciples' ($\mu\alpha\theta\eta\tau\alpha\acute{\iota}$) is not to be found in the account of the arrest of Jesus (as it is also not to be found in the following passion narrative). Whereas in the Gethsemane narrative we find 'the disciples' (Mark 14.32; Luke 22.45), Mark 14.47 has 'those who stood by', 14.50 'they all . . .', Luke 22.49 'those who were about him'. Jesus is therefore depicted 'during the arrest as being in the midst of a group which is not specifically described'. This observation also points to a break in the narrative.[8] There can therefore be very little doubt but that there was an early stage of the passion narrative which began with the arrest of Jesus.

The result of this comparison of the Johannine and Markan passion narratives is to give us an insight into the living growth of the tradition. If I Cor. 15.3b–5 is added to mark the initial stage, then *the following stages in the growth of the tradition* can be distinguished:

---

[1] Acts 3.13f.; 13.28.

[2] Mark 10.34; I Peter 2.23.

[3] Matt. 20.19; 26.2; Luke 24.7, 20; Acts 2.23, 36; 4.10; 5.30; 10.39; 13.29; I Cor. 1.17f., 23; 2.2; Gal. 3.1; I Peter 2.24.

[4] I Cor. 15.4; Acts 13.29.

[5] Also the expression 'the Lord Jesus on the night when he was betrayed' (I Cor. 11.23) with which Paul begins his account of the Lord's Supper shows that the betrayal at night belonged to the passion kerygma at an early time.

[6] See below, p. 99.

[7] F. Rehkopf, *Die lukanische Sonderquelle. Ihr Umfang und Sprachgebrauch* (Wissenschaftliche Untersuchungen zum Neuen Testament 5), Tübingen, 1959, 37.

[8] Rehkopf, *op. cit.*, 57f.

(1) At the beginning of our knowledge stands the early *kerygma* I Cor.
15.3b–5, originally drawn up in a Semitic language.[1]

(2) The second recognizable stage is the *short account*, beginning with
the arrest of Jesus.

(3) The third stage (the *long account*) is represented by the material
common to all four gospels. The material is supplemented back
to the triumphal entry. Further, the Peter tradition (Mark
14.26–42, 53f., 66–72), known to all four gospels, is inserted. The
narrative now contains in close succession the triumphal entry,
the cleansing of the temple, the question about Jesus' authority,
the Last Supper with the announcement of the betrayal, the
prophecy of the denial, Gethsemane, arrest of Jesus, trial before
the Sanhedrin, denial of Peter, the story of Barabbas, the condemnation by Pilate, the crucifixion, the empty grave. On the
whole this long account may well represent a reliable account of
the historical sequence of events. We have, however, no reason
to assume that this third stage of the tradition ever attained
written form.

(4) The passion narrative was expanded by the addition of particular
incidents and blocks of traditional material into the forms which
we now have in the four gospels.[2]

It goes without saying that these four stages are only milestones in a
much more colourful and complicated development.

THE ACCOUNTS OF THE LAST SUPPER

The picture which we have just drawn on a large canvas is repeated
on a smaller scale when the narratives of the Last Supper (Mark
14.12–26; Matt. 26.17–30; Luke 22.7–39; John 13.1–30) are sub-
jected to the detailed scrutiny of literary criticism. They are related
blocks of tradition composed out of very diverse elements.

This is especially clear in the case of *Mark*, who is closely followed
by Matthew. The three sections of his account of the Last Supper
belong to quite different strata of the tradition. (1) The preparation
of the passover room (Mark 14.12–16 par.) is a late section, as we

---

[1] See below, pp. 101ff.
[2] The way in which this filling-out process took place can best be seen by means
of a comparison of Matt. 21–28 with Mark 11–16.

have just seen,[1] that is not known to the long account. (2) The announcement of the betrayal at the supper (Mark 14.17–21 par.) is common to all four gospels and is therefore part of the long account.[2] Since Mark, Luke and John are independent of one another in their depiction of the announcement of the betrayal, the tradition that it took place at the Last Supper must be early. (3) When Mark and Matthew open the actual account of the Last Supper (Mark 14.22–25 par.) with a secondary,[3] redundant introduction (Mark 14.22 'as they were eating' competes with 14.18 'as they were at table eating'); when this account is unconnected with what precedes it in that it contains no reference to the preparations mentioned in verses 12–16; when Mark's plain narrative style gives place to a solemn, stylized language which piles up participles and finite verbs;[4] when words and constructions which Mark never uses elsewhere occur frequently[5] —all this is to be explained quite simply by the fact that any account of the Last Supper had to revert at this point to the liturgical formula, the wording of which had long been fixed and everywhere established by its use in the cult. This reversion to a liturgical formula was also a matter of course for Luke,[6] and Paul confirms the antiquity of the formula.

The *Lukan* account of the Last Supper (22.7–39) follows Luke's special source from verse 14 onwards. Luke has so constructed his gospel that he has introduced four blocks of Markan material into this source, as the following survey shows:

Lukan source	*Markan material*
1. Luke 1.1–4.30	—
—	2. Luke 4.31–6.11 = Mark 1.21–3.6

[1] See above, pp. 92f.

[2] See above, p. 93.

[3] See below, p. 113 n. 4.

[4] Mark 14.22a, for instance, appears almost as if it were a liturgical rubric, see below, p. 113; 'the fruit of the vine' is an established liturgical expression; further evidence below, pp. 177f. nos. 8 and 10. The accounts of the feeding of the multitudes (Mark 6.41; 8.6) bear out this stylization, as has often been observed; especially the traitorous αὐτά, Mark 8.7, shows that Mark has not composed the introduction to the account of the institution himself, 14.22, since this uses εὐλογεῖν absolutely (against N. Turner, 'The Style of St. Mark's Eucharistic Words', *JTS* 8 [1957], 108–11).

[5] Τοῦτό ἐστιν, πίνειν ἐκ, διαθήκη, ἐκχεῖν, ὑπὲρ πολλῶν, οὐκέτι οὐ μή, γένημα, ἄμπελος, ἕως . . . ὅτου, ἐν τῇ βασιλείᾳ τοῦ θεοῦ. Note also the absence of the historic present, of which Mark is so fond (151 occurrences in the gospel).

[6] See below, p. 155.

EWJ—G

Lukan source	Markan material
3. Luke 6.12–8.3 (except for 6.17– 19 = Mark 3.7–11a)	—
—	4. Luke 8.4–9.50 = Mark 4.1–25; 3.31–35; 4.35– 6.44; 8.27–9.40
5. Luke 9.51–18.14	—
—	6. Luke 18.15–43 = Mark 10.13–52
7. Luke 19.1–28	—
—	8. Luke 19.29–22.13 = Mark 11.1–14.16
9. Luke 22.14–24.53	—

The fact that the ninth block, the one which interests us particularly, does not come from Mark but from Luke's special source can be seen —apart from the fact of numerous variations from Mark in material, language and style[1]—from the following observation, fundamentally important for the analysis of Luke's gospel: whenever Luke follows the Markan narrative in his own gospel he follows painstakingly the Markan order, pericope for pericope. Up to the passion narrative there are only two insignificant deviations: Luke 6.17–19; 8.19–21.[2] But in these two small sections it is not the case that Luke has changed the Markan order but rather that he has introduced two things from a section of Mark which he otherwise omits, Mark 3.7–35, at what seemed to him to be appropriate places.[3] Luke was therefore, in contrast to Matthew, an enemy of rearrangement. Deviations in the order of the material must therefore be regarded as indications that Luke is not following Mark. Now, in the Lukan account of the Last Supper there are to be found a great many such deviations from the order of Mark: the 'eschatological prospect' is placed before the words of institution (22.15–18), the announcement of the betrayal (incidentally, correctly[4]) follows them (vv. 21–23); the lament over the

[1] Rehkopf, Die lukanische Sonderquelle.

[2] K. Grobel, Formgeschichte und synoptische Quellenanalyse (FRLANT 53), Göttingen, 1937, 87.

[3] H. Schürmann, 'Die Dubletten im Lukasevangelium', ZKTh 75 (1953), 339 n. 9; Der Paschamahlbericht Lk 22, (7–14.) 15–18 (NTA 19. 5), Münster, 1953 [= Paschamahlbericht], 2 n. 9; J. Jeremias, 'Perikopen-Umstellungen bei Lukas?', NTS 4 (1957–8), 116f.

[4] It seems that the Markan tradition intends to make things easier in that it puts the announcement of the betrayal before the words of institution and so removes the traitor from participation in the Lord's Supper itself. The change could also have been brought about by the influence of the eucharistic liturgy, which introduced the exclusion formula before the Eucharist (I Cor. 16.22; Did. 10.6, see below,

traitor (v. 22) precedes the speculations of the disciples (v. 23); the prophecy of the denial (vv. 33f.) comes before the departure to Gethsemane. These deviations in the order of the material show that the Lukan narrative from 22.14 onwards is no longer built upon a Markan basis but comes from *Urlukas*; only the preceding account of the preparation of the room (vv. 7–13) still belongs to the fourth block of Markan material.[1] We have therefore in Luke 22.14ff. an independent passion narrative which can be set beside Mark/Matthew and John. This conclusion, which will be confirmed when we come to the analysis of Luke 22.15ff.,[2] is very important for our investigation. So far as the account of the Lord's Supper in this source is concerned, it is characterized by the combination of the twofold eschatological prospect (vv. 15–18) and two eucharistic words (vv. 19f.), in which we can detect the different origins of the two sections because of the change from δεξάμενος (v. 17) to λαβών (v. 20), from the indefinite ποτήριον (v. 17) to τὸ ποτήριον (v. 20) and from the double εἶπεν (vv. 15, 17) to the double λέγων (vv. 19, 20).[3] The passover saying (vv.

---

pp. 118, 254). But the regulation that the make-up of a passover fellowship should not be changed after the slaughter of its passover lamb (Billerbeck IV, 44f.), makes it very improbable that Judas left the group after the preliminary course. Further on Judas's communion, see below, p. 237.

[1] The detailed evidence for the fact that Luke 22.7–13 is dependent upon Mark is offered by Schürmann, *Paschamahlbericht*, 75–110. He is wrong at only one point, in that he accounts the verse Luke 22.14 as Markan: Luke 22.14 and Mark 14.17 have actually only one word in common, the word 'and'.

It is my opinion that Luke has incorporated the Markan material into his own and not *vice versa*. For this hypothesis at least one reason may be mentioned here. Wherever Luke reports a story in a form different from that of Mark (e.g. the preaching at Nazareth, Luke 4.16–30; the call of Peter, 5.1–11; the anointing, 7.36–50; the greatest commandment, 10.25–28; the fig tree, 13.6–9, etc.), he has the relevant pericope in a context different from that in Mark (only the temptation story, 4.1–13, is in the same place as in Mark). In each of these cases Luke had the material before him in two different forms (the Markan and the divergent form in his own source), and in each case he prefers the form in his special source and abandons that of Mark. The striking thing in this is that Luke does not simply put his version in the place of the one in the text of Mark but rather brings it in at a quite different place. Since he is an enemy of rearrangement (see above in the text), this means *that the pericopes in question must already have had their fixed positions when he came to know the gospel of Mark*. On the problem of Proto-Luke cf. B. H. Streeter, *The Four Gospels. A Study of Origins*[5], London, 1936, 201–22 (ch. VIII: Protoluke), and M. Dibelius's review of the first edition of Streeter's book (1924), *ThLZ* 51 (1926), cols. 73–77.

[2] See below, pp. 161f.
[3] Schürmann, *Paschamahlbericht*, 47.

15–18) comes from the Palestinian tradition via the Lukan special source,[1] the words of interpretation (vv. 19f.) come, as we shall see below, pp. 155f., from the liturgical tradition. That the following section of sayings (vv. 24–38) is also diverse in origin is evident because of, among other things, the change from the earlier address 'Simon' (v. 31) to the later 'Peter' (v. 34), but it also can be seen by a comparison with the parallel texts.[2]

Finally, *John's* account of the Last Supper is composed of two elements, the feet-washing (13.1–20) and the announcement of the betrayal (13.21–30). The latter, as we know, formed part of the *long account*.[3] The feet-washing, which is found only in John, receives a double interpretation in verses 6–11 and 12–20, which shows that the material already has a history behind it.[4] Its early date is also shown by numerous semitisms.[5] In conclusion, the farewell discourse motif (cf. Luke 22.24–38) has been greatly expanded (John 13.31–17.26).

We obtain therefore the following picture:

(1) The earliest part of the accounts of the Last Supper are the words of interpretation (Mark 14.22–24 par.), whose antiquity approaches that of the early kerygma (I Cor. 15.3b–5).

(2) The announcement of the betrayal (Mark 14.17–21 par.) is an original part of the *long account*; it is common to all four gospels and in the synoptics is firmly embedded in its context.[6]

(3) Everything else is part early special tradition (so the avowal of abstinence, Luke 22.15–18; Mark 14.25; Matt. 26.29, and the feet-washing, John 13.1–20), part composition (so the Lukan table conversation, Luke 22.24–38) and part expansion (so the account of the preparation for the passover meal, Mark 14.12–16 par., which has its analogy in Jesus' miraculous foreknowledge, Mark 11.1–6).

---

[1] See below, pp. 161f.

[2] Vv. 24–27, 33f. have parallels in Mark and Matthew, vv. 28–30 only in Matthew, vv: 31f., 35–38 are found only in Luke. The promise of judgment over the twelve tribes, which Matthew rightly has earlier (19.28), can hardly have come after the announcement of betrayal by one of the twelve, cf. T. W. Manson, *The Church's Ministry*, London, 1948, 50 n. 1.

[3] See above, p. 93.

[4] Cf. the searching analysis by Bultmann, *Johannes*, 351f.

[5] The evidence given by Bultmann, *Johannes*, 352 n. 3, can be extended, e.g., βάλλειν ὕδωρ (v. 5): *hiṭṭil mayim* 'to throw water'; τὸν νιπτῆρα: emphatic form with the sense of an indefinite state.

[6] Mark 14.1–2, 10–11 par. Cf. John 13.2.

THE ACCOUNT OF THE INSTITUTION OF THE LORD'S SUPPER AS INDEPENDENT TRADITION

That the account of the institution of the Lord's Supper did actually circulate as an independent piece of tradition, as we have just suggested in our analysis of the Markan and Lukan accounts of the Supper, is confirmed by I Cor. 11.23–25. Paul here quotes the words: 'For I received of the Lord what I also delivered to you' (I Cor. 11.23). There should never have been any doubt that 'to receive' (παραλαμβάνειν) and 'to deliver' (παραδιδόναι) represent the rabbinical technical terms *kibbel min* and *masar le* (P. Ab. 1.1ff., etc.),[1] so that I Cor. 11.23 says nothing other than that the chain of tradition goes back unbroken to Jesus himself.[2]

Immediate proof of this is provided by I Cor. 15.1ff., where Paul similarly reminds the Corinthians of an old-established tradition, the kerygma, and in so doing uses the same terms 'to deliver' and 'to receive' (v. 3, 'For I delivered . . . what I also received'). For it can be established on linguistic grounds that the kerygma here quoted (which runs from I Cor. 15.3b 'Christ' to v. 5 'twelve' as is shown, e.g., by the syntactical break between vv. 5 and 6)[3] was not formulated by Paul. *Un-Pauline* is (a) the phrase ὑπὲρ τῶν ἁμαρτιῶν ἡμῶν, I Cor. 15.3 ('for our sins'). In the Pauline epistles ἁμαρτία ('sin') is to be found sixty-four times,[4] including three occasions in the Pastorals[5] and five times in Old Testament quotations.[6] In the remaining fifty-

---

[1] Cf. G. Kittel, *Die Probleme des palästinischen Spätjudentums und das Urchristentum* (BWANT 3.1), Stuttgart, 1926, 63f.; Dibelius, *Tradition*, 21, 206 n.; A. Schlatter, *Paulus, der Bote Jesu*, Stuttgart, 1934, 320; W. D. Davies, *Paul and Rabbinic Judaism*, London, 1948 =² 1955, 248f.; E. Käsemann, 'Anliegen und Eigenart der paulinischen Abendmahlslehre', *EvTh* 7 (1947–8), 272, reprinted in E. Käsemann, *Exegetische Versuche und Besinnungen* I, Göttingen, 1960, 21: ET, 'The Pauline Doctrine of the Lord's Supper', *Essays on New Testament Themes* (SBT 41), London, 1964, p. 120.

[2] Schlatter, *ibid.*; Hupfeld, *Abendmahlsfeier*, 67; E. Stauffer, *New Testament Theology*, London, 1955, 300 n. 552. On 'from the Lord', I Cor. 11.23, cf. further below, pp. 202f.

[3] Up to v. 5 there are ὅτι-clauses, from v. 6 onwards main clauses. Cf. A. von Harnack, 'Die Verklärungsgeschichte Jesu, der Bericht des Paulus (I Cor. 15.3ff.) und die beiden Christusvisionen des Petrus', *Sitzungsberichte der Preussischen Akademie der Wissenschaften, Phil.-hist. Klasse*, 1922, 62–80.

[4] Furthermore in variant readings at Col. 2.11; II Thess. 2.3.

[5] I Tim. 5.22, 24; II Tim. 3.6.

[6] Rom. 4.7 = Ps. 31.1 (LXX); Rom. 4.8 = Ps. 31.2 (LXX); Rom. 8.3, περὶ ἁμαρτίας, 'as a sin offering' = Lev. 5.6 (LXX), etc.; Rom. 11.27 = Isa. 27.9 (LXX); I Thess. 2.16 = Gen. 15.16 (LXX).

six places ἁμαρτία is used fifty times in the singular and absolutely,[1] because sin is for Paul a personified power[2] (for a particular sin Paul uses ἁμάρτημα and παράπτωμα). The six places where ἁμαρτία is used in the plural or with a genitive or a personal pronoun all show the influence of the general early Christian linguistic usage (I Cor. 15.3, the kerygma; I Cor. 15.17, reminiscence of the kerygma; Gal. 1.4, a christological formula; Rom. 7.5; Eph. 2.1; Col. 1.14), and are not specifically Pauline. Un-Pauline is (b) the expression 'according to the scriptures', I Cor. 15.3, 4, found nowhere else in Paul; he normally says 'as it is written' or the like. Also not found elsewhere in Paul are: (c) the perfect passive ἐγήγερται, which occurs only in I Cor. 15.4 and, clearly under the influence of this passage, in verses 12–14, 16f., 20, as also in the confessional formula II Tim. 2.8; (d) the report that Jesus rose on the third day, whereby the placing of the ordinal number after the noun (τῇ ἡμέρᾳ τῇ τρίτῃ) occurs only here in Paul;[3] (e) ὤφθη, found only in I Cor. 15.5–8 and in the confessional formula I Tim. 3.16; (f) the expression 'the twelve' (I Cor. 15.5, Paul normally says 'the apostles').[4] But more can be said. There are, if not strict proofs, at any rate signs that the core of the kerygma is *a translation of a Semitic original*.[5] The evidence is as follows: 1. The text contains numerous semitisms: (a) the structure in synthetic *parallelismus membrorum*:

> *that* Christ died for our sins   in accordance with the scriptures
>   and *that* he was buried
> and *that* he was raised on the third day
>   in accordance with the scriptures
>   and *that* he appeared to Cephas, then to the twelve.

One can see that the first and third *that*-clauses correspond to each other in length, in construction (verb, nearer definition, reference to scripture), in ending with 'according to the scriptures' and in being

---

[1] 'I.e. without a genitive, or an expression equivalent to a genitive, indicating the person who commits or bears the sin', E. Lohmeyer, 'Probleme paulinischer Theologie III. Sünde, Fleisch und Tod', *ZNW* 29 (1930), 2.

[2] Lohmeyer, *op. cit.*, 2f.

[3] Eph. 6.2, ἐντολὴ πρώτη, is only an apparent exception, because πρώτη here, as the absence of the article shows, is not an ordinal number but a designation of the commandment as 'especially important'.

[4] Gal. 1.19 (I Cor. 9.5); II Cor. 11.5; 12.11.

[5] In 'Artikelloses Χριστός in I Cor. 15, 3b–5', *ZNW* (in the press), I have clarified my position in view of some objections raised against it by H. Conzelmann and P. Vielhauer.

followed by a short *that*-clause (the second and fourth), the purpose of which is to warrant the reality of the preceding statement. Further indications of a Semitic original are (*b*) the absence of particles except καί; (*c*) the independence from the LXX of the reference to Isaiah 53 ('for our sins in accordance with the scriptures');[1] (*d*) the adversative καί at the beginning of the third line (cf. δέ, Acts 13.30); (*e*) the placing of the ordinal number after the noun in τῇ ἡμέρᾳ τῇ τρίτῃ, which is the only possible order in a Semitic language; (*f*) the use of the word ὤφθη instead of the more natural ἐφάνη, which is to be explained by the fact that Hebrew *nir'ah* and Aramaic *'ithame* have the double meaning 'he was seen' and 'he appeared'; (*g*) the introduction of the logical subject in the dative Κηφᾷ after a passive verb, instead of the expected ὑπό with the genitive.[2] These semitisms show that the kerygma was formulated in a Jewish-Christian milieu.[3] This is also suggested by the double reference to the Old Testament. 2. There are some features which do not possess an exact Hebrew or Aramaic equivalent, such as κατὰ τὰς γραφάς, 'in accordance with the scriptures', and the passive ἠγέρθη, 'he was raised'. Therefore we cannot say that the kerygma is a translation from a Semitic original in its present wording. It must have taken the shape it has now in a Greek-speaking environment. 3. Yet it cannot have originated there. With Paul's closing assertion, I Cor. 15.11, that his kerygma was identical with that of the first apostles,[4] and with the independence from LXX of the reference to Isaiah 53 (see above under *c*), it is a safe conclusion that the core of the kerygma was not formulated by Paul, but comes from the Aramaic-speaking earliest community.

Since Paul, as we have seen, speaks in I Cor. 11.23 exactly as in I Cor. 15.3 of 'receiving' and 'delivering', we may conclude that he owes the formulation of the account of the Lord's Supper, just as he does that of the kerygma, to tradition. In fact, it can be shown *that*

[1] That the *Hebrew* text of Isa. 53 is presupposed can be seen from the fact that in LXX Isa. 52.13–53.12 ὑπέρ is not found.

[2] Notice also the Aramaic form of the name Cephas. However, the use of this form proves little in the present connection because Paul, although he sometimes uses Peter (Gal. 2.7, 8), prefers Cephas (Gal. 1.18; 2.9, 11, 14; I Cor. 1.12; 3.22; 9.5 as well as in our passage, 15.5).

[3] Cf. Schlatter, *Paulus*, 395.

[4] Cf. also F. Büchsel's review of M. Dibelius, *Die Formgeschichte des Evangeliums*[2], Tübingen, 1933, in *ThLBl* 55 (1934), col. 98: 'I Cor. 15.3 ff., where Cephas and James, the authorities of the primitive Church, are specially mentioned as witnesses of the resurrection, certainly belongs as to its contents, and probably also as to its form, to Jerusalem.'

the account of the Lord's Supper also has idioms foreign to Paul. Only in I
Cor. 11.23–25 do we find in Paul παραδίδοσθαι used absolutely,
εὐχαριστεῖν used absolutely to designate grace at table, κλᾶν without an
object, καὶ εἶπεν,[1] ἀνάμνησις (twice), μετά with infinitive used as a
noun, δειπνεῖν, τοῦτο placed before the noun,[2] ὁσάκις (only I Cor.
11.25, 26).[3] Still weightier is the observation that Paul elsewhere uses
the central words of this account 'the body of Christ' in another
sense. For 'the body of Christ' in Paul elsewhere designates not the
earthly body of Jesus[4] but the community. (Even Rom. 7.4 uses the
expression in this sense, for 'through the body of Christ' here means:
'through [your incorporation by baptism into] the body of Christ'.)
Indeed, Paul connects the idea of the community as the body of
Christ even with the eucharistic words, as I Cor. 10.16f. shows. This
makes it even more clear that I Cor. 11.24 is couched in an idiom
foreign to him.[5] Here we really have to distinguish in Paul between
'Mishnah' and 'Gemara'.[6] In the Gemara 'body' designates the
community. The Mishnah is therefore pre-Pauline.

Although it is certain that in the Pauline account of the Lord's Supper
we have a pre-Pauline formula before us, we must not overlook the fact
that in Paul's time its text was not yet completely fixed. At any rate, there
are two places at which we have to reckon with the possibility that here we
have changes which Paul has introduced into the text: the positioning of a
prepositional attribute with an article after the noun, τὸ ὑπὲρ ὑμῶν, I Cor.
11.24, is a characteristically Pauline idiom,[7] and the placing of the personal
pronoun before the noun which we find twice in the words of interpretation
in Paul (v. 24: τοῦτό μού ἐστιν τὸ σῶμα and v. 25: ἐν τῷ ἐμῷ αἵματι) and
not at all in the other accounts, may also come from him.[8]

Since we can see also in both Mark and Luke that the account of
the institution comes from a separate tradition, we may conclude
that this circulated in the whole of the Early Church, down to the

---

[1] Schürmann, *Einsetzungsbericht*, 10, 59f.
[2] Schürmann, *Einsetzungsbericht*, 12.
[3] Cf. E. Lohmeyer, 'Vom urchristlichen Abendmahl [I]', *ThR* 9 (1937), 184.
[4] For this he uses other expressions, e.g., 'the body of his flesh' (Col. 1.22).
[5] Hupfeld, *Abendmahlsfeier*, 78f.
[6] This most apposite comparison was suggested by J. Héring, *Le Royaume de Dieu et sa venue*², Neuchâtel, 1959, 224 n. 1.
[7] This is shown by Schürmann, *Einsetzungsbericht*, 24–26. For the evidence see below, p. 167.
[8] Schürmann, *Einsetzungsbericht*, 40f. Paul is fond of the possessive adjective ἐμός (twenty-three times).

time of the composition of the gospels, as an independent liturgical tradition. It was formulated in the very earliest period; at any rate before Paul, since the version found in Paul could be shown to be a pre-Pauline formula.

For our purposes the most important result gained in this second section is that by means of literary critical analysis the independence and antiquity of the tradition of the eucharistic words of Jesus has been brought out, a result which will receive support from quite different considerations. Another significant result is that the accounts of the Last Supper in the four gospels, as we have them today, can be seen to represent the result of a living process of growth in the tradition.

IIII

THE INFLUENCE OF WORSHIP UPON THE TRANSMISSION OF THE EUCHARISTIC TEXTS

THE ESTABLISHMENT OF the fact that the account of the institution was transmitted as independent tradition turns our attention to the *Sitz im Leben* of this tradition: the eucharistic practice of the Early Church.

THE USE OF THE ACCOUNT OF THE INSTITUTION AT THE EUCHARIST

As he cites the account of the institution Paul adds a sentence: 'For as often as you eat this bread and drink the cup, you proclaim the Lord's death until he comes' (I Cor. 11.26). Because of the preceding 'for', 'you proclaim' must be understood as indicative, as is generally accepted; the verb (καταγγέλλειν) means 'to proclaim' and designates the 'proclamation, announcement of a completed event',[1] whereby the general usage suggests a proclamation in words.[2] Paul therefore establishes that in Corinth at every Eucharist ('as often as') the death of the Lord is proclaimed. An indication of how this 'proclamation of the death of Jesus' was carried out is gained when one observes that in Symmachus (Ps. 39[40].6) καταγγέλλειν represents the Hebrew *higgid*.[3] This verb is used for the recitation of the exodus credo, Deut. 26.5–9, at the passover.[4] If we may understand 'the proclamation of

---

[1] J. Schniewind, ἀγγελία κτλ., *TWNT* I (1933), 70.5.

[2] Schniewind, *op. cit.*, 70.23–71.6.

[3] The correspondence of these two verbs was noted by G. H. Box, 'The Jewish Antecedents of the Eucharist', *JTS* 3 (1901–2), 365 n. 1. More recently, D. Jones, 'ἀνάμνησις in the LXX and the Interpretation of 1 Cor. XI.25', *JTS* 6 (1955), 188f.

[4] Following Deut. 26.3, *higgadti*. Cf. Daube, *New Testament and Rabbinic Judaism*, 5.

the death of the Lord' at the Eucharist in an analogous manner, then it must have had the form of a recitation of the words of interpretation followed by an exposition.[1] In fact, we have in the New Testament an example of a eucharistic quotation with a following interpretation, John 6.51c–58.

Although the fourth gospel, in contrast to the synoptics, does not report the institution of the Lord's Supper in the context of its passion narrative, it is none the less not completely silent about the Supper, but devotes a passage to it in the discourse on the bread of life, John 6. This passage (6.53–58) is prepared for by the clause 6.51c, with which the discourse suddenly and surprisingly proceeds from an interpretation of the bread of life related to the person of Jesus to one related to his flesh. Because of its vocabulary, which comes from the language of the sacrament, the section 6.51c, 53–58 differs so radically from the preceding discourse that it appears to be quite alien to it. For this reason it has been widely accepted as a redactional insertion into the fourth gospel, a view formerly also shared by the present author. But it is so thoroughly Johannine in style[2] that one cannot deny that it comes from the evangelist; its special characteristics in comparison with the context in which it is set in the fourth gospel can be adequately explained by taking into account the fact that John may well have used traditional eucharistic expressions (perhaps even an actual eucharistic homily).[3]

The fact that in John 6.51c–58 traditional eucharistic material has been used is confirmed by an observation made by J. H. Bernard in 1928. He recognized *that we have in John 6.51c an independent version of Jesus' word of interpretation over the bread*.[4] One needs only to set John 6.51c and I Cor. 11.24b side by side to be convinced of the correctness of this insight:

---

[1] Cf. for the liturgical use of Jesus' words of interpretation at the Eucharist Justin, *Apol.* I 66.2, τὴν δι' εὐχῆς λόγου τοῦ παρ' αὐτοῦ εὐχαριστηθεῖσαν τροφήν, 'the food consecrated by the word of prayer coming from him'. E. R. Hardy translates similarly in C. C. Richardson, *Early Christian Fathers* (The Library of Christian Classics I), London, 1953, 286; others refer λόγος to Christ as the logos who descends at the *epiklesis*, cf. J. Quasten, *Monumenta eucharistica et liturgica vetustissima I* (Florilegium Patristicum 7), Bonn, 1935, 18 n. 1.

[2] E. Ruckstuhl, *Die literarische Einheit des Johannesevangeliums* (Studia Friburgensia N.F. 3), Freiburg (Switzerland), 1951, 220–71.

[3] J. Jeremias, 'Joh 6, 51c–58—redaktionell?', *ZNW* 44 (1952–3), 256f.

[4] J. H. Bernard, *Gospel according to St John* I[4], Edinburgh, 1953 (=[1] 1928), clxx f.; E. Lohmeyer, 'Vom urchristlichen Abendmahl [III]', *ThR* 9 (1937), 308; N. Johansson, *Det urkristna nattvardsfirandet*, Lund, 1944, cf. L. Fendt, *ThLZ* 73 (1948), col. 35.

John 6.51c	*I Cor. 11.24b*
the bread which I will give	this
is my flesh	is my body
for the life of the world	which is for you

It can be seen that the structure and content of the sentence is the same in both cases. John has only expanded it paraphrastically at the beginning and at the end. The whole sequence of thought in the discourse on the bread of life now becomes clearer: its conclusion (6.53–58) is a eucharistic homily, the theme of which is introduced by the word of interpretation to the bread (6.51c). John therefore, although he does not mention the institution of the Lord's Supper, introduces the word of interpretation to the bread in the context of a discourse by Jesus, without it thereby (as the history of the research shows) becoming immediately evident as such.

That we have in John 6.51c the Johannine version of Jesus' word of interpretation over the bread is an observation that will still concern us later. In this connection the point is that in John 6.51c, 53–58 we meet with a sequence of word of interpretation and its exposition. For here, we may assume, we have an example of the way in which the 'proclamation of the death of the Lord' was carried out at the celebration of the Lord's Supper (I Cor. 11.26).

The use of the account of the institution at the Eucharist had two consequences. On the one hand, the liturgical usage influenced the formulation of the accounts of the Lord's Supper (we can explain in this way a good many of the variations in form with agreement in substance which we find in the accounts of the institution); on the other hand, there was an ever-growing concern to protect from profanation the sacred formula which was used in the celebration. These two consequences must be examined more exactly.

THE INFLUENCE OF THE LITURGY ON THE FORMULATION OF THE EUCHARISTIC WORDS

The liturgical use of the accounts of the institution at the celebration of the Lord's Supper has influenced in many ways both the composition of its setting and the formulation of the words of institution themselves.

(a) *The ritual of grace at table before and after the meal*

Common to all the accounts of the Lord's Supper is the detailed description of the action of Jesus in connection with the bread, using three verbs ('he took the bread, blessed, broke') which we know, from the rabbinical literature, as technical terms for the *grace at table before the meal*.[1] In the case of the passover meal this grace was spoken at the beginning of the main meal, which followed upon the preliminary course and the first part of the passover liturgy.[2] The *paterfamilias* arose from his reclining position, took, as he sat,[3] a cake of unleavened bread ('he took bread', Paul; 'taking bread', Mark/-Matt./Luke)[4] and recited the blessing ('having said the blessing', Mark/ Matt.; 'having given thanks', Paul/Luke)[5] over it 'for all'[6] (i.e. in the name of all). This blessing runs: 'Praised be thou, O Lord, our God, king of the world, who causes bread to come forth from the earth'.[7] It is, however, very probable that Jesus gave this daily blessing a form of his own.[8] The table companions made this blessing their own by saying 'Amen'. Only after the amen had been said[9] did the *paterfamilias* break from the cake ('he broke', Paul/Mark/Matt./-Luke)[10] a piece at least the size of an olive[11] for each participant and give it to him ('gave it to them', Mark/Luke; 'giving it to the disciples', Matt.) it had to be passed from hand to hand to reach the more distant guests. Lastly, he broke a piece for himself and ate it, thus giving the table companions the sign to eat theirs too.[12] During the distribution, which normally took place in silence,[13] Jesus spoke the words of interpretation.[14]

The words introducing the word of interpretation over the wine (I Cor. 11.25a; Mark 14.23a; Matt. 26.27a; Luke 22.20a) describe the

---

[1] See below, p. 174 nn. 3, 4; p. 176 n. 3.

[2] See above, pp. 85f. [3] b. Ber. 51 b.

[4] In connection with the passover unleavened bread at the time of Jesus, we are not to think of the usual thin, hard-baked *maṣṣot* we know today; rather it could be as thick as the breadth of a hand (j. Pes. 2.29b.59f.), which indicates that it was soft bread.

[5] On 'give thanks' (εὐχαριστήσας) see below, pp. 113f. and 175. [6] Ber. 6.6.

[7] Ber. 6.1. It seems that a special word of praise over the unleavened bread was added at the passover meal.

[8] This conclusion is suggested as much by the Lord's prayer as by the early Christian graces: Did. 9–10. So now also J. P. Audet, 'Literary Forms and Contents of a Normal Εὐχαριστία in the First Century' in *Studia Evangelica* (TU 73), Berlin, 1959, 650.

[9] b. Ber. 47a.

[10] In view of what was said above, n. 4, about the unleavened bread we are to think of tearing off rather than actually breaking (cf. also Dalman, *Jesus-Jeshua*, 137f.); incidentally, in the East bread is never cut with a knife.

[11] j. Ber. 6.10a.51; b. Ber. 37b. [12] b. Ber. 47a; j. Ber. 6.10a.58.

[13] Dalman, *Jesus-Jeshua*, 139.

[14] This is shown most clearly by the word 'take' Mark 14.22.

rite of *thanksgiving after the meal* ('after supper', Paul/Luke) as it was carried out when wine had been drunk. The *paterfamilias* arose again[1] from his reclining position and, having taken the cup of watered wine[2] out of the hand of the one serving at table,[3] spoke, as he sat,[4] the exhortation-blessing which still today lives on in our eucharistic liturgies:[5] 'Let us praise the Lord, our God, to whom belongs that of which we have partaken', and the table companions replied 'Praised be our God for the food we have eaten'.[6] Then he took the 'cup of blessing' (I Cor. 10.16) in his right hand,[7] held it a hand's breadth above the table ('taking')[8] and with his eyes on the cup[9] said the grace 'for all'[10] (i.e. in the name of all). At the time of Jesus this grace was probably worded as follows:

(1) 'Blessed art thou, O Lord, our God, king of the universe, who feedest the whole world with goodness, with grace and with mercy.'

(2) 'We thank thee, O Lord, our God, that thou hast caused us to inherit a goodly and pleasant land.'

(3) 'Have mercy, O Lord, our God, on Israel, thy people, and on Jerusalem, thy city, and upon Zion, the dwelling place of thy glory, and upon thy altar and upon thy temple.[11] Blessed art thou, O Lord, thou who buildest Jerusalem.'[12]

The table companions made this prayer their own by saying 'Amen'.[13] After this Jesus—apparently himself not drinking, contrary to cus-

[1] See above, p. 109.   [2] See below, p. 221 n. 1.   [3] See below, p. 162.
[4] b. Ber. 51b.   [5] See below, pp. 116f.
[6] Ber. 7.3; b. Ber. 50a. The two formulae varied slightly according to the number of the participants, cf. p. 117 n. 2.
[7] According to b. Ber. 51a the cup is lifted up with both hands and then held in the right hand.
[8] j. Ber. 7.11c.63f.; b. Ber. 51a, b. Cf. V. Kurrein, 'Die Genuss-Symbolik in den rituellen Bräuchen [II]', *MGWJ* 67 (1923), 263.
[9] Kurrein, *ibid.*   [10] Ber. 6.6.
[11] Concerning the ancient additional passover prayer which was inserted into the third benediction, see below, p. 252.
[12] L. Finkelstein, 'The Birkat Ha-Mazon', *JQR* 19 (1928–9), 211–62, has collected the widely scattered evidence for the various forms of the grace after the meal and by means of a careful analysis has reconstructed the text quoted as presumably the earliest. At about 120 BC the triad of benedictions was firmly established, cf. the triad of benedictions after the meal of Abraham, Jub. 22.6–9. (The fourth benediction was only decided upon at Jamnia after AD 100, cf. Finkelstein, *op. cit.*, 217f., 221f.; C. Albeck, 'Die vierte Eulogie des Tischgebets' *MGWJ* 78 [1934], 430-7.)
[13] Ber. 8.8.

tom[1]—passed the cup round and spoke the word of interpretation as it circulated.[2]

(b) The development of a Christian liturgical language

That all the accounts are concerned with the ritual that we have just depicted, is shown by the material which all four of them have in common (see the italicized words in the following table). They none the less vary characteristically in the details of their formulation.

I Cor. 11.23–25	Luke 22.19f.	Mark 14.22–24	Matt. 26.26f.
ὁ κύριος ᾽Ιησοῦς	καὶ	καὶ ἐσθιόντων αὐτῶν	ἐσθιόντων δὲ αὐτῶν
the Lord Jesus	and	and as they were eating	as they were eating
ἐν τῇ νυκτὶ on the night ᾗ παρεδίδοτο when he was delivered up			
ἔλαβεν ἄρτον	λαβὼν ἄρτον	λαβὼν ἄρτον	λαβὼν ὁ ᾽Ιησοῦς ἄρτον
took bread	*taking bread*	*taking bread*	Jesus *taking bread*
καὶ εὐχαριστήσας and *having given thanks*[3]	εὐχαριστήσας *having given thanks*[3]	εὐλογήσας *having said the blessing*[4]	καὶ εὐλογήσας and *having said the blessing*[4]
ἔκλασεν *broke (it)*	ἔκλασεν *broke (it)*	ἔκλασεν *broke (it)*	ἔκλασεν *broke (it)*
	καὶ ἔδωκεν and gave (it) αὐτοῖς to them	καὶ ἔδωκεν and gave (it) αὐτοῖς to them	καὶ δοὺς and giving (it) τοῖς μαθηταῖς to the disciples
καὶ εἶπεν and *said*	λέγων *saying*	καὶ εἶπεν and *said*	εἶπεν *said*

[1] See below, pp. 208f. This is also perhaps suggested by the otherwise superfluous words 'and they all drank of it' in which the word 'all' (πάντες) is in the Greek placed in an emphatic position at the end of the sentence (καὶ ἔπιον ἐξ αὐτοῦ πάντες).

[2] See above, pp. 87, 109.

[3] [εὐχαριστήσας. This is an aorist participle and the above translation is an attempt to represent the force of this participle in English, cf. RSV 'when he had given thanks' and NEB 'after giving thanks to God'. Transl.]

[4] [εὐλογήσας. Again, this is an aorist participle and the above translation is an attempt to represent the force of this participle in English; it is the NEB translation of this word. The RSV, in view of its translation of εὐχαριστήσας (previous note), is inconsistent here and has 'and blessed'. Transl.]

I Cor. 11.23–25	Luke 22.19f.	Mark 14.22–24	Matt. 26.26f.
ὡσαύτως	καὶ τὸ ποτήριον	καὶ λαβὼν	καὶ λαβὼν
in the same way	and the *cup*	and taking	and taking
καὶ τὸ ποτήριον	ὡσαύτως	ποτήριον	ποτήριον
also the *cup*	in the same way	(the) *cup*	(the) *cup*
μετὰ τὸ δειπνῆσαι	μετὰ τὸ δειπνῆσαι		
after supper	after supper		
		εὐχαριστήσας	καὶ εὐχαριστήσας
		having given thanks	and having given thanks
		ἔδωκεν	ἔδωκεν
		he gave (it)	he gave (it)
		αὐτοῖς	αὐτοῖς
		to them	to them
		καὶ ἔπιον ἐξ αὐτοῦ πάντες	
		and they all drank of it	
λέγων	λέγων	καὶ εἶπεν	λέγων
saying	saying	and *he said*	saying
		αὐτοῖς	
		to them	

An analysis of the variations shows the influence of the liturgical usage everywhere at work. In *Paul*[1] the introductory words 'the Lord Jesus on the night when he was delivered up took bread, and having given thanks, he broke (it) and said' (I Cor. 11.23f.) have a solemn ring. The very first words are liturgical, for the phrase 'the Lord Jesus' is not used in narrative; it is therefore not found in any of the gospels,[2] but rather belongs to the liturgical confessional formulae (I Cor. 12.3; Rom. 10.9). Standing as it does as a pendant phrase at the very beginning of the sentence, it almost has the force of a proclamation.. The following 'in the night when he was delivered up' is also liturgical, for it is not a mere chronological statement.[3] The verb 'delivered up', used absolutely, refers to an action of God; the passive is thus a circumlocution for the divine name, as in Rom. 4.25.

[1] Cf. to what follows E. Lohmeyer, 'Vom urchristlichen Abendmahl [I]', *ThR* 9 (1937), 184f.
[2] It is first found in [Mark] 16.19 as a variant reading.
[3] See above, p. 74 n. 4.

We are to understand it as 'on the night when God delivered him up', and we cannot fail to hear the echo of Isaiah 53. The concluding detailed description of the rite of grace at table with its three verbs ('took bread and having given thanks broke') has exactly the character of a liturgical rubric. In the use of the verb 'to give thanks' (εὐχαριστεῖν), instead of 'to bless' (εὐλογεῖν)[1] which we would expect in this context (grace before the meal), we have the first example in the New Testament[2] of that Graecizing which caused the Lord's Supper to come to be known as the Eucharist. The concise 'in the same way also the cup', with which Paul introduces the word over the cup, sounds like an instruction for the celebrant, and the use of the article before 'cup' (noticeable in contrast to 'bread' in v. 23, which does not have the article) refers to the ritual 'cup of blessing' (I Cor. 10.16).

In *Mark* the passage begins with a genitive absolute (καὶ ἐσθιόντων αὐτῶν, 'and as they were eating', Mark 14.22) which competes with Mark 14.18[3] and is probably secondary.[4] This redundant beginning betrays a seam in the text; it incorporates the liturgical account into the narrative of the passion, and is therefore a redactional connecting link. The action of Jesus is described by Mark with the same three verbs as by Paul, but Mark has the earlier[5] 'having said the blessing' (εὐλογήσας). As a fourth verb 'and he gave (it) to them' is added, strengthening the impression that this is a liturgical rubric. The introduction to the word over the cup is, in contrast to Paul/-Luke, phrased in ceremonial liturgical language, using five verbs ('and taking . . . to them'); it is clear that it is an imitation of the introduction to the word over the bread, an instance of the tendency towards the development of parallels which is so extraordinarily characteristic of the accounts of the institution.

The *Matthaean* account keeps closely to Mark. However, the addition of 'Jesus' and 'the disciples' (Matt. 26.26) gives the introduction the character of a new beginning,[6] and because of this the liturgical tone of the whole becomes even more marked. In connecting λαβών

[1] See below, p. 178.

[2] Later instances are Mark 8.6; Matt. 15.36; Luke 22.17, 19; Acts 27.35; John 6.11, 23; Did. 9.1; 10.1.

[3] See above, p. 97.

[4] The originality of the simple 'and taking' is borne out not only by Luke 22.19, but also Mark 6.41; 8.6; 14.23 par. Matt. 26.27; Luke 24.43; Acts 27.35, cf. Schürmann, 'Lk 22, 19b–20 als ursprüngliche Textüberlieferung', *Biblica* 32 (1951), 385; *Einsetzungsbericht*, 44. It should be added that the genitive absolute is unknown in Semitic languages (see below, p. 184).

[5] See below, p. 175 n. 4.   [6] Lohmeyer, *op. cit.*, 177.

('taking') and εὐλογήσας ('having said the blessing') by καί ('and') and in substituting δούς ('giving') for ἔδωκεν ('gave'), the whole emphasis is laid upon the breaking of the bread: the κλάσις τοῦ ἄρτου ('breaking of the bread') has become the essential feature of the first act.

Luke shows affinity to the Pauline account in the introduction to the word over the cup, and to both the Pauline and Markan accounts in the introduction to the word over the bread. The affinities, which extend into the details, show that the liturgical language is becoming firmly established. In connection with the bread Luke has (22.19a) 'to give thanks' (instead of 'to say the blessing') as does Paul; he has the same verb in 22.17: this is influence of the Christian liturgical language, in which the Graecizing first found in Paul was rapidly adopted.[1]

In the variations between the four introductions which we have discussed we do not find for the most part literary corrections by the four authors, but rather the reflection of liturgical development.

So far as *Jesus' words of interpretation* are concerned, the detailed comparison which we shall undertake below, pp. 164–173, will also show the same influence of the liturgical usage everywhere at work. It is to be seen in the emergence of the command to repeat the rite, which in Paul even appears twice; in the commands to action ('eat', 'drink'); in the change of the third person ('many') into the form of direct address ('you'), which changes a statement into a formula of distribution; in clarifications, expansions and in references to the scriptures. Also the avoidance of semitisms, which to the Gentile-Christians were strange and in part unintelligible, and the concern to avoid possible misunderstandings must have been particularly important in the case of a text used liturgically. But of all the influences of the liturgical usage on the text the most enduring was the one we have not yet mentioned in this summary, namely the tendency to make parallel the word over the bread and the word over the cup. In the subsequent period, too, this tendency has been strongly at work, as is shown by the history of the eucharistic liturgies.

(c) *The diminishing of references to the passover*

Already on p. 67 we have seen that the use of the account of the institution at the Eucharist had as a consequence the diminishing of

[1] See above, p. 113 n. 2. Further, in Luke 22.19a we find λέγων ('saying') in place of εἶπεν ('he said', Mark/Matt./Paul), a smoothing of the style into conformity with the λέγων of Luke 22.20 which at the same time betrays the oft-noted tendency towards parallelization.

references to the passover; and the way in which Pes. 10 portrays the passover had confirmed the assumption that texts which become significant in liturgical practice have a tendency to relegate to the background that which is no longer practised, or no longer practicable, in order to concentrate attention on the continuing ritual. In exactly the same way the descriptive elements in the accounts of the institution (the frame of the words of interpretation) show no interest in historical details, beyond those which are necessary to the liturgy itself. This conclusion applies also to the introductory words I Cor. 11.23b, which at first glance create an impression to the contrary; we saw above, p. 113, that they are more than merely a bare chronological reference, they contain a significant theological statement. The freeing of the account of the institution from the concrete historical situation makes it timeless and brings to expression those elements whose validity transcends time.

(d) The celebration sub una

The Christian communities, whose members were mostly from the poorer strata of society, did not always have wine available. It is possible that at several places we have traces of a celebration in one kind (*sub una*): in the designation of the Eucharist as κλάσις τοῦ ἄρτου ('the breaking of bread'), κλᾶν ἄρτον ('to break bread'); in the limiting clause 'as often as you drink it' which Paul adds to the word over the wine (I Cor. 11.25); and in the absence of the command to repeat the rite in connection with the wine in the Lukan account (Luke 22.20; different in Paul).[1]

If the limitation to the bread of the command to repeat the rite in the Lukan account represents the earliest stage of the Pauline-Lukan tradition,[2] then one must go a step farther and conclude that celebration *sub una* not only was frequent in the earliest period but was actually the rule. This would agree very well with our conclusion that the earliest Christian meal celebrations were a continuation of the table fellowship of Jesus with his disciples,[3] for it is certain that wine was not usually drunk on these occasions.[4]

(e) The separation of the Eucharist from the meal proper

At the Last Supper itself the action with the bread and the wine surrounded the meal proper; the clearest evidence for this are the

[1] See above, p. 52 n. 3.　　[2] See below, p. 249.　　[3] See above, p. 66.
[4] See above, p. 52.

words 'in the same way also the cup after supper' (I Cor. 11.25). A quite different picture is, however, to be found in the middle of the second century: the two eucharistic actions have now come together and stand independently beside the meal proper, now called the *Agape* (earliest witness: Jude 12). The actual position of the Eucharist now varies: according to the Ethiopic text of the *Epistula Apostolorum* (AD 140-70)[1] the Eucharist follows the Agape; according to the Coptic text the Eucharist precedes the Agape;[2] according to Justin the Eucharist, separated from the Agape, is celebrated on Sunday morning.[3] The first of these arrangements (Agape-Eucharist; Eucharist-Agape; complete separation of the two) is the earliest. That the Eucharist was at first held following the meal proper can be seen from the three-part dialogue which from the early period introduced the celebration of the Eucharist. This runs, according to the Apostolic Tradition of Hippolytus:[4]

Bishop: The Lord be with you.

People: And with thy spirit.

Bishop: Lift up your hearts.[5]

People: We have them with the Lord.

Bishop: Let us give thanks unto the Lord.

People: [It is] meet and right.

Bishop: We render thanks unto thee, O God, through thy Beloved Child Jesus Christ . . .

[1] Ethiopic text published by L. Guerrier, *Le Testament en Galilée de Notre-Seigneur Jésus-Christ* (Patrologia Orientalis 9.3), Paris, 1913; Coptic and Ethiopic text with a German translation by C. Schmidt–I. Wajnberg, *Gespräche Jesu mit seinen Jüngern nach der Auferstehung. Ein katholisch-apostolisches Sendschreiben des 2. Jahrhunderts* (TU 43), Leipzig, 1919. A German edition according to both versions by H. Duensing, *Epistula Apostolorum* (KIT 152), Bonn, 1925. [English translation of the Ethiopic text by G. Horner, *The Statutes of the Apostles*, London, 1904.]

[2] *Epist. Apost.* 15 (26) (Eth. Guerrier 198 [ch. 26]; Schmidt 54.5f. Copt. Schmidt 55.9f.). Cf. Duensing, *op. cit.*, 13; Horner, *op. cit.*, 158.

[3] Justin, *Apol.* I 67.3-7.

[4] On the involved textual tradition of Hippolytus' *Apostolic Tradition*, usually called 'Church Order', see Jeremias, *Infant Baptism*, 13f.

[Prof. Jeremias now quotes the Greek text according to the retranslation into Greek from the Latin, Ethiopic and Syriac texts by H. Lietzmann, *Messe und Herrenmahl* (Arbeiten zur Kirchengeschichte 8), Bonn, 1926, 158 (= *Mass and Lord's Supper*, 125). We give the English version from G. Dix, *Apostolic Tradition of St Hippolytus*, London, 1937, 7. Transl.]

[5] Not 'to leave the travail of the world' (Lietzmann, *Mass and Lord's Supper*, 187), but: to meet the coming Lord!

This prayer is followed by the account of the institution with the words of interpretation over the bread and the wine. We are concerned with the fifth line ('let us give thanks unto the Lord', εὐχαριστήσωμεν τῷ κυρίῳ, gratias agamus Domino), which is transmitted in the same words in the ancient liturgies of the East and the West,[1] and so must have been early established and therefore very old. This call of the minister is nothing other than the exhortation formula which introduced the Jewish grace after the meal (we have already discussed this grace, above, p. 110) and the following eucharistic prayer is simply a Christian version of the grace after the meal:[2] the corresponding words 'let us give thanks' (εὐχαριστήσωμεν, line 5) / 'we render thanks' (εὐχαριστοῦμεν, line 7) are parallel to those in the Jewish grace after the meal (see above, p. 110), nebarek baruk let us bless' / 'blessed be'. We see therefore that the celebration of the Eucharist begins with the grace after the meal and therefore follows the meal proper. When, in some places, the Eucharist was later celebrated before the Agape[3] this was done from a desire to receive it in a state of fasting.[4] The same desire is determinative when in Rome (Justin) the Eucharist is linked with the morning worship.

But the drawing together of the two eucharistic acts and their separation from the preceding meal proper is considerably older than the earliest literary reference to this procedure in the *Epistula Apostolorum* in the middle of the second century. Already the *Didache* presupposes the practice of following the Agape with the Eucharist. Since the first publication of the *Didache* in 1883[5] a lively discussion has taken place as to whether the prayers in Did. 9–10 are for an

[1] So Hippolytus (Lietzmann, *Mass and Lord's Supper*, 125), the Apostolic Constitutions (p. 122), the liturgies of Basil (p. 137), Chrysostom (p. 138), James (p. 140), Mark (p. 154), etc. In the Didache this exhortation is missing; it should come after 10.1 ('in this manner give thanks') and may here have been just as much taken for granted as the missing 'Amen' after 9.2 and 9.4.

[2] Cf. Lietzmann, *Mass and Lord's Supper*, 187; Dix, *Liturgy*, 79f. According to Ber. 7.3 the exhortation formula varied slightly according to the number present at the table. The version which lives on in the eucharistic liturgy, 'Let us give thanks unto the Lord', corresponds to that which the rabbis prescribed for the occasions when there were ten ('Let us bless our God') or a hundred ('Let us bless the Lord, our God') persons present. Rightly, Dix points out, *Liturgy*, 80, that we may assume from this that in Jewish-Christian circles the celebration was not held privately but in the assembly of the community.

[3] *Epist. Apost.* 15 (26) Copt. (Schmidt 55.9f.; Duensing 14b; Horner, 158).

[4] Hippolytus, *Ap. Trad.* 28.1 (ed. Dix, 55). Cf. F. J. Dölger, *Der heilige Fisch in den antiken Religionen und im Christentum. Textband (ΙΧΘΥΣ II)*, Münster, 1922, 554.

[5] Ph. Bryennios, Διδαχὴ τῶν δώδεκα ἀποστόλων, Constantinople, 1883.

Agape[1] or for a Eucharist.[2] This may now be concluded by recognizing, mainly on the basis of an investigation by M. Dibelius, that neither of these alternatives is correct; we are dealing with an Agape which was followed by a celebration of the Eucharist:[3] Did. 9.1–10.5[4] has the prayers of the Agape before and after the meal, 10.6 the introductory liturgy to the following Eucharist.[5]

The same picture is presented by Acts 2.42:

> 'they were devoting themselves to the teaching of the apostles
> and to the κοινωνία
> to the breaking of bread
> and to the prayers.'

The interpretation of this verse must begin with the participle προσκαρτεροῦντες ('devoting themselves'). A manumission inscription from Panticapaeum (modern Kertch) on the Black Sea (to be dated AD 80) has the rare word προσκαρτέρησις, used to denote regular visits to the synagogue.[6] This corresponds to the use of the verb προσκαρτερεῖν in Acts, where it often means 'to attend worship regularly' (2.46 Temple worship; 1.14 communal prayer; 6.4 prayer and ministry of

---

[1] P. Ladeuze, F. Kattenbusch, P. Drews, V. Ermoni, van Crombrugghe, E. Baumgärtner, P. Cagin, R. Knopf, T. E. J. Ferris, W. Goossens, J. Brinktrine, R. H. Connolly, F. J. Dölger, F. L. Cirlot, G. Dix.

[2] P. Batiffol, J. Bricout, K. Völker, A. Greiff, O. Casel.

[3] M. Dibelius, 'Die Mahlgebete der Didache', *ZNW* 37 (1938), 32–41. The same was seen and supported by wholly correct arguments as early as 1884 by T. Zahn, *Forschungen zur Geschichte des neutestamentlichen Kanons und der altkirchlichen Literatur* III. *Supplementum Clementinum*, Erlangen, 1884, 293–8. Further: E .v. d. Goltz, *Das Gebet in der ältesten Christenheit*, Leipzig, 1901, 213; E. Hennecke, *Neutestamentliche Apokryphen*[2], Tübingen, 1924, 559; R. Stapper, *Katholische Liturgik*[5,6], Münster, 1931, 182; Hupfeld, *Abendmahlsfeier*, 1935, 77; Quasten, *Monumenta*, 9.12 n. 5; A. Arnold, *Der Ursprung des christlichen Abendmahls im Lichte der neuesten liturgiegeschichtlichen Forschung* (Freiburger Theologische Studien 45), Freiburg i. Br., 1937, 26–29; Bultmann, *Theology* I, 145; A. M. Schneider, *Stimmen aus der Frühzeit der Kirche* (Am Lebensstrom 5), Cologne, 1948, 23 n. 11; J.-P. Audet in *RB* 65 (1958), 394; *La Didachè. Instructions des Apôtres* (Études bibliques), Paris, 1958, 410–15, 431.

[4] Did. 10.5 belongs to the prayer after the meal, as the parallel to 9.4 shows.

[5] The main arguments are as follows: (1) There never was a Eucharist with the sequence Wine–Bread (Did. 9.2–4). (2) The liturgical ejaculations in 10.6, which greet the coming Lord, and the warning 'if anyone is holy, let him come; if he is not, let him repent' are meaningful only as the introduction to the Eucharist (not as the conclusion of an Agape or a Eucharist).

[6] Moulton and Milligan, *Vocabulary*, 548: χωρὶς ἐς τ[ὴ]ν προ[σ]ευχὴν θωπείας τε καὶ προσκα[ρτερ]ήσεω[ς], 'besides reverence and constancy towards the place of prayer'.

the word).[1] If one turns to 2.42 with this in mind, then the conclusion follows that the four phrases used here, in pairs and dependent on προσκαρτεροῦντες ('devoting themselves'), describe the sequence of an early Christian service: first the teaching of the apostles and the (table) fellowship, then the breaking of bread and the prayers. This conclusion can be supported by numerous observations: 1. That the meetings of the early Christian communities began with teachings is evidenced directly by Acts 20.7ff.; Justin, *Apol.* I 67.4; Acts of John 106–10,[2] etc., and also indirectly by the exhortation to the holy kiss which we find in Rom. 16.16; I Cor. 16.20; II Cor. 13.12; I Thess. 5.26; I Peter 5.14. This exhortation shows clearly that the celebration of the meal, introduced by the holy kiss, followed directly upon the reading of the letters; i.e. when an apostolic letter had been received this took the place of the teaching. 2. That, further, the celebration ended with psalms and prayers is to be concluded from Acts 2.46f., and this is supported by the eucharistic liturgies of the whole of the ancient church (Rome, Egypt, Africa), as well as indirectly by the evening prayer of the community, Acts 12.12.[3] 3. The context in which Acts 2.42 is set permits the interpretation of the verse in terms of early Christian worship without any kind of difficulty. After the report in 2.41 that at Pentecost 3,000 were baptized, in 2.42 it is added that from then on the newly baptized regularly took part in the assemblies of the community. 4. A final argument for our interpretation of Acts 2.42 is that it perhaps provides a solution for the problem of how the Lord's Supper came to be known as the 'breaking of bread' (Acts 2.42, 46; 20.7, 11). In Judaism, it should be noted, as J. Lightfoot (died 1675) saw long ago,[4] 'breaking of bread'

[1] The only exceptions are 8.13; 10.7: attachment to persons.

[2] [James, *The Apocryphal New Testament*, 266–8. Transl.]

[3] Cf. J. Müller-Bardorff, 'Nächtlicher Gottesdienst im apostolischen Zeitalter', *ZNW* 46 (1955), 275f. Haenchen's arguments (*Die Apostelgeschichte*[13], Göttingen, 1961 [= *Apostelgeschichte*], 153) against the interpretation of Acts 2.42 as referring to early Christian worship have not convinced me. Certainly the Christians taught publicly in the temple (Acts 5.21, 25, 42), but this does not preclude the idea that instruction of the community had a firm place at the beginning of the communal assembly (20.7, etc.). Equally certainly the Christians took part in the public prayers of the temple (3.1), but that does not mean that the meal celebrations of the community did not end with prayers of thanksgiving; the liturgies of the ancient Church witness to this. In the previous edition of this work I gave no arguments in support of my interpretation of Acts 2.42; I hope that the material I have given above will serve to meet Haenchen's objections.

[4] J. Lightfoot, *Exercitations* on Acts 2.42 (*Works* VIII, 384); cf. *Commentary* on Acts 2.42 (VIII, 60).

never refers to a whole meal but only (a) the action of tearing the bread, and (b) the rite with which the meal opened, as it is depicted above, p. 109.[1] How, then, did this become a technical term for the Lord's Supper? If we consider carefully the four expressions in Acts 2.42 (the teaching of the apostles, the κοινωνία, the breaking of bread, the prayers), then we must ask the question: To what exactly does κοινωνία refer, when it is used to describe a part of an early Christian meeting for worship? One could turn to Rom. 15.26, where κοινωνία is used in the sense of 'contribution', 'donation', and think of it as referring to a collection of contributions for the 'daily distribution' (Acts 6.1), which was taken after the apostolic instruction (so the second edition of this work [ET, 83 n. 3]). But it may well be better to translate κοινωνία '(table) fellowship'.[2] If the κοινωνία of Acts 2.42 refers to the Agape, then 'the breaking of bread' must mean the subsequent Eucharist.[3] The designation 'to break bread' was

[1] The constantly repeated assertion that 'breaking of bread' is an expression used in Jewish sources meaning 'to have a meal' is an error that it seems to be impossible to eradicate. Leenhardt, Le sacrement, 58, quotes as evidence b. Ber. 51b: 'She [sic] came to the house of Rab Nachman in order to break [sic] the bread.' In fact this reads: '(R.) Ula once entered the house of Rab Naḥman. He enveloped bread (kerok riphta, i.e. he took part in the meal [Soncino Talmud, 'They had a meal.' Transl.]).' When Billerbeck IV, 613, says, 'to break the bread' is synonymous with 'to have a meal', this is an oversight; as the evidence given p. 614 under 'e' clearly shows, instead of 'to break the bread' we should read 'to eat (the) bread' or 'to envelop bread'.

[2] Cf. Ecclus 6.10, κοινωνὸς τραπεζῶν ('table-friend'); Tob. 2.2 (Codex Sinaiticus), φάγεται κοινῶς μετ᾽ ἐμοῦ ('he shall eat together with me'); I Cor. 10.18, 20, κοινωνοὶ ('table-fellows', cf. H. Gressmann in ZNW 20 [1921], 226) τοῦ θυσιαστηρίου, τῶν δαιμονίων ('of the altar, of the demons'). So Lietzmann, Mass and Lord's Supper 204; A. Fridrichsen, 'Église et Sacrement dans le Nouveau Testament', RHPhR 17 (1937), 353; Ph.-H. Menoud, 'Les Actes des Apôtres et l'Eucharistie', RHPhR 33 (1953), 26.

[3] Luke 24.35, 'Then they told what had happened on the road, and how he was known to them in (ἐν) the breaking of the bread', is to be understood in a similar way. Here the breaking of bread could refer (1) to the act of breaking the bread in its literal sense. If this is accepted, then ἐν must be translated 'by' (so John 13.35; I John 4.2), and it must be taken to mean that Jesus had a special manner, characteristic for him, in which he tore the loaf (perhaps lifting his eyes to heaven, cf. Mark 6.41; so Hupfeld, Abendmahlsfeier, 87 n. 1). (2) However, the phrase 'to break bread' has also a wider meaning; it can be used of the whole ritual with which the meal opened: grace, breaking, distribution (b. Ber. 46a; 47a; Targ. I Sam. 9.13; etc.). This ritual joined the company at table into a fellowship. If the expression 'in the breaking of bread' (Luke 24.35) is understood in this way, then it may be assumed either (a) that just as he had given the disciples a prayer of their own in the Lord's prayer, so also Jesus had created a special form of the daily blessing at the breaking of bread (perhaps with abba as the address to God), by which the Emmaus disciples recognized him (so Dalman, Jesus-Jeshua, 136). Or (b)

appropriate for the Eucharist and conforms to the usual idiom, because this was not a meal, but rather consisted of the ritual which began the meal, united with that which ended it. It may therefore be assumed that the designation of the Lord's Supper as 'the breaking of bread' arose as a consequence of the separation of the Eucharist from the meal proper. If this is correct, then Acts already presupposes this separation (20.11: Eucharist after midnight is also evidence for this).

Recently a rather convincing suggestion has been made: that the separation of Agape and Eucharist is already presupposed in I Corinthians.[1] That the abuse of the celebration, against which Paul struggles in I Cor. 11.17–34, could have gained ground is more readily understandable if the communal meal proper, which was taken less seriously, preceded the sacramental act. Also the advice of the apostle, in certain circumstances to eat first at home (I Cor. 11.34, cf. 22), is best understood if the meal proper normally preceded the Eucharist.[2]

For the Eucharist (in the form of the carrying out of the two sacramental acts after the meal proper) to become an independent rite is a decisive change that could not but have left traces in the tradition of the eucharistic formula. Such traces are to be found in the fact that in Mark/Matthew the word over the bread and the word over the

---

one might remember that the blessing before the meal was said by the host (b. Ber. 46a); it would be unusual for Jesus, as a guest, to take the place of the master of the house, and the disciples might have recognized him by this. (3) But it is questionable whether Luke 24.35 'the breaking of bread' really means either the actual breaking of the bread (1) or the ritual of grace before the meal (2), since Luke does not use for 'to recognize by something', γινώσκειν ἔν τινι, but rather γινώσκειν ἔκ τινος (6.44) or γινώσκειν κατά τι (1.18). In view of the Lukan usage of 'the breaking of bread' (Acts 2.42) and 'to break bread' (2.46; 20.7, 11) it is more probable that the phrase refers to the Eucharist. The risen Lord grants the Emmaus disciples fellowship at his table and 'during the holy meal' (understanding the ἐν in Luke 24.35 as a temporal ἐν 'at, during', as in ἐν τῇ προσευχῇ, Matt. 21.22, further Luke 14.14; 20.33; Acts 7.13, cf. Bauer: A. and G., 259), 'their eyes were opened, so that they recognized him' (Luke 24.31). Cf. Jeremias, Weltvollender, 78, and below, p. 204 n. 3, on the table fellowship between the risen Lord and his disciples.

[1] A. M. Schneider, Stimmen, 23 n. 1; G. Bornkamm, 'Herrenmahl', ZThK 53 (1956), 312–49; E. Schweizer, 'Abendmahl I. Im NT', RGG³ I (1957), col. 11; C. Schneider, 'Abendmahlsstellen', in Abendmahlsgespräch, ed. by Evangelische Akademie der Pfalz, 1958, 32f.

[2] The words 'after supper' (I Cor. 11.25) are not necessarily irreconcilable with this conclusion. They were part of the old ritual and are simply preserved (not in Mark/Matthew), even though the ritual had already changed. The question as to how the separation of meal proper and Eucharist could have come about will concern us below, p. 133.

wine follow one another, whereas in Paul they are separated by the words 'after supper'. Furthermore, the 'as they were eating' at the beginning (Mark 14.18, 22 par. Matt. 26.21, 26) indicates that the meal proper preceded the Eucharist.

In the Lukan account the change of the Eucharist becoming independent of the meal proper is reflected in what seems at first glance to be a wholly unimportant change in word-order. Whereas in Paul we have, 'In the same way also (sc. he took) the cup after supper' (I Cor. 11.25), in Luke we read precisely the same words but with 'in the same way' (ὡσαύτως) now coming later, 'Also the cup (sc. he took) in the same way after supper' (22.20). In Paul it is said that the Lord 'in the same way (as before the meal he took bread) after the meal (took) the cup' and spoke the blessing over it. In Luke, on the other hand, the 'in the same way' is drawn to 'after supper', so that the interpretation is possible—and probably intended—'likewise after supper' he took the cup (i.e. he took both bread and cup 'after supper'); 'this, however, depicts a secondary meal practice of a later time in which the eucharistic breaking of bread had been moved to join the eucharistic cup at the end of the meal'.[1]

(f) The early Christian celebration of the passover[2]

Among the meal celebrations of the early Christian community the Eucharist held during the night of the passover stands out because of the unusual hour at which it was celebrated. We now have a more exact knowledge of the manner in which the Early Church celebrated the passover, since it has been shown (1) that the passover of the Early Church lived on in that of the Quartodecimanians,[3] and (2) that previous conceptions of the procedure and meaning of the Quartodecimanian passover festival were erroneous.[4]

In the generally accepted view of the Quartodecimanian passover the 'breaking of the fast' which characterized this celebration[5] came at three o'clock in the afternoon of Nisan 14, i.e. at the time of the death of Jesus according to the Johannine chronology, and from this the conclusion is drawn that the Quartodecimanian passover fast was

---

[1] Schürmann, Einsetzungsbericht, 34.
[2] See Jeremias, πάσχα, TWNT V (1954), 900–3.
[3] This has been shown by E. Schwartz, 'Osterbetrachtungen', ZNW 7 (1906), 10f., and K. Holl, 'Bruchstück', Gesammelte Aufsätze II, 214; cf. Lohse, Passafest, 74f., 76, 82–84, 89–93.
[4] Demonstrated by Lohse, Passafest, 44f.
[5] Eusebius, Hist. eccl. 5.23.1–25.

in remembrance of the Passion. This Quartodecimanian practice of ending the fast at 3 p.m. on Nisan 14 was held to be an important support for the Johannine chronology of the Passion, according to which Jesus was crucified on Nisan 14 (not 15), with the consequence that the Last Supper was not a passover meal. All these conclusions are erroneous. We now know that the Quartodecimanian 'breaking of the fast' at 3 p.m. on Nisan 14 is a modern fable, first propounded in 1856[1] and completely without foundation. The truth is that this 'breaking of the fast' came at cock-crow during the passover night, as has been established by the discovery of the *Epistula Apostolorum* (AD 140–70),[2] i.e. at about 3 a.m., as indeed the Eucharist was celebrated at 3 a.m. on Easter day in the great Church, too.[3] The passover celebration of the Quartodecimanians, and so of the early Jewish-Christian community whose practice lived on in that of the Quartodecimanians, took the following form:[4] 1. While the Jews were holding the passover meal in the night Nisan 14/15, the Christian community fasted representatively for Israel.[5] 2. Exodus 12 was read and explained. 3. After midnight, at about 3 a.m., the fast was broken by the celebration of the Lord's Supper (Agape and Eucharist). The unusual time of this celebration itself shows what the emphasis was at this early Christian passover: the primary concern was neither with the remembrance of the passion nor with the remembrance of the resurrection, but with the expectation of the Parousia! That the Messiah would come on the night of the passover was both a Jewish[6] and a Christian[7] hope. Each year, therefore, during the passover night the primitive community awaited until midnight, in prayer and fasting, the return of the Lord. They prolonged the waiting into the hours after midnight. If he had not come bodily by cock-crow, then they united themselves with him in the celebration of table fellowship.

If this sequence of the primitive Christian passover celebration is kept in mind, then it can easily be recognized in Luke 22.15–20. In this passage two independent bits of tradition have been brought

---

[1] By G. E. Steitz, 'Differenz', *ThStKr* 29 (1856), 721–809.
[2] *Epist. Apost.* 15 (26) (Duensing, 13). On this epistle see above, p. 116 n. 1.
[3] Evidence in Lohse, *Passafest*, 83 n. 2.
[4] Lohse, *Passafest*, 62–89.
[5] Evidence in Lohse, *Passafest*, 63–70; Jeremias, πάσχα, *TWNT* V (1954), 901 n. 51.
[6] See below, p. 206.
[7] See below, p. 206 n. 5.

together, namely the avowal of abstinence (vv. 15–18) and the words of interpretation (vv. 19f.). Mark has the opposite order; in his account the avowal of abstinence (14.25) follows the words of interpretation. Why does in Luke the fasting of Jesus in prospect of the kingdom of God come at the beginning? The answer may very well be: The tradition preserved in Luke has been influenced by the primitive Christian passover celebration. It portrays the Last Supper as the prototype of the Christian passover. As Jesus renounced the feast and the wine in prospect of the fulfilment of the passover in the kingdom of God (Luke 22.15–18), so the Christians fasted on passover eve and thereby prepared themselves for the coming of the kingdom in the Parousia. And as Jesus subsequently tendered bread and wine (Luke 22.19f.), so the Christians broke their fast when the cock crew by celebrating the Lord's Supper. Jesus is the founder of the new passover,[1] in which the Eucharist replaces the paschal lamb.[2] 'A community which continued the celebration of the Jewish Passover in a "new" Christian manner, sought the model for its new celebration in the last supper of Jesus.'[3] In this connection we must realize that a community which celebrated the Christian passover in the manner depicted above must have found this prototypal character of the passage Luke 22.15–20 much clearer than do we who have first to think ourselves back into the early Christian passover celebration.

At this point, however, we must utter an energetic warning against the possibility of a false conclusion. Although we may have established that the arrangement of the two bits of tradition (first, the avowal of abstinence, Luke 22.15–18, then the institution of the Lord's Supper, v. 19f.) corresponds to the sequence of the early Christian passover celebration, we must not overlook the fact that the early Christian practice of fasting in the passover night must, in turn, have developed out of Jesus' avowal of abstinence. How could the Christian community have felt called upon to fast while the Jews celebrated the passover joyously[4] if they were not following the pattern of the abstinence of Jesus? It is not the liturgy which stands at the very beginning, but the word and act of Jesus. From this was developed the early Christian passover practice; only secondarily has

[1] H. Schürmann, 'Die Anfänge christlicher Osterfeier', *Theologische Quartalschrift* 31 (1951), 414–25.

[2] Schürmann, *op. cit.*, 422.

[3] Schürmann, *op. cit.*, 424.

[4] Epiphanius, *Panarion* 70.11.3 (GCS 37.244.9ff.): 'while they are feasting you are to mourn, fasting for them.'

this, then, influenced the Lord's Supper tradition, at least in so far as it was the occasion for the transmission of the tradition concerning Jesus' avowal of abstinence. Precisely in the case of the avowal of abstinence we can see with especial clarity that the tradition goes back to a pre-liturgical stage.

So we can see that the liturgical usage has influenced the formulation of the accounts of the Lord's Supper in many ways. It should also be clear that this conclusion provides us with an important resource to help us in our endeavour to recover the very earliest tradition, the tradition that has not yet been influenced by the usage of the community.

THE PROTECTION OF THE SACRED FORMULA

The liturgical usage of the account of the institution not only influenced the formulation of the tradition, it also had another and quite different consequence, a consequence which becomes evident when one asks why the fourth gospel offers no account of the institution. This *silence of the gospel of John* is the more remarkable in that John 13.2ff. certainly describes the same meal as Mark 14.17ff.: namely the Last Supper, which is followed by the journey to Gethsemane by night and the arrest. The usual explanations for the omission of the account of the institution are quite unsatisfactory. Or are we intended to take seriously the suggestion that the apostle John 'composed his account of that night at a time . . . before it was possible to speak of a Christian Eucharist'?[1] Was there ever such a time? What features in John 13.1ff. suggest such an early date? No better is the contention that John's gospel has rejected the Eucharist or regarded it as superfluous.[2] Where in the history of the apostolic age do we find the slightest support for so weighty a thesis? All difficulties disappear, however, with the realization that the fourth evangelist consciously omitted the account of the Lord's Supper *because he did not want to reveal the sacred formula to the general public*. Or is this too bold an assumption?

(a) The esoteric element in Late Judaism and in primitive Christianity

The whole environment of primitive Christianity knows the element of the esoteric. For the hellenistic world we need only refer to the mystery religions,[3] the secret teachings of Gnosticism, the esoteric teachings of the

---

[1] Gottfr. Kittel, 'Wirkungen', *ThStKr* 96/97 (1925), 224.
[2] Bultmann, *Johannes*, 360.   [3] Batiffol, *Études* I, 10–15.

philosophic schools[1] and the world of magic.[2] Although it has been generally recognized that this is true of the hellenistic world, it has for a long time been little known that we also find an arcane discipline in Palestine in New Testament times. But the newly discovered *Essene texts* have disposed of the last doubt concerning this. We knew already from Josephus that among the Essenes the novices were admitted to the sacred washings only after a strict probationary year, and to acceptance in the order only after a further two years.[3] At his admission the new member had to bind himself with terrible oaths to protect the secret teachings of the order from non-members, to keep secret the—probably magical—names of the angels and to guard the secret writings of the order.[4] These secret writings contained, according to Josephus, medical and alchemistic secrets,[5] and probably also the angelic names.[6] The Damascus Document adds that no one was allowed to know anything of the 'rulings' of the community before his acceptance;[7] the Manual of Discipline prescribes the concealment of 'the counsel of the Torah in the midst of the men of deceit'.[8] The meals were also kept secret. Only after admission to the order was participation in them permitted;[9] no 'partisan of another faith' was allowed to enter the room,[10] and their meals were taken in such silence that 'it appeared to those outside the house like some tremendous mystery'.[11] Here we have arcane discipline *in the strict sense*.

But we do not need to confine ourselves to the sects in order to find esotericism in Palestine in New Testament times. The orthodox religious writings also exhibit similar characteristics, even if not arcane discipline in the strict sense. Here we must remember *apocalyptic*, which from the time of Daniel spoke in veiled pictures, in many cases for political reasons. All the apocalypses claim to be secret writings,[12] in order to explain their

---

[1] Mentioned, for example, by Clement of Alexandria, *Strom.* 5.10.65.1–66.5 (GCS 15.369.24–370.25).

[2] Cf. G. Bornkamm, μυστήριον, μυέω, *TWNT* IV (1942), 810–20, with copious references to further literature.

[3] Josephus, *Bell.* 2.137f. According to 1QS 6.12–23 the whole probationary period lasted only two years.

[4] Josephus, *Bell.* 2.141f.

[5] *Bell.* 2.136.

[6] *Bell.* 2.142. Whether the reference to 'prophetic sayings' which are to be found in the 'holy books' (2.159) is a reference to the prophecies of the OT or to the utterances of prophetically gifted members of the order cannot be decided from the report of Josephus.

[7] CD 15.10f. (C. Rabin, *The Zadokite Documents*[2], Oxford, 1958, 73).

[8] 1QS 9.17; cf. 5.15f.; 8.11f.

[9] Josephus, *Bell.* 2.138f.

[10] *Bell.* 2.129. The 'strangers' who according to 2.132 do take part in the meal should therefore be understood as foreign members of the order.

[11] *Bell.* 2.133.

[12] G. Box in Charles, *APOT* II, 614 (on IV Ezra 12.37).

pseudepigraphical character (they claim to come from a previous time). Daniel receives the order, 'shut up the words, and seal the book, until the time of the end' (12.4, cf. v. 9; 8.26). The Assumption of Moses is supposed to have been put away with other books in earthen vessels until the day of repentance in Jerusalem (1.16–18; 10.11–13). Pseudo-Ezra is told to publish only twenty-four books (the canonical books of the Old Testament) of the ninety-four that he has written, and to keep back the last seventy (the apocalypses) and give them only to the wise among the people.[1] Origen[2] and the Talmud[3] testify to the existence of Jewish apocalyptic secret writings and traditions.[4]

Even outside the apocalyptic tradition the esoteric element figures largely in late Judaism.[5] In another place[6] I have sought to show that the enormous influence of the scribes at the time of Jesus can only be understood if it is recognized that the respect paid to them is due to their being the bearers of a secret knowledge, the esoteric tradition.[7] Right down to the second century AD *the entire oral tradition* was treated as the secret of God,[8] being protected from the heathen by the interdict on writing it down.[9] The esoteric traditions of the rabbis in a narrower sense contained,

---

[1] IV Ezra 14.44–46, cf. 12.36–38; 14.26. According to IV Ezra 14.6 Moses was instructed to publish a part of the words of God (the Torah) and to keep a part (the apocalypses) secret.

[2] Origen, *Commentariorum series* 28 on Matt. 23.37–39: 'out of the secret books which are current among the Jews' (E. Klostermann, *Origenes Werke* XI. *Origenes Matthäuserklärung* II [GCS 38], Leipzig, 1933, 50.6f.), 'it is said . . . in writings not manifest' (50.23f.), among which are 'a secret book of Isaiah' (50.28), 'many of the secret books' (51.9), 'secret books which go under the name of the saints' (51.12). To this belongs also the remark of Origen, *op. cit.*, 55, on Matt. 24.36, concerning II Thess. 2.1f.: 'Perhaps it was because there were among the Jews some who declared to be informed about the times of the consummation, either from Scripture or from secret (sources), that Paul wrote this (II Thess. 2.1f.), teaching his disciples to believe none declaring such things' (124.17–20).

[3] E.g., b. B. M. 92a, etc.

[4] W. Bousset, *Der Antichrist*, Göttingen, 1895, has shown that the apocalyptic conceptions of late Judaism have largely come down to us only in late, and sometimes even very late, Christian sources, whereas the older reports are fragmentary. 'How are we to explain this? It seems to me that in very many cases the eschatological revelations were not handed down in a written form but orally, as secret teaching to be handled with fear and trembling' (p. 18).

[5] How completely this fact has been overlooked can be seen from, e.g., G. Anrich, 'Arkandisziplin', *RGG*[2] I (1927), cols. 530–3, which ignores this just as it does the material we have mentioned from the Palestinian sectarian literature and from apocalyptic.

[6] Jeremias, *Jerusalem*[3], 270–5.

[7] Cf. Jesus' rebuke of the scribes in Luke 11.52, 'you have taken away the key of knowledge'.

[8] Pesik. R. 5 (14b).

[9] H. L. Strack, *Introduction to the Talmud and Midrash*, London and New York, 1959, 12–18.

according to Ḥag. 2.1; Tos. Ḥag. 2.1, 7 (223f.), four groups of secret teaching: (1) the incest laws might not be expounded before more than two people; (2) the creation story might not be interpreted before more than one;[1] (3) the vision of the chariot (Ezek. 1, 10), i.e. the secrets of the divine nature, might only be taught with a veiled head,[2] in whispers,[3] and only to one person, who had to be a scholar and a man of mature judgment;[4] (4) it was altogether forbidden to give instruction about the cosmic topography, i.e. the depiction of the heavenly and subterranean world, and about the eternity existing before the creation and after the destruction of the world.[5] Origen delineates the esoteric material similarly when he says that the Jews reserved for truly mature readers the account of creation in Genesis, the theophany at the beginning and the description of the new temple at the end of the book of Ezekiel, and the Song of Solomon.[6] But the esoteric tradition was not limited to these subjects, which were kept secret in part for fear of gnostic influences. The most holy name was also preserved from profanation by a rule that, as is said in one place, permitted teachers to mention it to their pupils only once in each week;[7] the 'grounds of the Torah', i.e. the grounds of God's laying down the particular commandments, were not to be disclosed to the multitude.[8] Furthermore, certain passages from the Old Testament were either not to be read at all in synagogue worship, or only to be read in Hebrew without an accompanying translation into the Aramaic of the people;[9] certain regulations tending to relax the rules concerning purification, working on minor feast days, hallowing the Sabbath, were, for pedagogical reasons, not to be taught publicly;[10] certain teachings which had not attained validity were to be handed on only in a whisper.[11] Still more elaborate were, finally, the precautions taken in regard to the heathen. Josephus mentions, for

---

[1] It is said that Alexander the Great asked the elders in southern Palestine whether light or darkness was created first. He was given no answer, because 'this matter may not be explained' (b. Tam. 32a).

[2] Jeremias, *Jerusalem*³, 270.

[3] b. Ḥag. 14a; Gen. R. 3.4 on 1.3: secret teaching was given in whispers.

[4] On 'throne-mysticism' see Billerbeck I, 974–8; G. Scholem, *Major Trends in Jewish Mysticism*³, New York, 1954, 40–79. According to j. Ḥag. 2.77a.13ff. the second and third prohibitions go back to R. Aḳiba (died after AD 135), cf. P. Benoit, 'Rabbi Aqiba ben Joseph. Sage et héros du Judaïsme', *RB* 54 (1947), 70 (reprinted in Benoit, *Exégèse et Théologie* II, Paris, 1961, 358).

[5] On the combination of apocalyptic with theosophy and cosmogony see Scholem, *Mysticism*, 43.

[6] Origen, *Commentary on the Song of Solomon*, Prologue (W. A. Baehrens, *Origenes Werke* VIII [GCS 33], Leipzig 1925, 62.22–30).

[7] b. Ḳid. 71a.

[8] b. Sanh. 21b, etc.

[9] Meg. 4.10; Tos. Meg. 4.31ff. (228.5), cf. Jeremias, *Jerusalem*³, 272.

[10] Jeremias, *Jerusalem*³, 273.

[11] j. Beṣ. 1.61a.1.

example, that it was forbidden to speak of the worship of God in the Holy of Holies.[1] This survey shows that there were very different reasons for this secrecy in the various instances, but the primary reason was always the intent to protect the sacred from profanation.

We find a similar situation in the *Dispersion*. Philo demands in *De Cherub*. 42,[2] at the beginning of an interpretation of Gen. 4.12 (on 'the virtues . . . their conception and their birth-pangs'), that 'those who corrupt religion into superstition' should 'close their ears or depart': 'For this is a divine mystery and its lesson is for the initiated who are worthy to receive the holiest secret.' A little farther on he exhorts the worthy initiates: 'These thoughts, ye initiated, whose ears are purified, receive into your souls as holy mysteries indeed and babble not of them to any of the profane' (48 [Loeb, 36f.]). But if they meet one of the 'initiated' (into the sacred mysteries) they are to question him closely, 'lest knowing of some still newer secret he hide it from you; stay not till you have learnt its full lesson. I myself was initiated under Moses the God-beloved into his greater mysteries, yet when I saw the prophet Jeremiah and knew him to be not only himself enlightened, but a worthy minister of the holy secrets, I was not slow to become his disciple' (48f. [Loeb, 36f.]).

The role which the esoteric plays in the *teaching of Jesus* and in early Christianity is in accordance with all this. The most important elements may be briefly indicated.[3]

According to the account in the synoptic gospels the esoteric material in the teaching of Jesus comprised: 1. *Jesus' messiahship*. After Peter's confession Jesus reveals it to the disciples, but expressly enjoins silence upon them (Mark 8.30; 9.9 par.). Only once, before the Sanhedrin, did Jesus publicly proclaim himself as the Messiah (Mark 14.62 par.). The key notion of this part of Jesus' esoteric teaching is his self-description as 'son of man', which from Caesarea Philippi onwards invariably has an apocalyptic-messianic significance in Mark, and is, with one exception,[4] used esoterically until the unveiling before the Sanhedrin, Mark 14.62 par. 2. *The prediction of the Passion* (Mark 8.31f. par.; 9.31f. par.; 10.32–34 par., etc.), which,

---

[1] Josephus, *C. Ap.*, 82.

[2] [Loeb Classical Library, *Philo* II, 32ff., from which the translations here given are taken. Transl.]

[3] Words characteristic of esoteric teaching are, among others: ἄρρητος; γάλα (in the sense of elementary teaching)—βρῶμα; γάλα—στερεὰ τροφή; οἱ ἔξω (Mark 4.11); οὐκ ἐξὸν λαλῆσαι; ἐπιλύειν; ἐπιτιμᾶν (to urge *sc.* to say nothing); καλύπτειν; κατ' ἰδίαν; κρυπτός; μυστήριον (Rev. 17.5, 7); νοῦς (ὧδε ὁ νοῦς ὁ ἔχων σοφίαν, ὁ ἔχων νοῦν); οὖς (ὁ ἔχων ὦτα [ἀκούειν] ἀκουέτω; οὖς—δῶμα); παραλαμβάνειν (to take to the side); παρρησία; πνευματικός—σάρκινος—ψυχικός; σκοτία—φῶς; σοφία (ὧδε ἡ σοφία ἐστίν); τέλειος—νήπιος; τελειότης; φανερός (Mark 3.12); φανερόω (Mark 4.22); χωρεῖν (ὁ δυνάμενος χωρεῖν χωρείτω). Cf. below, p. 130 n. 2.

[4] Mark 8.34, but here the words 'the multitude with' probably do not belong to the original tradition, cf. its parallel Matt. 16.24.

according to Mark, also first begins with Peter's confession, and is in any case confined to the circle of the disciples. 3. *The eschatological prophecies*: when Jesus spoke about the signs of the end, he did so (according to Mark 13.3) only to his four most trusted disciples. 4. *Individual items of instruction* were couched by Jesus in enigmatic speech, as the saying about eunuchs (Matt. 19.12, 'He who is able to receive this, let him receive it') and the saying about the destruction and the rebuilding of the temple (Mark 14.58 par.). When Jesus followed the saying in Matt. 11.14, which declared that John the Baptist was Elijah, with 'He who has ears to hear, let him hear' (v. 15), that meant that there was also a hidden meaning: if the Baptist be Elijah, Jesus is Messiah. 5. Finally, mention is made, *in quite general terms* without specification of content, of secret teaching of Jesus which, according to Christ's will, is to be made public in the future, Matt. 10.27 par.; Mark 4.22f. Matt. 10.26bc also seems to have had this meaning originally.[1] Matt. 10.27 par. should be compared with the rabbinical custom in which the most sacred secret traditions are 'whispered'.[2] Even if one or the other of the passages and expressions quoted have been introduced by the evangelists, the general picture is no doubt correct.[3]

In the fourth gospel the farewell discourses are the main material for comparison (John 13.31–17.26): following his revelation to the world (2.1–12.50), Jesus reveals in private conversation with his disciples the meaning of his departure and of his mission. Further, we should recall John 3.1ff. K. Bornhäuser has rightly seen that Nicodemus did not come to Jesus by night for fear of the Jews—for nothing is said to this effect—but because he desires of the prophet in secret conversation a revelation about the mysteries of the kingdom of God (cf. 3.3).[4]

When we turn to the *early Christianity*, we repeatedly come across cryptic sayings and a concern to keep the most sacred things from profanation.[5] Paul,[6] who calls himself and his fellow workers 'stewards of the mystery of God' (I Cor. 4.1), speaks in general terms in I Cor. 2.6–3.2 of the divine 'wisdom' (σοφία) which can only be

---

[1] Cf. also the warning in Matt. 7.6 not to give what is holy to dogs, or to cast pearls before swine.

[2] K. Bornhäuser, *Die Bergpredigt* (BFChTh II 7), Gütersloh, 1923, 7, cf. above, p. 128 n. 3.

[3] The vocabulary of the esoteric teachings of Jesus has been collected by T. W. Manson, *The Teaching of Jesus*[2], Cambridge, 1948 (= 1935), 320–3.

[4] K. Bornhäuser, *Das Johannesevangelium, eine Missionsschrift für Israel* (BFChTh II 15), Gütersloh, 1928, 26.

[5] Of course, there is here no question of an elaborate arcane discipline in the way of the mystery religions.

[6] On Paul as a 'mystagogue' see H. Windisch, *Paulus und Christus* (UNT 24), Leipzig, 1934, 215–29, although his account is very one-sided.

imparted to the 'mature' (τέλειοι, 2.6), i.e. 'those who possess the spirit' (πνευματικοί, 2.13); it is 'a secret and hidden wisdom of God' (θεοῦ σοφία ἐν μυστηρίῳ, 2.7). Paul had been able to offer the Corinthians only milk (elementary teachings, 3.2), not yet the solid food of 'wisdom' for the 'mature' (3.2; 2.6). The concern of this 'wisdom' is with 'the depths of God' (2.10). That Paul had kept this from the Corinthians, although they had been Christians for years, shows that he would never have spoken of these final secrets before non-Christians. In particular we hear of the following themes which were treated, whether always or only occasionally, as esoteric traditions.

1. Certain *eschatological teachings*, which had to be kept secret, partly for political reasons. The book of Revelation affords a good deal of evidence for this, and its pictorial language is very largely cryptic.[1] The clearest example is the secret number in Rev. 13.18, which is, moreover, emphasized by the two phrases 'this calls for wisdom' [lit. 'here is wisdom'] and 'he who has understanding'. Only the initiate can explain the number: the interpretation of the Satanic beast as a man—'for it is the number of a man'—is intentionally veiled. When the reader finds in Rev. 13.9 the esoteric phrase 'if anyone has an ear, let him hear', he is at once warned that the preceding description of the beast and the subsequent mention of persecution is purposely put in enigmatic language. A similar esoteric phrase is found in the passage describing the 'great harlot' Babylon in Rev. 17.9, where the phrase 'this calls for a mind with wisdom' occurs just before the number seven is enigmatically applied to the seven hills and the seven kings. The woman, Babylon, and the beast on which she is seated, are a 'mystery' (17.5, 7); once more the reader is warned that the true meaning is hidden by enigmatic language. Similar to the veiled reference to Rome is that to Jerusalem in Rev. 11.8. In fact, according to Rev. 10.7, the entire book is a 'mystery'. Similar phenomena are found in other New Testament writings: Babylon is the pseudonym for Rome in I Peter 5.13. The noteworthy phrase 'let the reader understand' (Mark 13.14 par. Matt. 24.15) is another instance: the reader is reminded of contemporary events, in which the prophecy of the 'abomination of desolation' begins to be fulfilled, but which for political reasons must not be more clearly indicated.

[1] C. Clemen, 'Die Stellung der Offenbarung Johannis im ältesten Christentum', *ZNW* 26 (1927), 173–86.

2. The deepest *secrets of Christology* similarly belong to the esoteric material. The clearest evidence for this is Heb. 5.11–6.8. In this passage elementary Christian instruction, consisting of three parts: (*a*) repentance from dead works, (*b*) faith towards God, (*c*) the doctrine of baptism, of the laying on of hands, and of the last things (Heb. 6.1–2), is distinguished from instruction for those mature in the faith (τελειότης, 6.1), which is expounded in the Christological passages of Heb. 7.1–10.18. In addition there are secrets of Christology which no one ventures even to touch on: no gospel—apart from the heretical gospel of Peter—gives any description of how the resurrection of Jesus took place. This is probably the solution of the abrupt ending of Mark at 16.8. Although the appearances of the risen Lord formed a fixed part of the teaching of the faith, Mark felt that they were among the things which should not be disclosed to pagan readers. The same applies to Mark's account of the temptation (Mark 1.12f.): Mark here deliberately uses a veiled symbolic language. Jesus' victory over Satan is an event which 'may only be told to the faithful with holy awe, but which must not be portrayed in a book which might fall into the hands of unbelievers'.[1]

3. The *secrets of the divine nature* also belong to the material which had to be kept from profanation. A specially significant example is to be found in II Cor. 12.1–10. Only under compulsion and in circumlocutory expressions (cf. II Cor. 12.2, 'a man in Christ'; 12.3, 'this man'; 12.5, 'on behalf of this man') does Paul speak of his being caught up into Paradise, a matter concerning which he had kept silent for fourteen years (12.2). The things which he there heard he may not even hint at: they are 'things that cannot be told, which man may not utter' (12.4)—not even to the most trusted, and certainly not to the outsider.

(*b*) *The protection of the Eucharistic Words from profanation*

From a very early time we can detect an effort *to protect the eucharistic words from profanation and misconstruction*. (*a*) Already in the *oldest* tradition, which underlies all our accounts of the Lord's Supper,[2] some scholars detect a tendency to a veiled manner of speaking: 'The

---

[1] E. Meyer, *Ursprung und Anfänge des Christentums* I[4, 5], Stuttgart-Berlin, 1924 (reprint Darmstadt, 1962), 95. The fact that the Christ-hymn in I Tim. 3.16 begins with the enigmatic ὅς may be also due to an intentional obscurity. This is all the more probable since reference is made to 'the great mystery' (this has been suggested to me by Hugo Duensing).

[2] See below, p. 165.

essential word, "This is my body", is strictly unintelligible to the uninitiated reader' is the opinion of M. Goguel,[1] following A. Loisy.[2] (*b*) If it is the case, that the complicated formulation of the word over the wine in the *Pauline-Lukan tradition* is occasioned by an effort to guard the Lord's Supper against misinterpretation, or to rule out possible misrepresentations (drinking blood, etc., cf. p. 170), then this would be a clear example of the desire to protect the sacred formula. (*c*) Very early, probably *in the time of Paul* (pp. 121f.), the Eucharist was separated from the meal proper. Why should this have happened? Well, it would have been unavoidable that from time to time guests should have been present who were not members of the community.[3] It would have been absolutely contradictory to all the rules of hospitality in ancient times to have shown them the door. But since they could not be permitted to share the 'table of the Lord', it became customary to wait until they had left after the end of the meal and then to hold the breaking of bread and the blessing of the cup in the narrowest circle of the community. The sacred was protected from profanation by being isolated from the profane. (*d*) The same concern is evident in the work of *Luke* in the Acts of the Apostles. In the gospel, following his source, Luke quotes the eucharistic words; but in Acts, speaking for himself, he refers to the Lord's Supper[4] exclusively in allusions and ambiguous phrases: 'the breaking of bread' (Acts 2.42),[5] 'to break bread' (Acts 2.46; 20.7, 11),[6] perhaps also 'food'[7]

---

[1] M. Goguel, 'La relation du dernier repas de Jésus dans I Cor. 11, et la tradition historique chez l'apôtre Paul. Observations sur deux théories récentes', *RHPhR* 10 (1930), 64.

[2] Loisy, 'Les origines' in *Loisy-Festschrift*, 78f.

[3] Audet, *La Didachè*, 415. Cf. I Cor. 14.23–25, where, although the meal is not specifically mentioned, it is presupposed that non-Christians have access to the communal assemblies for worship.

[4] Luke seems to have taken the communal meals of the primitive community to be celebrations of the Lord's Supper; whether they originally were is another question (see above, p. 66).

[5] On 'the breaking of bread' as designating the Eucharist in distinction from the Agape, see above, p. 120. Cf. also Luke 24.35 and above, p. 120 n. 3.

[6] Acts 27.35, 'he took bread, gave thanks to God in the presence of all, and having broken it began to eat', is, on the other hand, probably a reference to an ordinary morning meal and not to a celebration of the Eucharist. In any case, it is quite incorrect to say that Paul alone ate (so, e.g., Völker, *Mysterium*, 28f., and others). The 'having broken it' rules this out, because the breaking of bread takes place to distribute the bread over which the blessing has been spoken to the table companions. The addition 'giving also to us' which some MSS. (sa, sy[harcl], *614, 1611, 2147, 2401, 2422*) have after 'began to eat' is therefore substantially correct. We are to think of the author of the 'we-sections' and of Aristarchus (Acts 27.2) as

and 'to taste'.[1] It is a natural conclusion that the intention is that the non-Christian should not understand the references. (e) The *epistle to the Hebrews* offers evidence pointing in the same direction. The conspicuous absence of any reference to the Eucharist in the list of subjects taught to beginners in the faith (Heb. 6.1f.) is probably to be explained by the consideration that eucharistic doctrine belonged to those elements which were reserved to the 'mature'.[2] (f) Especially significant is the evidence from the *Didache*. Its construction alone is significant. The first part (1–6), which is generally, and correctly, regarded as catechetical instruction, is followed by the instruction for Baptism (7) and only after this do we have a discussion of fasting and prayer (including the Lord's prayer!), meal celebration, church order and church discipline (8–15). Apparently the Lord's prayer and the Lord's Supper belong to the elements to be known only by the baptized.[3] So far as chapters 9 and 10 are concerned, we saw above[4] that, most probably, 9.1–10.5 contains the opening and closing prayers of the Agape, and 10.6 is the liturgy introducing the subsequent Eucharist.[5] But the Eucharist itself is not described and we are not told anything about the words and prayers used in connection with it; rather, the texts break off abruptly at the *maranata: amen* (10.6) of the introductory liturgy.[6] Even the section concerning the Sunday celebration of the Eucharist (14) restricts itself to emphasizing the need for mutual reconciliation beforehand. The only thing we are told is that the Eucharist is called a 'sacrifice' (14.1, 2, cf. 3). What followed the introductory liturgy (10.6)? How did the

---

taking part in this communal meal. The example of the Christian prisoner and his companions encourages the other travellers also to eat (Acts 27.36).

[7] τροφή, Acts 2.46. Cf. Justin, *Apol.* I 66.1, 2.

[1] γεύεσθαι, Acts 20.11. Cf. I Peter 2.3; Heb. 6.4.
[2] Cf. Goguel, *L'eucharistie*, 217; Goossens, *Les origines*, 222.
[3] T. W. Manson, 'The Lord's Prayer', *Bulletin of the John Rylands Library* 38 (1955–6), 102.
[4] See above, p. 118.
[5] Lietzmann, *Mass and Lord's Supper*, 192f., attempted to refer the whole passage to a uniform celebration of the Supper by transposing 10.6 before 9.5—without any kind of support in the text. Those who used Lietzmann's generally most excellent work have not always noticed that his fundamental thesis, that the Didache reflects a Jerusalem archetype of the Lord's Supper which, in distinction from the Pauline form, knows nothing of the memorial of the death of Jesus, must stand or fall with this arbitrary rearrangement of the text.
[6] Goetz, *Ursprung*, 8, suggests that the words of institution were omitted from the prayers in Did. 9.10 'for fear of profanation'.

'sacrifice' proceed? Were the words of institution recited? Were words of administration spoken? We are told nothing! (g) In Did. 9.5 for the first time the unbaptized are expressly excluded also from the meal proper, and this prohibition is grounded in the sharply expressed 'for concerning these the Lord has said: Give not that which is holy to the dogs' (Matt. 7.6). J.-P. Audet has shown that 9.5 is to be recognized, on stylistic grounds, as an insertion by the *author of the Didache*.[1] We see therefore that the circumstances were changing rapidly and that the tendency developed to exclude completely the unbaptized[2] from that which lay at the heart of the communal life, the meal celebration. (h) When *Pliny* mentioned in his letter to Trajan (AD 112–13) that the Christians examined by him had declared that the food at their communal meals was harmless ordinary food,[3] this is an implicit rejection of the slander that Christians held Thyestean meals,[4] but the slander itself was a consequence of the esoteric character of the eucharistic celebrations.[5] (i) The shorter form of the account of the institution read by a fraction of the textual witnesses in Luke, which has to be considered in this connection (see below, p. 159), indicates the sacred formula only indirectly by quoting the words with which they begin. (k) *Justin Martyr, Apology* I 66.1 (150/5) confirms the fact that only the baptized might participate in the Eucharist. He goes on to speak of the meaning of the Eucharist, and even to quote the words of interpretation,[6] but this he does apparently to refute the wild rumours to which the esoteric character of the celebration had given rise. Still he quotes the word over the cup only in the abbreviated form, 'This is my blood.'[7] (l) Completely expressed in symbolic-mysterious language is the *inscription of Abercius*, from the end of the second century AD.[8] Here we find, in reference to the

---

[1] Audet, *La Didachè*, 414.

[2] As also the heretics: compare II Peter 2.13 with Jude 12.

[3] Ep. 10.96.7. [Pliny, *Letters* II (Loeb Classical Library 59).]

[4] A similar allusion may be found already in the mention of false accusations in I Peter 2.12; 4.12–19.

[5] F. Blanke, Zürich, has kindly reminded me of the fact (postcard dated February 2, 1941) that, according to the letter of Pliny, baptism must also have belonged to the ceremonies incriminated by the heathen.

[6] *Apol.* I 66.3.   [7] *Ibid.*

[8] This date for the Abercius inscription is arrived at because of the use made of it in the Christian inscription of a certain Alexander from Hieropolis, dated AD 216 (J. B. Lightfoot, *Apostolic Fathers*, Pt 2, vol. 1², London, 1889, 493–6). The Christian character of the Abercius inscription seems to me, as to the majority of scholars (F. L. Cross, *Oxford Dictionary of the Christian Church*, Oxford, 1957, 5), to have been established beyond question.

Eucharist: 'And everywhere (faith) set before me for food a fish[1] from the fountain, mighty and stainless, which a pure virgin[2] had caught, and gave this to friends to eat always, having good wine and giving the mixed cup with bread.'[3] (m) Finally, *Hippolytus of Rome* in his Apostolic Tradition (about 215), which is concerned to portray the older usage, concludes the section on Baptism and the Eucharist with the words, 'He shall not tell this to any but the faithful.'[4]

From this evidence we can see that, as early as the first century, a concern *to protect the sacredness of the Eucharist and the eucharistic words from profanation* made itself felt in different places, arising locally out of the concrete situation, but growing in intensity, although the accounts of the Lord's Supper in the synoptic gospels and in Justin's *Apology* are a salutary warning against mistaking this concern for a fully developed and strictly applied arcane discipline like that of the mystery religions or of the Essenes. The development leads from the earliest rudiments of an enigmatic manner of speaking about the Lord's Supper to the Acts of the Apostles (pseudonyms for the Eucharist), to Hebrews (reservation of eucharistic teaching to the 'mature'), to the Didache (silence about eucharistic procedure), then to the shorter text of Luke (limitation to the first words of the formula) and to the symbolic representation of the Eucharist in the Abercius inscription, and finally to the secrecy imposed upon the whole baptismal and eucharistic procedure by Hippolytus. A corresponding change in the liturgical practice went hand in hand with these developments in the transmission of the eucharistic words. This begins with the separation of the Eucharist from the meal proper in order to exclude the unbaptized from the Eucharist, and quickly leads to the reservation of even the meal proper to the baptized alone (Did. 9.5; Pliny).

The *gospel of John* also fits into the framework of this development. This gospel includes (6.51c, 53–58) a homily on the eucharistic words (which would, however, have been intelligible only to the initiated) but most conspicuously omits the account of the institution: the sacred text must be protected.[5]

---

[1] Christ.

[2] Mary.

[3] Greek text with English translation in Lightfoot, *op. cit.*, 496f.

[4] Hippolytus, *Ap. Trad.* 23.14 (Dix, 43). Cf. J. Leipoldt, 'Arkandisziplin', *RGG*[3] I (1957), col. 607.

[5] Eisler, 'Das letzte Abendmahl [I]', *ZNW* 24 (1925), 185; H. N. Bate, 'The "Shorter Text" of St Luke XXII 15–20', *JTS* 28 (1926–7), 367f.; Huber, *Herrenmahl,*

In summary we may say: we have seen that the use of the eucharistic texts in worship has influenced their transmission and their formulation in many ways. It has led to the situation that the eucharistic words of Jesus are available to us exclusively in the form of liturgical texts. But however important the results of our investigation may be for the history of the Lord's Supper in apostolic times, about which we have elsewhere only very limited information, for our purpose the really important thing is the fact that the investigation of the liturgical influence on the transmission of the eucharistic words reveals an element that cannot be derived from the worship, *a preliturgical stratum of tradition*. Belonging to this are, for example, the prayers before and after the meal, together with the words of interpretation (for already the Corinthian rite no longer seems to have agreed with the sequence: breaking of bread—meal—blessing of cup),[1] also the passover elements (because the earliest community celebrated the Lord's Supper daily, later weekly),[2] and finally the two avowals of abstinence (for these gave rise to the early Christian passover fast).[3] These conclusions justify the expectation that it must be possible, by means of a comparison of the different forms of the eucharistic words, to which we shall now turn, with all due caution to remove a secondary layer under which the original tradition lies hidden.

92; W. Oehler, *Das Johannesevangelium eine Missionsschrift für die Welt*, Gütersloh, 1936, 28f.; W. L. Knox, *Some Hellenistic Elements in Primitive Christianity* (Schweich Lectures, 1942), London, 1944, 66; G. D. Kilpatrick, 'Luke XXII. 19b–20', *JTS* 47 (1946), 52f.; J. Leipoldt, 'Das Christentum', in *Handbuch der Religionswissenschaft* I. 4, Berlin, 1948, 52; A. M. Schneider, *Stimmen aus der Frühzeit der Kirche* (Am Lebensstrom 5), Cologne, 1948, 23 n. 11; C. H. Dodd, *The Interpretation of the Fourth Gospel*, Cambridge, 1953, 260 n. 1; 342 n. 3.

[1] See above, pp. 121f.
[2] See above, p. 62.
[3] See above, p. 124, and below, p. 212.

IV

THE OLDEST TEXT
OF THE EUCHARISTIC WORDS OF JESUS

THE EUCHARISTIC SAYINGS of Jesus are transmitted to us in a fourfold form:

1. I Cor. 11.23–25 is from a literary point of view the oldest account. Paul wrote it probably in the spring of 54.[1]

2. Mark 14.22–25. Matt. 26.26–29 repeats the Markan account with trivial deviations and expansions.

3. Luke 22.15–20.

4. John 6.51c which we have judged (pp. 107f.) to be the Johannine form of the word over the bread.[2]

Before we can go on to a comparison of the five texts we must answer a preliminary question:

---

[1] In an essay entitled, 'Sabbathjahr und neutestamentliche Chronologie', *ZNW* 27 (1928), 98–103, I have attempted to show that the chronology of the Sabbatical year strongly suggests the year 55 as being the date of the imprisonment of the Apostle Paul. The zeal with which Paul sponsored the gathering of the collection for Jerusalem on his so-called third missionary journey makes it probable that the Sabbath year 54/55 was anticipated with special apprehension after the bad experiences of the last Sabbath year 47/48; II Cor. 8.13–15 (cf. 9.12) is, among other things, evidence for this supposition: the gathering of the collection was occasioned by a concrete necessity of the congregation. It is to be observed further that, apart from the collection gathered on the third missionary journey, we only hear of one other collection (Acts 11.27–30) and that this first collection was made in order to alleviate the famine intensified by the Sabbath year 47/48. The imprisonment of Paul in Jerusalem is dated in the year 55 by the new chronological school, and among others by K. Lake in the principal investigation, 'The Chronology of Acts', in F. J. Foakes Jackson and K. Lake, *The Beginnings of Christianity* I, vol. 5, London, 1933, 445–74; and last by Haenchen, *Apostelgeschichte*, 64.

[2] The account of Justin, *Apol.* I 66.3, has no independent value; concerning it, cf. p. 139 n. 5.

LUKE: SHORT TEXT OR LONG TEXT?

The Lukan text of the eucharistic words is transmitted to us in a twofold form: a longer and a shorter text.[1] At first both forms read Luke 22.15–18, but then diverge: in the longer text there follow verses 19–20, in the shorter text only verse 19a—the text breaks off abruptly after 'my body'. The problem is therefore this: are verses 19b–20 ('which is given for you. Do this in remembrance of me. 20. And likewise the cup after supper, saying, "This cup which is poured out for you is the new covenant in my blood" ') original or not? The question is not simply a subordinate text-critical problem; anyone who knows the history of the investigation of the Lord's Supper of the last eighty years is aware that the question of the Long Text or Short Text of Luke has time and again been a crucial issue and that a basically different understanding of the Lord's Supper has repeatedly resulted according to the answer given to this. We will first establish the attestation of the two forms.

(a) The witnesses

The Long Form is attested: (1) by all the Greek MSS. (the earliest being at present P[75], AD 175/225) except D, (2) by all the versions[2] with the exception of the Old Syriac (syr[cur sin], see below, pp. 143f.) and a part of the Itala,[3] and (3) by all early Christian writers, beginning with Marcion,[4] Justin[5] and Tatian.

As to *Tatian's Diatessaron*, we do not possess its original text. The attempt to reconstruct the text of Tatian, which is so necessary and urgent

---

[1] The most important forms of the texts are printed in Merx, *Markus und Lukas*, 441–8.

[2] sa bo (with the exception of one MS.) vg syr[pesh] (v. 17f. are omitted) arm georg aeth, cf. P. Benoit, 'Le récit de la Cène dans Lc. XXII, 15–20', *RB* 48 (1939), 358.

[3] The Long Text is read by the Itala MSS. (c) *f q r*[1] (*r*[2]) *aur* δ (interlinear Latin text of the Greek gospel MS. *Δ*); for *c r*[2] and *q aur* δ, cf. below, p. 142 n. 6.

[4] According to Tertullian, *Adversus Marcionem* 4.40 (Ae. Kroymann, *Quinti Septimi Florentis Tertulliani Opera* III [CSEL 47], Vienna-Leipzig, 1906, 560.13f.), it is certain that Marcion read v. 20 (probably with the omission of 'new').

[5] Justin, *Apol.* I 66.3, has a text with the command to repeat the rite applied to the bread. He follows Luke (not I Cor. 11.24f.), for he (1) has the command to repeat the rite *only* with the bread, (2) reads with the Lukan word-order καὶ τὸ ποτήριον ὁμοίως, (3) permits μου to follow σῶμα and αἷμα, and (4) calls his source 'the Memoirs (of the Apostles) which are called Gospels'.

for New Testament textual criticism, has been interrupted time and again in a tragic way by the deaths of the editors E. Preuschen (d. May 25, 1920), A. Pott (d. February 24, 1926) and D. Plooij (d. July 5, 1935). We today, however, already see more clearly, since in the last decades there have appeared further additions to the long-known witnesses. We have: 1. Tat^{ephr}: Ephraim's (d. 373) Commentary on the Diatessaron, preserved completely only in Armenian.[1] 2. Tat^{aphr}: the gospel quotations in the Demonstrationes (337–45) of the Syrian theologian Aphraates.[2] 3. Tat^{arab}: the Arabic version of the Diatessaron, ascribed by several MSS. (probably incorrectly) to 'Abdullah Ibn aṭ-Ṭayyib (d. 1043), resting on a Syrian *Vorlage*, with strong accommodation to syr^{pesh}.[3] 4. Tat^{fuld}: gospel harmony which is offered in place of the four gospels by the manuscript Bonif. 1 of the Landesbibliothek, Fulda, which was written in 540–6 for Bishop Victor of Capua, with the Vulgate text.[4] 5. Tat^{ned}: especially valuable, best represented by the Liège Diatessaron.[5] The Dutch text goes back to a Latin Diatessaron, which offered essentially the Old Latin text, and therefore stands nearer to Tatian's original text than Tat^{fuld} with its Vulgate text. 6. Tat^{ven} and Tat^{tusc}: two early Italian harmonies based upon a Latin *Vorlage*. The Tuscan stands very near to Tat^{fuld}, while the text of the Venetian is thought to go back to an archetype which is older than the Vulgate.[6] 7. Tat^{pers}: a thirteenth-century version (after 1223) of a Syriac

[1] L. Leloir, *Saint Éphrem. Commentaire de l'évangile concordant. Version arménienne* (Corpus Scriptorum Christianorum Orientalium 137 [Text], 145 [Translation]), Louvain, 1953, 1954. Part of the Syriac text has recently been discovered, but it is as yet unpublished (cf. L. Leloir, 'L'original syriaque du Commentaire de S. Éphrem sur le Diatessaron', *Biblica* 40 [1959], 959–70).

[2] Text and translation: J. Parisot, *Aphraatis Sapientis Persae Demonstrationes* (Patrologia Syriaca I. 1), Paris, 1894.

[3] German: E. Preuschen–A. Pott, *Tatians Diatessaron aus dem Arabischen übersetzt*, Heidelberg, 1926. New edition: A. S. Marmardji, *Diatessaron de Tatien. Texte arabe établi, traduit en français, collationné avec les anciennes versions syriaques, suivi d'un évangéliaire diatessarique syriaque*, Beirut, 1935. Cf. P. E. Kahle, *Cairo Geniza*[2], 283–304.

[4] Edition: E. Ranke, *Codex Fuldensis*, Marburg-Leipzig, 1868.

[5] Edition: D. Plooij–C. A. Phillips–A. J. Barnouw–A. H. A. Bakker, *The Liège Diatessaron* (Verhandelingen der Koninklijke Nederlandse Akademie van Wetenschappen, Afd. Letterkunde, Nieuwe Reeks, 31), Amsterdam, Parts 1–6, 1929, 1931, 1933, 1935, 1938, 1963. The six parts which have appeared offer the text up to Matt. 23.7 (with a very full, but unfortunately not always error-free, apparatus). For the remainder we must be content with the older edition of J. Bergsma, *De levens van Jezus in het Middelnederlandsch* (Bibliotheek van Middelnederlandsche Letterkunde 54, 55, 61), Groningen, 1895, 1896, 1898, which reproduces the text of the Liège Diatessaron (L) besides that of a Flemish gospel harmony of the Landesbibliothek, Stuttgart (Cod. theol. et phil. oct. 140, Bergsma: S) with the apparatus of additional MSS.

[6] Texts: V. Todesco–A. Vaccari–M. Vattasso, *Il Diatessaron in volgare italiano. Testi inediti dei secoli XIII–XIV* (Studi e Testi 81), Vatican City, 1938.

text, which deviates widely in wording and construction from the original Diatessaron.[1]

In view of the fact that we now possess the account of the Lord's Supper in the Diatessaron in Syriac, Arabic, Latin, Middle Dutch, early Italian and Persian tradition, we can say today with certainty that Tatian chose Matthew/Mark as the basis of his text of the Lord's Supper. It nevertheless exceeds Matthew and Mark in the following ways: (1) The phrase 'the new covenant' (Tat[aphr,2 arab,3 fuld,4 ned,5 pers,6 ven,7 tusc8]), in which it is characteristic for Tatian that he places it in apposition to 'my blood',[9] and (2) the command to repeat the rite (Tat[aphr,10 arab,11 fuld,12 ned,13 pers,14 ven,15 tusc16]). This follows—in this all witnesses with the exception of Tat[pers17] are agreed among themselves—the eschatological prospect and therefore stands after the command over the cup (so only Paul!),[18] while after the bread (so Luke/Paul!) it is missing; besides, in Aphraates it has the striking form: 'Thus should you do in my memory, as often as you congregate' (Tat[ned]: 'as often as you do it'), a free reworking of I Cor. 11.25: 'This do, as often as you drink it, in remembrance of me'.[19] From this Plooij has concluded that Tatian in his account of the Lord's Supper may have worked together Matthew/Mark and Paul.[20] Yet this conclusion is not

---

[1] Text and translation: G. Messina, *Diatessaron persiano* (Biblica et Orientalia 14), Rome, 1951.

[2] Aphraates, *Demonstr.* 12.6 (Parisot, 516.27–517.1): *hnw dmy dytk' ḥdt'*, 'this is my blood, the new covenant'. This apposition becomes a characteristic mark of the Syriac eucharistic tradition from that time on.

[3] Marmardji, *op. cit.*, 430, 431; Preuschen–Pott, *op. cit.*, 206 (likewise in apposition as in Tat[aphr], although in Arabic it is grammatically offensive).

[4] Ranke, *op. cit.*, 138.35: *sanguis meus noui testamenti* (Genitive, not apposition, which says nothing for the early text of Tatian, because Tat[fuld] offers the Vulgate text).

[5] Bergsma, *op. cit.*, 244.5f. (S): *dit es mijn bloet een niewe testament* (apposition again).

[6] Messina, *op. cit.*, 311.27f.: *Questo è il bicchiere del nuovo patto* ('covenant' is translated twice), *il mio sangue* (apposition also, but with transposition).

[7] Todesco in Todesco–Vaccari–Vattasso, *op. cit.*, 136.8 (genitive).

[8] Vattasso–Vaccari in Todesco–Vaccari–Vattasso, *op. cit.*, 335.9f. (genitive).

[9] Tat[aphr arab ned], cf. p. 194 n. 1.   [10] Aphraates, *Demonstr.* 12.6 (Parisot, 517.2–4).

[11] Marmardji, *op. cit.*, 430, 431; Preuschen–Pott, *op. cit.*, 206.

[12] Ranke, *op. cit.*, 139.3.   [13] Bergsma, *op. cit.*, 244.9f. (S); 225.9f. (L).

[14] Messina, *op. cit.*, 311.25.

[15] Todesco in Todesco–Vaccari–Vattasso, *op. cit.*, 136.17.

[16] Vattasso–Vaccari in Todesco–Vaccari–Vattasso, *op. cit.*, 335.13f.

[17] In Tat[pers] the command to repeat the rite follows the word over the bread.

[18] In the citation in Aphraates, *Demonstr.* 12.6, the command to repeat the rite directly follows the command about the cup. The eschatological prospect is lacking.

[19] D. Plooij, *A Further Study of the Liège Diatessaron*, Leiden, 1925, 8.

[20] Plooij, *ibid.* Likewise earlier, T. Zahn, *Forschungen zur Geschichte des neutestamentlichen Kanons* I. *Tatians Diatessaron*, Erlangen, 1881, 204f., who has, however, revised his view (see below, p. 142 n. 5).

tenable, for: 1. It is in itself completely improbable that a gospel harmony should have been harmonized with Paul and not with a gospel such as Luke.[1] 2. From the addition, 'as often as you congregate', in Aphraates (cf. Tat[ned]) not too much is to be deduced, because, as F. C. Burkitt showed,[2] it recurs in the Nestorian Liturgy of Theodore (sixth century): Aphraates probably follows in the addition the eucharistic liturgy of his time,[3] while Tat[ned] accommodates in a secondary manner to I Cor. 11.25. 3. Tatian does not give the command to repeat the rite twice (as Paul), but only once (as Luke), although not after the word over the bread (as Luke), but rather after the word concerning the 'fruit of the vine,' i.e. at the very end, no doubt because he related it to both acts.[4] In this way Tatian thus obviously harmonized Matthew/Mark with the Long Text of Luke (not with Paul). *Tatian is therefore a witness for the long form of the text of Luke.*[5]

The *Short Text* (Luke 22.15–19a) is read by D *a d ff*[2] *i l*,[6] further by *b e* (with the sequence of verses 15, 16, 19a, 17, 18).[7] It is disputed whether the Old Syriac is derived from the Short[8] or the Long Text.[9] This question can be answered with certainty.

Syr[cur] reads verses 15, 16, 19 (without 'given'), 17, 18; syr[sin] reads the same text with five additions which are put in parentheses and italics in the following text:

[1] H. Schürmann, 'Lk 22, 19b–20 als ursprüngliche Textüberlieferung [I]', *Biblica* 32 (1951), 370.

[2] F. C. Burkitt, *Evangelion Da-Mepharreshe* II, Cambridge, 1904, 300.

[3] Thus also F. Hamm, *Die liturgischen Einsetzungsberichte im Sinne vergleichender Liturgieforschung untersucht* (Liturgiegeschichtliche Quellen und Forschungen 23), Münster, 1928, 7f.

[4] Brought to my attention by E. Haenchen. That the one command to repeat is related to both eucharistic deeds is general eucharistic tradition, cf. Hamm, *op. cit.*, 72f., 87f.

[5] T. Zahn, *Das Evangelium des Lucas*[3,4], Leipzig-Erlangen, 1920, 671 n. 34; P. Benoit, 'Le récit de la Cène dans Lc. XXII, 15–20', *RB* 48 (1939), 359; H. Schürmann, 'Lk 22, 19b–20', *Biblica* 32 (1951), 369–71.

[6] According to the careful investigation of G. D. Kilpatrick, 'Luke XXII. 19b–20', *JTS* 47 (1946), 49–56, the archetype of *c* should be added (in the present form of *c* vv. 19b–20 are added according to the Vulgate Text) and probably that of *r*[2]. According to Merx, *Markus und Lukas*, 437, the same is true for *q aur δ*.

[7] The placing of v. 19a earlier in *b e* aims at establishing the sequence bread-wine, and at avoiding the very difficult transition from v. 19a to 21.

[8] Burkitt, *Evangelion Da-Mepharreshe* II, 300–2; W. Sanday, *Outlines of the Life of Christ*, Oxford, 1911, 159; Lietzmann, *Mass and Lord's Supper*, 177.

[9] Merx, *op. cit.*, 416ff., 432ff.; Benoit, *op. cit.*, 372–8, who sees in the Old Syriac a compromise between the Short and Long Text (376); E. Schweizer, 'Das Abendmahl eine Vergegenwärtigung des Todes Jesu oder ein eschatologisches Freudenmahl?', *ThZ* 2 (1946), 85.

15, 16, 19. And he took the bread and recited the benediction over it and broke it and gave it to them and said (+ *de* [see below]) : 'This is my body, which (+ *I give*) for your sakes. Do this in remembrance of me.'

17. And (+ *after they had eaten supper*) he took the cup and recited the benediction over it and said: 'Take this. Divide it among yourselves (+ *This is my blood, the new covenant*).

18. (+ *For*) I say unto you, that I from now on shall not drink of this $\begin{Bmatrix} \text{cur: product of the vine} \\ \text{sin: fruit} \end{Bmatrix}$ until the kingdom of God shall come.'

It is quite certain: 1. That the text of the syr^{sin} is based upon that of the syr^{cur}, for syr^{sin} (with the exception of two meaningless variants[1]) *offers exactly the wording of* syr^{cur}, only supplemented in five places.[2] The problem is simplified by this fact and can now be phrased: does the syr^{cur} go back to the Short or Long Text? 2. Already the agreement of the very same sequence of verses 15, 16, 19, 17, 18 with the witnesses of the Short Text *b e*[3] establishes *for certain* that the syr^{cur} goes back to the Short Text. Moreover, the syr^{cur} cannot go back to the Long Text, because in verse 19, after the words, 'This is my body, which (is) for you', the word 'given' is omitted, which *all* the witnesses to the Long Text of Luke read without exception; therefore, the words, 'which for your sakes. This do in remembrance of me' (v. 19 syr^{cur}) derive not from the Long Text of Luke (22.19), but from I Cor. 11.24. The conclusion that the syr^{cur} does not in any case go back to the Long Text plainly finds cogent confirmation finally in the fact that syr^{cur} shares with the witnesses of the Short Text D *e* two singular special readings which are in themselves insignificant.[4] This means that syr^{cur} *has the Short Text* and this, to be sure, in the form of *b e* (15, 16, 19a, 17, 18) with the enlargement of verse 19 from I Cor. 11.24. 3. There still remains the question as to the source of the five additions with which the text of syr^{cur} is expanded by syr^{sin} (in parentheses above). Do they derive from the Long Text which in the meantime must have been known in Syria? That is not the case, for on the one hand the words of Luke 22.20 'which is poured out for you' are lacking in syr^{sin}, and on the other syr^{sin} reads an apposition: 'This is my blood, the new covenant', while the Long Text has

[1] 1. Verse 16 is read in syr^{cur}: 'until it will be accomplished in his reign', syr^{sin} on the contrary lacks 'in': 'until the reign be accomplished'. 2. In v. 18 the phrase 'product of the vine' (syr^{cur}) is replaced in syr^{sin} by the more usual 'fruit'—thereby the syr^{cur} again exhibits itself as the older text!

[2] Also the two specific variants of the Short Text, which are cited in n. 4, reappear in syr^{sin}.

[3] See above, p. 142.

[4] 1. The omission of 'and' before 'divide' in v. 17 (omitted only in D *e* sa bo syr^{cur} ^{sin}). 2. The omission of 'to the man' in v. 22 (omitted only in D *e* syr^{cur} ^{sin}). I am indebted to the Rev. E. Kerlen for this important observation.

'This cup is the new covenant in my blood'.[1] *Neither* syr^cur *nor* syr^sin *shows any acquaintance with the Long Text. Both Old Syriac versions are much more to be regarded as expanded Short Texts.* This fact dates the Short Text in the second century.

The Short Text, therefore, is attested not only by D it, but also by the Old Syriac, from which the following development can be established:

D *a d ff² i l*: 15–19a (original form of the Short Text);

b e: 15, 16, 19a, 17, 18 (restoration of the bread-cup sequence);

syr^cur: 15, 16, 19a (+ I Cor. 11.24b), 17, 18 (enlarged with assistance of I Cor. 11.24);

syr^sin: Same as syr^cur, plus the five additions.

Since the two Old Syriac versions are not independent witnesses, much more does their text of the Lord's Supper present an advanced development of the form of the text reached by the Itala witnesses *b e*, and since the Western witnesses preponderantly read the Long Text, we may conclude that *the Short Text is attested solely by one branch of the Western text.*

It is clear that the weight of the evidence lies with the Long Text: it is noteworthy that of all the Greek manuscripts only one (D) offers the Short Text! To hold the Short Text as original would be to accept the most extreme improbability, for it would be to assume that an identical addition to the text of Luke (22.19a–20) had been introduced into every text of the manuscripts with the exception of D *a b d e ff² i l* syr^cur sin![2] In other words *the attestation speaks decisively for the originality of the Long Text.*

---

[1] What is the source of the five additions of syr^sin? (*a*) The *de* is the introduction of direct discourse; (*b*) 'I give' derives probably neither from Luke ('which was given') nor John 6.51, it is rather added for stylistic reasons; (*c*) 'after they had eaten supper' derives from I Cor. 11.25; (*d*) 'this is my blood, the new covenant' is from Matt. 26.28 syr^sin pal; (*e*) 'for' from Matt. 26.29 syr^sin. The most important addition, namely (*d*), is a specifically Syriac phrase in the text of the Lord's Supper, which probably goes back to the Diatessaron (cf. p. 141 n. 2).

[2] From a practical standpoint it could scarcely be imagined other than that the primitive exemplar itself had been interpolated and that only in the West did a non-interpolated copy come to be circulated.

(b) Shortened Text of Luke in D it (vet-syr)[1]

The following section deals with the problem of the so-called 'Western non-interpolations' in Luke, one of which is Luke 22.19b–20. This unfortunate name, which already contains in itself a text-critical judgment whose validity is going to be examined in this paragraph, stems from B. F. Westcott and F. J. A. Hort.

Luke 22.19f. is not the only place in Luke where a Long Text stands opposite a Short Text attested by D it vet-syr. It should be evident that Luke 22.19f. should not be isolated, but rather that all cases in which D it vet-syr offer a shortened text of Luke must be examined. Only then will a decisive answer to the question 'Long Text or Short Text?' be possible.

The problem in each of the passages to be discussed presently is the same as that in Luke 22.19b–20: is the Long or Short Text original? If the Long Text is original, then we have before us in D it vet-syr a text shortened in the West; if the Short Text is original, then all the ecclesiastical provinces with the exception of the West read an interpolated text. It must once more be emphasized that we are not dealing in this with two possibilities which are on the same level from the text-critical point of view: the assumption that the archetype of D it vet-syr offered a shortened text is simple, whereas from the standpoint of the history of the transmission it is difficult to assume that an interpolation could have been introduced into *all* the Greek manuscripts except D. Only on compelling grounds will one occasionally need to reckon, therefore, with the originality of the Short Text.

Before we take up the individual passages of the gospel of Luke in which D it (vet-syr) have a shortened text, a word must be said about *Marcion and Tatian*, since, as we have seen, they repeatedly offer the same Short Text as D it (vet-syr). First, *Marcion*: When we encounter in a variant reading the combination D it (vet-syr) Marcion, we do not have before us the influence of Marcion upon the text read in the West, but simply that text which Marcion found in Rome *c.* AD 140. The independent and confirmatory studies by A. Pott[2] and A. von Harnack[3] have definitely established

---

[1] The sign 'it' will be employed in the following section even when only a part of the Itala manuscripts are concerned. For the sake of completeness passages will also be cited in which only D it (without vet-syr) attest a shortened text.

[2] Finally in E. Preuschen–A. Pott, *Tatians Diatessaron aus dem Arabischen übersetzt*, Heidelberg, 1926, 13–19.

[3] A. von Harnack, *Marcion: Das Evangelium vom fremden Gott* (TU 45), Leipzig, [1]1921, 222*–30*; [2]1924 (reprint Darmstadt, 1960), 242*–8*.

this.[1] This pre-Marcionite Western text is characterized in its text of Luke by numerous assimilations to Matthew (and Mark).[2] Already before Marcion, therefore, there ruled in Rome the tendency to harmonize the synoptic gospels by assimilation; it is no accident that Tatian at that very place had the idea of constructing a harmony of the gospels. With regard to *Tatian*, what was valid for Marcion can be applied equally to the combination D it (vet-syr) Tat, namely that we do not have before us influences of Tatian upon the text read in Rome, but that text which Tatian found in Rome during his stay (*c.* 150–72). The greatest evidence for this is that among the witnesses for the Western special readings not seldom Marcion and Tatian appear side by side. Numerous instances of this kind have already been collected by A. Pott.[3] An examination of the text of the Tat[ned] as published in the first five parts of the edition of D. Plooij–C. A. Phillips–A. J. Barnouw–A. H. A. Bakker[4] yielded further confirmatory examples. Luke 16.22–23 may be noted as an especially indicative example for such concord by Marcion and Tatian. By the loss of the 'and' which connects both verses there arose in one small branch of the tradition the nonsensical 'he (the rich man) was buried in Hades'—thus only in Marcion Tat[ned ven tusc fuld] ([aphr]) it vg (syr[sin pal A]).[5]

[1] As over against 200–300 regular instances, Harnack finds only eight exceptions where Marcionite readings may have been introduced into the Western text (2nd ed., 247*); these are correctly disputed by Pott, *op. cit.*, 17f.

[2] The text of Luke alone in manuscript D has more than 500 harmonistic readings (list in H. J. Vogels, *Die Harmonistik im Evangelientext des Codex Cantabrigiensis* [TU 36.1a], Leipzig, 1910, 87–105). Cf. further Harnack, *op. cit.*, 2nd ed., 243*f., and the list which he published only in the first edition, 223*–6*. Harnack's list is completed and confirmed by Pott's collection of the harmonizations which Marcion and Tatian have in common (*op. cit.*, 18f.).

[3] A. Pott, 'Marcions Evangelientext', *Zeitschrift für Kirchengeschichte* 42 (1923), 220–2; Preuschen–Pott, *op. cit.*, 18f.

[4] See above, p. 140 n. 5.

[5] Examples of the concord of D Marcion Tat[ned] (the page numbers of the Plooij–Phillips–Barnouw–Bakker edition are in parentheses):

Luke 4.34 ἔα—omitted by D Marcion Tat[ned] *33* it syr[sin pal] sa bo (107).
      6.5 The whole verse is omitted by D Marcion Tat[ned tusc], is added after 6.10 in D Marcion.
      6.12 'of God'—omitted by D Marcion Tat[ned] (165).
      6.26 'all'—omitted by D Marcion Tat[ned arab pers] W 𝔑 *al* syr (66).
           'for'—omitted by D Marcion Tat[ned pers] lat (66).
    10.1 ἀνέδειξεν—ἀπέδειξεν D Marcion Tat[ned ephr ar fuld pers] it vg[codd] syr sa (151).
    11.38 'was astonished to see'—'he began to doubt within himself saying' D Marcion Tat[ned] ([ven]) [tusc] *pc* lat syr[cur] (214).
    12.47 'make ready or'—omitted by D Marcion Tat[ned] ([pers]) P[45] *69 d* Ir[lat] Or Adamantius Ambr Cyr Chr Basilius (367).
    12.49 ἐπί—εἰς D Marcion Tat[ned ven tusc pers] P[45] 𝔑 *Δ* lat syr (367).
    16.23 'in his bosom'—+ 'resting' D Marcion Tat[ned] ([ven]) Θ it arm Or Aug[pt] (357).

If, however, Marcion and Tatian both used the Western text which was read in Rome around the middle of the second century, then this destroys the so-called Tatian hypothesis of Hermann von Soden[1] who wanted to make Tatian responsible for almost all the divergencies from the original text in the Greek texts, the versions and the Fathers; that this hypothesis presupposed a maximum number of im- probabilities had long been recognized. The influence of Tatian upon the text of the New Testament was essentially limited to Syria; syr^cur and syr^sin were influenced to a strong degree by the Diatessaron.[2] For our question we may conclude that wherever we meet the combination D it vet-syr Tatian, we do not have before us the influence of Tatian upon the

---

20.36 ἀποθανεῖν δύνανται—ἀποθανεῖν μέλλουσιν DWΘ syr^harc mg; *incipient mori e* Cypr; *morientur q ff*[2] *i l (c)* Tert; *morituri a* Marcion; *selen steruen* Tat^ned L (473).

Examples of the concord of Marcion and Tat^ned without D:

7.24 εἰς τὴν ἔρημον θεάσασθαι—θ. εἰς τὴν ἔρημον Marcion Tat^ephr ned tusc (145).
8.25 ὅτι καί—ὅς Marcion Tat^ned; ὅς καί *251* Tat^ar (113).
10.5 'first'—omitted by Marcion Tat^ned ven pers D² *579 r* Or (91).
10.21 ἐξομολογοῦμαί σοι—εὐχαριστῶ σοι Marcion Tat^ephr ned ven syr (153).
10.22 'chooses to reveal'—'reveals' Marcion Tat^ned Ju Ir^pt Tert Cl Or Eus Didymus Cyr (154).
11.8 Before 'I tell you'—*eñ deghene die buten steet hi sal bliuen roepende eñ cloppende vor die dore* Tat^ned ven; *et ille si (si i.* vg^cl) *perseveraverit pulsans* it vg^cl Tat^tusc (84). Plooij, *op. cit.*, noted that Marcion's (and Tertullian's) text likewise mentions 'the door': Tertullian, *Adversus Marcionem* 4.26 (Ae. Kroymann, *Quinti Septimi Florentis Tertulliani Opera* III [CSEL 47], Vienna-Leipzig, 1906, 510.24): *cuius ianuam norat; De praescriptione haereticorum* 12 (Ae. Kroymann, *Quinti Septimi Florentis Tertulliani Opera* II 2 [CSEL 70], Vienna-Leipzig, 1942, 8f.): *etiam pulsator ille vicini ianuam tundebat.* That in this an acquaintance with the Tatianic form of Luke 11.8 is expressed is possible, but not certain, since the door is mentioned also in 11.7 ('the door is now shut').
11.28 'keep it'—'do it' Marcion *2145* (a minuscule manuscript influenced by Tatian) *q* syr^pesh codd arm. Tat^ned adds both readings: *en dat behouden eñ dar na werken* (130).
12.3 ὁ ἐλαλήσατε—*quae intra se mussitarent* Marcion (Tertullian, *Adv. Marc.* 4.28 [Kroymann, CSEL 47, 516.19f.]); 'what you have whispered' Tat^ar syr; *dat ic v rune* Tat^ned (95).
12.47 'that'—omitted by Marcion Tat^ned pers syr sa.
13.15 βοῦν . . . ὄνον—ὄνον . . . βοῦν Marcion Tat^ned L *69* aeth (329).

---

[1] Hermann von Soden, *Die Schriften des Neuen Testaments in ihrer ältesten erreichbaren Textgestalt*, I. 1, Berlin, 1902; I.2, 1907; I.3, 1910; II Göttingen, 1913. Cf. especially I.2, 1535–1648.
[2] The proof was advanced by Burkitt, *Evangelion Da-Mepharreshe* II, 173–212 ('The Diatessaron and the Old Syriac'); also M. Black, 'The New Testament Peshitta and its Predecessors', *Studiorum Novi Testamenti Societas Bulletin*, 1950, 51.

text read in the West, but rather the text which Tatian in his stay at Rome found there and utilized.[1]

After this preliminary survey let us turn to the individual passages in Luke. When we disregard irrelevant omissions and minor abbreviations of the text (for the most part harmonizing omissions), major lacunae occur in D it vet-syr in the following passages of Luke:

5.39—is missing from D it^{codd} (syr$^{cur sin}$ *desunt*) Marcion Ir Eus. We have before us one of the assimilations to the parallels in the other synoptic gospels of the pre-Marcionite Western text of Luke: Luke 5.39 has no parallel in Mark and Matthew. The omission of the offensive verse, for whose antiquity speaks the semitism of the positive χρηστός in place of the comparative, may have been encouraged by encratite tendencies (disapproval of the use of wine). The Long Text is therefore, as is generally acknowledged, the original.

7.7a, 'therefore I did not presume to come to you'—missing in D *pc* it syr^{sin} (syr^{cur} *deest*). These words have no parallel in Matthew—for a good reason! According to Matt. 8.5 the centurion came personally to Jesus. Luke 7.1–10 knows nothing of such a personal encounter; according to Luke the centurion first sent Jewish elders (7.3), then friends (7.6) to Jesus and based his personal absence on the words quoted above. Tatian has harmonized Matthew and Luke by allowing the centurion to come to Jesus together with the elders of the Jews.[2] In view of the basic rule stated above about the combination D it syr Tat, it is highly probable that Tatian did not have 7.7a in the Lukan text which lay before him. The omission of 7.7a is probably one of the many assimilations to Matthew of the text of Luke used in Rome about 150. The reason for this omission in any case was the contradiction to Matt. 8.5. Once more the Long Text is certainly original. This is universally accepted.

7.33, 'bread', 'wine'—missing in D φ *al* it syr$^{cur sin}$ arm Tat^{ned}. Both words have no parallel in Matt. 11.18—a harmonizing omission.[3]

10.41f., 'you are anxious and troubled about many things; (42) one thing is needful'—missing in D (except 'you are troubled') it syr^{sin}.[4] 10.42 'for'—missing in D *270* lat syr$^{sin cur}$ arm Tat$^{ned ven tusc}$ Ambr Hier.

---

[1] Already recognized by Burkitt, *op. cit.*, II, 5, 209f., 240. Whenever the Old Latin and Old Syriac agree, we have before us 'the old Greek text of Rome, which Tatian has used in the Diatessaron'; such is the correct judgment of A. Jülicher, 'Der echte Tatiantext', *JBL* 43 (1924), 170.

[2] On this agree Tat$^{ephr arab}$.

[3] 'The frequent assimilation to Matthew' (Preuschen–Pott, *op. cit.*, 43 n. 1).

[4] Also in syr^{cur} the words were originally omitted (Burkitt, *op. cit.*, II, 242, 294), cf. the omission of 'for' in 10.42 by syr^{cur}.

Presumably homoioteleuton caused the short text 'Martha, Martha, Mary has chosen the good portion' (it syr^{sin}).[1]

11.35f.—missing from D it; v. 36 missing in syr^{cur}. All the witnesses cited read Matt. 6.23b in place of the omission. We are dealing therefore again with an assimilation of the Western text. Again, as is generally recognized, the Long Text is original.

12.19, 'laid up ($\kappa\epsilon i\mu\epsilon\nu\alpha$) for many years ($\epsilon\tau\eta$); take your ease, eat, drink'—missing in D it. Linguistic usage speaks for the originality of the Long Text.[2]

12.21—missing in D a b. Probably an omission by accident.[3]

12.39, 'he would ($\overset{\circ}{\alpha}\nu$) have been awake and would not'—'he would ($\overset{\circ}{\alpha}\nu$) not' $\aleph$* (D) e i syr$^{cur\ sin}$ sa arm Marcion. Pre-Marcionite Western text (scribal omission, prompted by the subsequent $\overset{\circ}{\alpha}\nu$?).

19.25—missing in D W 69 pc it syr$^{sin\ cur}$ bo. The verse is missing in Matthew. It is therefore probably a harmonizing omission of the Western text.

21.30, 'you see for yourselves ($\overset{\cdot}{\alpha}\phi'\ \overset{\cdot}{\epsilon}\alpha\upsilon\tau\hat{\omega}\nu$)'—missing in D lat syr$^{sin\ cur}$ Marcion Tat$^{ned\ ven}$. The words are characteristically Lukan: $\overset{\cdot}{\alpha}\phi'\ \overset{\cdot}{\epsilon}\alpha\upsilon\tau\hat{\omega}\nu$ ('for yourselves') is found in the synoptics only in Luke (12.57; 21.30). Since the words are missing in Mark (13.28) and Matthew (24.32), we are dealing with a pre-Marcionite harmonizing omission of the Western text.

24.6, 'he is not here but has risen'—missing in D it.[4] That these words are originally Lukan and not a harmonizing interpolation in an originally Short Text is suggested by the independence of the formulation from Matthew and Mark: only Luke 24.6 has the antithesis.

24.12, 'but Peter rose and ran to the tomb; stooping and looking in, he saw the linen cloths lying (omitted by $\aleph$ B al) alone (omitted by $\aleph$* A K al) and he went home ($\kappa\alpha i\ \overset{\cdot}{\alpha}\pi\hat{\eta}\lambda\theta\epsilon\nu\ \pi\rho\grave{o}\varsigma\ \alpha\overset{\cdot}{\upsilon}\tau\acute{o}\nu$ [$\overset{\cdot}{\epsilon}\alpha\upsilon\tau\acute{o}\nu\ \aleph\ \aleph\ \Theta\ pl$]) wondering at what had happened'—missing in D it (syr)[5] Marcion Tat$^{arab\ fuld\ ned}$ $^{ven\ tusc}$. Many regard this verse to be a summary of John 20.3–10 which was inserted here, so that we would have before us an instance in which D it Marcion Tat preserved the original text of Luke. But the reasons given

[1] Similarly G. D. Kilpatrick, 'Three Recent Editions of the Greek Testament [II]', JTS 50 (1949), 151.

[2] *Ἔτος is a favourite word of Luke (once in Matthew, twice in Mark, three times in John, twenty-six times in Luke–Acts), $\kappa\epsilon\hat{\iota}\sigma\theta\alpha\iota$ is a favourite word of the Vorlage of Luke. Kilpatrick judged the text of Luke 12.19 similarly (op. cit.).

[3] Zahn, Lucas, 499 n. 24.

[4] Only 'he has risen' (with the omission of the other four words) is read by Marcion sa bo.

[5] Verse 12 may have been lacking originally in syr$^{cur\ sin}$, for only in this place in the entire gospel of Luke do syr$^{cur\ sin}$ render the Greek Petros by Šm'wn; this argues for the later insertion of the verse.

are not very convincing: 1. The verbal similarities with John 20.4–6,10 are indeed striking, but not without parallels;[1] precisely in the Passion and Easter accounts Luke has numerous points of contact with John.[2] It must be added that over against the agreement there stands a considerable deviation, in so far as, according to Luke 24.12, Peter hastens to the tomb alone, while John speaks of two disciples. 2. It is certain that the words ὀθόνιον ('linen cloth'), παρακύπτειν ('to stoop down'), ἀπέρχεσθαι πρὸς ἑαυτόν ('to go home') are not found elsewhere in Luke. Also, however, in John ὀθόνιον is found only in 19.40; 20.5, 6, 7; παρακύπτειν only in 20.5, 11; ἀπέρχεσθαι πρὸς ἑαυτόν only in 20.10. The use of these words is required by the nature of the material and there can be no question of a specifically Johannine idiom. On the contrary, Luke 24.12 exhibits Lukan idiom: ἀναστάς ('rose'), used pleonastically as a semitic idiom without its strict meaning is completely lacking in John. Matthew has it once, Mark five times, Luke (with Acts) on the contrary twenty-eight times; θαυμάζειν ('to wonder') belongs to the words favoured by Luke (cf. esp. Luke 8.25; 9.43; 11.14, with the parallels in Mark 4.41; 9.30; Matt. 12.22; θαυμάζειν with the accusative is found in the New Testament only in Luke 7.9; 24.12; Acts 7.31; John 5.28; Jude 16); τὸ γεγονός ('what had happened') is met, with the exception of Mark 5.14, only in Luke (five times in the gospel, three times in Acts); the verse is really 'a sentence in good Lukan style'.[3] The frequency of Lukanisms compels us to conclude that Luke 24.12 is the original text of Luke. 3. For the originality of Luke 24.12 the reference back to this verse in verse 24 (with the plural τινές) speaks conclusively). 4. Only a hitherto unobserved difficulty seems to oppose this conclusion: the present tense of βλέπει. On the whole Luke avoids the historic present. Mark has it 151 times; Luke has removed it ninety-two times from the portions of Mark taken over by him and only allows it to stand once (8.49) and, besides, writes it only eleven times in the gospel[4] and thirteen times in Acts.[5] The difficulty, however, is only on the surface: the historical

---

[1] Cf., e.g., John 12.8 with Mark 14.7.

[2] Easter story: Luke 24.9–11/John 20.2, the message of the women (woman); Luke 24.18/John 19.25, the name Cleopas (Clopas) occurs only in these two passages in the New Testament; Luke 24.24/John 20.3–10, ascertaining the empty tomb; Luke 24.25/John 20.27, rebuke of unbelief; Luke 24.36/John 20.19, appearance before the Twelve on Easter eve; Luke 24.39/John 20.27, invitation to touch the stigmata; Luke 24.40/John 20.20, showing of the stigmata; Luke 24.41/John 21.5, 'Have you something to eat?'; Luke 24.42/John 21.10, serving of the fish; Luke 24.49/John 20.21, commission; Luke 24.49/John 20.22, (promise of) the gift of the Spirit. Cf. J. Schniewind, *Die Parallelperikopen bei Lukas und Johannes*, Leipzig, 1914; F. Hauck, *Das Evangelium des Lukas*, Leipzig, 1934, 6f.

[3] Harnack, *Marcion*[2], 247*, cf. 238*.

[4] Luke 7.40; 11.37, 45; 13.8; 16.7, 23, 29; 17.37; 19.22; 24.12, 36; eleven times, of which seven times are λέγει (-ουσιν, 17.37), one is φησίν (7.40).

[5] J. C. Hawkins, *Horae Synopticae*[2], Oxford, 1909, 149.

present goes back to the *Vorlage* used by Luke, which he has stylistically refined much less basically than the text of Mark taken over by him, as the historic presents directly show (cf. p. 150 n. 4). The result is that Luke 24.12 is the original text of Luke.

24.21, σὺν πᾶσιν τούτοις ('besides all this')—missing in it syr[sin cur pesh] Tat[(arab)] ned [pers]. σύν is a favourite word of Luke (Matthew four times, Mark six times, John three times, Luke–Acts seventy-five times); an amplifying σύν for the introduction of a new point ('*im* = 'apart from') appears only here in the New Testament; this semitism has a parallel in the New Testament in the synonymous ἐν πᾶσι τούτοις in Luke 16.26. The words are therefore certainly the original text of Luke.

24.36, 'and said to them, "Peace to you" '—missing in D it. That this half-verse recurs verbatim in John 20.19 does not necessarily speak for its being an interpolation. The salutation of the resurrected one could have been just as well an old essential part of the report about the Christophany before the disciples (cf. John 20.19, 21, 26). On the historic present λέγει, cf. above on 24.12, and p. 150 n. 4.

24.40, 'and when he had said this, he showed them his hands and his feet'—missing in D it syr[sin cur] Marcion. Is this an interpolation from John 20.20? There 'his side' stands in place of 'his feet'. So Luke 24.40 is probably rather a harmonizing omission in the Western text due to the supposed contradiction with John 20.17, unless it is simply a scribal oversight.

24.50, ἕως—missing in D lat. Ἕως with a preposition following is found in the New Testament only in Luke (Acts 17.14; 21.5; 26.11) and is therefore original.

24.51, 'and was carried up into heaven'—missing in ℵ* D it syr[sin] (syr[cur] *deest*). The Short Text eliminates the ascension on Easter evening for harmonizing purposes, because it seems to contradict the account in Acts 1.1–11, which allows the ascension to follow forty days later (1.3). Equally possible is the still simpler explanation that the Short Text arose from the fact that the eye of a scribe became diverted by the letters *NKAIA* which recur in Luke 24.51.[1] The Short Text also makes a break in style: verses 50 and 52f. offer the description in two co-ordinate clauses; the same structure is to be expected also for v. 51.[2]

24.52, 'worshipped him'—missing in D it syr[sin] Tat[ned].

[1] G. D. Kilpatrick expressed this conjecture in a lecture at Göttingen on July 2, 1959.
[2] The following scholars argue for the originality of the Long Text of Luke 24.51: W. Bauer, *Das Leben Jesu im Zeitalter der neutestamentlichen Apokryphen*, Tübingen, 1909, 275; Zahn, *Lucas*, 732; L. Brun, *Die Auferstehung Christi in der urchristlichen Überlieferung*, Oslo, 1925, 91; M. Goguel, *La foi à la résurrection de Jésus dans le christianisme primitif* (Bibliothèque de l'École des Hautes Études. Sciences religieuses 47), Paris, 1933, 348 n. 2; Hauck, *Lukas*, 299; M.-J. Lagrange, *Critique*

The result is that in the great majority of these cases of the Short Text of Luke which have been discussed Marcion or Tatian, or both, add their testimony to the witnesses D it vet-syr; it follows from this that we are dealing with readings of the Western text from the time before and around 150. In most instances high probability speaks for the originality of the Long Text: the disputed verses or words exhibit in part Lukan style; in several passages the tendency toward assimilation to Matthew (and Mark) which characterizes the old Western text speaks for the assumption of a shortening in that text, also once perhaps an encratite tendency is at work; also abbreviations due to scribal oversight must be reckoned with. Only in two instances (Luke 24.36, 40) must the decision remain *in suspenso*. 'It is not reasonable to suppose that the original text was preserved in a pure form only in the West and was wholly obliterated in the East, from which it came,' judged one of the best authorities.[1] The fact that in Acts, too, the Western readings are secondary throughout supports this judgment.

This conclusion is quite important for the originality of the Long Text of the Lukan account of the Lord's Supper.[2]

(c) *In spite of the evidence—objections to the originality of the Long Text?*

Since the year 1881, the view has nevertheless asserted itself increasingly that the Short Text may be the original text of Luke;[3] it was also advanced in the first edition of this book. [Not in the earlier English version which was from the second German edition. Transl.] The grounds are weighty enough. 1. That the Short Text is the more difficult is clear from the first glance. What could have caused the

---

textuelle II. *La critique rationnelle* (Études bibliques), Paris, 1935, 69; V. Larrañaga, *L'Ascension de Notre-Seigneur dans le Nouveau Testament* (Scripta Pontificii Instituti Biblici), Rome, 1938, 171–3; A. N. Wilder, 'Variant Traditions of the Resurrection in Acts', *JBL* 62 (1943), 311; P. Benoit, 'L'ascension', *RB* 56 (1949), 189; P. A. van Stempvoort, 'The Interpretation of the Ascension in Luke and Acts', *NTS* 5 (1958–9), 36.

[1] F. G. Kenyon, *The Text of the Greek Bible*, London, 1937, 220 [Rev. ed. Naperville, 1958. Transl.].

[2] The context also speaks for the originality of the Long Text of the Lord's Supper in Luke: the adversative πλὴν ἰδού in Luke 22.21 is harsh as the continuation of verse 19a, but makes a smooth connection to ὑπὲρ ὑμῶν in verse 20: the 'for you' is not valid for the traitor (cf. H. Schürmann, 'Lk 22, 19b–20', *Biblica* 32 [1951], 386f.).

[3] First: B. F. Westcott–F. J. A. Hort, *The New Testament in the Original Greek*, Cambridge–London, I, 1881, 177 (Text); II, 1882, Appendix, 63f.

deletion of 19b–20? The addition is on the contrary easy to understand, because the text which breaks off sharply at 19a cries out for a supplement. The two basic rules of textual criticism, 'The shorter text is the older', and 'The more difficult reading is to be preferred', unanimously commend the Short Text. 2. It seems to argue for an interpolation of verses 19b–20 that against the Lukan origin of these one and a half verses two weighty considerations are raised: (a) a comparison with the parallel texts proves that the Long Text from 'which is given for you' to 'in my blood' (vv. 19b–20) is identical with I Cor. 11.24–25, except for slight stylistic polishing[1] and two insignificant inversions;[2] while 19a (to 'my body') and the concluding phrase of the Long Text 'which is poured out for you' (which takes the place of the second Pauline command to repeat the rite)[3] agrees essentially with Mark 14.22, 24.[4] In addition, the Long Text of Luke exhibits secondary features over against Paul as well as Mark: over against Paul because of stylistic polishing and the attempt to parallel the word over the bread and the wine;[5] over against Mark because of traces of liturgical development.[6] The Long Text therefore seems to be a *compilation of Paul and Mark*. Among the words which agree with Paul the similarity in the connecting clause 'In the same way also the cup' (Luke: 'And the cup in the same way') is especially noteworthy and a strong proof for the close relationship of the two texts, because connecting clauses are more subject to change than the words of Jesus himself. These close contacts with Paul seem to exclude tracing the Long Text to Luke; for nowhere do we find in him a literary borrowing from Paul, or even only the most insignificant

[1] Luke 22.19b adds 'given'. The addition of 'given' to the word over the bread in Luke corresponds to 'poured out' in the word over the wine.

[2] Luke 22.20: 'and the cup in the same way' (I Cor. 11.25: 'and in the same way also the cup'); 22.20: 'in the blood of me' (I Cor. 11.25: 'in my blood'). Furthermore, in 22.20b the copula ἐστίν is missing, which Paul reads in I Cor. 11.25.

[3] On the omission of the command to repeat the rite of the cup, see above, p. 52 n. 3.

[4] Yet in v. 19a Luke has εὐχαριστήσας (instead of εὐλογήσας, Mark/Matt.) and λέγων (instead of εἶπεν, Mark/Matt.); also, he lacks λάβετε (Mark/Matt.). Further Luke has ὑμῶν (instead of πολλῶν, Mark/Matt.) in v. 20 as do I Cor. 11.24 and Luke 22.19b—corresponding to liturgical style. Finally, the passive participle ἐκχυννόμενον is placed at the end, corresponding to διδόμενον in 19b which stands at the conclusion. These deviations from Mark permit us to see the liturgical development of the eucharistic formula.

[5] See note above re v. 19b. Cf. also the double ὑπέρ-phrase in Luke (in Paul only with the bread).

[6] See note above, re v. 19a.

indications that he knew the Pauline letters. (*b*) Besides, linguistic-stylistic observations show that the Long Text cannot have been formed by Luke. First: to the words which agree with Paul the words 'which is poured out for you' are added with great clumsiness; they are widely separated from the related word 'cup'.[1] Further, one would have expected the participial expression to stand in the dative: the blood was shed (so Mark/Matt.), not the cup! Can the striking nominative instead of the demanded dative be explained by saying that the words stem from a text in which 'blood' (as Mark 14.24; Matt. 26.28) stood in the nominative?[2] The mechanical preservation of the nominative would then have created the anomaly that the Lukan Long Text speaks of the shed cup instead of the shed blood. A compilation with such a piece of stylistic clumsiness is not Lukan. Furthermore, that in Luke 22.19b–20 non-Lukan style is actually present is substantiated by many further observations. Only in 19b–20 of the two Lukan writings is $\dot{v}\pi\acute{e}\rho$ used of the atoning work of Christ and only here in Luke does one meet the (quite infrequent) $\dot{a}v\acute{a}\mu\nu\eta\sigma\iota\varsigma$ (cf. Acts 10.4: $\mu\nu\eta\mu\acute{o}\sigma\nu\nu o\nu$). Luke uses the possessive pronouns $\dot{e}\mu\acute{o}\varsigma$, etc., predicatively and pronominally, never attributively as in 19.[3] Καὶ . . . ὡσαύτως (in v. 20) is contrary to Lukan word order; instead he places καί afterward: ὡσαύτως δὲ καί (20.31), cf. also ὁμοίως (δὲ) καί (5.10, 33; 10.32; 22.36); the sole καὶ . . . ὡσαύτως which he found in Mark (12.21), he has changed to ὡσαύτως δὲ καί (20.31).[4] Beyond these examples also striking is the article before ποτήριον ('cup') (22.20a), since ποτήριον[5] and ἄρτος ('bread') are anarthrous in 17a and 19a. Finally, the copula ἐστίν is lacking in Luke 22.20b, although Paul reads it;[6] the omission of the copula, however, is not Lukan style; it is rather Luke's habit to add a verb if the copula is omitted in his *Vorlage*;[7] in four cases it can be certainly shown,[8] in four more it is

---

[1] [Prof. Jeremias is quoting the Greek which we are translating as far as possible for the benefit of the more general reader. The order of Luke 22.20 in the Greek is: 'This cup (is) the new covenant in my blood, which is poured out for you.' Transl.]

[2] Dibelius, *From Tradition to Gospel*, 209 n. 1.

[3] G. D. Kilpatrick, 'Luke XXII. 19b–20', *JTS* 47 (1946), 51.

[4] H. Schürmann, 'Lk 22, 19b–20', *Biblica* 32 (1951), 368, 383; *Einsetzungsbericht*, 35f.

[5] The variant in 17 (add τό) A D W Θ *al* is secondary.

[6] F. C. Burkitt, 'On Luke XXII 17–20', *JTS* 28 (1926–7), 180.

[7] H. J. Cadbury, *The Style and Literary Method of Luke* (Harvard Theological Studies 6), Cambridge, Mass., 1920, 149. Examples of the opposite are quite infrequent.

[8] Cf. Luke 9.8, 19; 18.27; 20.24 with the Markan *Vorlage*.

made probable through comparison with the synoptics.[1] On the basis of all this evidence there is high probability that Luke 22.19b–20 do not stem from Luke. Verses which do not stem from Luke—the conclusion appears unavoidable—cannot be part of the original text of Luke!

This conclusion breaks down, however, as soon as it is realized that we are dealing in Luke 22.19–20 with a *liturgical text*.[2] Luke is indeed not writing *extempore*; rather he is following his *Vorlage*. While he, however, normally improves this stylistically, in this particular instance the idea hardly even occurred to him. At the most, if he changed the text at all he may have decided to use the liturgical formula which was familiar to him. This is what Paul himself did, for we have seen (p. 104) that his account of the Lord's Supper in I Cor. 11.23–25 bears the marks of a language usage completely foreign to him. *Therefore Lukan style is not to be expected in the case of the words of institution.*

In a liturgical text the incongruence of the participial construction τὸ ὑπὲρ ὑμῶν ἐκχυννόμενον ('which is poured out for you') (nominative instead of expected dative) is not intolerable. The sacral language, the phrase-by-phrase speech employed in the worship service,[3] which allows the concluding phrase to be regarded as an exclamation in its own of independent right,[4] the parallelism to the corresponding participial construction about the bread which stands in the nominative, the familiarity with the old-established formula[5]—all of this probably removed the feeling of incongruity in liturgical usage. But can we speak at all of an incongruity? The extremely striking fact of the complete absence of a stylistic emendation proves that in the Early Church no one took offence at the nominative in the participial phrase. The association of cup, wine and blood was apparently so customary an idea in the Lord's Supper that the reference of 'which is poured out for you' to the cup offered no difficulty.

Finally, in a liturgical text also the close contact of Luke 22.19b–20 with Paul loses its strangeness. Paul, indeed, expressly said that he owes the words of institution to tradition (I Cor. 11.23). Therefore

---

[1] Cf. Luke 3.22; 7.25; 17.35; 22.42 with the synoptic parallels. Schürmann, *Einsetzungsbericht*, 37, counts four more instances (Luke 6.3; 7.8; 22.3; 23.50) in which a participle is supplemented by Luke.

[2] E. Lohmeyer, 'Vom urchristlichen Abendmahl [I]', *ThR* 9 (1937), 178.

[3] E. Lohmeyer in a letter dated September 17, 1937.

[4] Schlatter, *Lukas*, 422.

[5] On the age of the participial construction, see below, p. 196.

Luke need not have known I Corinthians to have written 22.19b–20. It is more natural to explain the agreement between Luke and Paul by church tradition. That even holds good for the striking connection of the handling of the bread and the wine in both by the concise 'in the same way also the cup after supper' (I Cor. 11.25; Luke 22.20); for the comparison with John 6.11b; 21.13b shows that the 'in the same way' in the accounts came to be used formally. Indeed, we can judge here with more certainty that the literary dependence of the Long Text upon Paul is directly excluded by the observation that it exhibits two deviations from Paul which betray greater originality.[1]

On account of the close connection with the formula used in Corinth the Long Text could stem from a region of the Pauline missionary territory, but probably more likely—because it exhibits at the same time strong connection with the Marcan tradition stemming from Palestine[2] and has the ὑπέρ-phrase with the bread in common with John 6.51c—from Luke's Syrian home church to which Paul is also indebted for his account of the Lord's Supper.[3] We have before us therefore in Luke 22.19–20 not a literary compilation from Mark and Paul, but rather a 'third variant'[4] of the liturgical eucharistic formula, a variant which beyond all question presents against Mark and Paul an advanced stage which none the less in individual features is more original.[5] This means that neither the non-Lukan linguistic character of the Long Text nor its contacts with Paul and Mark offer an argument against its originality.

(d) How did the puzzling Short Text arise?

Our previously stated conclusion that the Long Text is original can only then be held as certain if the puzzling Short Text can successfully be derived from it.

The Short Text of Luke 22.15–19a is highly peculiar because of its surprising abrupt ending. This abrupt ending with the words, 'This is my body', cannot possibly be explained by saying that Luke knew nothing of the explanatory words over the wine: that is excluded by

---

[1] That holds in each case for the absence of the copula ἐστίν (Luke 22.20), and also for the absence of the second command to repeat the rite: Schürmann, Einsetzungsbericht, 36–39, 69–72.

[2] See below, pp. 173–85.

[3] See pp. 185f. A Syrian origin was conjectured also by Schlatter, Lukas, 421; Héring, Le royaume de Dieu et sa venue[2], 227.

[4] Dibelius, From Tradition to Gospel, 210.

[5] See above, n. 1; below, p. 161 n.

that fact that he had Mark's gospel before him and therefore his account of the Lord's Supper as well. The Short Text of Luke can in no way be grounded in a *communio sub una*,[1] because in vv. 17f. it presupposes the enjoyment of the wine. No more can the Short Text finally be explained by saying that it presupposes a Lord's Supper in the order wine-bread (Luke 22.17–19a); such a Lord's Supper has never happened.[2] We see that it is difficult to believe that the Short Text is original. One best sees how great the difficulty is from the fact that the majority of the scholars supporting the Short Text strike out 19a as a secondary addition[3]—an outrageous and inadmissible act,[4] because 19a is read by all textual witnesses.

Thus the question is raised whether the Short Text can be understood under the assumption that it may have arisen from the Long Text by the deletion of 19b–20. The question is to be answered in the affirmative. The popular view that the Short Text arose because of the exception taken to the two cups (Luke 22.17f., 20) and that the second cup was deleted because of the supposed repetition is not satisfactory. For it cannot explain why, conforming to the sequence of the supper, one did not rather delete the first mention of the cup which is much less significant theologically and liturgically and—above all—why 19b was deleted, for which there was no reason whatsoever! *The deletion of 19b* ('which is given for you') *is the real problem* when one attempts to derive the Short Text from the Long Text. For this extremely striking deletion there is only *one* explanation (since the assertion 'Luke altogether avoids the concept of an atoning sacrifice'[5] is already shattered by Acts 20.28[6] and since the assumption

---

[1] On *communio sub una*, see p. 115.

[2] See p. 118 n. 5.

[3] G. Loeschcke, 'Zur Frage nach der Einsetzung und Herkunft der Eucharistie', *ZWTh* 54 (1912), 196; Meyer, *Ursprung und Anfänge* I, 178 n. 1; J. Wellhausen, *Das Evangelium Lucae*, Berlin, 1904, 121f.; Bertram, *Leidensgeschichte*, 27; K. L. Schmidt, 'Abendmahl I. A. Im Neuen Testament (Urchristentum)', *RGG*[2] I (1927), cols. 7–10; H. N. Bate, 'The "Shorter Text" of St Luke XXII 15–20', *JTS* 28 (1926–7), 362–8; Huber, *Herrenmahl*, 68; Bultmann, *Tradition*, 266 n. 1, cf. 431 (Supplement).

[4] Otto, *Kingdom of God and Son of Man*, 269, calls this 'caprice' and 'contrary to sense'.

[5] L. von Sybel, 'Das letzte Mahl Jesu', *ThStKr* 95 (1923–4), 123; M. Kiddle, 'The Passion Narrative in St Luke's Gospel', *JTS* 36 (1935), 277f. A similar view on Luke's theology is held by R. A. Hoffmann, *Das Gottesbild Jesu*, Hamburg, 1934, 167–77, esp. 172f.

[6] That Luke knew and affirmed the concept of the atoning sacrifice follows further from his references to Isa. 53: Luke 22.37 ('with the transgressors') = Isa. 53.12; Acts 8.32f. ('as a sheep', 'as a lamb', 'his judgment') = Isa. 53.7f.; Acts 3.13

of a scribal mistake—the eye of the copyist may have slid from 'which is given for you' to 'which is poured out for you'[1]—has against it that both ὑπέρ-phrases are omitted in the Short Text): that we have before us in 19a the abbreviation of a liturgical text. How often in antiquity in texts, scriptural quotations or prayers only the beginning words are cited! In our case the shortening took place in order to protect the Eucharist from profanation;[2] the 'for you' over the bread and all that follows was deleted so that only the beginning words, as signifying the beginning of a verse of the holy text, remain, an *aposiopesis* which is clear enough to each Christian, but for the uninitiated remains impossible to understand.[3] If in this way the word over the wine was completely omitted, then another factor could have played a part in the omission, namely the desire to avoid misinterpretation (blood drinking). That means that the Short Text belongs to the above-

---

('glorified his servant', cf. Isa. 52.13); 3.14; 7.52; 22.14 ('the Just One', cf. Isa. 53.11); 2.23; 3.18; 13.27, 29; 17.11; 26.22f. (the suffering of the Messiah predicted in the Scripture). E. Schweizer has further indicated that the expression 'to hang upon a tree' (Acts 5.30; 10.39, cf. 13.29 = Deut. 21.22) is probably used 'in recollection of thoughts like Gal. 3.13' ('Das Abendmahl eine Vergegenwärtigung des Todes Jesu oder ein eschatologisches Freudenmahl?', *ThZ* 2 [1946], 100 n. 94).

[1] H. I. Bell in a discussion of C. S. C. Williams, *Alterations to the Text of the Synoptic Gospels and Acts*, Oxford, 1951, *JTS* 3 (1952), 262.

[2] As a student I heard from J. Leipoldt in the Winter Semester of 1919–20 this explanation, that the Short Text of Luke goes back to an esoteric tradition (cf. the allusion which J. Leipoldt gives in *Die urchristliche Taufe im Lichte der Religionsgeschichte*, Leipzig, 1928, 33 n. 5; further, 'Das Christentum als Weltreligion', in *Handbuch der Religionswissenschaft* I. 4, Berlin, 1948, 52).

[3] In a substantial essay, 'Luke XXII. 19b–20', *JTS* 47 (1946), 49–56, G. D. Kilpatrick judged that we have before us in Luke 22.19a a catchword 'which the faithful would know how to supplement, but which would tell the uninitiated little. This explains the abrupt ending of the account at τοῦτό ἐστιν τὸ σῶμά μου. The abruptness of the ending is deliberate in order to preserve the *arcanum* of the rite' (p. 53). On the technique of obscuration by allusion, cf. Apuleius, *Metamorphoses*, XI—Apuleius, *Golden Ass* (Loeb Classical Library 44), 581—concerning the consecration to Isis: 'You, kind reader, will now probably be curious and ask what was said and what was done; how gladly would I tell you if I were permitted; you would certainly be informed if you were permitted to hear it. However, ears and tongue would have to pay the penalty for any such foolhardy curiosity. Yet I do not want to keep your pious thirst for knowledge in suspense too long. Listen, therefore, but also believe, for this is true. "I approached the boundary of death, crossed the threshold of Proserpine, passed through all the elements and returned. At midnight I saw the sun shining with a bright light, I saw the gods of the lower world and the upper world face to face and I worshipped them from the closest proximity." See, I have explained it to you. But have you understood it? By no means!'

described[1] series of witnesses which intended the defence of the Supper in the most varied ways. As the actual reason for the abbreviation it can be suggested that a pagan around the middle of the second century[2] requested a copy of the gospel of Luke; the copyist, however, was hesitant to deliver over to him the complete text of the sacramental formula and therefore omitted it after the beginning words. A small group of old Western and Syriac MSS., among which is D, goes back to the abbreviated text; so we do not have to do with a general occurrence within the broad area of diffusion of the gospel of Luke, but rather with an occurrence confined to one branch of the tradition in the West and to Syria. That D in Matthew and in Mark did not hesitate to present the full text of the Supper, whereas in Luke he offers only the disguised Short Text, does not contradict this explanation. The abbreviation had not been proposed by the scribe of D himself (i.e. fifth to sixth century) but much earlier, around the middle of the second century.[3] The archetype of D, however, is a collection of independent manuscripts of the four gospels and Acts which in their turn go back to a time in which there was still no established four-gospel corpus; we see this, e.g., in that D in Matthew and Mark writes almost exclusively Ἰωάννης (with two ν), in Luke/Acts on the contrary twenty-seven/twenty-one times Ἰωάνης (with one ν), and once/twice Ἰωάννης.[4] In the collection of manuscripts for the archetype of D the Luke exemplar was accidentally one with the Short Text. If our explanation of the rise of the Short Text is correct—the one which derives this from the Long Text—then decisive objections to the originality of the Long Text advanced by textual criticism cannot stand. For, as may be again emphasized as in conclusion, the decisive argument in favour of the Long Text is its overwhelming attestation.[5]

[1] See pp. 132–6.
[2] The date is determined from the fact that it vet-syr (late second century) have the Short Text, see pp. 142–4.
[3] See the previous note.
[4] F. Blass, *Euangelium secundum Lucam sive Lucae ad Theophilum liber prior*, Leipzig, 1897, VII, on the basis of an observation by E. Lippelt.
[5] Recently R. D. Richardson, 'Supplementary Essay. A Further Inquiry into Eucharistic Origins with Special Reference to New Testament Problems', in Lietzmann, *Mass and Lord's Supper*, 217ff. (in the process of publication), has again emphatically maintained the originality of the Short Text. He has to pay a high price for this: he regards not only Luke 22.19b–20 but also I Cor. 11.23–26 as an interpolation (p. 285). Instead of being the oldest literary account of the Last Supper, I Cor. 11.23–26 is thus relegated to post-Marcionite times as a late liturgical formula. Although Richardson's essay has not yet been completed it may

COMPARISON OF THE TEXTS

After this preliminary work we are now in a position to compare the eucharistic words of Jesus in the five texts (I Cor. 11.23–25; Mark 14.22–25/Matt. 26.26–29; Luke 22.15–20; John 6.51c) in order to discover the oldest attainable form of the tradition.

(a) *The prospect of the meal of the consummation*

Mark 14.25/Matt. 26.29 and Luke 22.15–18 offer the so-called eschatological prospect; in Paul at least one reference to it is found in the last three words of I Cor. 11.26: 'For as often as you eat this bread and drink the cup, you proclaim the Lord's death until he comes.'

Luke differs from Mark and Matthew in two respects: 1. In his order: according to Luke the eschatological prospect is at the beginning of the passover, according to Mark and Matthew it is placed at the end of the grace after the meal toward the end of the celebration. 2. In the doubling of Jesus' prospect of the meal of the end-time (Luke 22.16, 18). Scholars have recently been inclined to see in the deviations merely the redactional work of the third evangelist.[1] Luke, who often 'transposes' especially in his account of the Passion, is said to have placed the eschatological prospect of Mark 14.25 at the beginning of his account of the Supper and enlarged it by the free invention of the parallel words of 22.16, in order to accent more strongly the eschatological character.[2] This view can be conclusively

---

already be seriously doubted whether this *tour de force* which runs counter to all of the manuscript evidence concerning I Cor. 11.23–26 will meet with much approval.

[1] Lietzmann, *Mass and Lord's Supper*, 175f.; Klostermann, *Lukasevangelium*, 208; Hans von Soden, *Sakrament und Ethik bei Paulus*, Gotha, 1931, 29 n. 2 (also in *Urchristentum und Geschichte* I, Tübingen, 1951, 265 n. 37); Dibelius, *From Tradition to Gospel*, 210; Hauck, *Lukas*, 262; Finegan, *Überlieferung*, 11f.; E. Schweizer, 'Das Abendmahl eine Vergegenwärtigung des Todes Jesu oder ein eschatologisches Freudenmahl?', *ThZ* 2 (1946), 96–98; W. G. Kümmel, *Promise and Fulfilment* (SBT 23), London 1957, 31.

[2] P. Benoit, 'Le récit de la Cène dans Lc. XXII, 15–20', *RB* 48 (1939), 380, supports this thesis by reference to three Lukanisms: 1. ἐπιθυμίᾳ ἐπεθύμησα (22.15), cf. on this construction Acts 5.28; 23.14 (4.17 *v. l.*). 2. παθεῖν (22.15), cf. Luke 24.46; Acts 1.3; 3.18; 17.3. 3. διαμερίζειν (22.17) appears outside of Mark 15.24 only in Luke (11.17, 18; 12.52, 53; Acts 2.3, 45). But we find πάσχειν used absolutely also in Heb. 2.18; 9.26; I Peter 2.23, and διαμερίζειν has the meaning 'to distribute' only in Acts 2.45. Above all, however, Lukan style may not be used as evidence for Lukan creation, because, as we shall see immediately, we are dealing with a Lukan reworking of sources.

disproved. We have already seen that Luke is an enemy of transpositions;[1] this can be seen with full certainty from his dealing with the Markan material. Deviations in sequence of material which Luke exhibits against Mark are always signs that Luke follows his *special source* (see above, pp. 97ff.). That is confirmed in the present instance by the parallelism between verses 16 and 18; it is quite unbelievable that Luke could have created it, because he tends to strike out parallelisms where he finds them in his source.[2] The fact that the unit is stamped quite strongly with the linguistic and stylistic peculiarities of the Lukan source speaks decisively against the thesis that Luke 22.15–18 is an expansion of Mark 14.25 operated by Luke himself. Its distinguishing signs are: καὶ εἶπεν as the opening of the pericope;[3] ἐπιθυμεῖν with the infinitive;[4] λέγω γὰρ ὑμῖν (twice);[5] οὐ μή (twice);[6] ἕως ὅτου;[7] ἀπὸ τοῦ νῦν.[8] We possess, therefore, the so-called eschatological prospect *in a twofold tradition*: in a short form in Mark (/Matthew) and in a valuable[9] longer form in Luke.[10]

Both forms go back to a *Semitic original.* The content as well as the linguistic form argue for this fact. As far as the content is concerned it is Palestinian: the 'eating of the Passover', the table ritual with the

[1] See above, p. 98.

[2] Cf. among others, E. Norden, *Agnostos Theos*[2], Leipzig–Berlin, 1923 (reprint Darmstadt, 1956), 357–60; Hauck, *Lukas*, 9.

[3] Καὶ εἶπεν is a favourite phrase of the Lukan source (thirty-five cases). The following are such pericope openings: Luke 11.5; 13.20; 17.5 (καὶ εἶπαν); 22.35.

[4] Luke 15.16; 16.21; 17.22; 22.15 (otherwise not found in Luke/Acts).

[5] Λέγω ὑμῖν (σοί) the Lukan source has not less than forty-one times, of which six are λέγω γὰρ ὑμῖν: 3.8; 10.24; 14.24; 22.16, 18, 37 (λέγω γὰρ ὑμῖν is otherwise never in Luke/Acts; λέγω ὑμῖν is in Acts only once: 5.38).

[6] In Acts only in LXX quotations (three times); twelve times in the Lukan source.

[7] Luke 12.50; 13.8; 22.16 (otherwise not in Luke/Acts).

[8] Luke 1.48; 5.10; 12.52; 22.18, 69 (in Acts only at 18.6); cf. Rehkopf, *Die lukanische Sonderquelle*, 92, no. 14.

[9] Verse 18 in Luke has the organic connection which is missed in Mark (see below, pp. 191f.).

[10] Schürmann, *Paschamahlbericht*, 1–74, comes to the same result on the basis of a minute word-for-word analysis of Luke 22.15–18. Previously the following men had come to the same conclusion: H. E. D. Blakiston, 'The Lucan Account of the Institution of the Lord's Supper', *JTS* 4 (1902–3), 548–55; W. Bussmann, *Synoptische Studien* I, Halle, 1925, 191f.; Schlatter, *Lukas*, 137, 420f.; W. Goossens, *Les origines de l'Eucharistie*, Gembloux–Paris, 1931, 105f., 194f.; Bultmann, *Tradition*, 266, 278, 279 (otherwise 435 [Supplement to 276]: 'edited versions of the Mark text'); E. Lohmeyer, 'Vom urchristlichen Abendmahl [I]', *ThR* 9 (1937), 178, 194; V. Taylor, *Jesus and His Sacrifice*, London, 1943 (= 1937), 175; C. H. Dodd, *The Parables of the Kingdom*, London, [4]1938 (= [2]1936), 56 n. 1; J. Behm, κλάω κτλ., *TWNT* III (1938), 731; Rengstorf, *Lukas*, 241–4.

liturgical phrase 'fruit of the vine',[1] the concept of the eschatological 'fulfilment' and the avowal of abstinence (see pp. 212ff.). As to the linguistic aspects, for Mark 14.25 one may refer to pp. 182–4 for a collection of the semitisms. In Luke 22.15–18 the following semitisms are found: the parallelism between vv. 16 and 18; v. 15: τὸ πάσχα φαγεῖν = akal pasha, 'to eat the passover lamb';[2] v. 16: the passive πληρωθῇ which paraphrases the name of God; v. 17: δεξάμενος ποτήριον εὐχαριστήσας is a stock formula,[3] in which δεξάμενος designates the receiving of the cup from the hand of the one waiting on the table;[4] v. 18: the omission of the 'more' to be expected with οὐ μή is typically Semitic;[5] the same is true for the paraphrase 'fruit of the vine' for wine,[6] and the phrase that the Kingdom of God 'is coming'.[7] The expression gives life to what is inanimate in that it ascribes an activity to the Kingdom of God; that is reverent speech about God. One says, 'The Kingdom of God is coming'; this means, 'God is coming.'

Nevertheless Luke is linguistically more strongly reworked than Mark. Several graecisms are found in his writing: v. 15: τοῦτο τὸ πάσχα φαγεῖν has unsemitic word order and the accusative in place of a preposition (Hebrew *be*, Aramaic *min*); παθεῖν used absolutely is scarcely translatable back into Hebrew or Aramaic,[8] it is the linguistic idiom of the Early Church;[9] v. 16: φάγω αὐτό, on the accusative cf. v. 15; τοῦ θεοῦ stands in place of an expected paraphrase of the name of God; v. 17: εὐχαριστήσας is a graecism;[10] v. 18: τοῦ θεοῦ (cf. v. 16). The comparison of Mark 14.25 with Luke 22.18 shows above all, however, that the text of Luke is more strongly graecized than that of Mark, since several of Mark's phrases which are non-Greek are not found in Luke:

---

[1] See below, p. 183.

[2] E.g., Targ. II Chr. 30.18, *akalu yat pisha*. Examples easily surveyed in C. K. Barrett, 'Luke XXII.15: To Eat the Passover', *JTS* 9 (1958), 305–7. On the vocalizing *pasha* (above in the text), see above, ch. 1, first note.

[3] See below, p. 178 n. 8.

[4] Cf. Siphre Deut. 38 to 11.10, *kibbelo* = 'he received it (the cup)'.

[5] P. Joüon, *L'Évangile de Notre-Seigneur Jésus-Christ*, 102, on Matthew 15.32. The observation is also valid for v. 16, where the variant οὐκέτι is to be regarded as secondary.

[6] See below, p. 183.

[7] Dalman, *Words*, 107; *Jesus-Jeshua*, 182.

[8] Dalman, *Jesus-Jeshua*, 128.

[9] See above, p. 160 n. 2.

[10] The literal translation of *barek* is εὐλογεῖν, see below, p. 175.

Mark 14.25	Luke 22.18	(Luke 22.16)
ἀμὴν λέγω ὑμῖν	λέγω γὰρ ὑμῖν	λέγω γὰρ ὑμῖν
Truly *I say to you*	For *I say to you*	For I say to you
ὅτι		ὅτι
that		that
οὐκέτι οὐ μὴ πίω	οὐ μὴ πίω ἀπὸ τοῦ νῦν	οὐ μὴ φάγω
I shall not drink again	*I shall not drink* from now on	I shall not eat
ἐκ τοῦ γενήματος	ἀπὸ τοῦ γενήματος	αὐτὸ
of *the fruit*	from *the fruit*	it
τῆς ἀμπέλου	τῆς ἀμπέλου	
of *the vine*	of *the vine*	
ἕως τῆς ἡμέρας ἐκείνης	ἕως οὗ	ἕως ὅτου
until that day	*until*	until
ὅταν		
when		
αὐτὸ πίνω καινὸν ἐν		πληρωθῇ ἐν
I drink it new in		it is fulfilled in
τῇ βασιλείᾳ τοῦ θεοῦ.	ἡ βασιλεία τοῦ θεοῦ	τῇ βασιλείᾳ τοῦ θεοῦ.
the kingdom of God.	*the kingdom of God*	the kingdom of God.
	ἔλθῃ	
	comes.	

The common words are italicized. If the differences are compared it can be seen that: ἀμήν (Mark) has fallen out and is replaced by γάρ;[1] the barbaric οὐκέτι οὐ μή[2] of Mark does not return in Luke,[3] who reads instead οὐ μή . . . ἀπὸ τοῦ νῦν; the phrase πίνειν ἐκ which is impossible in Greek when it is followed by the mention of the beverage[4] is softened into πίνειν ἀπό; also the semitizing phrase in Mark ἕως τῆς ἡμέρας ἐκείνης[5] is not found in Luke. The graecizing of the tradition, which we observe in Luke 22.15–18, belongs at least in part already to the pre-Lukan form of the pericope.[6]

[1] Matthew also replaces the ἀμήν in our passage (26.29: δέ). The extraordinarily strong inclination of the synoptic tradition to efface or replace ἀμήν (J. Jeremias, 'Kennzeichen der *ipsissima vox* Jesu', in *Synoptische Studien* [A. Wikenhauser-Festschrift], Munich, 1954, 90–92), which is opposed by only very few examples of the addition of ἀμήν (Matt. 19.23; 24.2), confirms the conclusion that ἀμήν in Mark 14.25 represents the older tradition.
[2] See below, p. 182 no. 18.
[3] Also not in v. 16, where οὐκέτι (D W φ 𝔑) is not the original reading; it is omitted by ℵ A B C Θ sa bo.
[4] See below, p. 183 no. 20.
[5] See below, p. 183 no. 22.
[6] This is evident from two observations: 1. εὐχαριστήσας used absolutely (Luke

To sum up: The doubling of the eschatological prospect as we have it in Luke 22.15–18 is probably original. Nevertheless, the wording in Mark, as far as it may be compared, is more original than Luke.[1]

(b) The words of interpretation

The expression 'word of interpretation' (*Deutewort*) is retained because it has become familiar in Germany. It may be expressly noted that it is intended to designate merely the form and structure of the words of Jesus and will not be used as though the words of Jesus exhaust themselves in interpreting the bread and wine.

Immediately a first glance at the texts (see below pp. 165, 168) permits us to recognize their extensive agreement in all essentials. On closer study it appears, however, that two types oppose one another: Paul and Luke exhibit themselves as related through the structure of the words over the wine, also in that they alone offer the phrase μετὰ τὸ δειπνῆσαι and the command to repeat the rite, and finally through the connection of the ὑπέρ-phrase with the word over the bread; John shows his relationship to this first type in that he also, as Paul and Luke, joins the ὑπέρ-phrase to the word over the bread. Mark and Matthew represent the second type.

22.17) is difficult to trace back to Luke, since he connects the word in Acts 27.35 and 28.15 with a dative object. 2. Luke deals with ἀμήν very carefully, as his reworking of Mark shows: he allows it to stand (three times: Luke 18.17 = Mark 10.15; Luke 18.29 = Mark 10.29; Luke 21.32 = Mark 13.30) or translates it with ἀληθῶς (twice: Luke 9.27, cf. Mark 9.1; Luke 21.3, cf. Mark 12.43), but never deletes it. Quite the contrary is the handling of ἀμήν in the remaining parts of Luke which stem from the special source which makes up about three-quarters of the whole gospel. To be sure, ἀμήν is found three times (Luke 4.24; 12.37; 23.43) and once the translation with ἀληθῶς (12.44); in the remainder, however, ἀμήν is avoided in different ways. It is translated with ναί (7.26; 11.51; 12.5) or ἐπ' ἀληθείας (4.25), replaced with γάρ (22.16, 18) or completely omitted (7.9, 28; 10.12, 24; 12.59; 15.7, 10; 22.34); repeatedly the whole phrase ἀμὴν λέγω ὑμῖν is replaced by merely καί (11.29; 12.10), δέ (16.17; 22.28), πλήν (10.14), πλὴν ἰδού (22.21) or completely deleted (13.25; 17.6). The extensive avoidance of ἀμήν is not Lukan; especially the substitution in our passage by γάρ (Luke 22.18, cf. 16) does not correspond to the peculiarity of Luke, cf. Jeremias, 'Kennzeichen der *ipsissima vox* Jesu', in *A. Wikenhauser-Festschrift*, 90f.

[1] The question whether the so-called eschatological prospect has its correct place in Luke (at the beginning of the meal) or Mark (end of the meal) can only be answered by the exegesis of the passage, see below, p. 212 n.1.

(a) The word of interpretation over the bread

On the setting (I Cor. 11.23–24a; Mark 14.22a par.), see p. 109.

I Cor. 11.24	Luke 22.19	John 6.51c	Mark 14.22	Matt. 26.26
			λάβετε	λάβετε
			Take	Take
				φάγετε
				eat
τοῦτό	τοῦτό	ὁ ἄρτος δὲ	τοῦτό	τοῦτό
This	*This*	*The bread*	*this*	*this*
		ὃν ἐγὼ δώσω		
		which I shall		
		give		
μού ἐστιν	ἐστιν	ἡ σάρξ μού	ἐστιν	ἐστιν
of me is	*is*	*the flesh of me*	*is*	*is*
τὸ σῶμα	τὸ σῶμά	ἐστιν	τὸ σῶμά	τὸ σῶμά
the body	*the body*	*is*	*the body*	*the body*
	μου		μου	μου
	of me		*of me*	*of me*
τὸ ὑπὲρ ὑμῶν	τὸ ὑπὲρ ὑμῶν	ὑπὲρ τῆς τοῦ		
which (is)	which for you	for the of the		
for you				
	διδόμενον	κόσμου ζωῆς		
	(is) given	world life		
τοῦτο ποιεῖτε	τοῦτο ποιεῖτε			
this do	this do			
εἰς τὴν ἐμὴν	εἰς τὴν ἐμὴν			
in my	in my			
ἀνάμνησιν	ἀνάμνησιν			
remembrance	remembrance			

In our table the material common to all five texts is italicized. If one disregards the fact that John paraphrases the τοῦτο, to which already his context compelled him, then it follows that *all witnesses transmit the sentence*: τοῦτό ἐστιν τὸ σῶμά μου / ἡ σάρξ μου ('This is my body/my flesh').

As to the *surplus* there follows: 1. The *invitation* to take (Mark/Matthew) and to eat (Matthew). The expansion in Matthew as opposed to Mark (+ φάγετε) suggests at first sight the conjecture that we are dealing probably in λάβετε as in φάγετε with amplifications which could easily have arisen with the liturgical use of the words of the Lord's Supper. This is correct[1] for φάγετε (Matthew) in spite of the ancient asyndeton;[2] this is not so for λάβετε (Mark/Matthew); for this is only apparently lacking in Luke; he has used it immediately before (22.17). The inscription on the famous Jewish golden beaker in the Vatican Library ΛΑΒΕ ΕΥΛΟΓΙΑ (μετα των) ΣΩ(ν π)ΑΝΤΩΝ[3] shows that such invitation formulas were used, at any rate as the cup was circulated. It is true, however, that there are no known examples of the use of such a formula in connection with the bread;[4] for this reason another explanation for the λάβετε of Mark 14.22/Matt. 26.26 is preferable.[5]

2. *The ὑπέρ-phrase.* It is found in Paul, Luke, and John; is lacking in Mark/Matthew—yet only apparently; for the first and second

---

[1] The addition of φάγετε hangs together with the corresponding imperative πίετε ἐξ αὐτοῦ πάντες (Matt. 26.27), on whose secondary character, cf. below, p. 171.

[2] Λάβετε φάγετε. Cf. Midr. Lam. on 1.4 (G. Dalman, *Aramäische Dialektproben*, Leipzig, 1927², 16, line 2 from the bottom): *sab pelag*, 'take, carve' (at table); further see below, pp. 174 n. 3, 177 n. 2.

[3] Most recently published by E. R. Goodenough, *Jewish Symbols in the Greco-Roman Period* (Bollingen Series 37) III, New York, 1953, no. 978; previously by R. Eisler, 'Das letzte Abendmahl [II]', *ZNW* 25 (1926), plate IV.5 before p. 33; K. H. Rengstorf, 'Zu den Fresken in der jüdischen Katakombe der Villa Torlonia in Rom', *ZNW* 31 (1932), plate before p. 33; J.-B. Frey, *Corpus Inscriptionum Iudaicarum* I (Sussidi allo studio delle antichità cristiane 1), Vatican City–Rome–Paris, 1936, 377f. no. 515; W. G. Kümmel, 'Die älteste religiöse Kunst der Juden', *Judaica* 2 (1946), plate 4b before p. 16. The different attempts at interpretation which are enumerated by Goodenough, *op. cit.*, II, New York, 1953, 115f., need not be repeated here. By far the most preferred interpretation, which was also represented in the second edition of this work [ET, p. 109. Transl.], which supplies a ν after εὐλογία ('take the [cup of] blessing with all your own'), appears to me to be untenable; for—quite apart from the uncertainty of the supplement of the ν—we have no example for the view that Judaism has designated the cup with εὐλογία, or *berakah*. The correct interpretation appears, in my opinion, from a comparison with other inscriptions. From Jewish grave inscriptions we read: ΕΥΛΟΓΙΑ ΠΑΣΙΝ (Frey, *op. cit.*, I, 124–6 no. 173, Rome; Goodenough, *op. cit.*, III, no. 977, Nicomedia in Asia Minor) as independent wishes of blessing. Since we know from the Pauline greetings that in wishes of blessing μετὰ πάντων can stand in place of the dative πᾶσιν (ἡ χάρις . . . μετὰ πάντων ὑμῶν, II Thess. 3.18; Titus 3.15; ἡ ἀγάπη μου μετὰ πάντων ὑμῶν, I Cor. 16.24, cf. II Cor. 13.13; Rom. 16.20), we should translate: 'Take! Blessing to all of your own!' The correctness of the independent conception of λάβε is cogently confirmed by the analogous, independent πίε, which is constantly repeated on Jewish as well as Christian inscribed beakers: πίε ζήσῃς—'Drink! May you live!' We have therefore before us on the golden beaker the same invitation formula without an object (λάβε) as in Mark 14.22/Matt. 26.26 (Luke 22.17) (λάβετε).

[4] A. Wünsche, *Neue Beiträge zur Erläuterung der Evangelien aus Talmud und Midrasch*, Göttingen, 1878, 331: It was 'not customary for the head of the house expressly to invite his guests [sic!] to eat the bread that was offered'.

[5] See p. 219.

evangelists have it with the word over the cup (where Luke repeats it). It is therefore presented by all five witnesses. Must we content ourselves with establishing that its position vacillates? Or is there any evidence to help in answering the question whether the ὑπέρ-phrase belonged originally to the bread or the cup? With due caution attention may be directed to four observations which permit a conjecture.

(a) The Pauline short form τὸ ὑπὲρ ὑμῶν hardly stems from a Semitic tradition, for its retranslation back into Aramaic is impossible,[1] and also in Hebrew a participle could hardly be omitted.[2] On the contrary, in Greek the phrase is inoffensive. Since such postpositive attributes with the article are characteristic of the style of Paul (cf., e.g., II Cor. 7.12, τὴν σπουδὴν ὑμῶν τὴν ὑπὲρ ἡμῶν; 9.3, τὸ καύχημα ἡμῶν τὸ ὑπὲρ ὑμῶν), the phrase τὸ ὑπὲρ ὑμῶν in I Cor. 11.24 can in this form go back to Paul himself.[3]

(b) Also the Lukan form of the ὑπέρ-formula (τὸ ὑπὲρ ὑμῶν διδόμενον/ ἐκχυννόμενον) is—at any case in the word order—unsemitic, while Mark 14.24 offers the postpositive form of the prepositional phrase corresponding to the Semitic idiom.

(c) Paul/Luke, who attach the ὑπέρ-phrase to the bread, have ὑπὲρ ὑμῶν; Mark/Matthew have ὑπὲρ (περὶ) πολλῶν. As a semitism (see below, pp. 179ff.) πολλῶν has to be regarded as the older.

(d) These three linguistic observations speak already unanimously for the originality of the Markan form of the ὑπέρ-phrase; a fourth consideration definitely decides the issue in its favour. We are referring to the noteworthy asymmetry which results in the Markan tradition of the words of interpretation from the fact that the word over the bread in Mark remains without any theological interpretation, so that the emphasis lies quite one-sidedly on the word over the cup. This enigmatical 'emptiness'[4] of the word over the bread called for a completion. It must have been the more disturbing as the tendency to parallel the words over the bread and wine increasingly

[1] Dalman, *Jesus-Jeshua*, 144f.
[2] On the question whether Jesus spoke the eucharistic words in Aramaic or in Hebrew, see pp. 196ff.
[3] Schürmann, *Einsetzungsbericht*, 24–26; G. Friedrich, 'Ursprung, Urform und Urbedeutung des Abendmahls', in *Abendmahlsgespräch*, ed. by the Evangelische Akademie der Pfalz, 1958, 21: 'Pauline gloss'. Early it was attempted to explain this concise clause by the addition of a participle, as the variants to I Cor. 11.24 show (+ κλώμενον ℵ³F G ℜ *pl* it sy, θρυπτόμενον D*, διδόμενον sa bo arm).
[4] W. Michaelis, letter of July 28, 1949.

asserted itself in liturgical practice. Moreover, when one cele-brated *sub una*, the need for a theological interpretation with the word over the bread must have been felt to be pressing. A movement of the ὑπέρ-phrase from the wine to the bread is therefore more easily conceivable than the reverse procedure.

3. *The command to repeat* (the words of institution) is found only in Paul and Luke. It also can hardly be an ingredient in the oldest formula,[1] since its addition is more easily understandable than its deletion.

4. Finally we will have to regard ἐστίν also as an addition. The copula is read, to be sure, in the word over the bread in all five witnesses, but it is lacking in Luke in the word over the cup, and that is a reminiscence of the old Semitic form.

As the presumably oldest text we have thus: (λάβετε·) τοῦτο τό σῶμά μου/ἡ σάρξ μου ('[Take]; this [is] my body/my flesh').

(β) *The word of interpretation over the wine*

On the setting (I Cor. 11.25a; Mark 14.23 par.), see pp. 109ff.

I Cor. 11.25	*Luke 22.20*	*Mark 14.24*	*Matt. 26.27b–28*
			πίετε ἐξ αὐτοῦ Drink of it πάντες all (of you)
τοῦτο τὸ ποτήριον This cup	τοῦτο τὸ ποτήριον This cup	τοῦτό This	τοῦτο this γάρ for
ἡ καινὴ διαθήκη the new *covenant*	ἡ καινὴ διαθήκη the new *covenant*		
ἐστὶν is		ἐστιν is	ἐστιν is
ἐν τῷ ἐμῷ in *my*	ἐν τῷ αἵματί in *the blood*	τό αἷμά μου the blood of me	τὸ αἷμά μου the blood of me
αἵματι.[2] blood	μου of me		
		τῆς διαθήκης of the covenant	τῆς διαθήκης of the covenant

---

[1] That was discerned long ago. Already Schleiermacher expressed doubt: F. Schleiermacher, *The Christian Faith*, Edinburgh, 1928, 643 (§ 139.3).

[2] P46 A C al, ἐν τῷ αἵματί μου.

I Cor. 11.25	Luke 22.20	Mark 14.24	Matt. 26.27b–28
	τὸ ὑπὲρ ὑμῶν which (is) for you	τὸ ἐκχυννόμενον which (is) poured out	τὸ περὶ πολλῶν which (is) for many
	ἐκχυννόμενον poured out	ὑπὲρ πολλῶν for many	ἐκχυννόμενον poured out
			εἰς ἄφεσιν to the forgiveness
			ἁμαρτιῶν of sins
τοῦτο ποιεῖτε this do			
ὁσάκις ἐὰν πίνητε as often as you drink (it)			
εἰς τὴν ἐμὴν in my			
ἀνάμνησιν remembrance			

The great disparity in the *common words*, which are again italicized, is only superficial. When Paul/Luke, who agree as in the words over the bread, say 'This cup is the new covenant in my blood', while Mark/Matthew on the contrary say 'This is my blood of the covenant', then both formulations signify substantially the same thing. That becomes clear when the subject and predicate of both formulations are separately compared. The subject in Mark/Matthew is the red wine contained in the cup, and the same holds for Paul/Luke—with τοῦτο τὸ ποτήριον they do not mean the cup, but its contents. Also the predicate agrees substantially in both formulations. Just like Mark/Matthew (the wine 'is my blood of the covenant'), so also Paul/Luke (the wine 'is the new covenant by virtue of [causal ἐν][1] my blood') compare the wine with the blood, through whose out-pouring the new covenant is established. The common text is therefore: 'This (wine) (is) my blood (shed for the concluding) of the covenant.'

There thus remains only the very difficult and disputed question of whether the form in Paul/Luke or in Mark/Matthew is the more original form of the common words. In favour of Paul/Luke speaks on first glance the striking asymmetry which exists in them between

[1] Schlatter, *Lukas*, 422.

the word over the bread and the cup. No factor has influenced the formulation of the words of interpretation as strongly as the striving towards harmonization, and since in Mark/Matthew the words over the bread and wine are structured symmetrically, their form appears to express itself immediately as secondary. Very considerable grounds are needed in order to shatter this conclusion. Such are actually at hand. In this connection we do not concern ourselves so much with the support that Mark/Matthew finds in the Epistle to the Hebrews (9.20, τοῦτο τὸ αἷμα τῆς διαθήκης, cf. Mark/Matthew: τοῦτό (γάρ) ἐστιν τὸ αἷμά μου τῆς διαθήκης)[1] and in the gospel of John (6.51c–58); for this is evidence only for the diffusion, but not for the age, of the Mark/Matthew form. Also we are not concerned that the asymmetry in the sentence structure which makes the Paul/Luke form so striking corresponds to an asymmetry in Mark/Matthew, namely, the different lengths of the sentences ('empty' word over the bread, fullness at the end of the word over the wine).[2] More important is the fact that the equation of the cup with the new covenant by Paul/Luke is a 'peculiar',[3] not immediately understandable, way of speaking and gives the impression of a later form. The decisive argument in favour of the Mark/Matthew form is, however, that it is in substance the more difficult. The words 'this is my blood' were susceptible to the misunderstanding that they spoke of the drinking of blood,[4] which, particularly for born Jews, was a dark animistic abomination.[5] It is a likely assumption that the strangely complicated formulation of the word over the wine in Paul/Luke ('this cup is the new covenant') was occasioned by the intention of warding off the misunderstanding that the Lord's Supper was a Thyestian meal where blood was drunk.[6] This consideration weighs very heavily in favour of the form in Mark/Matthew; 'Exactly that which seems scandalous will be

[1] In Heb. 9.20 the LXX of Ex. 24.8 is cited: ἰδοὺ τὸ αἷμα τῆς διαθήκης. The replacing of ἰδού (LXX) by τοῦτο is caused by the influence of the eucharistic formula (cf. O. Michel, *Der Brief an die Hebräer*[11], Göttingen, 1960, 210).

[2] See pp. 167f.

[3] Dalman, *Jesus-Jeshua*, 161.

[4] Cf. John 6.60, 'this is a hard saying', and the Ep. of Pliny 10.96.7 (Pliny, *Letters* II [Loeb Classical Library 59]).

[5] Gen. 9.4; Lev. 3.17; 7.26f.; 17.10–14; 19.26; Deut. 12.16, 23f.; 15.23, cf. I Sam. 14.32–34; Acts 15.20, 29; Josephus, *Ant.* 3.260. For Rabbinic parallels see Billerbeck II, 737.

[6] Dalman, *Jesus-Jeshua*, 161. Also T. H. W. Maxfield, *The Words of Institution*, Cambridge, 1933, 20; P. Benoit, 'Le récit de la Cène dans Lc. XXII, 15–20', *RB* 48 (1939), 363; W. D. Davies, *Paul and Rabbinic Judaism*, 250.

historical.'[1] Nevertheless it may be stressed that the decision as to which of the two forms of the word over the wine is to be regarded as more original will become important only in a later part of our investigation, since, as we shall see on pp. 190f., the primitive form lies behind the cleavage. Here, where we are dealing with the establishment of the text common to both forms, the question can rest.

The elements not common to both are: 1. *The invitation* to drink (Matthew). This is secondary, as the comparison with Mark shows. Matthew likes to transpose the narrative report of Mark into direct speech.[2] That in our text too the address (Matt. 26.27b, 'Drink of it, all of you') is secondary over against the narrative form (Mark 14.23b, 'and they all drank of it') is confirmed by the consideration that the words 'of it, all of you' in Matthew are superfluous (cf. the mere 'eat' of Matt. 26.26); they are to be regarded as 'Markan remnants'.[3] It is, however, difficult to regard the change to direct speech as merely a stylistic alteration. For the change from the indicative (Mark) into the imperative 'Drink of it, all of you' (Matthew) results in a *formula of distribution*,[4] which has its counterpart in the invitation formula over the bread. But we have seen repeatedly that the influence of the rite[5] and the attempt to harmonize the words over the bread and wine[6] are signs of a secondary formulation of the words of interpretation. 2. Likewise secondary is 'for' (Matt. 26.28), which is made necessary by the invitation 'Drink of it, all of you.' It produces a radical shift of emphasis, because now the following words of interpretation are only the foundation of the invitation to drink upon which the whole stress is laid.[7] This shift of the emphasis to the formula of distribution is clearly conditioned by liturgical usage. 3. The further definition of 'this' by 'the cup' (Paul/Luke) is explanatory. 4. Likewise explanatory is the further definition of the 'covenant' by 'new' (Paul/Luke), a reference to Jer. 31.31–34. The addition is certainly pre-Pauline, as the agreement of Paul with Luke shows, but presumably first arose on hellenistic soil, since the

---

[1] Dalman, *Jesus-Jeschua* (German edition), 143. [The English translation has modified this sentence, p. 157. Transl.]

[2] Matt. 3.2; 12.10; 13.10; 15.15, 25; 16.22; 17.9; 18.1; 21.33a; 26.1f., 15, 66. Examples of the opposite trend are rare: 8.18; 20.20, 32.

[3] Finegan, *Überlieferung*, 10.

[4] Cf. from the profane sphere the stereotyped phrase πίε ζήσῃς recurring on the golden beakers (see above, p. 166 n. 3).

[5] See pp. 108ff., 153 n. 4, 187.

[6] See pp. 114, 153, 167f., 187.

[7] E. Lohmeyer, 'Vom urchristlichen Abendmahl [I]', *ThR* 9 (1937), 176f.

position of the adjective 'new' before 'covenant' is unsemitic. 5. The addition of the copula ἐστίν (Paul, Mark/Matthew) is for smoothness; Luke (cf. also Heb. 9.20) stands nearest here to the Semitic original. 6. *The command to repeat the rite* (Paul) does not belong to the old formula (see above, p. 168); its repetition with the cup (only Paul, not Luke) is a further instance of the tendency toward harmonization.[1] 7. *The ὑπέρ-phrase*. It is lacking in Paul, but is placed by him with the word over the bread. We saw, pp. 166ff., that several different observations argue that it originally belonged to the word over the wine. The only question remaining is how the words originally read. We read in

Mark:	Τὸ ἐκχυννόμενον	ὑπὲρ πολλῶν
	which is poured out	for many
Matthew:	Τὸ	περὶ πολλῶν ἐκχυννόμενον εἰς ἄφεσιν ἁμαρτιῶν
	which	for many is poured out for the forgiveness of sins
Luke:	Τὸ	ὑπὲρ ὑμῶν ἐκχυννόμενον
	which	for you is poured out

Here it can be said with great certainty that Mark offers the oldest text. For (*a*) the placing of the participle before the prepositional phrase (thus only in Mark) corresponds to the Semitic word order; Matthew and Luke wished presumably with the transposition to avoid the hiatus. (*b*) Also πολλῶν ('many') (Mark/Matthew) has as a semitism (pp. 179ff.) to be considered as older than ὑμῶν ('you') (Luke, cf. Paul). The substitution of πολλῶν by ὑμῶν is primarily neither the rejection of the semitism, nor still less a limitation of the atoning work of Jesus to the community arising out of theological reflection; it is rather a consequence of liturgical usage. In practice the address came to replace the statement; thus the ὑμῶν acts so that each of the worshippers knows himself personally addressed by the Lord.[2] The

---

[1] See p. 249. Cf. also p. 52 n. 3, for Schlatter's hypothesis that the explanation of 'as often as you drink it' in the second command to repeat the rite (I Cor. 11.25) is to be found in the fact that wine was seldom available for the celebrations of the community. This observation shows—presuming the correctness of Schlatter's explanation—that the formulation of the command to repeat the rite with the cup reflects the situation of the communities.

[2] Cf. E. Lohmeyer, 'Das Abendmahl in der Urgemeinde', *JBL* 56 (1937), 243; J. Leipoldt, *Der Gottesdienst der ältesten Kirche jüdisch? griechisch? christlich?*, Leipzig, 1937, 39.

word of interpretation becomes a formula of distribution. (Under no. 1 above we have observed in Matthew the same process of the development of a formula of distribution as here with Paul/Luke.) (c) ὑπέρ (in Mark, Luke, cf. Paul, John; see pp. 166f.) or περί (Matthew)? Since Matthew stands alone and since he has taken over the text of Mark literally with insignificant changes, it is as a matter of course probable that the divergence goes back to him. Actually Matthew shares the general predilection of the New Testament (Paul only dissents) for περί: in his entire gospel ὑπέρ with the genitive is found a single time (5.44), against περί with the genitive twenty times.[1] (d) 'for the forgiveness of sins' (Matthew) is probably an addition—substantially correct—which makes use of a liturgical formula which perhaps stems from the baptismal rite.[2] Therefore the following appears as the oldest form of the tradition of the words of interpretation attainable by a comparison of the texts:

1.	(Λάβετε·)	τοῦτο τὸ σῶμά μου/ἡ σάρξ μου
	(Take)	This my body / my flesh
		τὸ αἷμά μου τῆς διαθήκης
2.	Τοῦτο	my blood of the covenant
	This	ἡ διαθήκη ἐν τῷ αἵματί μου
		the covenant in my blood
3.	Τὸ . . .	ὑπὲρ πολλῶν
	Which . . .	for many

SEMITISMS

(a) Mark

We take a further step in the quest for the oldest tradition when we give attention to the semitisms and to the Palestinian idioms. They are found in Mark in a strikingly large number. All other texts, including the Matthaean text of the words of the Lord's Supper which is so close to the text of Mark, have been graecized in comparison with Mark.

---

[1] Also, in addition, in the New Testament περί occasionally takes the place of ὑπέρ (Blass-Debrunner, § 229.1), while the reverse exchange (ὑπέρ for περί) is less frequent (§ 231.1).

[2] Mark 1.4 par.; Acts 2.38.

(a) *The setting*

Concerning the word over the bread

1. 14.22, καί ('and') as beginning of the pericope. Mark is unique among our gospels in that, apart from a few exceptions, it allows pericope after pericope to begin monotonously with καί. That is an established characteristic of Palestinian historical writing. From Genesis on to I Maccabees every pericope in the Palestinian historical books with relatively few exceptions begins with 'and'. *In the liturgical use of such pericopae in Palestine the 'and' at the beginning of pericopae was left unchanged.* In the Greek historical writing on the contrary the καί is only seldom found at the beginning of a new section; here δέ is customary. Also in Luke the καί is retained (22.19). Matthew has removed it, replacing it with the unsemitic δέ[1] (26.26). In place of καί ('and'), Paul offers the sonorous 'The Lord Jesus on the night in which he was betrayed' (I Cor. 11.23).

2. 14.22, καὶ ... ἔκλασεν καὶ ἔδωκεν ... καὶ εἶπεν ... 23, καὶ ... ἔδωκεν ... καὶ ἔπιον ... 24, καὶ εἶπεν ('and ... he broke and gave ... and said ... 23, and ... gave ... and they drank ... 24, and he said'). Connection with καί is, of course, common to popular idiom of all times, yet the uniformity with which in Mark the finite verbs are connected by καί is a semitic usage.[2] Instead of these six 'ands', Matthew, who alone can be compared here (because in Paul and Luke the introduction to the word over the cup is reduced to a comprehensive expression), has only two 'ands' connecting finite verbs.

3. 14.22, λαβὼν ἄρτον εὐλογήσας ('having taken bread and blessed') is an established phrase for the action of the Jewish head of the household in the grace before meals; cf. Mark 6.41 par.; 8.6 par.; Luke 24.30; John 6.11. 'Take (the bread) and say grace.'[3] 'He takes the bread and pronounces the blessing over it.'[4] The elevation of the bread[5] introduces the grace.[6] Although λαβὼν ἄρτον ('having taken

---

[1] J. Wellhausen, *Einleitung in die drei ersten Evangelien*[2], Berlin, 1911, 10.

[2] Cf. Blass-Debrunner, § 458; M. Black, *An Aramaic Approach to the Gospels and Acts*[2], Oxford, 1954, 51.

[3] j. Ber. 8.12a.45; 6.10a.63, *sb bryk.*

[4] j. Ber. 6.10a.49. Cf. j. Ber. 6.10a.9: 'He took an olive and pronounced the blessing'; j. Ber. 6.10a.45: 'He took a lupine and pronounced the blessing over it.'

[5] What is meant is the simple act of lifting the bread. A 'consecrating elevation or waving' (Goetz, *Die heutige Abendmahlsfrage in ihrer geschichtlichen Entwicklung*[2], 191, on I Cor. 11.23) is out of the question.

[6] Thus is John 21.13 to be understood.

bread') in our text is meaningful in so far as it describes the elevation of the bread, nevertheless this detailed form of expression will have to be designated as typically Semitic. Λαμβάνειν belongs namely to those verbs which in a Semitic language describe, in a way which is cumbersome and superfluous for our idiom, a movement (or attitude) which is preparatory to the action on which the stress lies; that is true for the Hebrew *laḳaḥ, naṭal* as for the Aramaic *nesab*, e.g. Matt. 13.31, ὃν λαβὼν ἄνθρωπος ἔσπειρεν ('which a man took and sowed'); 13.33, ἣν λαβοῦσα γυνὴ ἐνέκρυψεν ('which a woman took and hid'); 14.19; 15.36; 17.27; 21.35, 39; 25.1; 26.26, 27; 27.24, 48, 59; Mark 6.41; 8.6; 9.36; 12.3, 8; Luke 6.4; 9.16; 13.19, 21; 24.30, 43; John 6.11; 13.4, 26; 19.1, 6, 23, 40; 21.13; Acts 9.25; 16.3; 27.35; I Cor. 11.23; Rev. 8.5. Used analogously to λαβών are: ἀναστάς, ἀπαγαγών, ἀπελθών, ἀπερχόμενος, ἀφείς, ἐγερθείς, εἰσελθών, ἐλθών, ἐρχόμενος, ἑστώς, καθίσας, καταλιπών, πορευθείς, σταθείς.

4. 14.22, εὐλογήσας ('having blessed'). In secular Greek εὐλογεῖν has quite predominantly the meaning 'to praise or glorify someone' and is constructed with a personal or impersonal object. In the meaning 'bless', as in the special meaning 'to say grace', it is a semitism (= Hebrew *berak*, Aramaic *barek*). The omission of the object is also a semitism. How strange the absolute use of εὐλογεῖν must have appeared to the non-Palestinian is shown by Luke 9.16, where it speaks of fish and bread: εὐλόγησεν αὐτούς; here by the transposition of the object (which belongs in the *Vorlage*, Mark 6.41, to κατέκλασεν) the grace has become a consecration.[1] This linguistic misunderstanding of the Semitic εὐλογεῖν in Greek circles has had far-reaching consequences in the history of the Lord's Supper. The replacement of εὐλογήσας by εὐχαριστήσας in the parallels I Cor. 11.24; Luke 24.19a is a translation variant[2] which graecized the semitism.[3]

5. 14.22, ἔκλασεν καὶ ἔδωκεν ('He broke and gave'). The breaking of the bread took place for the purpose of distribution (see above, p. 109). Presumably, 'he broke and gave' is a set phrase. 'Rab (d. 247) was accustomed, when he had *broken* the bread, to eating (his piece immediately) with his left hand and (simultaneously) to *dis-*

---

[1] Analogous to Mark 8.7, εὐλογήσας αὐτά, on which see p. 97 n. 4.

[2] H. Schürmann, 'Die Semitismen im Einsetzungsbericht bei Markus und bei Lukas (Mk 14, 22–24/Lk 22, 19–20)', *ZKTh* 73 (1951), 74.

[3] Paul is—accidentally to be sure—the sole witness to the fact that the daily grace was designated as εὐχαριστεῖν in hellenistic Judaism (Rom. 14.6; I Cor. 10.30; I Tim. 4.3f.).

tributing with his right hand.'[1] Cr. Mark 6.41 par.; 8.6 par.; Luke 24.30; John 6.11.[2] The omission of the subject is striking. How did it come about that the liturgical formula, which indeed formed an independent unit, appears to have been transmitted without a subject in Mark as well as Luke? Is it because the name of Jesus, analogous to the practice of avoiding the name of God in Judaism, should not be named out of reverence (cf. Acts 5.41; III John 7, ὑπὲρ τοῦ ὀνόματος 'for Him', further the variant Βαρσουμα ['Son of the Name'] syr^{pesh} Ephr in Acts 13.6, Βαριησοῦς, and the textual apparatus for Matt. 27.17)? As noteworthy as this explanation is, we would like to prefer to it still another (p. 192). Matthew (ὁ Ἰησοῦς) and Paul (ὁ κύριος Ἰησοῦς) independently of each other offer the supplied subject.

6. 14.22, ἔκλασεν ('broke'). κλᾶν, Hebrew *baṣaʿ*, more seldom *paras*, Aramaic *ḳeṣa*, is a technical term[3] for the Jewish practice of breaking the bread[4] before the meal;[5] it followed only when the 'Amen' of the company, answering the grace, had died away.[6] The phrase κλᾶν ἄρτον ('to break bread') is strange to classical Greek.[7] The absolute use of κλᾶν is also Semitic.[8]

---

[1] j. Ber. 6.10a.62. It deals with a courtesy: The host's act of eating opened the meal and Rab wished to avoid keeping his guests waiting until he has finished with the distribution of the bread (cf. on the passage, Billerbeck IV, 622 under 'o').

[2] Cf. also John 21.13, 'and took the bread and gave it to them'. Here, also, 'gave' refers to the distribution of the broken pieces of bread.

[3] Jer. 16.7 LXX (cf. note below); Lam. 4.4; j. Ber. 8.12a.45: 'He gave him a loaf of bread that he might break it. He said, Take and say grace.'

[4] The translation of κλᾶν with 'to sacrifice with blessing, to consecrate' (Goetz, *Abendmahlsfrage*, 186–8) is linguistically and materially impossible; cf. J. Jeremias, 'Das paulinische Abendmahl — eine Opferdarbringung?', *ThStKr* 108 (1937–8), 124–41.

[5] *paras leḥem* was already used in Jer. 16.7 (where instead of *yiphresu lahem* is to be read *leḥem* with the LXX κλασθῇ ἄρτος) as a designation for the breaking of the bread for condoling of persons. For Talmudic examples of the rite of breaking of the bread, cf. Billerbeck I, 687; II, 619f.; IV, 621f.; Dalman, *Jesus-Jeshua*, 136f. Further b. R. H. 29b; b. Ber. 46a.

[6] b. Ber. 47a. Since the time of F. Spitta, *Zur Geschichte und Litteratur des Urchristentums* I, Göttingen, 1893, 238, there has been cited over and over again (finally by A. Greiff, *Das älteste Pascharituale der Kirche, Did. 1–10, und das Johannesevangelium* [Johanneische Studien I], Paderborn, 1929, 149) b. Pes. 115b, 116a as evidence for the assertion that in the passover—contrary to usual usage—first the bread was broken and after this the prayer of blessing pronounced. Concerning the erroneousness of this assertion, see pp. 68f.

[7] T. Schermann, 'Das "Brotbrechen" im Urchristentum', *Biblische Zeitschrift* 8 (1910), 33–52; 162–83, established on pp. 39f.: 'In classical literature σχίζω or ψωμίζω (the latter, however, mostly with the meaning 'to nourish'), also μερίζω and διαμερίζω, seem to have been employed instead of κλάω. It is true, however, that I have found only one place in which mention is made of the dividing of

7. 14.22, καὶ ἔδωκεν αὐτοῖς ('and gave to them'). Ἔδωκεν has no direct object, since ἄρτον, because of the absolutely used εὐλογήσας (see above on no. 4), cannot be attracted to all four verbs. 'To give' in the sense of 'to pass out' without the accusative object is a Semitic idiom.[1]

Concerning the word over the cup

8. 14.23, λαβὼν ποτήριον εὐχαριστήσας ('having taken the cup and given thanks') is a set phrase, cf. Luke 22.17: δεξάμενος ποτήριον εὐχαριστήσας. 'Take (the cup) and speak the eulogy.'[2] 'He took the cup and spoke the eulogy.'[3] With λαβών is meant thereby the elevation of the cup about a hand's breadth above the table,[4] an action by which the grace was introduced. On λαβών, see further number 3. Λαβών in Mark 14.23 and δεξάμενος in Luke 22.17 could be variants in translation; it is more probable, however, that δεξάμενος designates taking of the cup from the hands of the attendant,[5] λαβών designates the elevation of the cup before the benediction.

9. 14.23, εὐχαριστήσας ('having given thanks'). Hebrew and Aramaic know only *one* expression for the prayer before and after the meal: *berak/barek*, εὐλογεῖν. The use of εὐχαριστήσας for the thanksgiving after the meal is tolerable.[6] It is otherwise with εὐχαριστήσας in

---

something baked, in an inscription from a cult of Samothrace: the priest offers the sacrificial cake ([τὸ πέμμ]α), after he has divided it (σχίξας), and pours forth the drink for the mystae (καὶ ἐγχέει [τὸ ποτὸν τοῖ]ς μύσταις).' (On this inscription cf. also A. Dieterich, *Eine Mithrasliturgie*[2], Leipzig–Berlin, 1910, 105.) Κλᾶν ἄρτον is therefore a strange phrase in classical Greek. On the passage in the great Paris Magical Papyrus, Bibliothèque Nationale, Suppl. gr. 574: καταλιπὼν ἀπὸ τοῦ ἄρτου, οὗ ἐσθίεις, ὀλίγον καὶ κλάσας ποίησον εἰς ἑπτὰ ψωμούς (K. Preisendanz, *Papyri Graecae Magicae. Die griechischen Zauberpapyri* I, Leipzig–Berlin, 1928, 118, no. IV 1392–4), J. Behm, κλάω κτλ., *TWNT* III (1938), 727 n.2, correctly remarked that it is of little weight, because the magical papyrus exhibits Jewish-hellenistic as well as Christian influences.

[8] An established usage: Tos. Suk. 4.23 (200.9); j. Ber. 6.10a.62; b. Ber. 46a (lines 6, 9, 11, 12 [twice]); 47a.

[1] Gen. 3.6; Judg. 14.9; Matt. 19.21; Luke 11.7; 15.16 (cf. p. 208); j. Hor. 3.48a.44: 'Go and sell his half (of the field) and give to them'; Mek. Ex. 19.6: 'They took from them and gave to the priests.'
[2] j. Ber. 7.11c.5; 8.12a.46; Lev. R. 9.3 on 7.11, *sb bryk*.
[3] j. Ber. 7.11b.62.
[4] j. Ber. 7.11c.63f.; b. Ber. 51a, b, cf. Ps. 116.13.
[5] See p. 162 n. 4.
[6] Cf. the wording of the second benediction of the grace after the meal: 'We thank Thee . . .' (see above, p. 110).

I Cor. 11.24; Luke 22.17, 19a (Prayer *before* the meal) (cf. no. 4). At any rate the omission of an object is a semitism (cf. no. 4).[1]

10. 14.23, εὐχαριστήσας ἔδωκεν αὐτοῖς ('having given thanks he gave to them') uses likewise a set phrase: 'He said grace and gave R. Naḥman the cup of blessing.'[2] On the omission of the object with ἔδωκεν, see no. 7.

(β) The words of interpretation

11. 14.22, τὸ σῶμά μου ('my body'). The translation variant ἡ σάρξ μου ('my flesh') in John 6.51c points to a Semitic *Urtext* (see below, p. 199). Furthermore, the pair of terms σῶμα/σάρξ—αἷμα is a semitism.[3] The position of the personal pronoun in Mark corresponds to the Semitic suffix; the placement of the pronoun before the noun (I Cor. 11.24, τοῦτό μού ἐστιν τὸ σῶμα) is only possible in Greek.

12. 14.24, τὸ αἷμά μου ('my blood'). On the pair of terms σῶμα/-σάρξ—αἷμα and on the position of the pronoun (I Cor. 11.25, ἐν τῷ ἐμῷ αἵματι), see no. 11.

13. 14.24, ἐκχυννόμενον ('[which is] poured out'). Ἐκχύννειν is the rendering of *heʿerah* in Isa. 53.12 (see below, p. 226). The primitive Hebrew text is used, not the LXX (παρεδόθη). The striking present tense is explained by the fact that, contrary to Greek, Hebrew and Aramaic possess no participial forms which distinguish time. The participle is atemporal. Its time sphere is determined by the context. In Aramaic the participle is often used for an event expected in the near future.[4] Now to be sure, in Greek too the present participle can

---

[1] Schürmann, *Paschamahlbericht*, 55; Schlatter, *Lukas*, 137 (examples from Josephus of εὐχαριστεῖν with an indirect object in the dative). The scarce hellenistic examples of the absolute use of εὐχαριστεῖν are restricted to the meaning 'to be thankful' (T. Schermann, 'Εὐχαριστία und εὐχαριστεῖν in ihrem Bedeutungswandel bis 200 n. Chr.', *Philologus* 69 [1910], 376f.).

[2] b. Ber. 51b.

[3] See pp. 199f., 222f.; P. Fiebig, 'Die Abendmahlsworte Jesu', *Neues Sächsisches Kirchenblatt* 42 (1935), col. 374.

[4] C. F. Burney, *The Aramaic Origin of the Fourth Gospel*, Oxford, 1922, 94f.; P. Joüon, *L'Évangile de Notre-Seigneur Jésus-Christ* (Verbum salutis V), Paris, 1930, 69; W. B. Stevenson, *Grammar of Palestinian Jewish Aramaic*, Oxford, 1924, 56, § 21.9; H. Odeberg, *The Aramaic Portions of Bereshit Rabba* II. *Short Grammar of Galilæan Aramaic* (Lunds Universitets Årsskrift N. F. I 36.4), Lund–Leipzig, 1939, 101, § 439. As to the use of the *passive* participle as a designation of an expected event: for Hebrew, cf.W. Gesenius–E. Kautzsch–G. Bergsträsser, *Hebräische Grammatik*²⁹ II, Leipzig, 1926, 69, 72, § 13 dᶜ, hᵈ; for the Aramaic may be mentioned as examples Dan. 2.13 (*mitḳaṭṭelin*); G. Dalman, *Aramäische Dialektproben*², Leipzig, 1927, 15.9 (*mitbene*); M. L. Margolis, *Lehrbuch der aramäischen Sprache des babylonischen Talmuds*, Munich, 1910, 80.10 (*mitbeʿena*).

designate a relatively future action; it nevertheless then has definite nuances (descriptive, characterizing, final).[1] Since these are not to be found in our passage (Mark 14.24 par. Luke 22.20), and also not in the remaining synoptic passages (Mark 10.30; Matt. 3.11; 11.3 par.; Luke 1.35; 13.23; 22.19), all instances will have to be called semitisms.[2] Our passage will therefore have to be translated: '(my blood) that (soon) *will* be shed'. Failure to notice this fact has led to serious misunderstandings, especially to the view that Jesus speaks of a pouring out of his blood at the Supper—not on the Cross![3]

14. 14.24, ὑπέρ ('for') can be recognized already as a rendering of a Semitic equivalent by the fact that ὑπέρ with the genitive is lacking in the LXX of Isa. 53 (where διά with the accusative and περί with the genitive stand). Moreover, a translation variant may be seen in ἀντὶ πολλῶν in Mark 10.45, a variant which likewise points to a Semitic *Urtext*.

15. 14.24, πολλῶν ('many'). While 'many' in Greek (as in English) stands in opposition to 'all', and therefore has the exclusive sense ('*many, but not all*'), Hebrew *rabbim* can have the inclusive sense ('*the whole, comprising many individuals*'). This inclusive use is connected with the fact that Hebrew and Aramaic possess no word for 'all'.[4]

The form *with the article* has throughout the inclusive meaning.[5] *Harabbim* is in the entire Talmudic literature the constant expression for '*the whole community*'.[6] In the Essene texts *hrbym* designates the guild of the fully qualified members.[7] This usage passed over into

---

[1] Blass-Debrunner, § 339.2a–c.

[2] In John are found the following examples: 1.29; 5.45; 12.25; 13.11; 16.13; 17.20; 18.4; 21.20.

[3] Principally Catholic authors have been led astray to this misunderstanding (e.g. H. Lamiroy, *De essentia ss. missae sacrificii* [Universitas Catholica Lovaniensis. Dissertationes ad gradum doctoris in Facultate Theologica consequendum conscriptae II 8], Louvain, 1919, 206–13; F. Ruffenach, 'Hoc est corpus meum, Hic est sanguis meus', *Verbum Domini* 4 [1924], 266: 'sacrificium praesens sit oportet'), in which case considerations of a dogmatic nature may have been determinative.

[4] Hebrew *kol*/Aramaic *kolla* is distinguished from our word 'all' in that it designates the totality, but not the sum. Accordingly, it has no plural.

[5] Since I have presented in πολλοί, *TWNT* VI (1959), 536–45, for the inclusive use of *rabbim* / πολλοί a detailed collection of material striving for completeness with reference to the Old Testament, New Testament and late Judaism, I am giving in the following only some examples.

[6] E.g., P. Ab. 5.18: Moses *zikkah et harabbim,* Jeroboam *heḥeṭi et harabbim*; R. H. 1.6; 3.8; 4.9; Tos. Sanh. 13.5 (434.23); Siphre Deut. 27 on 3.24 and very frequently.

[7] Jeremias, *op. cit.*, 538.15–30.

Jewish Greek, as Josephus shows.[1] In the New Testament, Rom. 5.15 is the clearest example for this inclusive use of οἱ πολλοί: 'For if many (οἱ πολλοί) died through one man's trespass, much more have the grace of God and the free gift in the grace of that one man Jesus Christ abounded for many (εἰς τοὺς πολλούς).' Here the meaning of οἱ πολλοί as 'all men' is secured not only by the double contrast with 'the one', but also by the meaning: 'the many died' must mean 'all men died' (οἱ πολλοί in 5.15a = πάντες ἄνθρωποι in 5.12 = πάντες in I Cor. 15.22). The same holds true for Rom. 5.19 (twice ὁ εἷς = Adam-Christ stands over against οἱ πολλοί = 'mankind'). Further, cf. Mark 9.26, τοὺς πολλούς 'all persons present'; Rom. 12.5, οἱ πολλοὶ ἓν σῶμά ἐσμεν ἐν Χριστῷ, 'we are all one body in Christ'; similarly I Cor. 10.17a, ἓν σῶμα οἱ πολλοί ἐσμεν (parallel to οἱ πάντες in v. 17b); I Cor. 10.33, 'not seeking my own advantage, but that of many (τὸ τῶν πολλῶν 'all'), that they may be saved'; Heb. 12.15, 'and by it the many (οἱ πολλοί 'the whole community') become defiled'.[2] It is used adjectivally in Luke 7.47: 'her sins which are many (αἱ πολλαί) are forgiven', 'God (see below, p. 202) has forgiven her her sins, as many as they are'.

But also the form *without the article* can have the same inclusive meaning.[3] I Enoch 62.3, 5 paraphrases the anarthrous *rabbim* of Isa. 52.14 with 'all the kings and the mighty, and the exalted and those who hold the earth'.[4] In the New Testament Mark 1.34, 'and he healed many (πολλούς)', is to be compared: it can hardly be said that Jesus healed only some of the sick, cf. par. Matt. 8.16, πάντας; Luke 4.40, ἑνὶ ἑκάστῳ (Mark 1.34 is therefore to be rendered perhaps with: 'great was the number of the ones who were healed'); further, cf. Mark 10.48, πολλοί par. Matt. 20.31, ὁ ὄχλος, and elsewhere.[5] In John 1.29 the anarthrous *rabbim* of Isa. 53.12 is replaced with ὁ

---

[1] Examples are given in Schlatter, *Matthäus*, 701; Jeremias, *op. cit.*, 539 n. 19. In Greek the use of οἱ πολλοί in the sense of 'the crowd, the masses, the people' (II Macc. 1.36), 'the populace' (2.27) comes close to the inclusive use ('all'), very often with the derogatory connotation: 'the common people, the (much too) many, *plebs*' (e.g. τῶν πολλῶν εἷς). Nevertheless the derogatory nuance does show that it has nothing to do with the inclusive usage.

[2] Cf. A. Seeberg, *Der Brief an die Hebräer*, Leipzig, 1912, 136, 140.

[3] For OT examples, see Jeremias, *op. cit.*, 537.3–9.

[4] Charles, *APOT* II, 227. Further examples from the non-canonical literature can be found in Jeremias, *op. cit.*, 539.8–23.

[5] Jeremias, *op. cit.*, 541.18–542.12.

κόσμος ('the world').¹ When IV Ezra 8.3 reads *multi quidem creati sunt,*
pauci autem salvabuntur ('Many have been created, but few shall be
saved', RSV), the first clause 'many have been created' obviously
embraces *all* men;² similarly the anarthrous πολλοί in the strictly
analogously constructed sentence 'For many (πολλοί) are called, but
few are chosen' (Matt. 22.14) is to be understood inclusively as 'all'.
The first clause, πολλοὶ γάρ εἰσιν κλητοί 'for all are called (to the
salvation meal)', does not speak therefore of God's selection by pre-
destination, but of the boundlessness of his invitation. That may be
the solution to this *crux interpretum!*³ Even *rabbim*/πολλοί used
adjectivally can have the inclusive sense. When Abraham in Rom.
4.17–18 is called 'father of many nations' (citation of Gen. 17.5),
the preceding interpretation, 'father of us all' (v. 16), and the universalistic rabbinic exegesis of Gen. 17.5 show that what is meant is
that Abraham is the father of *all nations.*⁴ In II Cor. 1.11, the
adjectival and substantival anarthrous πολλοί stand successively in the
inclusive sense:⁵ 'so that many (ἵνα ἐκ πολλῶν προσώπων, 'through
many persons = out of everyone's mouth') will give thanks on our
behalf for the blessing granted us in answer to many prayers (διὰ
πολλῶν, 'through many = through the entire community)'. Of
especial importance for our passage is Mark 10.45 par., λύτρον ἀντὶ
πολλῶν 'a ransom for many'.⁶ That πολλοί has here the inclusive
meaning 'all' is shown by the reference in Mark 10.45 to Isa.
53.10–12,⁷ as well as by the parallel in I Tim. 2.6: ἀντίλυτρον ὑπὲρ

¹ John 1.29: 'who takes away the sin of the world', is a free citation of Isa. 53.12:
'he bore the sin of many'.
² Likewise IV Ezra 4.34: 'You do not hasten faster than the Most High [to
precipitate the end of the world], your haste is for yourself, but the Highest hastens
on behalf of many' (RSV) (lat. *pro multis*; Arabic ed., J. Gildemeister, *Esdrae liber*
quartus arabice e cod. Vat., Bonn, 1877: 'for the sake of the whole number'). With the
word 'many' mankind is meant. In the (lost) Greek *Vorlage* πολλοί certainly stood,
probably without the article.
³ K. L. Schmidt, καλέω κτλ., *TWNT* III (1938), 496.
⁴ Billerbeck III, 211; H. Lietzmann, *An die Römer*⁴, Tübingen, 1933, 55 on
4.17; J. Jeremias, πολλοί, *TWNT* VI (1959), 539.29–32; 542.31–35. Probably to
be regarded as inclusive is the adjectival πολλοί of Heb. 2.10, where it says of God:
πολλοὺς υἱοὺς εἰς δόξαν ἀγαγόντα, '(in his intention) to lead many sons (i.e. the great
troop of sons) to glory'.
⁵ E. Lohmeyer referred to this passage in 'Vom urchristlichen Abendmahl [I]',
ThR 9 (1937), 191.
⁶ J. Jeremias, 'Das Lösegeld für Viele (Mk. 10,45)', *Judaica* 3 (1947–8), 249–64.
⁷ The omission of the article before πολλῶν in Mark 10.45 is explained by the
fact that the LXX in Isa. 53.11, 12b offers the anarthrous πολλοί (Targum on both
passages has *saggi'in*, therefore likewise anarthrous).

πάντων, 'a ransom for all'.[1] Just as Mark 10.45, so also our passage Mark 14.24[2] is to be interpreted *in the inclusive sense.* πολλῶν is therefore a semitism.

16. 14.24, τὸ ἐκχυννόμενον ὑπὲρ πολλῶν ('the [blood] poured out for many'). The placing of the prepositional phrase at the end corresponds to Semitic word order. That it is placed between the article and the participle independently of each other in Matthew as well as in Luke shows that the position at the end sounds harsh in Greek.

(γ) *The avowal of abstinence*

17. 14.25, ἀμήν = amen. Matt. 26.29 graecizes with δέ, Luke 22.18 with γάρ.[3] This use of ἀμήν is a characteristic of the *ipsissima vox.*[4] Mark 14.25 is the twelfth of the thirteen Marcan ἀμήν-sayings.

18. 14.25, οὐκέτι οὐ μή (emphatic 'not again'). This accumulation of negatives, 'a form of barbaric Greek',[5] (eleven times in the LXX for *lo ʿod* or *lo* or *en*, elsewhere in the New Testament in Rev. 18.14; Luke 22.16 *v.l.*), is caused by the translator's clumsiness. Translators who render into a foreign tongue easily seize upon expressions which are too strong.

19. 14.25. Instead of οὐκέτι οὐ μὴ πίω ('I will not drink again') D *a d f* arm read οὐ μὴ προσθῶ πεῖν (lit. 'I will not add to drink'), and Θ reads οὐ μὴ προσθῶμεν πιεῖν (lit. 'we will not add to drink'). This verbal paraphrase of 'further', 'furthermore' (cf. Luke 20.11, 12) is a semitism (D = *oseph lemište*; Θ = *noseph lemište*). The first person plural 'we' for 'I' (Θ) corresponds to the usual Galilean-Aramaic usage.

Which of the two variants (οὐκέτι οὐ μὴ πίω or οὐ μὴ προσθῶ[μεν] π[ι]εῖν) may be held as the original depends upon how one evaluates the semitisms among the special readings of D. The question has been quite recently reintroduced into the discussion,[6] and there are two views concerning it. The first says that προσθῶ(μεν) π(ι)εῖν is a secondary biblicism;[7] now, it is surely correct that προστιθέναι with

---

[1] Cf. Rom. 8.32, ὑπὲρ ἡμῶν πάντων παρέδωκεν αὐτόν, 'he delivered him for us all'.

[2] See below, p. 229. For the omission of the article what is said above, p. 181 n. 7, is applicable. Moreover, one has to bear in mind that in Aramaic the strong distinction between the definite and indefinite form recedes.

[3] Cf. further above, p. 163 nn. 1, 3.

[4] See pp. 163 n. 1, 201f.

[5] P. Benoit, 'Le récit de la Cène dans Lc. XXII, 15–20', *RB* 48 (1939), 379.

[6] By A. J. Wensinck and M. Black.

[7] Schürmann, *Paschamahlbericht*, 35, n. 154.

the infinitive is met frequently in the LXX, but the idiomatic first
person plural προσθῶμεν is not to be explained in this way. On the
other hand, J. Wellhausen represents the view that there have
survived in D a number of semitisms, of which the text has otherwise
been continuously cleansed;[1] but it is absolutely improbable that of
all the uncials only D and Θ should have preserved the original text.
This objection is avoided by the modification of Wellhausen's thesis
by M. Black: semiticizing variants in the text of the gospels may go
back to 'extra-canonical versions' of the words of Jesus.[2] In other
words, the variants of D Θ al in Mark 14.25 stem from oral tradition.
If this thoroughly obvious solution proposed by Black is correct, the
οὐκέτι οὐ μὴ πίω, οὐ μὴ προσθῶ πεῖν and οὐ μὴ προσθῶμεν πιεῖν represent
equivalent variations of tradition and translation. The wording of
each of these three variants as well as the existence of three concurring
translations points to a Semitic original.

20. 14.25, οὐ μὴ πίω ἐκ τοῦ γενήματος τῆς ἀμπέλου ('I shall not drink
again of the fruit of the vine'). 'I shall not drink again of wine' is not
Greek. In Greek ἐκ with πίνειν refers to the vessel from which someone drinks; the drink is referred to in the accusative or the partitive
genitive. The non-Greek character of the construction is confirmed
by Luke 22.18, where πίνειν ἐκ is softened into πίνειν ἀπὸ τοῦ γενήματος
τῆς ἀμπέλου. To the contrary, in Hebrew and Aramaic the usual
reference to the drink is with min. Cf. Gen. 9.21, wayyešt min hayyayin
(LXX, καὶ ἔπιεν ἐκ τοῦ οἴνου); Midr. Koh. 3.4 on 3.2, štwn mn hdyn
ḥmr', 'drink this wine', and elsewhere.[3] In the New Testament
compare John 4.13, ὁ πίνων ἐκ τοῦ ὕδατος τούτου; v. 14, ὃς δ' ἂν πίῃ ἐκ
τοῦ ὕδατος . . .; Rev. 14.10, πίεται ἐκ τοῦ οἴνου; 18.3, ἐκ τοῦ οἴνου . . .
πέπωκαν.

21. 14.25, τὸ γένημα τῆς ἀμπέλου ('the fruit of the vine') for 'wine' is
in the Judaism of the time of Jesus a set liturgical formula at the
blessing of the cup, both before and after the meal. Before the drinking of the wine, God is praised as bore peri haggephen, Ber. 6.1; Tos. Ber.
4.3 (8.24f.); b. Pes. 103a; 106a, and elsewhere. On the presence of the
article, cf. Dan. 5.1, ḥamra šateh, 'drinking wine'.

22. 14.25, ἕως τῆς ἡμέρας ἐκείνης ('until that day'). Ἐκεῖνος ('that')
does not stand here in the emphatic position, but is entirely unstressed. It owes its existence most probably to a pleonastically placed

[1] Wellhausen, Einleitung, 9.
[2] Black, Aramaic Approach[2], 214.
[3] Further rabbinic parallels in Schlatter, Johannes, 120, on John 4.13.

Aramaic[1] or Hebrew[2] demonstrative pronoun. Mark 14.21 par. offers a further example for this use of ἐκεῖνος.[3] The rendering of this completely unstressed correlative of the relative pronoun into Greek with ἐκεῖνος must be called a mistranslation.

23. 14.25, ἐν τῇ βασιλείᾳ τοῦ θεοῦ ('in the kingdom of God'). Βασιλεία does not signify in this phrase the kingdom as something spatial, to which it would approximate in the Greek understanding, but has rather—as always *malkut*—a dynamic significance. One should compare the chronological statement in Dan. 6.29: *bemalkut Doryaweš* 'under the reign (lordship, dominion) of Darius'. Correspondingly, 'in the kingdom of God' is not a local, but a temporal declaration: 'when God will have set up his rule'.[4]

On the contrary the number of graecisms in Mark is small.

14.22, ἐσθιόντων αὐτῶν ('as they were eating'). The genitive absolute is unknown in Semitic. It is no accident that this graecism can be recognized as a redactional connecting link (see p. 113).

14.23, εὐχαριστήσας ('having given thanks'). A graecized semitism (see nos. 4, 9).

14.25, καινόν ('new'). The predicative καινόν would be as unusual in Hebrew as in Aramaic.[5]

(b) Matthew

The Matthaean form is a graecized reworking of the text of Mark.

---

[1] Examples may be found in F. Schulthess–E. Littmann, *Grammatik des christlich-palästinischen Aramäisch*, Tübingen, 1924, 25, § 190.2b; Dalman, *Grammatik*, 113f., § 17.9; *Jesus-Jeshua*, 63, 181; Odeberg, *Aramaic Portions of Bereshit Rabba* II, 77, § 340; A. Ungnad, *Syrische Grammatik* (Clavis Linguarum Semiticarum 7), Munich, 1913, 31, § 15c; M. L. Margolis, *Lehrbuch der aramäischen Sprache des babylonischen Talmuds*, Munich, 1910, 72, § 51b; Th. Nöldeke, *Mandäische Grammatik*, Halle, 1875 (reprint Darmstadt, 1964), 344 with n. 2, § 239; P. Joüon, 'Quelques aramaïsmes sous-jacents au grec des évangiles', *Recherches de science religieuse* 17 (1927), 213f.; *L'Évangile*, 162, 263.

[2] E.g., I Sam. 17.28.

[3] Superfluous demonstrative pronouns: Matt. 5.19; 10.23, 42; 18.14; 24.14; 25.40, 45 (on Matt. 25.40, 45, cf. Jeremias, *Parables*, 203); 26.29a; Mark 4.11; 9.42; 13.24; Luke 12.47; 19.27. It is rather frequent in John.

[4] Most of the semitisms enumerated above are found also elsewhere in Mark (which is not surprising, since he wrote a strongly semitized Greek). That N. Turner, 'The Style of St Mark's Eucharistic Words', *JTS* 8 (1957), 108–11, on the basis of this fact, doubts that Mark in 14.22ff. used a formula is difficult to understand. That Mark employed such a formula is incontestably assured by the parallel tradition, principally I Cor. 11.23–25, and beyond this is confirmed by the observations stated on p. 97 (cf. especially n. 4 on Mark 8.7 and n. 5).

[5] Cf. Dalman, *Jesus-Jeshua*, 182. In addition it may be asked whether Jesus said 'of God' or did not rather use a circumlocution of the divine name.

(c) Luke

(α) The setting

In the Lukan setting (22.15a, 17a, 19a, 20a), as far as can be compared, most of the semitisms noted for Mark recur (nos. 1, 3, 5, 6, 7, cf. 8). Nevertheless, a light graecizing is evident: 22.15, πρὸς αὐτούς (instead of the dative), a typical peculiarity of Luke; 22.17, 19, εὐχαριστήσας (cf. under no. 4); 22.19, 20, λέγων (cf. under no. 2).

(β) The words of interpretation

Here in Luke there emerges a new, very remarkable semitism: the omission of the copula with the word over the cup (22.20). Also the causal ἐν (τῷ αἵματί μου) is semitizing (be, 'by virtue of'). Over against this there stands, however, a rather severe graecizing of the Lukan text of the words of interpretation: ὑμῶν has entered in place of πολλῶν (vv. 19, 20, cf. no. 15), ὑπὲρ ὑμῶν is twice placed before the participle (vv. 19, 20, cf. no. 16), and the addition of καινή (v. 20) stands in an unsemitic way before the related noun διαθήκη.

(γ) The avowal of abstinence

We have seen on pp. 162f. how strongly graecized the avowal of abstinence is in Luke as compared with Mark 14.25. There we had already established that the graecizing, at least in part, is pre-Lukan. The fact is true also of the Lukan graecisms in the setting and the words of interpretation; to the degree that these are already found in Paul (εὐχαριστήσας, λέγων, ὑμῶν, position of καινή), they are pre-Lukan.

(d) Paul

Of the twenty-three semitisms of the text of Mark, nos. 17–23 belong to the verse Mark 14.25, which Paul has not reproduced in extenso. Of the remaining sixteen semitisms, only three (nos. 3, 6 and 14) reappear in Paul. The remaining are partly graecized in Paul (I Cor. 11.23 offers a sonorous introduction with the naming of the subject instead of the καί which is ugly to Greek feeling; in v. 24 εὐχαριστήσας stands in place of εὐλογήσας, which could be misunderstood by the Greek reader; ὑμῶν clarifies the Semitic πολλῶν; twice the personal pronoun is placed before its related noun for the sake of greater stress), partly avoided. If one adds the fact already mentioned,[1] that the word over the bread in Paul has a form not possible

[1] See above, p. 167.

in a Semitic language, then it follows that the Markan account of the Lord's Supper is linguistically more original.[1] The same picture results when one compares the Pauline form of the eucharistic words with the Lukan: the Pauline has been more strongly graecized on the one hand by the introduction of the personal pronoun and by placing it twice before the noun, and on the other hand by the addition of the copula ἐστίν (I Cor. 11.25, different in Luke 22.20).[2]

The account of Paul presents therefore linguistically a transformation of the old semitizing tradition with respect to the understanding of the readers who speak Greek—or more correctly, congregations, for in Paul already we are dealing with a set liturgical formulation.[3]

We stand therefore before the following result: of all forms of the account of the Lord's Supper that of Mark shows by far the strongest Semitic speech colouring; the Lukan form has already been more assimilated to Greek style; in Paul—although his account is the oldest from a literary perspective—the graecizing has advanced the farthest. This result is of far-reaching significance for the question of the age of the tradition of the eucharistic words of Jesus.

THE AGE OF THE TRADITION

We establish summarily:

1. The Markan tradition and the Pauline/Lukan tradition are independent of each other and do not go back to the same Greek source: the variations are too great for such a conclusion. On the other hand, we have seen[4] that in their main features both forms are essentially the same.[5] They go back therefore to a *common eucharistic tradition lying behind both forms of the text*; we have before us 'two versions

---

[1] From the linguistic point of view the thesis of G. Loeschcke, 'Zur Frage nach der Einsetzung und Herkunft der Eucharistie', *ZWTh* 54 (1912), 197, is already shattered. He writes: 'The account of Mark is welded together out of the old synoptic text preserved by Luke [22.15–18 is meant] and the (Pauline) words of institution customary in the cultic practice of the Pauline congregations.'

[2] H. Schürmann, 'Lk 22, 19b–20 als ursprüngliche Textüberlieferung [I]', *Biblica* 32 (1951), 383.

[3] See above, pp. 101–4.

[4] See above, pp. 164–73.

[5] Lietzmann, *Mass and Lord's Supper*, 185: 'As a result of our investigations we may affirm that Paul is familiar with the same tradition of the Last Supper of Jesus as that followed by Mark.' Dibelius, *From Tradition to Gospel*, 206, 211; Finegan, *Überlieferung*, 66f., and others.

of the same tradition, independent of each other'.[1] This *primitive tradition*, as the linguistic study of Mark shows,[2] was formulated in *Aramaic or Hebrew*.

2. In *Paul*[3] we have a transformation and development of the oldest tradition, and this in both linguistic (pp. 185f.) and material aspects which, among other things, had Greek-speaking congregations in mind.

In this process of transformation, whose result is the Pauline formulation, there are different, partially overlapping, motives at work, which may be briefly summarized: 1. *In liturgical usage* the tendency soon appeared to harmonize the words over the bread and wine; 'which is for you' moved to the bread and the command to repeat the rite is cited twice. The celebration *sub una* assisted in the reinforcing of the word over the bread already mentioned and in the restriction of the second command to repeat the rite ('as often as you drink') (see p. 52 n. 3). In the change from 'many' to 'you' (p. 172) is reflected the use of the words of interpretation as *a formula of distribution*. 2. *A tendency toward clarification* may be recognized: the semitisms εὐλογήσας (p. 175) and πολλῶν (pp. 179ff.) could be misunderstood by non-Jews and were replaced. The second 'this' was clarified by 'cup', 'covenant' by 'new'. 3. This last-mentioned addition, a reference to Jer. 31.31–34, shows the emerging *theological reflection*. 4. Finally, the complicated construction which the word over the cup has in Paul may be traced to an *apologetic motif* (p. 170).

These changes cannot be attributed to Paul himself; his account of the Lord's Supper is certainly not yet completely hard and fast,[4] but it is 'clearly traditional material long since rounded off'.[5] That

---

[1] Lietzmann, *op. cit.*, 178; Goossens, *Les Origines*, 345–52.

[2] See above, pp. 173–84.

[3] Loisy, 'Les origines' in *Loisy-Festschrift*, 83f., has—with reservations—expressed and attempted to prove the hypothesis that the account of the Lord's Supper in I Cor., together with its context, was interpolated about the time of the Didache (p. 85). His reasons are surprisingly slight. On the one hand, Loisy doubted that so soon after the departure of the Apostle such an 'unheard-of disorder' could develop at the celebrations of the Lord's Supper in Corinth as is described in I Cor. 11.17–34 (p. 84). On the other hand, he doubted that Paul and the Christianity of his time could have already around 55 or 56 possessed a 'redemption gnosis' (*Erlösungsgnosis*), such as the eucharistic account of I Cor. 11.23–25 presupposes (p. 85). Loisy is sufficiently consistent to confess that if one shares the second doubt, the other passages in the Pauline corpus which contain this 'redemption gnosis' must also be explained as interpolations. How indeed the rise of Christianity is to be thought of and explained if one strikes out the cross from its oldest kerygma remains Loisy's secret.

[4] See above, p. 104.

[5] Otto, *Kingdom of God and Son of Man*, 326.

follows with certainty from the un-Pauline usages in I Cor. 11.23–25[1]
and from the wide agreement of the Pauline formula with the Lukan
form (which from a literary standpoint is independent of Paul).[2]

3. The Pauline account of the Lord's Supper, the oldest written
form of a pronouncement of Jesus himself, was probably written in
the spring of 54.[3] When Paul said that he has transmitted orally the
words of the account to the Corinthians (I Cor. 11.23, 'what I also
delivered to you'), this brings us back to the autumn of 49, i.e. the
beginning of the missionary work in Corinth. The further statement
of the Apostle that the report was transmitted to him (11.23, 'for I
received from the Lord') points back still farther.[4] When did Paul
himself receive the eucharistic tradition? At his conversion? That is
quite probable! If one pays heed to the *formulation*, however, one will
have to answer: the wording given in I Cor. 11.23–25 is later.
That the tradition attested by Paul was formed in hellenistic circles,[5]
and that there are contacts of the Pauline form with the Lukan[6]
and the Johannine,[7] suggests that Paul in I Cor. 11.23–25 offers
that form of the eucharistic words which was customary *in the
Antioch congregation*.[8] This conclusion is confirmed by a further
observation: The Johannine form is related to that of Ignatius of
Antioch.[9] Since Paul moved to Antioch at the latest *in the middle of
the fourth decade* (Acts 11.26), his form of the eucharistic words must
be at least that old.

4. Luke, however, is at two points—the one linguistic (see p. 185
c β) and the other material (omission of the second command to
repeat the rite)—more original than Paul; he goes back therefore to a
pre-Pauline stage of the Pauline form of the tradition. Mark leads us
still farther back, since he has preserved at any rate with regard
to language a considerably older form of the tradition than Paul and
also than Luke. Of all the accounts of the Lord's Supper transmitted
to us, therefore, Mark with his numerous semitisms stands linguistic-

---

[1] See above, p. 104.
[2] See above, p. 156.
[3] On the date, see above, p. 138 n. 1.
[4] See above, p. 101.
[5] See above, p. 186.
[6] See above, pp. 152f.
[7] John and Paul agree in having the ὑπέρ-phrase with the bread, and both omit
the participle.
[8] See above, p. 156. Cf. Schlatter, *Lukas*, 421; Otto, *Kingdom of God and Son of
Man*, 326; Héring, *Le Royaume de Dieu et sa venue*[2], 227.
[9] See below, p. 199.

ally nearest to the original tradition. These observations are of great importance for dating the tradition. We have seen that the Pauline formulation is the result of an arrangement and transformation of the eucharistic tradition effected *in the years before* AD *45* on hellenistic soil. Out of this process of transformation, which took place at the beginning of the fourth decade, the Lukan text arose. Behind it lies the Semitic tradition which Mark most truly reflects linguistically. It belongs therefore to *the first decade after the death of Jesus*.

THE OLDEST ATTAINABLE FORM OF THE TRADITION

(a) *The plurality of variations*

From the fact that the *Markan tradition* is linguistically the most ancient one could be tempted to draw the conclusion that Mark has preserved for us intact the original form of the tradition. But that would be in this form an improper conclusion. For, on the one hand, Mark has also paid tribute to the development (e.g., in the drawing together of the words over the bread and the wine), and, on the other, all other forms (with the exception of the Matthaean account which is dependent upon Mark) preserve elements which are older than Mark. For Paul we need mention only the phrase 'after supper', for Luke the doubling of the so-called eschatological prospect and the omission of the copula with the word over the wine, and for John the translation-variant 'flesh'.[1]

H. Schürmann finds the oldest text of the words of interpretation *in Luke* rather than Mark. His minute and careful investigation, *Der Einsetzungsbericht Lk 22, 19–20* (NTA 20.4), Münster, 1955, which dedicates no less than 153 pages to these two verses, comes to the following result: If one disregards two corrections which presumably go back to Luke himself (he places λέγων in 22.19a for καὶ εἶπεν and adds in 20b τὸ ὑπὲρ ὑμῶν ἐκχυννόμενον) and a further correction which Luke already found (transposition of ὡσαύτως in 20), then one has in Luke 22.19–20 the 'primitive account' ('Urbericht', p. 131), which already lay before Paul (p. 132). Concerning this it may be said that it is to Schürmann's credit that he has elevated to a deserved place the Long Text of Luke, which earlier had been estimated to be of little value. It is certain that the current text of Luke with its twofold ὑπέρ-phrase is a late form; that does not exclude the possibility that one

[1] See below, p. 199.

may find linguistically in its core a form which is prior to the Pauline account.[1] But none the less the Lukan form is, on the one hand, assimilated to a considerably stronger degree to the Greek idiom than Mark. That is most clearly shown to us by a comparison of Luke 22.18 with Mark 14.25;[2] the same is true, as we have seen on p. 185, for the setting and words of interpretation. Schürmann in part wrongly contested this point (his attempt to reclaim for the original account ὑμῶν as opposed to πολλῶν and εὐχαριστήσας as opposed to εὐλογήσας appears to me in no way successful), and in part did not see it (non-semitic word order). The graecisms of the Lukan form are to a great degree pre-Lukan, even pre-Pauline, and can therefore only to a small degree be traced back to Luke himself.[3] It is to be added that the secondary transformations noted on p. 187 (excluding the second command to repeat the rite) reappear in Luke. Quite apart from all that, one should perhaps be more cautious with reference to the hope that we are in a position to reconstruct an 'original account' word for word. The tradition is too complex for that. I am happy to be able to add that H. Schürmann has informed me that he would today no longer use the expression 'primitive account' for the pre-Lukan form of the Lukan text presupposed by him.[4]

We will do well in the quest for the primitive form of the eucharistic words to proceed from the fact that they come to us *in three lines of tradition* which substantially agree, but which differ characteristically in the formulation: a Markan, a Pauline-Lukan and a Johannine. When we further recall that two semitizing translation-variants (οὐ μὴ προσθῶ πεῖν/οὐ μὴ προσθῶμεν πιεῖν) appear for the phrase οὐκέτι οὐ μὴ πίω in Mark 14.25, both of which stem most probably from the oral tradition,[5] then we must reckon with the fact *that already in the Semitic stage of tradition the number of current variations of the eucharistic words was greater than our texts allow us to discern*. In the translation into Greek which followed in different places and at a time when the formulation was still not liturgically fixed, there arose then further deviations in the oral tradition. Its primitive form lies *behind* the division of the tradition into these variations. We cannot entertain

---

[1] See above, p. 156.
[2] See above, pp. 162f.
[3] See above, p. 185.
[4] Letter of March 25, 1959.
[5] See above, p. 182 no. 19.

the hope that we can succeed in reconstructing its wording in detail. We must rather be content with the belief that Mark linguistically stands nearest to it. From this, however, we can, on the basis of the aforementioned results, venture several pronouncements about the oldest tradition lying behind the division. We distinguish thereby again between the setting and the eucharistic words themselves.

(b) Liturgy or historical account?

As to the *setting*, the agreement of all accounts (Mark/Matthew, Paul, Luke) in the *word over the bread* is so extensive—the reader is requested to be convinced of this by looking at the table on p. 111 —that we must conclude that we have here before us an exceedingly ancient tradition. It is especially impressive that all four accounts feature by feature show small deviations, but agree in *one* place: all four have the strongly stressed ἔκλασεν ('he broke') as a finite verb. As to the introduction of the *word over the cup*, we must ascribe to the phrase 'after supper' a very great age, because it contradicts the early drawing together of the bread and the wine in the rite[1] and because it betrays nothing of the tendency to assimilate the framing of the word over the wine to that over the bread; furthermore, the variant formulation μετὰ τὸ ἐμπλησθῆναι (Did. 10.1) speaks for the great antiquity of the phrase μετὰ τὸ δειπνῆσαι. Nevertheless, the Markan introduction to the word over the cup is also quite old as, together with the semitisms[2] and the omission of the article before ποτήριον,[3] the inversion καὶ ἔπιον . . . καὶ εἶπεν (in the real order of events the word of interpretation belongs *before* the drinking by the disciples) shows. If we turn finally to the setting of the so-called eschatological prospect, it becomes evident that Mark 14.25 is connected 'unorganically' to v. 24;[4] the verse even appears as a 'torso',[5] a 'rudiment'.[6] Especially if we are dealing with a solemn avowal of abstinence,[7] we can scarcely dispense with an introduction like that in Luke 22.17. It may have fallen out by the addition of Mark 14.25

---

[1] See above, pp. 115–22.
[2] See above, pp. 177f.
[3] It is otherwise in I Cor. 11.25 and Luke 22.20 due to the influence of liturgical language (cf. p. 113).
[4] G. Loeschcke, 'Zur Frage nach der Einsetzung und Herkunft der Eucharistie', ZWTh 54 (1912), 197. F.-J. Leenhardt, *Le sacrement*, 41: 'lack of cohesion'.
[5] W. Haupt, *Worte Jesu und Gemeindeüberlieferung*, Leipzig, 1913, 135.
[6] Schürmann, *Paschamahlbericht*, 42.
[7] See below, pp. 207–18.

(which as Paul and Luke show, did not belong to the old liturgical formula) to the words of interpretation out of consideration for Mark 14.23. It may therefore be said that the framing words of Luke 22.15a, 17a (so-called eschatological prospect), Mark 14.22a (word over the bread) and I Cor. 11.25a (word over the wine) stand materially nearest to the oldest form of the setting.

We have still not mentioned, however, the most important observation on the setting. It follows from the comparative investigation of the *general introduction to the whole pericope*. While Paul offers a sonorous introduction ('the Lord Jesus on the night when he was betrayed'), we find in Luke only a scanty καί ('and'), which is expanded in Mark/Matthew by a redactional[1] genitive absolute (ἐσθιόντων αὐτῶν, 'as they were eating'), and which in Matthew is replaced, moreover, by δέ. We must remember here what was said earlier. The Pauline form, as we have seen, is a liturgical stylizing which employs a confessional formula;[2] the omission of the personal pronoun after ὁ κύριος points to extra-Palestinian territory.[3] Καί as the beginning of a pericope, on the contrary, is to be regarded as a certain indication of the semitic historical report;[4] its antiquity is confirmed by the fact that it is attested by two strands of tradition independent of each other, viz. the Markan-Matthaean (Mark 14.22), as well as the Pauline-Lukan (Luke 22.19). This introductory καί is pre-liturgical and leads us, however insignificant it may seem, to a far-reaching judgment: *at the beginning there stands not liturgy, but historical account.*

The omission of the subject—again in both strands of the tradition (Mark 14.22; Luke 22.19)—leads to the same judgment. For it is very improbable that the name of Jesus belonged originally to the liturgical formula, and that it should have dropped out when this was used in the Passion narrative. For the secondary addition of the subject in Paul ('the Lord Jesus') as in Matthew ('Jesus') shows that the tendency went not in the direction of the deletion of the subject, but of supplying it. On the contrary, it is typical for the Semitic narrative style that it is economical with the repetition of the name which forms the subject, often to the point of giving rise to mis-

[1] See above, p. 113.
[2] See above, p. 112.
[3] Dalman, *Words*, 326: 'To speak of "the Lord" with no suffix is contrary to Palestinian usage.'
[4] See above, p. 174.

understanding. Thus also the omission of the subject points back to a very old pre-liturgical narrative tradition.

(c) Old additions to the words of interpretation?

As to *the words of Jesus themselves,* the substantial agreement of the different accounts in the avowal of abstinence by Jesus, as well as in his words of interpretation, is so extensive[1] that we must conclude that the common substance of the accounts leads us into the closest approximation to the original form. In only two places, if one surveys the common substance of the tradition (pp. 164, 169), is the question raised as to whether in the earliest time an older wording has been expanded, namely, in the thought of the covenant and in the statement about substitution. The comparison of the text (pp. 164–73) showed with certainty that *after* the disruption of the tradition additions were made. Here, however, we are dealing with two pronouncements, both of which are given in all available texts, and which, therefore, if they are expansions, must have been added *before* the disruption of the tradition into strands, therefore in the oldest time.

1. The question as to whether an addition may have been made is raised first of all by the phrase 'my blood of the covenant' (Mark 14.24). This phrase is very difficult in a literal translation into Hebrew and Palestinian Aramaic: a noun with a pronominal suffix can generally tolerate no genitive after itself.[2] How unusual the phrase sounds for Semitic idiom is observed in the Syriac versions. Mark 14.24 syr[sin] and Matt. 26.28 syr[palA] are the only texts before the Peshitta which venture a literal rendering. All others solve the

---

[1] See especially above, p. 173.
[2] Cf. Wellhausen, *Evangelium Marci,* 114; Dalman, *Jesus-Jeshua,* 160f. Not comparable to Mark 14.24 is the completely different genitive after a proleptic pronominal suffix (e.g. Mark 6.22, τῆς θυγατρὸς αὐτῆς τῆς Ἡρῳδιάδος; Aramaism). A formal analogy to Mark 14.24 is offered in Gen. 9.5 LXX: τὸ ὑμέτερον αἷμα τῶν ψυχῶν ὑμῶν, but in the Hebrew we read *et-dimekem lenaphšotekem,* in which the preposition *le* has an epexegetical function and introduces a qualification of the suffix ('your *own* blood'). On 1QS 10.4, *ḥsdyw 'wlm,* no great weight can be laid, because *'wlm* as a substantive is very trite and the manuscript at this place is very faulty. Best for comparison (with H. F. D. Sparks in R. H. Fuller, *The Mission and Achievement of Jesus* [SBT 12], London, 1954, 69) is Dan. 2.34 (Aramaic), where after the suffix a genitive (*di*) follows as a designation of material. For the Syriac, J. A. Emerton ('The Aramaic Underlying τὸ αἷμά μου τῆς διαθήκης in Mk. XIV.24', *JTS* 6 [1955], 238–40) has brought together several examples for the noun with the pronominal suffix and the following genitive, especially from the Syriac version of the Psalms. But even in Syriac the construction is hardly 'a perfectly natural one' (p. 239), otherwise the rendering of τὸ αἷμά μου τῆς διαθήκης would have offered no such difficulties for the older Syriac versions.

problem by taking—quite artificially—the τῆς διαθήκης as apposition:
'This is my blood, the new covenant'[1] or by changing the personal
pronoun of the first person into that of the third person: 'This is his
(*sc.* covenant) blood, that of the new covenant.'[2] Therefore the
expression 'my blood of the covenant' in its present form does not
sound Palestinian. Thus the question is raised whether 'of the
covenant' is not an old theological interpretation,[3] which (with the
use of Ex. 24.8 and Jer. 31.31–34) designates Jesus' expiatory death
as a covenant sacrifice for the inauguration of the final salvation. In
truth, however, this linguistic objection to the use of the phrase 'my
blood of the covenant' rests upon a wrong inference which I (in view
of the second edition of this book [ET, p. 134. Transl.]) herewith
retract completely. The error lies in the implied presupposition that
the sequence of words in Greek must have been also that of the
Semitic original. To be sure, one can appeal for this presupposition
to the Syriac translators, but the fact that these men felt slavishly
bound to the order of words out of respect for the Greek text lying
before them does not give us the right to repeat their error. In truth
the Semitic requires another word order than the Greek,[4] for in
Hebrew as well as in Aramaic, a construct state combination tolerates
the suffix only at the end (therefore not with the governing noun but
with the governed noun); it is related then, however, to the whole
expression (test case: Heb. 5.7, αἱ ἡμέραι τῆς σαρκὸς αὐτοῦ does not mean
'the days of his flesh', but rather 'his flesh days'; analogously in 1.2,
ἐπ᾽ ἐσχάτου τῶν ἡμερῶν τούτων does not mean 'at the end of these days',
thus of the present aeon, but 'in this end-time,' thus at the beginning

---

[1] Tat[aphr arab ned], cf. Tat[pers] (see above p. 141), likewise Matt. 26.28 syr[sin pal]
([cur] *deest*); Luke 22.17 syr[sin]; Syriac Anaphora of the Twelve Apostles (cf. Merx,
Matthaeus, 385). This form of the text has completely taken root in Syria and can
therefore by no means be explained as a scribal oversight (omission of *d* before
dytk̲ owing to haplography, as Emerton, *op. cit.*, 239f.). It should be noted that the
difficulty of rendering τὸ αἷμά μου τῆς διαθήκης was felt not only in Eastern Syriac,
but also in Western (Matt. 26.28 syr[pal]).

[2] Matt. 26.28 syr[palc].

[3] W. Wrede, 'Τὸ αἷμά μου τῆς διαθήκης', *ZNW* 1 (1900), 69–74; G. Hollmann,
Die Bedeutung des Todes Jesu, Tübingen–Leipzig, 1901, 145–8; W. Heitmüller,
'Abendmahl I. Im Neuen Testament', *RGG*[1] I (1909), cols. 31f.; Dalman, *Jesus-
Jeshua*, 161 ('possible'); Clemen, *Religionsgeschichtliche Erklärung*, 177f.; Völker,
Mysterium und Agape, 27, 39–50; H. Windisch, review of J. Jeremias, *Die Abendmahls-
worte Jesu*[1], *Deutsche Literaturzeitung* 6 (1935), cols. 979f.; R. Bultmann, 'Die Frage
nach der Echtheit von Mt. 16, 17–19', *ThBl* 20 (1941), col. 272.

[4] I thank my former assistant Reinhard Deichgräber for this reference, which
prompted me to renewed scrutiny of the problem.

of the new aeon). Correspondingly, we can presuppose as the Hebrew original of 'my blood of the covenant' the expression *dam beriti*, Aramaic *adam ḳeyami* ('my covenant blood'), which in Greek could be rendered regularly and correctly only with the transposition of the personal pronoun. Then, however, the phrase 'my blood of the covenant' gives no pretext for linguistic objections to its originality. As to its contents, the possibility that Jesus spoke of the covenant at the Last Supper cannot be disputed. The thought of the covenant, to be sure, played no part in the old passover liturgy, yet there is found outside of it occasionally the connection of passover and covenant.[1] It is of greater weight that we learn through the Essene writings, especially the Damascus Document, how vital the promise of the new covenant (Jer. 31.31–34) was in the days of Jesus.[2] It is thereby important that in the Essene texts the community which has entered into the new covenant is described under the images of the building, of the planting, of the Temple and of the flock. Since Jesus speaks of the community of the time of salvation under the same images, the thought of the new covenant was not far from his thoughts, even when it is not otherwise attested expressly in the tradition of his words.[3]

2. One can similarly ask whether the ὑπέρ-phrase is an interpretative element.[4] For this view appeal certainly cannot be made to Justin,[5] in whose writings the words of interpretation have the short form: 'This is my body' and 'This is my blood'.[6] Justin is too late for that and, furthermore, he quotes in an abbreviated form.[7] But the vacillating position of the ὑπέρ-phrase, which Paul and John offer with the bread, Mark and Matthew with the cup, and Luke with the bread and the cup, calls forth doubt as to its originality. Words which move around are suspect; in most cases we are dealing

---

[1] See below, p. 225 n. 5.
[2] Cf. further Bar. 2.35; Jub. 1.17f., 23–25. That Jer. 31.31–34 is only relatively seldom cited in the rabbinic literature (Billerbeck I, 243; III, 89f., 704, 848; IV, 832, 850 [twice], 918) and with the exception of a late passage (Pesiḳ. 12, ed. S. Buber, Lyck, 1868, 107a par. Tanḥuma Ex. *Ytrw*, ed. S. Buber, Wilna, 1885, 38b) always so that the thought of the new covenant is avoided, is to be explained, as is evident from Midr. S. of S. on 1.14, as due to polemic against Christianity (Billerbeck II, 279, esp. 280 n. 1).
[3] Luke 22.29 (διατίθεμαι) is a reminiscence of διαθήκη.
[4] R. Bultmann, 'Die Frage nach der Echtheit von Mt. 16, 17–19', *ThBl* 20 (1941), col. 272; E. Schweizer, 'Abendmahl I. Im NT, 3', *RGG*[3] I (1957), cols. 13f.
[5] Bultmann, *Theology of the N.T.* I, 146.
[6] *Apol.* I 66.3.
[7] See above, p. 135. So already Wrede, *op. cit.*, 70.

in them with marginal glosses which then settle at different places in the text. Nevertheless, in the ὑπέρ-phrase the derivation from a marginal gloss is impossible because the different strands of tradition cannot be traced to one literary archetype. Besides, we saw on pp. 166ff. that several different considerations support the presupposition that it belonged originally to the cup. In any case, linguistic objections to the ὑπέρ-phrase cannot be permitted; on the contrary, its outspoken Semitic character (pp. 178–82) speaks for its great age.

One may reckon (to be sure, without linguistic pretext) with the possibility of an individual addition already in the earliest time; but one may hardly assume essential blurring of the substance of the tradition, in no case free invention. For the primitive Semitic tradition, as we established on pp. 188f., is traceable back into the first decade after the death of Jesus with the assistance of exact philological observation. That in this early time one should have freely created the ritual of the Lord's Supper and should have freely fabricated the account of the Lord's Supper as an aetiological cult legend for the rite is completely improbable.

THE ORIGINAL LANGUAGE

(a) Aramaic or Hebrew?

Jesus' words in the gospels permit us even in their Greek dress to recognize with certainty that Jesus spoke Aramaic. For example, the Lord's Prayer goes back to an Aramaic original, because sin is designated as 'debt' (ḥoba, ὀφείλημα) only in Aramaic, not in Hebrew. It was therefore natural that G. Dalman, in his attempt to translate the eucharistic words of Jesus back into their original language, fell back on Palestinian Aramaic,[1] for whose investigation he had performed the basic pioneer work through his excellent grammar.[2] Yet he was sufficiently cautious to leave open the possibility that Jesus spoke the benediction over the bread and wine and the attached words of interpretation in Hebrew.[3] M. Black[4] has considered this

---

[1] In *Jesus-Jeshua* Dalman gives the retranslations of the following parts of the eucharistic tradition: Luke 22.15, p. 126; 22.16, p. 129; 22.17, p. 158; 22.18, p. 182; Mark 14.22 par., pp. 140f., 145; 14.24 par., pp. 159, 160f., 171; 14.25 par., p. 181; I Cor. 11.24b, 25b (Luke 22.19b), p. 177.

[2] G. Dalman, *Grammatik des jüdisch-palästinischen Aramäisch*[2], Leipzig, 1905 (reprint Darmstadt, 1960).

[3] Dalman, *Jesus-Jeshua*, 163.

[4] *Aramaic Approach*[2], 268f.

possibility anew. It will indeed have to be earnestly examined, as the Essene texts have shown us how much Hebrew was in use as a *lingua sacra*.

The following considerations argue for a *Hebrew* basis of the eucharistic words: (1) the *figura etymologica*, ἐπιθυμίᾳ ἐπεθύμησα, 'with desire I have desired', in Luke 22.15, which imitates the Hebrew infinitive absolute;[1] (2) the verb πληροῦσθαι in Luke 22.16;[2] (3) perhaps also πολλοί in Mark 14.24.[3] Furthermore, one could cite the liturgical formula 'the fruit of the vine' (Mark 14.25; Luke 22.18), probably correctly, since it is transmitted only in Hebrew (see p. 183); nevertheless, the possibility that the grace over the wine, from which the formula descends, may have also been spoken in Aramaic is not to be eliminated with certainty. Finally, also, *amen* (Mark 14.25) is Hebrew (Aramaic would be *min ḳušṭa* or *beḳušṭa*); nevertheless, this familiar word is used so frequently by Jesus that no conclusion can be drawn from it as to the language in which Jesus spoke the eucharistic words.

On the other hand, the reading οὐ μὴ προσθῶμεν πιεῖν (Mark 14.25 Θ) goes back unequivocally to an *Aramaic* original; for the use of the first person plural for 'I' corresponds not only to the customary Galilean-Aramaic idiom, but is even demanded by it.[4] To be sure the reading is only attested by Θ. If, however, as was argued on pp. 182f.,

[1] Dalman, *Words*, 34: 'The Hebrew mode of emphasizing the finite verb by adding its infinitive or cognate substantive . . . is in the Palestinian Aramaic of the Jews . . . apart from the Targums . . . quite unknown.' Cf. Black, *Aramaic Approach*[2], 269.

[2] In Jewish literature it is nowhere said of the passover that it 'is fulfilled', no more than of the Kingdom of God, but it can be said of a promise. Probably 'promise' must be supplied as the subject of the passive πληροῦσθαι in Luke 22.16: 'until (the promise) be fulfilled in the Kingdom of God'. The passover (more exactly: the release from Egyptian slavery which ensued at passover) is therefore regarded as a promise which will be fulfilled (cf. Dalman, *Jesus-Jeshua*, 130). For the fulfilment of the Word of Yahweh the Old Testament says *mille*, 'to replenish;' the Aramaic, on the contrary, uses a completely different form, *itḳayyam*, 'to be put on the feet, to be confirmed'. Πληρωθῇ points to a Hebrew original; from an Aramaic original something like σταθῇ would be expected.

[3] Black, *Aramaic Approach*[2], 269: 'The allusion [to Isa. 53.11f.] would have been much more impressive, however, in Hebrew, while the inclusive meaning of *rabbim* would then be in no doubt.' Dalman was led to the possibility that Jesus could have spoken the eucharistic words in Hebrew by the observation that the Aramaic word for 'covenant' (*ḳeyam*) is to be found only in the Targums. Outside the Targums we find only the Hebrew *berit* for 'covenant' (*Jesus-Jeshua*, 163). It follows from this only that *ḳeyam* had not penetrated into everyday speech. Jesus could know the Aramaic word from the synagogue service.

[4] Dalman, *Jesus-Jeshua*, 127.

it stems from the oral tradition of the eucharistic words (and all probability speaks for that), then it has the full weight of an independent tradition.

So the quest for the original language of the eucharistic words will have to remain open and we must be content with the conclusion that they have been transmitted in the early period in Hebrew as well as Aramaic. However, we must reckon quite seriously with the possibility that Jesus spoke the solemn avowal of abstinence, the table prayers, and the words of interpretation in the Hebrew *lingua sacra*.

(b) The Semitic equivalent of σῶμα ('body')

The translation of the eucharistic words back into Hebrew or Aramaic offers no difficulties[1] if one disregards several difficulties already discussed (παθεῖν, Luke 22.15, see p. 162; τὸ ὑπὲρ ὑμῶν, I Cor. 11.24, see p. 167; τὸ αἷμά μου τῆς διαθήκης, Mark 14.24, see pp. 193ff.; καινόν, Mark 14.25, p. 184). The only disputed question is that of the Semitic equivalent to σῶμα. There are many statements on this question in the modern investigations of the eucharistic words, but one does not have the impression in every case that they rest upon independent knowledge of the subject. The question is of great importance, because the answer has far-reaching consequences for the exposition of the words of interpretation.

Most authors join G. Dalman, who, in 1922, proposed *guph* as the equivalent of σῶμα,[2] although already in 1878 A. Wünsche had rejected this rendering as impossible.[3] In the Old Testament this word designates a corpse; in post-biblical Hebrew and Aramaic, however, it generally (under hellenistic influence) designates the (living or dead) body in contrast to the soul; but the dichotomous antithesis body-soul is certainly not present in the word of Jesus. When Dalman appealed for the correctness of his thesis to the texts which speak of *gupho šel pesah*,[4] and added: 'It was evidently usual to differentiate between the lamb as the "body" of the passover, and the feast. Our Lord might have been influenced by this to point to his body at the distribution of the bread, while not bringing it into direct

---

[1] Retranslation into Hebrew: J. Salkinson–C. D. Ginsburg, *Habberit haḥadašah²*, Vienna, 1886, *ad loc.*; F. Delitzsch, *Siphre habberit haḥadašah¹⁴*, Berlin, 1923, *ad loc.* Retranslation into Aramaic: Dalman, *Jesus-Jeshua, passim* (see above, p. 196 n. 1).

[2] Dalman, *Jesus-Jeshua*, 141f.

[3] Wünsche, *Neue Beiträge zur Erläuterung der Evangelien aus Talmud und Midrasch*, 331f.

[4] Pes. 10.3; Tos. Pes. 10.9 (173.7).

conjunction with the passover lamb'[1]—then this highly respected scholar unfortunately cannot completely be spared the reproach that 'Dalman has abused some of these texts'.[2] For it stands linguistically certain beyond any doubt that *gupho šel pesaḥ* signifies not the 'body of the passover lamb', but 'the passover lamb itself' (in distinction from the other food of the passover meal) and nothing else.[3] By this the possibility of seeing in σῶμα a rendering of *guph* is completely eliminated.

Only the Hebrew *basar* and Aramaic *bisra* really come into question as equivalents of σῶμα, as already long ago (although actually on insufficient grounds) A. Wünsche[4] and (simultaneously with me in the second edition of the present work) J. Bonsirven[5] have seen. Two considerations argue for this claim: 1. On pp. 107f. we have seen that in John 6.51c we have before us the Johannine form of Jesus' word of interpretation over the bread. Once more we place alongside each other John 6.51c and I Cor. 11.24 (Luke 22.19):

John 6.51c	*I Cor. 11.24 (Luke 22.19)*
ὁ ἄρτος δὲ ὃν ἐγὼ δώσω the bread which I shall give	τοῦτό (= this bread) This
ἡ σάρξ μού ἐστιν is my flesh	μού ἐστιν τὸ σῶμα is my body
ὑπὲρ τῆς τοῦ κόσμου ζωῆς for the life of the world	τὸ ὑπὲρ ὑμῶν (Luke + διδόμενον) which (is) for you (Luke + given)

The comparison of the two forms shows that there is, besides the tradition which speaks of 'body' and 'blood' (Paul, Mark, Matthew, Luke) another one which speaks of 'flesh' and 'blood' (John, Ignatius,[6] Justin[7]). In all probability we have before us a translation variant which points back to Hebrew *basar*, or Aramaic *bisra*; 'flesh' is the literal, 'body' the idiomatic Greek translation. 2. A quite

---

[1] *Jesus-Jeshua*, 143.
[2] J. Bonsirven, 'Hoc est corpus meum. Recherches sur l'original araméen', *Biblica* 29 (1948), 217 n. 1.
[3] So Dalman himself, *Jesus-Jeshua*, 143; Wünsche, *op. cit.*, 330 n.*; Strack, P^esaḥim, 32f.; Bonsirven, *op. cit.*, 215 n.1; 217 n.1; Billerbeck IV, 63.
[4] Wünsche, *op. cit.*, 332.
[5] Bonsirven, *op. cit.*, 205–19.
[6] Ignatius, *Smyrn.* 7.1; *Rom.* 7.3; *Philad.* 4.1; *Trall.* 8.1.
[7] *Apol.* I 66.2. Justin also knows the 'body'-form (66.3).

different consideration leads to the same result. Paul already sees in body-blood a pair of terms (I Cor. 10.16; 11.27); the coupling of the two words with the pair of terms 'bread-wine', that is, with the grace before and after the meal, is evidence that they formed such a pair from the beginning. It is true that the two words of interpretation were separated by the meal itself, and through this interval of time each one of them attains a significance of its own. In this connection, however, we must not overlook the close relationship between these words. This relationship is given to them by the fact that they summarize Jesus' passover haggadah, which preceded both of them and which itself presents an overall unity. But then we must again reject *guph* as an equivalent of 'body', because its complement is *nowhere* 'blood'.[1] If we ask what pair of terms is formed with 'blood', then we meet the following connections: *deber-dam*, 'plague and blood',[2] *mayim-dam*, 'water and blood',[3] *ḥeleb-dam*, 'fat and blood',[4] *dam-abarim*, 'blood and sacrifice',[5] and—found extremely frequently—*baśar-dam*, 'flesh and blood'.[6] For Jesus' words of interpretation only the last-named pair comes into question. It is also recorded in Aramaic in isolated examples: *biśra udema*.[7] There corresponds to it in Greek σάρξ-αἷμα,[8] σῶμα-αἷμα[9] and κρέας-αἷμα.[10]

The linguistic possibility that *baśar*, or *biśra*, lies at the base of the 'body' of Jesus' words of interpretation is incontestable and is confirmed many times: the LXX renders Hebrew *baśar* mostly with 'flesh' (143 times), but in twenty-three cases with 'body'; indeed, 'body' renders *baśar* predominantly in the LXX, where it does not designate a corpse; Paul can use 'body' directly for 'flesh' (Rom.

---

[1] The pair of terms formed with *guph* are rather: *gupha-naphša* (Lev. R. 18.1 on 15.1; 21.7 on 16.3; 34.3 on 25.35; b. Sanh. 91a; Siphre Deut. 306 on 32.2), or *guph-nešamah* (Mek. Ex. 15.1 [ed. J. H. Weiss, Vienna, 1865, 44b.23f.] and elsewhere) (body and soul), *guph-roš* (Zeb. 16.6) (torso and head), *guph-mamon* (b. Ber. 61b) (body and money).

[2] Ezek. 5.17; 28.23; 38.22 (LXX: θάνατος καὶ αἷμα).

[3] Ex. 4.9 and elsewhere; John 19.34; I John 5.6; Rev. 11.6.

[4] Num. 18.17; II Sam. 1.22; Ezek. 44.7, 15 and elsewhere.

[5] Yoma 3.5.

[6] Ezek. 39.17. For examples from the Mishna, cf. below, pp. 221 n. 10, 222 n. 1.

[7] b. Tam. 32b; Targ. Esther II 1.4 (Dalman's remark, *Jesus-Jeshua*, 142 n. 1: 'but never in Aramaic', is incorrect).

[8] See below, p. 222 n. 3. Further: LXX Lev. 17.11–14; Ezek. 44.7 AB (σάρκας καὶ αἷμα); John 6.53–56 and elsewhere.

[9] For examples, see below, p. 222 n. 4; further: LXX Job 6.4.

[10] Very often in the LXX; cf. Philo, *Leg. ad Gaium* 356; *De spec. leg.* 1.268: κρέας (sing. or pl.)–αἷμα.

8.13); 'body' and 'flesh' appear as variations of the tradition:[1] in Hebr. 13.11 syr^{pesh} renders σῶμα with biśra.

The freer translation ('body') was perhaps occasioned out of regard for Gentile Christians who must have rejected the word 'flesh', which in Greek has a completely different ring from baśar-biśra in a Semitic language;[2] 'body' avoids the pejorative connotation of 'flesh'.[3] Moreover, the similar sounds of the endings of σῶμα ('body') and αἷμα ('blood'),[4] as well as the parallelism of the twofold τοῦτο (σάρξ would have demanded αὕτη) have contributed to the favouring of 'body'.

Since the Greek copula ἐστίν has no equivalent in Hebrew and Aramaic,[5] and accordingly is lacking in Luke 22.20 (cf. Heb. 9.20), the words of interpretation (if what has just been presented is conclusive) read, according to Mark, in Hebrew zeh beśari and zeh dami, and in Aramaic den[6] biśri and den[6] idmi.

INDICATIONS OF THE ipsissima vox

It is astonishing that in the few lines which the eucharistic words occupy we come upon not less than three peculiarities which present the most distinctive characteristics of Jesus' manner of speaking.[7]

1. Ἀμὴν λέγω ὑμῖν ('Truly I say to you') for the introduction and strengthening of his own speech (Mark 14.25) is a completely new

---

[1] Gospel of the Hebrews Fr. 22 (E. Klostermann, Apocrypha II [KlT 8]³, Berlin, 1919, 11), compared with Luke 24.39. On this, cf. A. Resch, Agrapha² (TU 15.3–4), Leipzig, 1906, 97f.

[2] J. Bonsirven, 'Hoc est corpus meum. Recherches sur l'original araméen', Biblica 29 (1948), 218.

[3] J. Dupont, ' "Ceci est mon corps", "Ceci est mon sang" ', Nouvelle Revue Théologique 80 (1958), 1030.

[4] W. Michaelis, letter dated July 28, 1949.

[5] Because there was no particular reason to distinguish the distributed bread from other bread. Not until later Aramaic is hu inserted when no emphasis is present (Jer. Targumim, Palestinian Talmud). Thus correctly Dalman, Jesus-Jeshua, 141. When Dalman, nevertheless, in his translation of the words of interpretation into Aramaic rendered ἐστίν with hu, unconscious dogmatic considerations have apparently been at work, cf. quite similarly below, p. 211 n. 2.

[6] Or dena. As the 1Q Genesis Apocryphon found at the Dead Sea shows, in the Palestinian Aramaic around the beginning of our era den and dena are used side by side (E. Y. Kutscher, 'Dating the Language of the Genesis Apocryphon', JBL 76 [1957], 289).

[7] J. Jeremias, 'Kennzeichen der ipsissima vox Jesu', in A. Wikenhauser-Festschrift, 86–93.

idiom of Jesus, which is without parallel in the entire Jewish literature and in the New Testament outside the gospels.[1]

2. $\Pi\lambda\eta\rho\omega\theta\hat{\eta}$ ([until] 'it is fulfilled') (Luke 22.16). The use of the passive for the reverent circumlocution of the activity of God (e.g. Matt. 5.4, $\pi\alpha\rho\alpha\kappa\lambda\eta\theta\eta\sigma\sigma\nu\tau\alpha\iota$, 'God will comfort them'; 5.6, $\chi\sigma\rho\tau\alpha\sigma\theta\eta\sigma\sigma\nu\tau\alpha\iota$, 'God will make them satisfied'; 5.7, $\dot{\epsilon}\lambda\epsilon\eta\theta\eta\sigma\sigma\nu\tau\alpha\iota$, 'God will [on the Last Day] send mercy upon them'; Mark 2.5, $\dot{\alpha}\phi\dot{\epsilon}\epsilon\nu\tau\alpha\iota$, 'God forgive') is met only very seldom in rabbinic literature. Dalman, in 1898, adduced only a single example,[2] to which Billerbeck, in 1922, added 5,[3] and Dalman himself in 1930 added a further example.[4] Even if the material is not exhausted,[5] nevertheless, the rabbinic examples are extremely sparse. The frequency of the passive for the circumlocution of the name of God, which is found in the words of Jesus in all five lines of tradition represented in the gospels (Mark, Sayings tradition, Matthaean special material, Lukan special material and John), is completely without parallel and therefore is to be taken as an indication of his own manner of speaking.

3. The predilection for similitudes, comparisons and parabolic expressions which is presupposed in the words of interpretation is likewise an express peculiarity of Jesus.[6]

These observations confirm the reliability of the statement of Paul, that he received the eucharistic words 'from the Lord' ($\dot{\alpha}\pi\dot{o}$ $\tau\sigma\hat{v}$ $\kappa\nu\rho\dot{\epsilon}ov$) (I Cor. 1..23). If Paul did not construe $\pi\alpha\rho\alpha\lambda\alpha\mu\beta\dot{\alpha}\nu\epsilon\iota\nu$ (= $kibbel$ min, see above, p. 101) with $\pi\alpha\rho\dot{\alpha}$, as elsewhere (Gal. 1.12; I Thess. 2.13; 4.1; II Thess. 3.6), but with $\dot{\alpha}\pi\dot{o}$, this was for a good reason. $\Pi\alpha\rho\dot{\alpha}$ indicates those who hand on the tradition;[7] $\dot{\alpha}\pi\dot{o}$, on the contrary, the originator of the tradition.[8] Paul therefore stressed in I Cor. 11.23

---

[1] The synoptic tradition shows a strong tendency to replace or completely to efface this unusual $\dot{\alpha}\mu\dot{\eta}\nu$, see above p. 163 nn. 1, 6. Also in the parallels Matt. 26.29 ($\delta\dot{\epsilon}$); Luke 22.18 ($\gamma\dot{\alpha}\rho$) it is replaced.

[2] G. Dalman, *Die Worte Jesu* I[1], Leipzig, 1898, 184.

[3] Billerbeck I, 443.

[4] G. Dalman, *Die Worte Jesu* I[2], Leipzig, 1930, 383. [Cf. ET *Words*, 225.] The five targumic examples on p. 382 are not exact parallels in so far as they indeed are passive, but name God ('because by God . . .').

[5] I note further: P. Ab. 2.8a: 'for thus you have been created'; b. Meg. 12b: 'he knocked on the gates of mercy and they were opened to him'; Targ. Isa. 9.5; 53.8; Targ. Hos. 3.1; further the formula $dkyr$ $l\d{t}b$, cf. below, p. 244; the old '$Kaddi\check{s}$ of the service'; LXX Isa. 19.2; Ps. 77(78).60 according to Symmachus; Ps. Sol. 3.11.

[6] From Hillel ($c.$ 20 BC) we possess, e.g., only two comparisons (Lev. R. 34.3 on 25.35), no narrative similitudes, although Hillel is the one pre-Christian scholar from whom $me\check{s}alim$ are transmitted in the rabbinic literature (Billerbeck I, 654).

[7] Gal. 1.12; I Thess. 2.13; II Tim. 1.13; 2.2; 3.14.

[8] Examples in Bauer: A. and G., 87 ($\dot{\alpha}\pi\dot{o}$ V, 4).

with the help of the preposition ἀπό that the eucharistic words cited by him out of the tradition go back to Jesus himself.

If we remember in addition that we have met something corresponding to a pre-liturgical stage of tradition by the investigation of the influence of the service upon the eucharistic tradition, as well as by linguistic analysis (pp. 137, 174, 192f.), then we have every reason to conclude that the common core of the tradition of the account of the Lord's Supper—what Jesus said at the Last Supper—is preserved to us in an essentially reliable form.

V

THE MEANING
OF THE EUCHARISTIC WORDS OF JESUS

THE MEAL

'AND WHEN IT was evening he came with the twelve' (Mark 14.17). This meal of Jesus with his disciples must not be isolated, but should rather be seen as one of a long series of daily meals they had shared together. For the oriental every table fellowship is a guarantee of peace,[1] of trust, of brotherhood. Table fellowship is a fellowship of life.[2] Table fellowship with Jesus is more. This becomes especially evident in the case of that table fellowship which Jesus celebrated with sinners and outcasts. The oriental, to whom symbolic action means more than it does to us, would immediately understand the acceptance of the outcasts into table fellowship with Jesus as an offer of salvation to guilty sinners and as the assurance of forgiveness.[3] Hence the passionate objections of the Pharisees (Luke 15.2: 'This man receives sinners and eats with them'; Mark 2.15–17, cf. Matt. 11.19), who held that the pious could have table fellowship only with the righteous. They understood the

---

[1] From very earliest times to the present day, cf. Gen. 43.25–34; Josh. 9.1–15.

[2] Dalman, *Arbeit und Sitte in Palästina* VII (BFChTh II 48), Gütersloh, 1942, 220.

[3] Cf. II Kings 25.27–30: Jehoiachin is freed from prison by the king of Babylon and invited to the king's table; Josephus, *Ant.* 19.321: King Agrippa I has Silas, who had fallen into disgrace, brought to his table to signify that he had forgiven him. The fact that the risen Lord eats with the disciples who had forsaken him (Luke 24.30, 35, 43 [where the word ἐνώπιον 'before' originally, as in 13.26, signifies the table fellowship]; Acts 1.4; 10.41; John 21.13) means that the disciples are readmitted into the old fellowship and it is a visible sign of his forgiveness. The anti-Docetic use of this element is secondary: Luke 24.41–43, cf. especially the variants in vv. 42–43 (where the restitution of the remainder of the honeycomb is apparently meant to convince the disciples of the impress made by his teeth). N. Johansson, *Det urkristna nattvardsfirandet*, Lund, 1944, is right to stress the centrality of the conception that table fellowship with Jesus signifies a guarantee of forgiveness.

intention of Jesus as being to accord the outcasts worth before God[1] by eating with them, and they objected to his placing of the sinner on the same level as the righteous.

The regular table fellowship with Jesus must have assumed an entirely new meaning for the disciples after Peter's confession at Caesarea Philippi. From this time onward every meal with Jesus was for his followers a symbol, a pre-presentation, indeed an actual anticipation of the meal of the consummation.[2] The request of the sons of Zebedee to be allowed to keep, at the meal of the salvation time, the places of honour which they had occupied on earth (cf. John 13.23) is clear evidence that the disciples were aware of this (Mark 10.35–37), and the continuation of the daily table fellowship after the death of Jesus as a sacred rite[3] can be understood *only on this basis*. The self-humiliation of Jesus in ministering to his disciples like a slave (John 13.1–17; Luke 22.27) can be seen in its true depth only when it is realized that this is the Messiah serving at the Messiah's meal. After Peter's confession (Mark 8.29f. par.) the acceptance of out-casts and renegades into the table fellowship signifies more than it did before: in them is now represented the eternal and perfected community of the 'saints'.[4] After Peter's confession every act of eating and drinking with the master is table fellowship of the re-deemed community with the redeemer, a wedding feast, a pledge of a share in the meal of the consummation; so also the meal on Maundy Thursday.

This meal on Maunday Thursday none the less stands out as a special one among these Messianic meals. It is the passover meal, the table celebration of the whole people of God, the high point of the year. The solemn setting, the reclining on couches, the festal wine, the paschal lamb, the liturgy of the feast, mark it as a meal of re-joicing[5]—in the characteristic distinction from the Samaritan passover: there the hour of the exodus is repeated, here the freedom achieved is celebrated. The Jewish passover celebration at the time of Jesus is both retrospect and prospect. At this festival the people of God remember the merciful immunity granted to the houses marked

---

[1] This intention is especially discernible in Luke 19.1–10.

[2] Cf. Hupfeld, *Abendmahlsfeier*, 57.

[3] See above, p. 66.

[4] Cf. E. Lohmeyer, *Kultus und Evangelium*, Göttingen, 1942, 37; 'Das Abend-mahl', *JBL* 56 (1937), 217–26.

[5] Ex. R. 18.11 on 12.41: 'This night is one of rejoicing for the whole of Israel'. This is rightly emphasized by M. Barth, *Das Abendmahl*, 7f.

with the blood of the paschal lamb and the deliverance from the Egyptian servitude. But that is only one aspect. At the same time the passover is *a looking forward to the coming deliverance* of which the deliverance from Egypt is the prototype.[1] This typology is a concept which 'most comprehensively determined already in early times, as no other did, the form that the doctrine of final salvation took'.[2] The Messiah comes in the passover night! 'In that night they were redeemed and in that night they will be redeemed', is an old saying.[3] 'The Messiah, who is called "first" (Isa. 41.27), will come in the first month.'[4] 'It is a tradition of the Jews', reports Jerome, 'that the Messiah will come at midnight according to the manner of the time in Egypt when the Passover was (first) celebrated.'[5] An ancient passover poem, '*The Four Nights*', depicts four events, all of which take place in the night Nisan 14/15. This was the night of creation, of the covenant with Abraham and of the deliverance from Egypt, and it will consequently be the night of redemption: Moses and the Messiah, with the *memra* of Jahweh between them, will come in this night on the summit of a cloud (*bereš 'anana*, cf. Dan. 7.13).[6] 'Then

---

[1] See above, pp. 58–60; Billerbeck II, 256; Moore, *Judaism* II, 42; Dalman, *Jesus-Jeshua*, 183f.; Schlatter, *Matthäus*, 732; Zolli, *Il Nazareno*, 212–14; H. Riesenfeld, *Jésus transfiguré* (Acta Seminarii Neotestamentici Upsaliensis 16), Copenhagen, 1947, 29–53.

[2] Billerbeck I, 85. Cf. L. Goppelt, *Typos* (BFChTh II 43), Gütersloh, 1939, 131–9.

[3] Mek. Ex. 12.42 (ed. Lauterbach, Philadelphia, 1933, I, 115), ascribed to R. Joshua b. Hananiah, *c.* 90. Cf. Targ. Jer. I Ex. 12.42.

[4] Ex. R. 15.1 on 12.2. The context is: 'God who is called "the first" (Isa. 44.6) will come and build the Temple which is also called "first" (Jer. 17.12), and will exact retribution from Esau, who is also called "first" (Gen. 25.25). Then the Messiah, who is called "first" (Isa. 41.27), will come in the first month (Nisan), as it is said: This month shall be unto you the beginning of the months (Ex. 12.2).' Nisan is the month of the first and of the final redemption: Targ. Hos. 3.2; b. R. H. 11a, b; Pesik. 5, ed. S. Buber, Lyck, 1868, 47b; Eleazar b. Kalir, cf. Dalman, *Der leidende und sterbende Messias der Synagoge im ersten nachchristlichen Jahrtausend* (Schriften des Institutum Judaicum in Berlin 4), Berlin, 1888, 63 n. 2.

[5] Jerome, *Commentary on Matthew* IV on 25.6 (MPL 26 [1866], col. 192). He adds: 'Whence I think also the apostolic tradition has persisted that on the day of the paschal vigils it is not permitted to dismiss before midnight the people who are expecting the advent of Christ.' This 'apostolic tradition' that Christ would come 'during the paschal vigils' was widespread, cf. R. Eisler, 'Das letzte Abendmahl[I]', *ZNW* 24 (1925), 180 n. 3 (where instead of 'Isid. Hisp. VI 16' one should read: Isidore of Seville, *Etymologiarum* 6.17.12 [MPL 82 (1878), col. 248]); Lohse, *Passafest*, 78–84. The oldest occurrence is *Epistula Apostolorum* (AD 150–60), 15–17 Schmidt = 26–28 Guerrier.

[6] Targ. Jer. II Ex. 15.18 (M. Ginsburger, *Das Fragmententhargum*, Berlin, 1899, 36f.), cf. *ibid.* Ex. 12.42 (pp. 82, 105), quoted by Black, *Aramaic Approach*[2], 172f.

will the night turn to day because the creation light shines.'[1] So the night of the Passover is called the 'sign' through which God guarantees the coming of the Messiah.[2] The passover traditions variously reflect the vitality of this Messianic hope,[3] just as do the revolts against Rome which repeatedly took place at the passover.[4]

The gravity of the hour in which the Twelve, the living symbol of the new people of God,[5] celebrate the passover with Jesus stands in sharp contrast with the normal elation of this festival. This is for them the final meal, the farewell meal, and what Jesus said and did at this last meal must be understood against the background of this contrast.

On that evening Jesus said more than has been preserved for us. Yet two things impressed themselves especially upon the disciples, partly because in them Jesus, to their surprise, deviated from established custom: the avowal of abstinence and the words of interpretation.

JESUS' AVOWAL OF ABSTINENCE[6]

According to Luke 22.15 Jesus began the Last Supper with the words, 'I have earnestly desired to eat this passover with you before

---

[1] Ex. R. 18.11 on 12.42 (Billerbeck IV, 55).

[2] Ex. R. 18.12 on 12.42: 'Let this sign be in your hands: on the day when I wrought salvation for you, on that very night know that I will redeem you.' All these expectations are based on Ex. 12.42 where the passover night is called 'a night of watching'.

[3] The eschatological interpretation of the four passover cups in terms of the four cups of punishment and reward at the End time, as well as the eschatological interpretation of the unleavened bread, was discussed above, pp. 59f. On the eschatological interpretation of the *hallel* (Pss. 113–18) see below, p. 256 n. 3; on the Messianic prayer which on the passover evening was inserted into the grace after the meal see below, p. 252. Cf. Dalman, *Jesus-Jeshua*, 183f.; Zolli, *Il Nazareno*, 212–14. On the age of these hopes see especially pp. 258ff.

[4] Josephus, *passim*. In the NT cf. Luke 13.1–3 (that this took place at passover follows from the fact that lay people were sacrificing; only in the case of the passover sacrifices were laymen permitted to play an active part, cf. Philo, *De decal.* 159; *De spec. leg.* 2.145; *De vita Mos.* 2[3].224f.) and Mark 15.7; Luke 23.19 (the Barabbas revolt seems to have taken place within the last few days, as is suggested by the vivid interest taken by the people); also John 6.15; Luke 22.38 show an atmosphere of passover. Cf. further A. Strobel in ZNW 49 (1958), 187ff.

[5] The number twelve included the lost nine and a half tribes of the northern kingdom and is therefore not a symbol for empirical Israel but for the eschatological people of God, cf. Jeremias, *Jesus' Promise*, 21.

[6] In the second German edition, and so in the first English edition, the term 'vow of abstinence' was used, which is the usual translation of *issar*. However, Jesus does not employ one of the formulae which served to introduce a vow (cf. Mark 7.11 par.) but prefixes his declaration of renunciation by ἀμήν (Mark 14.25).

I suffer.' In this connection it must be noted that the words 'to eat this passover' can only mean 'to eat this passover lamb' (not 'to celebrate this year's passover' or the like).[1] Further, concerning the use of ἐπιθυμεῖν, 'to desire', with an infinitive, this is a favourite construction in Luke's special source, for it occurs there four times (15.16; 16.21; 17.22; 22.15) and only once elsewhere in the New Testament, in Matt. 13.17. In Luke 17.22 the construction clearly expresses an unfulfilled wish ('you will desire to see one of the days of the Son of man, and you will not see [it]') as it does in Matt. 13.17. Accordingly a similar meaning is to be assumed for Luke 15.16 ('and he would have been only too glad to fill his belly with the carob-beans with which the swine were fed [sc. but he was too disgusted to do so], and no one gave him [sc. anything to eat]')[2] and 16.21 ('He would gladly have satisfied himself with the [pieces of bread] which the rich man's guests [used to wipe their hands and then] threw on the ground').[3] Our text (22.15) also must be understood in a similar manner, as concerned with an unfulfilled wish,[4] and therefore translated: 'I would very gladly have eaten this passover lamb with you before my death.'[5] The reason why for Jesus this wish remained unfulfilled is given in v. 16: 'for I tell you I shall not eat it until it is fulfilled in the kingdom of God.'

Luke continues, 'And he took the cup, and when he had given thanks (i.e. said the blessings for the feast day and for the cup, see p. 85) he said, "Take this and divide it among yourselves" ' (Luke 22.17). The cup was normally passed around in silence; at most a 'take' would be appropriate.[6] The unusual[7] instruction, 'Take this and divide it among yourselves', should therefore most probably be

---

I shall therefore rather use 'avowal of abstinence' as a less technical expression (cf. Dalman, *Jesus-Jeshua*, 155; Kuhn, 'The Lord's Supper' in *The Scrolls and the New Testament*, 265 n. 81).

[1] C. K. Barrett, 'Luke XXII.15: To Eat the Passover', *JTS* 9 (1958), 305–7.
[2] Jeremias, *Parables*, 129.
[3] Jeremias, *Parables*, 184.
[4] Rightly seen by F. C. Burkitt–A. E. Brooke, 'St Luke XXII 15, 16: What is the General Meaning?', *JTS* 9 (1907–8), 569–72.
[5] Πάσχειν, 'to suffer' = 'to die'; see above, p. 160 n. 2.
[6] See above, p. 166.
[7] P. Fiebig, 'Die Abendmahlsworte Jesu', *Neues Sächsisches Kirchenblatt* 42 (1935), col. 376.

understood as indicating that Jesus did not share in the cup.[1] The reason why Jesus, who blessed the cup, should exclude himself from it, contrary to custom, he himself gives in v. 18, 'for I tell you that from now on I shall not drink (οὐ μὴ πίω) of the fruit of the vine until the kingdom of God comes'.

The two parallel arguments in vv. 16 and 18 are usually called the 'eschatological prospect', and the sayings of Jesus, that he will eat the passover meal and drink wine again only in the kingdom of God, are commonly understood as predictions of his death. But there are two reasons why this understanding is difficult to maintain: 1. A prediction of his death is no foundation for the direction given in v. 17: 'Divide the cup among you for I must soon die'—this scarcely makes sense. 2. Anyone who understands vv. 16 and 18 as predictions of Jesus' death misses the real difficulty in these verses, namely that they are in the *form of a careful declaration of intent, almost an oath*.

1. Reference has to be made first to the οὐ μή (Luke 22.16, 18; Mark 14.25; Matt. 26.29). Previous investigation of this (classical) emphatic form of denial has shown that it is far more common in the New Testament than in classical or contemporary Greek, but that this disproportionate use is due to its frequency in the quotations from the LXX and in the sayings of the earthly and risen Lord. For these two groups account for almost 90 per cent of the occurrences of οὐ μή in the New Testament.[2] J. H. Moulton explains this unusual frequence as due to 'a feeling that inspired language was fitly rendered by words of a peculiarly decisive tone'.[3] But we must go a step further than this. Of the nine οὐ μή-passages in Mark, no less than five (including Mark 14.25)[4] are linked with the oath formula ἀμήν;[5] the other gospels provide further instances of these[6] and similar[7] combinations. Moreover, if we examine the passages from the gospels where

---

[1] This exegesis is widely accepted; cf. the commentaries by B. Weiss, T. Zahn, E. Klostermann, A. Schlatter, K. H. Rengstorf, *ad loc.*; P. Volz, 'Ein heutiger Passahabend', *ZNW* 7 (1906), 251; Dalman, *Jesus-Jeshua*, 158f.; P. Fiebig, *ThLZ* 60 (1935), col. 343 (reviewing Jeremias, *Die Abendmahlsworte Jesu*[1]); E. Lohmeyer, 'Das Abendmahl in der Urgemeinde', *JBL* 56 (1937), 246f.; Dodd, *Parables*, 60; Dibelius, *Jesus*, 133; Dix, *Liturgy*, 54. So also almost all of the modern Roman Catholic exegesis, but on the basis of 'dogmatic, not exegetical considerations' (H. Vogels, 'Mk. 14, 25 und Parallelen', in *Vom Wort des Lebens* [M. Meinertz Festschrift] [NTA, Ergänzungsband 1], Münster, 1951, 98; but cf. pp. 96–99).

[2] J. H. Moulton, *Grammar of New Testament Greek* I. *Prolegomena*[3], Edinburgh, 1908, 187–92.

[3] Moulton, *op. cit.*, 192.

[4] Mark 9.1, 41; 10.15; 13.30; 14.25.

[5] 'Amen implies oath, acceptance of words and confirmation of words' (b.

someone other than Jesus or the angel of God (Luke 1.15) uses οὐ μή, we always find it in oath-like assurances (Mark 14.31 par.; Matt. 16.22;[1] John 13.8; 20.25), with the one exception, John 11.56. In I Cor. 8.13 we find οὐ μή in a (hypothetical) vow of abstinence. The remainder of the total of ninety-seven instances of οὐ μή in the New Testament, with but few exceptions, consist of *oath-like assurances, promises or threats* by God[2] or Jesus. Noteworthy in our passage is the connection of οὐ μή with ἀμήν and the intensifying οὐκέτι (Mark 14.25).

2. The nuances of meaning to be found in the ἀμήν . . . οὐ μή of our text are indicated by the γάρ at the beginning of Luke 22.18. Jesus explains in v. 18 why he does not drink: 'Take this and divide it among yourselves; for (γάρ) I tell you that from now on οὐ μὴ πίω of the fruit of the vine until (ἕως) the kingdom of God comes' (vv. 17–18). The translation of οὐ μὴ πίω as a future ('I shall not drink') gives no reason for Jesus' not drinking. Only a *resolve* would provide a reason here. In fact, the Aramaic imperfect underlying the Greek φάγω, πίω (Luke 22.16, 18; Mark 14.25; Matt. 26.29) is used with a future sense in Galilean Aramaic only very occasionally; it almost always has jussive, final or modal[3] forces.[4] Also in Hebrew the modal or potential use of the imperfect is an established practice. In our text it is used to express intention: 'Divide it among yourselves, for (the Lukan source here, as often,[5] omits the oath-substitute ἀμήν found in Mark 14.25) I tell you from now on I do not intend to drink again until God[6] establishes his kingdom.' Such is the case too in v. 16.

3. It agrees with the facts mentioned under 1 and 2 that ἀπὸ τοῦ νῦν, 'from now on', has a tendency to be used in solemn declarations (cf. Acts 18.6; Luke 5.10), and that a deadline (ἕως, 'until') belongs to the termi-

---

Shebu. 36a par.). In late Judaism 'amen' serves *exclusively* as corroboration of a blessing or oath. Jesus uses it in place of an oath (Dalman, *Words*, 229).
[6] With ἀμήν: Matt. 5.18, 26; 10.23; 18.3; 24.2; Luke 18.17; John 8.51; 13.38.
[7] With λέγω γὰρ (δὲ) ὑμῖν, Matt. 5.20; 23.39; 26.29; Luke 13.35; 22.16, 18; with λέγω δὲ ὑμῖν ἀληθῶς, Luke 9.27; with λέγω σοι, 12.59; with ἰδού, 10.19.

[1] Peter's horrified exclamation, Matt. 16.22, has the force of an adjuration.
[2] Through the quotation of scripture or by the word of an angel.
[3] Expressing intent, desiderative, optative, permissive (e.g. Matt. 5.43b, 'but you do not need to love your enemy'), prohibitive (Matt. 7.4, 'how dare you . . .'), etc.
[4] W. B. Stevenson, *Grammar of Palestinian Jewish Aramaic*, Oxford, 1924, 49f.; Odeberg, *The Aramaic Portions of Bereshit Rabba* II, 93, 146–50. Judaean Aramaic (the Targums) is different, for there the imperfect more often has a future meaning, having been influenced by Hebrew.
[5] See above, p. 163 n. 6.
[6] The expression 'the kingdom of God comes', which ascribes an activity to the abstract expression 'kingdom of God', is a circumlocution for the activity of God.

nology of the vows of abstinence: he who makes the vow states for how long it is to last.[1]

In other words, Jesus expresses a twofold declaration of intent to abstain,[2] to which he may have given an especially ceremonial flavour by choosing Hebrew as his language.[3] 'I would very much have liked to eat this passover lamb with you before my death. (But I must deny myself this wish.)[4] For I tell you I do not intend to eat of it again until God[5] fulfils (his promises) in the kingdom of God ... Take (this cup) and divide (it) among you; for I tell you I do not intend from now on to drink of the fruit of the vine until God[6] establishes his kingdom' (Luke 22.15–18).[7] If we have understood v. 15 correctly as the expression of an unfulfilled wish, the first declaration of intent to abstain can only have come before the beginning of the meal, and the second immediately following at the

---

[1] Cf. '*ad*, I Sam. 14.24; ἕως οὗ, Acts 23.12, 14, 21; *donec* in the vow of James, the Lords' brother (see below, p. 215).

[2] First precisely formulated by C. P. Coffin, *Indications of Source for the Accounts of the Last Supper as given by the Synoptists and by St Paul*, Evanston, Ill., 1937, 6f. Earlier, Zahn, *Lucas*, 673. Correctly M. Barth, *Das Abendmahl*, 42: the words of Jesus 'have the form and significance of an oath'. Dalman, *Jesus-Jeshua*, 155f., also recognizes that Jesus excludes himself from the wine drinking, that he expressed a renunciation, that we have here an 'avowal of renunciation' (*issar*). But then, as in the instance given above, p. 201 n. 5, doctrinal considerations intervene ('Is it possible to ascribe this kind of avowal to our Lord?') and prevent Dalman from drawing the correct conclusion.

There is here no contradiction of Matt. 5.33–37. In that passage Jesus forbids the use of oaths to guarantee the truth of one's own words. As we shall see immediately below (pp. 213f.), neither Paul nor the Early Church understood Matt. 5.33–37 as indicating that Jesus also intended to forbid avowals of abstinence (Acts 21.13f.; 18.18; I Cor. 8.13, cf. 7.5).

[3] See above, pp. 196f.

[4] Bauer: A. and G., 151, *s. v.* γάρ: 'Often the thought to be supported is not expressed, but must be supplied from the context.'

[5] The passive is used to signify the activity of God (cf. above, p. 202).

[6] See above, p. 210 n. 6.

[7] There remains for mention the form given to Luke 22.15 in the Gospel of the Ebionites according to Epiphanius, *Panarion* (*Against Heresies*) 30.22.4 (GCS 25.363.4–6). The disciples ask, 'Where will you have us prepare for you to eat the passover?' (cf. Matt. 26.17), to which Jesus replies by asking indignantly, 'Have I earnestly desired to eat flesh, this passover, with you?' In this modification of Luke 22.15, in which Jesus altogether denies the eating of flesh, there are certainly encratite tendencies at work which are completely foreign to Jesus. None the less, if our understanding of Luke 22.15 as an avowal of abstinence is correct, this modification is not, as has heretofore been supposed, purely arbitrary, but rather goes back to a remembrance of the fact that Jesus had not partaken of the passover lamb at the Last Supper, a remembrance which had been supported by the fasting in the Easter Night (see above, p. 124).

passing of the first cup (see p. 85).[1] At the Last Supper therefore Jesus neither ate of the passover lamb nor drank of the wine; probably he fasted completely.

This understanding of Luke 22.15–18 par. Mark 14.25, however unusual it may appear, receives strong support from the words of interpretation. For it is very unlikely that Jesus himself should have eaten of the bread that he referred to as his body, or drunk of the wine that he referred to as his blood. In addition to this, our interpretation is supported by the earliest church history. In Asia Minor towards the end of the first century the Christians celebrated the Passover at the same time as the Jews;[2] but whereas the Jews reclined to a ceremonial meal at table, the Christian community fasted and first broke the fast with a celebration of the Eucharist at cock-crow.[3] We have seen that this Quartodecimanian practice goes back to the earliest community.[4] There can scarcely be any other explanation for this non-holding of the passover meal than that the early community is following the example of Jesus.[5]

The fact that Jesus excluded himself from the passover meal must have seriously disturbed his disciples. What was his intention when he made this strange twofold declaration of intent to abstain? The text offers no information on this point. An attempt to answer the question can therefore be made only after an examination of the contemporary sources.

The basic regulations of the Law concerning vows of abstinence (*issar*[6]) are found in Num. 30.2–17. Examples of such vows are found in the Old Testament: I Sam. 14.24b, 'Saul laid an oath on the people, saying, "Cursed be the man who eats food until it is evening and I am avenged on my enemies" '; Ps. 132.2–5, David swears not to enter his house or to get into his bed, indeed to forgo sleep altogether until he has found a place for the house of God; II Sam. 11.11 (Uriah's vow of abstinence), etc.

---

[1] Luke has therefore placed the words in their proper place. This confirms the observations made on p. 191 on Mark. 14.25.

[2] Eusebius, *Hist. Eccl.* 5.24.16.

[3] *Epistula Apostolorum* 15 (26). See above, p. 123.

[4] See above, p. 122 n. 3. First seen by E. Schwartz, 'Osterbetrachtungen', *ZNW* 7 (1906), 27.

[5] See pp. 124f. A further support for our interpretation is perhaps offered by Mark 15.23; Matt. 27.34. When Jesus refused the wine mingled with myrrh which was offered to him as a narcotic the reason could have been that he was bound by his declaration of intent to abstain.

[6] The closing sentence of Meg. Taan. says *esar bişlo*, 'abstention by vow'.

In *late Judaism* such renunciations play a large part.[1] They are used in relation to all kinds of food (for a limited or an unlimited period),[2] to all kinds of drink,[3] *especially wine*,[4] to certain kinds of clothing,[5] to sexual intercourse,[6] to sleep,[7] to speaking,[8] to bathing,[9] to business with and profit from others (e.g., by buying or selling),[10] to entry into a house,[11] or a town,[12] etc.

1. As we can see simply from this enumeration of examples, these renunciations were connected with religion only in so far as they possessed the binding power of vows; the motives for them were rather, in everyday life, of a very secular kind. Very often they were caused by anger[13] or hate[14] and in such cases simply expressed a refusal to have any further dealings with someone (wife, father, business partner);[15] they were intended to reinforce one's own statement as by an oath.[16] In bargaining buyer and seller used them as a means of influencing the other to yield.[17] They were used in an attempt by one person to put pressure on another, e.g. to make him accept[18] or present[19] a gift. Almost always they were an *expression of the irrevocability of the resolution made*.[20] This is also the meaning of the vow of abstinence taken by more than forty men not to eat or to drink until they had killed Paul (Acts 23.12, 14, 21). The same thing probably lies behind

---

[1] In what follows we shall limit ourselves to vows of abstinence (in which someone renounces something); the vows of interdiction (in which someone compels another person to renounce something, e.g. Mark 7.11), which also belong to the *issarim* (vows of abstinence), are discussed by Billerbeck I, 713–17.

[2] Ned. 1.1, 3f.; 2.1f.; 4.1, 5, 7f.; 6.1–10; 7.1f., 6–8; 8.6; 9.8; 11.2; Ḥul. 8.1. Cf. I Sam. 14.24 (see above, p. 211 n.1).

[3] Ned. 3.2; 6.5, 7, 9; 8.1, 5; 9.8.

[4] Ned. 6.7–9; 8.1, 5; 9.8; Naz. 2.3, etc. The Nazirite vows constitute a special case of these vows of abstinence. Renunciation of wine alone did not make a man a Nazirite, for a Nazirite was also bound not to cut his hair and to guard himself from defilement.

[5] Ned. 7.3, 8.

[6] Ned. 2.1, 5; 3.2, 4; 8.7; 9.5; 11.12; Ket. 5.6. Cf. I Sam. 21.6; II Sam. 11.11; I Cor. 7.5.

[7] Ned. 2.1. Cf. Ps. 132.2–5 (see above, p. 212).

[8] Ned. 1.4; 2.1.

[9] Ned. 11.1.

[10] Philo, *De spec. leg.* 2.16; Ned. 3.6–11; 4.1–7; 5.1ff.; 9.2, 7, 10; 11.3, 11.

[11] Ned. 7.4f.; 9.2f.

[12] Ned. 7.5.

[13] Ned. 4.6; 7.3.

[14] Ned. 9.4.

[15] Philo, *De spec. leg.* 2.16; Ned. 4.6; 9.4.

[16] Ned. 3.2, 4.

[17] Ned. 3.1.

[18] Ned. 8.7.

[19] *Ibid.*

[20] Of a refusal: Ned. 8.7; 9.2; of a decision to seek a divorce: Ned. 9.9, etc. Cf. from ancient times: Gen. 24.33; Ps. 132.2–5.

Acts 18.18, if Paul is here the subject in 'he cut his hair';[1] since the cutting of the hair took place in Cenchreae immediately after leaving Corinth, it may be assumed that, by means of a vow not to cut his hair before his departure, Paul had made it plain to the Corinthian church that his decision to go was irrevocable; although they pressed him to stay.

2. But there are many indications that the avowals of renunciation had none the less in no way lost their religious significance. 'He makes atonement for the sins of ignorance by fasting', say the Psalms of Solomon of the righteous man.[2] The fear of sinning while intoxicated, the fight against the evil impulse (e.g., vanity), the resolution to mortify the flesh, are all given in the rabbinical literature as reasons for the renunciation of wine[3] or for the taking of the Nazirite vows so frequent in the time of Jesus.[4] Paul says that if by eating meat he is in danger of causing a brother to sin, then he is prepared to renounce meat for ever (I Cor. 8.13). The Nazirite dedicates himself to God.[5] *Dedication of oneself to God* is also the intent of those who renounce marriage for the sake of the kingdom of God (Matt. 19.12).[6] No different is the case of Anna the prophetess when she, like Judith,[7] renounces a second marriage and serves God with prayer and fasting (Luke 2.37). The Christian couples in Corinth who for a time refrain from marital intercourse do so in order to devote themselves without distraction to prayer (I Cor. 7.5).[8] Similarly, when John the Baptist renounces the eating of flesh and the drinking of wine (Mark 1.6; Luke 7.33), the reason most probably is a desire to devote himself completely to his mission.

3. To these motives for taking a vow of abstinence may be added a third. 'For thou, O God, hast heard my vows', says Ps. 61.6. The word 'vows' is used here as meaning 'prayers'. The thought is of vows that are spoken in connection with a petitionary prayer. The suppliant promises a sacrifice or a gift dedicated to the temple, should his prayer be heard. Such a vow used to reinforce a prayer need not, however, be the promise of a gift; from the earliest times it could just as well be a vow of abstinence. Saul made his warriors swear that none of them would eat before the

---

[1] So Billerbeck II, 747; Lake–Cadbury in *Beginnings* IV, 229; Kuhn, *Sifre zu Numeri*, 692; Haenchen, *Apostelgeschichte*, 478, 481f. Aquila is held to be the subject by Wendt, Zahn and Bauernfeind in their commentaries on this passage, but does the account have such an interest in Aquila?

[2] Ps. Sol. 3.8.

[3] Evidence in Billerbeck II, 748. Further, Test. Jos. 3f., 9f.

[4] Historical evidence collected by Billerbeck II, 87f., 748f., 755f.; Heinemann, *Philons griechische und jüdische Bildung*, 91f.; Schlatter, *Theologie des Judentums*, 117. Cf. Acts 21.23f.; Luke 1.15; Eusebius, *Hist. eccl.* 2.23.4f.

[5] Josephus, *Ant.* 4.72: 'they dedicate themselves to God'.

[6] Cf. Rev. 14.4.

[7] Judith 8.4–6.

[8] Scribes used to renounce marital intercourse for a time for the sake of their study of the Torah (Billerbeck III, 372).

evening, until victory should be won (I Sam. 14.24). This renunciation was intended to gain God's grace. David fasted in order that God should spare the life of his sick child (II Sam. 12.15–23, esp. v. 22). That the practice of making a vow of abstinence to ensure God's hearing continued into New Testament times is evidenced on every side. Josephus says that it was customary for 'those who were plagued by serious illness or by any other distress' to take upon themselves a thirty-day Nazirite vow,[1] and there are numerous rabbinical reports of vows of fasting, sometimes for long periods, which were made because of personal or national emergencies, or to ensure that prayers were heard.[2] 'He who prays without being heard should fast.'[3] According to the Gospel of the Hebrews the Risen Lord appeared first to his brother James, 'for James had sworn that he would not eat bread from that hour in which he had drunk the Lord's cup until he should see him rising again from among them that sleep'.[4] James certainly expected that Jesus would be resurrected (that can be seen from the 'until') and vows not to partake of food until then; the fasting is obviously meant as prayer-fasting. The petitionary prayer was especially linked with prayer-fasting. Fasting was undertaken for the sick,[5] and for the people as a whole.[6] 'Ezra . . . went to the chamber of Jehohanan the son of Eliashib, where he spent the night, neither eating bread nor drinking water; for he was mourning over the faithlessness of the exiles.'[7] 'R. Zadok (I, before AD 70) observed fasts for forty years in order that Jerusalem might not be destroyed.'[8] Enlightening is Billerbeck's suggestion[9] that the pious who fasted twice weekly (on Monday and Thursday, Luke 18.12: 'I fast twice a week') did so for their people. They 'felt themselves called to cast themselves into the breach which the sins of the broad mass of the people was

---

[1] Josephus, *Bell.* 2.313. Queen Helena of Adiabene undertook to live as a Nazirite for seven years if her son should return safely from the war (Naz. 3.6). We hear of husbands vowing to become Nazirites if a child or a son should be born to them (Naz. 2.7).

[2] Billerbeck II, 241–4; IV, 94–96. For the wording of a fasting vow, Billerbeck IV, 97 under 'e'. Cf. Ps. 69.11; 109.24; Dan. 9.3; 10.2f.; Tob. 12.8; Test. Jos. 3.4f.; 4.8; 9.2; 10.1f.; Test. Benj. 1.4. Prayer combined with fasting in the NT, Mark 9.29 *v. l.*; Luke 2.37 *v. l.*; Acts 10.30 *v. l.*; 13.2f.; 14.23; I Cor. 7.5 *v. l.*

[3] j. Ber. 4.8a.2.

[4] Jerome, *De viris illustr.* 2. Klostermann (*Apocrypha* II [KIT 8], 10f.) is probably correct in viewing the words quoted as an addition by Jerome to the text of the Gospel of the Hebrews. The old Greek translation of *De viris illustr.* has 'the Lord had drunk the cup' for 'he had drunk the Lord's cup' (see above, p. 46 n. 8), a dogmatic correction occasioned by the idea that the brother of the Lord, not a member of the Twelve, should have taken part in the Last Supper.

[5] Ps. 35.13; Tos. Taan. 3.3 (219.4); cf. Mark 9.29 *v. l.*

[6] Dan. 9.3ff.

[7] Ezra 10.6.

[8] b. Giṭ. 56a.

[9] With reliance upon Meg. Taan. 13.

always creating between God and Israel, in order that the atoning power
of their fasting might turn away the wrath of God and protect the people
from national catastrophe'.[1] In all these cases listed under 3 the mortifi-
cation of the flesh is intended to strengthen the *insistency of the prayer*.

We ask again: can we venture a conjecture as to Jesus' intention
in making his avowal of renunciation? All the motives we have
mentioned could have played a part, for they are not mutually
exclusive, but rather they supplement one another. Jesus may have
intended to make clear to his disciples the irrevocable nature of his
decision to prepare the way for the kingdom of God by his vicarious
suffering. He burns his bridges, forswears feasting and wine, prepares
himself with resolute will to drink the bitter cup which the Father
offers him. In his renunciation there would thus be already something of the dreadful tension of the struggle at Gethsemane and of the
depth of his dereliction on the cross. At the same time Jesus may have
wished to make clear to his disciples how completely his life was
detached from this aeon. His life is dedicated completely to God
(John 17.19) and belongs already to the coming kingdom of God,
to the passover of the consummation. Finally, Jesus may have desired
to impart to his disciples a sense of the certainty of the nearness of the
kingdom of God by means of a symbolic and urgent prayer for the
consummation of the passover, almost by a wrestling with God.

All these possibilities were mentioned in the previous edition of
this work [p. 171. Transl.] and they are all real possibilities. But in
the meantime recent research[2] has given us a new possibility with
regard to the explanation of Jesus' renunciation, and this points
in a different direction. We must remind ourselves once more that
the Christian communities in Asia Minor about AD 100 fasted on
passover evening, whereas the Jewish families sat at their festive
passover meals. We must also realize that this practice goes back to the
earliest community, and that the passover fasting of the earliest community was apparently a continuation of the example of Jesus.[3]
Now the question becomes important: what did the early Christians
intend by their passover fast? The answer of the oldest sources
is completely unanimous.[4] Epiphanius of Salamis (d. 403) quotes

---

[1] Billerbeck II, 243.
[2] Lohse, *Passafest*, 62–75.
[3] See above, p. 124.
[4] Cf. to what follows Lohse, *Passafest*, 63–68.

from the *Diataxeis of the Apostles*[1] (to be dated shortly after AD 200):
'The same apostles say, "While they (the Jews) are feasting (in the
passover night) you are to fast, mourning for them".'[2] The *Apostolic
Constitutions* give the following regulations for the passover fast:
'fasting . . . all of you with fear and trembling, *praying for those that
are perishing*'.[3] 'He (the risen Lord) therefore charged us himself to
fast these six days (of the passover week) *on account of the impiety and
transgression of the Jews*, commanding (us) withal to bewail over them
and to lament for their perdition.'[4] In the Syriac *Didascalia* we find
in chapter 21, which deals with the passover and the resurrection:
'Therefore, when you fast, so pray and petition *for the lost*'; '*for the
sake of your brothers* . . . (you) should do it.'[5] In the *Didache* (1.3) we
find the general rule: 'Fast for those who persecute you.'[6] This
fasting for Israel certainly began in Jewish Christian circles. When
we consider in addition that, as we have seen,[7] it was a widespread
Jewish practice to link petitionary prayer, especially prayer for the
guilt of the people, with fasting, then we may conclude: the reason
which the earliest community gives for its passover fast shows us what
moved Jesus to his avowal of abstinence at the Last Supper.

The glory of God has drawn very near. The Passion of Jesus will be
the beginning of the last great hour of temptation for the whole earth
(Mark 14.38), which will usher in the dawn of the day of salvation
(14.58). So the hour is at hand in which the celebration of the passover year after year will cease, and God will inaugurate in its place
the eternal passover of the fulfilment (Luke 22.16, '[until] it is fulfilled'), for which the people of God look longingly as they celebrate
the yearly passover. The next meal of Jesus with his disciples will be
the Messianic meal on a transformed earth. It will be a fulfilment of
the apocalyptic saying: 'The Lord of Spirits will abide over them,
and with that Son of Man shall they eat, and lie down and rise up

[1] This is the *Didascalia* or a preliminary stage of that work. The following
quotation is not found in the Syriac *Didascalia*.
[2] Epiphanius, *Panarion*, 70.11.3 (GCS 37.244.9–11).
[3] *Ap. Const.* 5.13.3f. (F. X. Funk, *Didascalia et Constitutiones Apostolorum* I, Paderborn, 1905, 271.5–7).
[4] *Ap. Const.* 5.14.20 (Funk, 279.1–4).
[5] Ed. H. Achelis–J. Flemming, *Die ältesten Quellen des orientalischen Kirchenrechts* II.
Die syrische Didaskalia (TU 25.2), Leipzig, 1904, 105.24f.; 107.8f.
[6] In what we have said here we do not deny that this reason for the passover fast
in the Early Church was soon supplemented by another one: it was also explained
to be in remembrance of Jesus' suffering.
[7] Above, pp. 215f.

for ever and ever' (I Enoch 62.14). Jesus will drink the wine 'new', adds Mark (14.25). To be 'new' is a mark of the redeemed world and of the time of salvation, of the transformed creation.[1] When Matthew, with equal correctness, adds 'with you' (26.29) he is expressing the idea that the passover of the consummation will be a consummation of the fellowship of the community of the redeemed with the redeemer. On a transformed earth, where perfect communion with God will have become a reality through a transformation of the body, Jesus will again, as now at the Lord's Supper, act as *paterfamilias* and break the blessed bread and offer them the cup of thanksgiving—he himself being once more the giver and the server,[2] and his own the recipients, who in eating and drinking receive the salvation gift of God: eternal life.

But, the hour of the dawning of the consummation is at the same time the hour of the final judgment, in which Israel's guilt will reveal itself. She has rejected one commandment of God after another. From the blood of Abel, the innocent, to that of Zechariah, slain in the holy place, she has burdened herself with the guilt of one capital crime after another. Now the tenants of the vineyard are prepared even to attack the son of their master. The last generation, who with this final rejection bring the weight of sins to its eschatological breaking-point, must assume the totality of guilt (Luke 11.49–51 par. Matt. 23.34–36).

The one thing that Jesus can still do, now that Israel has shown that she does not know what will make for her peace (Luke 19.42), is to throw himself into the breach with his intercession. With a love that is a completely selfless surrender, Jesus seeks to make this intercession for his deluded people as urgent as possible, and to impress it upon his disciples as much as he can. Therefore he unites with it a renunciation of the festival celebration and of the wine. He fasts for those who persecute him (Did. 1.3). Jesus begins the last passover meal as the servant of God who makes intercession for the transgressors (Isa. 53.12).

THE WORDS OF INTERPRETATION

After the *ḳidduš* and the blessing of the cup (see p. 85) the meal

---

[1] J. Behm, καινός κτλ., *TWNT* III (1938), 451f. [Also R. A. Harrisville, *The Concept of Newness in the New Testament*, Minneapolis, 1960. Transl.]

[2] Cf. Luke 12.37; 22.27.

began with the preliminary course.[1] Then the passover lamb was
served and the second cup was mixed. But before the meal proper
began Jesus, as *paterfamilias*, held the passover meditation, the kernel
of which was the interpretation of the special elements of the meal
in terms of the events of the exodus from Egypt: the unleavened
bread was usually explained as a symbol of the misery that was
endured, the bitter herbs as representing the slavery, the fruit-purée
which resembled clay as recalling the forced labour, the passover
lamb as a remembrance of God's merciful 'passing over' Israel. At the
same time there were other interpretations, especially eschatological
interpretations, of these elements.[2] The wording of Jesus' meditation
on this occasion has not been preserved.[3] But it is of the greatest
importance to remember that Jesus' words of interpretation were not
for his disciples, as they are for us, something isolated, but that they
were prepared for by the interpretations which Jesus, following the
normal custom, had given to the special elements of the meal during
the meditation.

The passover devotions were followed immediately by the grace
over the unleavened bread, the eating of the passover lamb and the
grace over the cup. Surprisingly for the disciples Jesus now added,
however, further words after the two graces. It is true that he had
already added the unusual[4] 'Take' to the grace before the meal, at
any rate according to Mark (14.22), but this was understandable; as
the comparison with the analogous, more complete instruction
given with the *ḳidduš* cup (Luke 22.17)[5] shows, it was apparently
occasioned by the fact that Jesus, although he pronounced the blessing, did not partake of the bread.[6] But that Jesus should have spoken
a word of interpretation after each of the graces[7] must have been as
unexpected by the disciples as his avowal of abstinence at the beginning of the celebration, because it was contrary to all custom. Words
of interpretation belonged to the passover meditation, not to the

[1] Mark/Matthew link the designation of the traitor with the preliminary course
(Mark 14.18–21); however, Luke (22.21–23, pointing out of the traitor after the
meal) is probably here the one who has the original order of events, see p. 98 n. 4
and p. 237.
[2] See above, p. 59.
[3] For a hypothesis, see below, pp. 222f.
[4] See above, pp. 109 n.13, 166 n.4.
[5] See above, p. 208.
[6] So Dalman, *Jesus-Jeshua*, 141; P. Fiebig, *Neues Sächsisches Kirchenblatt* 42
(1935), col. 376; E. von Severus, 'Brotbrechen', *RAC* II (1954), col. 621.
[7] See above, p. 87.

graces. The unusual nature of Jesus' action certainly helped to impress it on the disciples more deeply than other details of that evening. What is the meaning of the two words of interpretation? Why were they spoken at the distribution of the bread and wine?

(a) Jesus, the passover lamb

In the two sentences *zeh beśari* and *zeh dami*, or *den biśri* and *den idmi*, *zeh/den* is the subject and *not* the predicate,[1] which corresponds to the usual word order in a Semitic nominal clause,[2] as it does in the case of the ancient Aramaic passover formula interpreting the unleavened bread, *ha laḥma 'anya*,[3] and as is shown, and this is the decisive point, by the way in which the primitive Church uniformly understood the words of interpretation from the beginning.[4]

We consider first the subject (τοῦτο, *den*, 'this'). There is a widespread opinion that Jesus meant by τοῦτο the *action* of breaking the bread and of pouring out the wine. This interpretation, which in any case is incompatible with the τοῦτό ἐστιν ('this is'), would only be feasible if the actions named coincided with the words of interpretation. But that is not the case. As regards the bread-word, the fact that it is preceded by λάβετε ('take') shows that Jesus said it not as the bread was being broken, but as it was being distributed. It is even clearer that the wine-word had nothing to do with the pouring out of the wine. For between the pouring of the wine out of the mixing

---

[1] The opposite view, that 'my body' and 'my blood' are the subjects, is taken by, among others, K. G. Goetz, *Abendmahl*, 58–61; 'Der Einfluss des kirchlichen Brauches auf die Abendmahlstexte des N.T.', in *Vom Wesen und Wandel der Kirche* (E. Vischer Festschrift), Basel, 1935, 21ff., 32; 'Zur Lösung der Abendmahlsfrage', *ThStKr* 108 (1937–8), 81ff., 108, 120. He interprets as follows: eating and drinking my flesh and blood, i.e. my person, means for you 'what eating and drinking [means] for ordinary people', namely 'the means of gaining strength and refreshment' (*Abendmahl*, 84). Also Lohmeyer, *Markus*, 306f., who understands it as follows: 'just as my body has been the centre and core of the fellowship of disciples, so is now the common eating of the bread' (p. 307); Dibelius, *Jesus*, 133, who sees 'this is' as having the same meaning as 'behold' in John 19.26f., viz. 'this is from now on to be'.

[2] Cf. the numerous examples in Dalman, *Jesus-Jeshua*, 141; *den, da, dena* is always the subject.

[3] See above, p. 54. Obviously *ha* is the subject.

[4] The earliest evidence is I Cor. 11.24, τοῦτό μού ἐστιν τὸ σῶμα τὸ ὑπὲρ ὑμῶν: the insertion of ἐστίν between μου and τὸ σῶμα shows that τοῦτο is the subject and all that follows the predicate. Equally unambiguous is I Cor. 11.25, τοῦτο τὸ ποτήριον ἡ καινὴ διαθήκη ἐστὶν ἐν τῷ ἐμῷ αἵματι: the insertion of ἐστίν between ἡ καινὴ διαθήκη and ἐν τῷ ἐμῷ αἵματι again shows that τοῦτο τὸ ποτήριον is the subject and all the rest the predicate.

bowl[1] into the 'cup of blessing' and Jesus' word of interpretation there came the grace at the end of the meal, which consisted of the elevation of the cup (Mark 14.23),[2] an invitation to the table companions to join in the prayer,[3] the grace itself, consisting of several benedictions,[4] and the response (Amen) of the table companions. (By way of comparison it should be remembered that, as was shown on p. 85, the pouring out of the second cup was separated from its consumption by the whole of the passover *haggadah*, a period of time to be estimated at between a quarter and half an hour.)[5] It was not the action of breaking the bread or of pouring out the wine that Jesus interpreted, but rather *the bread and the wine itself*. This is supported by two observations: first, that the interpretation of the special elements in the Jewish passover rite, which was the precedent for the form of Jesus' words of interpretation,[6] is not concerned with any actions, but with the components of the meal themselves; and secondly, that the whole Early Church has from the beginning understood the τοῦτο as referring to the bread and wine (cf. I Cor. 11.25 τοῦτο = τοῦτο τὸ ποτήριον = 'this wine').

Although an interpretation of the unleavened bread, and probably also of the wine,[7] had already been given during the devotions, Jesus now interprets both again as he says grace, and this time in reference to his own person. For this purpose he used the twin concept *baśar wadam* or *biśra udema*.[8] This expression has a twofold meaning: (1) it designates, for the first time in Ecclesiasticus,[9] man as a transient being in contrast to God or to supernatural powers;[10] (2) it also designates, as already in ancient Hebrew, the two component parts of the body, especially of sacrificial animals, which are separated

---

[1] On the mixing of the wine cf. Dalman, *Jesus-Jeshua*, 149f.; Billerbeck IV, 58.
[2] See above, p. 177 no. 8.
[3] See above, p. 110.
[4] The probable usual wording of this prayer at the time of Jesus is given above, p. 110.
[5] See above, p. 84 n. 5: little children have to be watched lest they fall asleep during the *haggadah*.
[6] See above, pp. 55–61.
[7] See above, p. 59.
[8] See above, p. 200.
[9] 14.18; 17.31.
[10] Matt. 16.17; I Cor. 15.50; Gal. 1.16 (in the reverse order: Eph. 6.12; Heb. 2.14). Three times in the Mishnah: Naz. 9.5 (twice), fear of flesh and blood (fear of God); Soṭ. 8.1, strength of flesh and blood (strength of God). Frequently in rabbinical texts, especially in parables: evidence, e.g., in Billerbeck I, 141, 725, 726, 730f., etc.; Schlatter, *Matthäus*, 108, 230, 505.

when it is killed.[1] The cultic significance given under (2) is present in the twin concept in all three Greek forms: κρέας-αἷμα ('flesh'-'blood'),[2] σάρξ-αἷμα ('flesh'-'blood')[3] and (note the examples from Philo previously overlooked) σῶμα-αἷμα ('body'-'blood').[4] Only this second, cultic, meaning comes into question when Jesus speaks of 'his flesh' and 'his blood'. He is applying to himself *terms from the language of sacrifice*, as is also the case with the participle ἐκχυννόμενον ('poured out', Mark 14.24).[5] Each of the two nouns presupposes a slaying that has separated flesh and blood.[6] In other words: *Jesus speaks of himself as a sacrifice*.[7]

It can be assumed with a high degree of probability that Jesus had prepared the way for this comparison of himself with the sacrifice earlier, in the passover meditation. It is certain that the interpretation of the passover lamb belonged to the passover *haggadah*. How did Jesus interpret the passover lamb? Since he interpreted the bread and wine in terms of himself, as the words of interpretation show, it is a likely assumption that in the preceding passover devotions he had *also interpreted the passover lamb in terms of himself*. It should be remembered that already the pre-Pauline passover *haggadah* preserved in I Cor. 5.7f.[8] calls Jesus 'our passover (lamb)' and that Paul presupposes as self-evident the familiarity of the Corinthian community

---

[1] Gen. 9.4; Lev. 17.11, 14; Deut. 12.23; Ezek. 39.17–19; Heb. 13.11 (the bull of the sin offering and the scapegoat); Zeb. 4.4 (three times: burnt offerings, sin offering of a bird); 13.8 (sin offering); Ker. 6.1 (three times), 2 (guilt offering); Meil. 1.2 (three times: most holy offering, sin offering); 4.3 (reptile); Maksh. 6.5 (the same); Par. 4.3 (red cow); cf. also Pes. 7.5 (passover lamb, slaughtered offering).

[2] E.g., LXX, Gen. 9.4; Lev. 6.20; Num. 18.17f.; Deut. 12.27 etc.; Philo, *Leg. ad Gaium* 356; *De spec. leg.* 1.268.

[3] E.g., LXX, Lev. 17.11–14; Ezek. 44.7 AB (σάρκας καὶ αἷμα).

[4] Philo, *De spec. leg.* 1.231f., in reference to the young bull of the sin-offering, Lev. 4.2ff.: 'to pour the . . . blood . . . to burn the . . . body'; 4.122, in reference to animals slaughtered in a non-kosher manner: '. . . entombing in the body the blood . . .'; cf. 1.62, in reference to divination from 'entrails and blood and dead bodies' of animals; Heb. 13.11 in reference to the animals sacrificed on the Day of Atonement: 'the bodies of those animals whose blood is brought into the sanctuary . . . are burned'.

[5] Ἐκχεῖν αἷμα is used in the LXX, apart from its use of murder or the domestic slaughter of cattle, only when speaking of sacrifice.

[6] Fiebig, 'Die Abendmahlsworte Jesu', *Neues Sächsisches Kirchenblatt* 42 (1935), col. 374; 'Nochmals: Die Abendmahlsworte Jesu', *ibid.*, cols. 475f.; Jeremias–Fiebig, *ibid.*, cols. 517f. I withdraw my objections to this part of Fiebig's contentions.

[7] On comparison with a sacrifice cf. Billerbeck II, 275, 279; III, 260f.

[8] See above, pp. 59f.

with this comparison, a comparison widespread in the early Christian literature.[1] The comparison is also to be found outside the New Testament in an ancient interpretation of the paschal lamb which Justin traces back to Ezra, but which is actually an early Christian interpretation: 'This passover is our saviour and our refuge'.[2] The very great age of this comparison of Jesus with a sacrificial animal is evidenced finally by the following observation: a language usage, which must be pre-Pauline because it is common in early Christianity (Paul, I Peter, Hebrews, I John, Revelation), sums up the saving power of the death of Jesus in the phrase 'his blood'. But the crucifixion itself was a bloodless form of execution. The phrase therefore does not come from a reminiscence of the form of the execution but rather from the language of sacrifice, and it became generally accepted despite the fact that it did not correspond to what actually happened at Golgotha. The simplest explanation of this is that it was already a given fact to the earliest community.

With the words *den biśri*, 'this is my (sacrificial) flesh', and *den idmi*, 'this is my (sacrificial) blood', Jesus is therefore most probably speaking of himself as the paschal lamb.[3] He is *the eschatological paschal lamb*, representing the fulfilment of all that of which the Egyptian paschal lamb and all the subsequent sacrificial paschal lambs were the prototype. The *tertium comparationis* in the case of the bread is the fact that it was broken,[4] and in the case of the wine the red colour. We have already seen, above p. 53, that it was customary to drink red

---

[1] I Peter 1.19; Rev. 5.6, 9, 12; 12.11; John 1.29, 36; 19.36. I Cor. 10.14–21 also belongs here: when Paul puts the Lord's Supper side by side with the Jewish and pagan sacrificial meals he presupposes the comparison of Jesus with a sacrifice.

[2] Justin, *Dial.* 72.1.

[3] A view presented vigorously by G. Walther, *Jesus, das Passalamm des Neuen Bundes*, Gütersloh, 1950. Earlier presentations: R. H. Kennett, *The Last Supper*, Cambridge, 1921, 38; A. Schweitzer, *Mysticism of Paul the Apostle*, New York, 1931, 251; W. Niesel, 'Vom heiligen Abendmahl Jesu Christi', in *Abendmahlsgemeinschaft?* (Beihefte zur *Ev Th* 3), Munich, 1937, 47; Zolli, *Il Nazareno*, 232; H. Sasse, 'Das Abendmahl im N.T.', in *Vom Sakrament des Altars*, 44, 70, 75; A. Oepke, 'Jesus und der Gottesvolkgedanke', *Luthertum* 42 (1942), 49, 61 n. 79; M. Barth, *Abendmahl*, 13–15; F.-J. Leenhardt, *Le sacrement*, 31, 37; *Ceci est mon corps* (Cahiers théologiques 37), Neuchâtel–Paris, 1955, 24 [ET in Cullmann–Leenhardt, *Essays on the Lord's Supper*, London, 1958]; R. Stählin, 'Die neutestamentliche Lehre vom heiligen Abendmahl', *Evangelisch-lutherische Kirchenzeitung* 2 (1948), 62; A. J. B. Higgins, *The Lord's Supper in the New Testament* (SBT 6), London, 1952, 49–51; W. Manson, *Jesus the Messiah*, London, 1943, 145; G. Stählin, 'Die Gleichnishandlungen Jesu', in *Kosmos und Ekklesia* (W. Stählin Festschrift), Kassel, 1953, 15.

[4] So expressly the ancient variant κλώμενον 'broken' in I Cor. 11.24 (see above, p. 167 n. 3).

wine at the passover,[1] a custom for which support was found in Prov. 23.31 which speaks of wine that 'is red'. The comparison between *red wine* and blood was common in the Old Testament (Gen. 49.11; Deut. 32.14; Isa. 63.3, 6), further Ecclus 39.26; 50.15; I Macc. 6.34; Rev. 14.20; b. Sanh. 70a, etc.

We have therefore a double simile of Jesus here,[2] which has its formal analogy in the manner in which the prophets of the Old Covenant announce future events parabolically (Ezek. 4.1–17; 5.1–17; Jer. 19.1–15). Its meaning is quite simple. Each one of the disciples could understand it. Jesus made the broken[3] bread a simile of the fate of his body, the blood of the grapes a simile of his out-poured blood. 'I go to death as the true passover sacrifice', is the meaning of Jesus' last parable. The fact that Jesus expresses the same thought in a double simile is in accord with his predilection for pairing parables and especially similes: one recalls the twin parables of the lost sheep and the lost coin (Luke 15.1–10), or of the tower-builder and the king (Luke 14.28–32), and the great number of paired similes.[4] In our case the synthetic parallelism was occasioned by the twin terms: flesh and blood.

According to Mark/Matthew the bread-word completely lacks any detailed explanation of its meaning. Further, it is separated from its supplement, the cup-word, by the whole meal. This has led some to question whether the bread-word itself could have had for the disciples the full content of meaning: I am the eschatological paschal lamb whose death initiates the time of salvation. But such questioning overlooks the fact that Jesus must have said more than has been preserved in our brief, liturgical texts. Above all, insufficient attention is paid to the fact that Jesus' passover meditation preceded the words of interpretation. These words therefore did not meet the disciples unprepared. For the disciples the surprising thing must have been something else, namely that the interpretation given during the meditation was repeated at the grace before and after the meal. We will later ask what it could have been that led Jesus to this unusual linking of the words of interpretation with the graces.[5]

---

[1] Cf. Dalman, *Jesus-Jeshua*, 159.

[2] This has been justly stressed by A. Jülicher, 'Zur Geschichte der Abendmahls-feier in der ältesten Kirche', in *Theologische Abhandlungen* (C. von Weizsäcker Festschrift), Freiburg i. Br., 1892, 243. From Lietzmann to Dalman all are agreed on this.

[3] See above, p. 109 n. 10.   [4] Jeremias, *Parables*, 90–92.

[5] See below, pp. 231–7.

Only the fact of his vicarious death is announced by Jesus in the simile, not the details of its manner. None the less we can see from the simile and from the use of ἐκχυννόμενον[1] that Jesus did expect a violent death. Mark 14.25 par. makes it clear that Jesus was certain that God would vindicate his death by his resurrection and the establishment of the kingdom.

Yet the words of interpretation involve more.

(b) A statement about the meaning of Jesus' death

By comparing himself with the eschatological paschal lamb Jesus describes his death as a *saving death*. It is true that the passover of later times was not an expiatory[2] but an ordinary sacrifice; its blood was not sprinkled on the horns of the altar of burnt-offering, but poured on its base. It was indeed 'well pleasing before God',[3] but it could not be accepted as a substitute for the obligatory sin-offerings. But at the passover meal the attention was directed *not* to the 'passover of the generations', i.e. to the celebration which had been repeated year after year, but to the one 'passover of the exodus' for the sake of which God had mercifully 'passed over' the houses of the Israelites. The blood of the lambs slaughtered at the exodus from Egypt had *redemptive power*[4] and made *God's covenant* with Abraham operative.[5]

---

[1] Cf. Josephus, *Ant.* 19.94, αἷμα . . . περὶ τὸν σταυρωθέντα ἐκκεχυμένον.

[2] Cf. Wünsche, *Neue Beiträge*, 333; Dalman, *Jesus-Jeshua*, 123, 168.

[3] Jub. 49.9, 15; Pes. 10.6; Zeb. 4.6 (this last instance in Billerbeck IV, 49f.).

[4] Pirḳe Rabbi Eliezer 29 (ed., Warsaw, 1878, 51): 'For the merit of the covenant blood of the circumcision and of the passover blood, I have redeemed you out of Egypt, and for their merit will you be redeemed at the end of the fourth (Roman) world empire (i.e. in the days of the Messiah)' (Billerbeck IV, 40).

[5] Targ. Zech. 9.11 (ed., Wilna, 1893): 'You also, for whom a covenant was decided upon over blood, have I redeemed from servitude in Egypt.' Cf. also Dalman, *Jesus-Jeshua*, 167: 'the direct reference is to the blood of the *passover lambs*, which brings into fruition God's "covenant" at the redemption from Egypt' (my italics). Mek. Ex. 12.6: ' "And you shall keep it until the fourteenth day of the same month." Why did the scripture require the purchase of the paschal lamb to take place four days before its slaughter? R. Matia b. Ḥeresh (*c*. AD 125) used to say: Behold it says: "Now when I passed by thee, and looked upon thee, and, behold, thy time was the time of love" (Ezek. 16.8). [As so often, the most important words of the quotation for the present context are not given: "I spread my skirt over thee, and covered thy nakedness: yea, I plighted my troth to thee and entered into a covenant with thee."] This means, the time had arrived for the fulfilment of the oath which God had sworn unto Abraham, to deliver his children (Gen. 15.14). But as yet they had no (obligatory) commandments to perform by which to merit redemption (by keeping the commandments), as it further says: "thy breasts were fashioned, and thy hair was grown; yet thou wast naked and bare" (Ezek. 16.7), which means bare of (the keeping of) any commandments. Therefore God gave

As a reward for the Israelites' obedience to the commandment to spread blood on their doors, God manifested himself and spared them, 'passing over' their houses.[1] For the sake of the passover blood God revoked the death sentence against Israel;[2] he said: 'I will see the blood of the passover and make atonement for you.'[3] In the same way the people of God of the End time will be redeemed by the merits of the passover blood.[4] Jesus describes his death as this eschatological passover sacrifice: *his vicarious* (ὑπέρ) *death brings into operation the final deliverance*, the new covenant of God. Διαθήκη ('covenant') is a correlate of βασιλεία τῶν οὐρανῶν ('kingdom of heaven').[5] The content of this gracious institution which is meditated by Jesus' death is perfect communion with God (Jer. 31.33–34a) in his reign, based upon the remission of sins (31.34b).

The addition to the wine-word τὸ ἐκχυννόμενον ὑπέρ πολλῶν, Hebr. *hannišpak be'ad rabbim*, Aram. *demištephek 'al saggi'in*, 'which will be shed[6] for many', continues the comparison with the sacrifices: ἐκχυννόμενον is taken from the language of sacrifice.[7] It makes clear *for whom the atoning and redeeming power of Jesus is effective*. It is linked with an Old Testament passage: Isa. 53.12, 'because he poured out (*he'erah*) his life to death, and was numbered with the transgressors;

---

them two commandments: the blood of the paschal sacrifice and the blood of the circumcision, which they should perform so as to be worthy of redemption. For thus it is said: "And when I passed by thee, and saw thee wallowing in thy two kinds of blood" [Ezek. 16.6; *bedamayik* is understood as a dual by the Midrash: passover blood and circumcision blood]. Further it is said: "As for thee also, because of the blood of thy covenant I will send forth thy prisoners out of the pit wherein is no water" (Zech. 9.11).' Passover blood and circumcision blood are the blood of the covenant for the sake of which the deliverance out of Egypt was granted. So also Ex. R. 17.3 on 12.22.

[1] Mek. Ex. 12.13 par. 12.23.
[2] Ex. R. 15.12 on 12.10. 'It is as if a king said to his sons: Know you that I judge persons on capital charges and condemn them. Give me therefore a present, so that in case you are brought before my judgment seat I may set aside the indictments against you. So God said to Israel: I am now concerned with death penalties, but I will tell you how I will have pity on you and for the sake of the passover blood and the circumcision blood I will atone for you (*mkpr 'l npšwtykm*).'
[3] Ex. R. 15.12 on 12.2.
[4] See note above, beginning 'Targ. Zech 9.11'.
[5] J. Behm, διαθήκη B, *TWNT* II (1935), 137.
[6] See above, pp. 178f. no. 13.
[7] See above, p. 222 n. 5.

yet he bore the sin of many (*rabbim*) and made intercession for the transgressors' (the reference is to the Hebrew text of this passage, a fact to be kept in mind as evidence of the age of the tradition).[1] This allusion to the Old Testament passage on the suffering servant is supported by the fact that the word *rabbim/πολλοί* is almost a *leit-motiv* in Isa. 52.13–53.12.[2]

So if we wish to discover whom Jesus meant by the 'many' for whom his blood would be shed, we must first ask how the word *rabbim* (LXX πολλοί) in Isa. 52.14; 53.11, 12a, 12b was understood at the time of Jesus. It is difficult to understand why it should be that this question seems only recently to have been raised.[3] In answering it a distinction must be made between the views of the pre-Christian and post-Christian writings of Judaism. With regard to the latter, the first thing to be considered is the paraphrase of Isa. 52.13– 53.12 in the Targum on the prophets.[4] Here the 'many' are understood as: the house of Israel (Targ. Isa. 52.14), many sinners (53.11), many peoples (53.12a), many transgressions (53.12b).[5] Although the 'many' here are in part understood to be Jews and in part Gentiles, yet it is significant that in those cases where the reference is to the salvation wrought by the servant for the many (Isa. 53.11, 12b) the interpretation seems to be limited to *Israel*. The same is true for the remaining rabbinical interpretations of the 'many' in Isa. 53.11, 12b:

[1] See above, p. 179 no. 14.
[2] That Jesus was thinking in terms of Isa. 53 during the Last Supper is not only presupposed by Luke 22.37 but also by the pre-Markan passion tradition; cf. C. Maurer, 'Knecht Gottes und Sohn Gottes im Passionsbericht des Markusevangeliums', *ZThK* 50 (1953), 1–38. On the question whether Jesus regarded himself as the suffering servant, cf. Jeremias, *Servant of God*, 98–104. Further, cf. W. Staerk, *Soter* I (BFChTh II 31), Gütersloh, 1933; Otto, *Kingdom of God and Son of Man*; N. Johansson, *Parakletoi*, Lund, 1940; Jeremias, *Judaica* 3 (1947–8), 249–64. See also below, p. 230.
[3] Since the previous edition of this book there has appeared H. Hegermann, *Jesaja 53 in Hexapla, Targum und Peschitta* (BFChTh II 56), Gütersloh, 1954, 68f., 91–93, 96f.; J. Jeremias, πολλοί, *TWNT* VI (1959), 536–45.
[4] A critical edition of the text of this passage, based upon ancient MSS. and the 1517 Venice edition is given by Dalman, *Dialektproben*, 10f., and, along with a translation, by J. F. Stenning, *The Targum of Isaiah*, Oxford, 1949, 178–81. A very well-arranged synoptic table of the texts, M.T., LXX, Targum, Peshitta, Aquila, Theodotion, Symmachus, printed side by side in seven columns, is given by Hegermann, *op. cit.*, in an appendix.

[5] Isa.						
52.14	MT	*rabbim*	LXX	πολλοί	Targ.	*bet yiśrael*
53.11	MT	*harabbim*	LXX	πολλοί	Targ.	*saggi'in*
53.12a	MT	*harabbim*	LXX	πολλοί	Targ.	*'amemin saggi'in*
53.12b	MT	*rabbim*	LXX	πολλοί	Targ.	*saggi'in*

almost without exception the reference is understood to be to Israel. Seder Eliyyahu Rabbah 14 interprets the 'many', Isa. 53.11, as the rich and poor in Israel without distinction,[1] *ibid.* 25 as the 'contemporaries' (each particular generation of Israel). The 'many' in Isa. 53.12b are interpreted in Siphre Num. 131 on 25.13 as 'the children of Israel', in b. Soṭ. 14a as those who are guilty of the sin of the golden calf, i.e. the people of Israel as a whole, in Siphre Deut. 355 on 33.21 as the whole people of Israel. An exception is the late collection of homilies Pesiḳta Rabbati, where alongside the narrower interpretation, in chapter 36, the conception is to be found that all who are called into life by the will of God are those thought of as the recipients of salvation in Isa. 53.[2]

But all these post-Christian explanations of the 'many' in Isa. 53 are of little importance to our purpose. No other passage from the Old Testament was as important to the Church as Isa. 53, and for this reason no other passage has suffered as much from Jewish polemics. One can see in the Targum on the prophets[3] how much ingenuity has been exercised to eliminate the suffering of the Messiah. So the pre-Christian interpretations of the 'many' in Isa. 53 are the more important. I Enoch interprets the 'many' in Isa. 53 as the kings, the mighty, the strong, the sinners (I Enoch 46.4–5), as 'the kings of the earth and the strong who possess the land' (48.8), similarly 55.4; 62.1, 3, 6, 9; 63.1–11. Here therefore it is certain that the 'many' are understood as *Gentiles*. The Wisdom of Solomon 5.1–23, cf. 2.19–20, interprets the 'many' (Isa. 52.14f.) as the sinners who have afflicted (5.1) and derided (5.3f.) the righteous, as the presumptuous and the insolent (5.8), as those who live an evil life (5.13), as the godless (5.14; 2.19f.). Since no distinction is made in this passage between Jews and Gentiles, it is probable that the reference is to the *godless among both the Jews and the Gentiles*,[4] although

[1] The passage 'the righteous one, my servant, shall make many to be accounted righteous' (Isa. 53.11) is interpreted as referring to a true teacher who 'teaches Israel publicly' and makes his teaching accessible to all, irrespective of social differences.

[2] The passage has been printed, e.g., by Dalman, *Der leidende Messias*, 61. Isa. 53 is not specifically quoted in this passage, which describes how the Messiah, before the creation of the world, declares himself prepared to undergo vicarious suffering for the redemption of the world. But it is certain that the description is based upon Isa. 53.

[3] English translation in Stenning, *op. cit.*, 178, 180; Jeremias, *Servant*, 68–70.

[4] F. Feldmann, *Das Buch der Weisheit*, Bonn, 1926, 44.

in view of Wisd. 1.1ff. and Isa. 52.15 primarily to the latter. The pre-Christian interpretations are especially important because of their agreement with the meaning of the original text.

However, one reservation must certainly be made here. The 'many' envisaged in I Enoch and the Wisdom of Solomon are the 'many' of Isa. 52.14f., i.e. the Gentiles[1] who become silent in repentance and shame before the servant of God, not the 'many' of 53.11, 12b whose sins were born by the servant. But according to the Isaiah text there is no difference between these two. The 'many' who are seized by astonishment and terror (52.14f.) are the very ones who confess that they have failed to recognize the servant because he had neither form nor comeliness, and whose eyes are opened to the fact that it was *their* griefs that he bore, *their* sorrows that he carried, *their* iniquity that God laid on him (53.2ff.). They are the ones who acknowledge: 'upon him was the chastisement that made us whole' (53.5). In fact, the Peshitta renders Isa. 52.15, 'he will purify many peoples'. If the Peshitta version of the Old Testament is pre-Christian (which is probable),[2] then we have here an example of the inclusion of the Gentiles in the group of the 'many' for whom the atoning work of the servant is effective.[3] It is most unlikely that Jesus would have interpreted Isa. 53 differently, if he knew himself to be the servant of God of whom it is said in Isa. 49.6 that he would not only restore the preserved of Israel but also be a light to the Gentiles, in order that the salvation of God might reach to the end of the earth. The 'for many' of the eucharistic words is therefore, as we have already seen,[4] not exclusive ('many, but not all'), but, in the Semitic manner of speech, inclusive ('the totality, consisting of many').[5] The Johannine tradition interprets it in this way, for in its equivalent to the bread-word (see above, pp. 107f.) it paraphrases 'for many' as 'for the life of the world' (John 6.51c). Translating according to the sense therefore, τὸ ἐκχυννόμενον ὑπὲρ πολλῶν is to be rendered, '*which will be shed for the peoples of the world*'.

This is a concept unheard of in contemporary rabbinical thought.

---

[1] Cf. especially Isa. 52.15, *goyim rabbim*. If Dan. 12.3 refers to Isa. 53.11b, then we have also a pre-Christian interpretation of this text. Dan. 12.3 regards the many (*harabbim*) as those from Israel who are led to righteousness.

[2] Jeremias, πολλοί, *TWNT* VI (1959), 544f.

[3] Hegermann, *Jesaja 53*, 96f.

[4] See above, pp. 179–82.

[5] Cf. on this, Jeremias, *ibid*.

Late Judaism concerned itself extensively with the conception of atonement.[1] Tos. Yoma 5.6ff. (190.15ff.)[2] gives the following scale:

(a) Penitence—atones for the breaking of a positive commandment.

(b) Penitence and the day of atonement—atones for the breaking of a prohibition.

(c) Penitence, day of atonement and suffering—atones for a sin worthy of death.

(d) Penitence, day of atonement, suffering and death—atones for the profanation of the name of God.

In reality, however, the means of atonement were far more numerous. In addition to the four given above there are: public and private sacrifice,[3] fasting,[4] indemnification,[5] the High Priestly robes,[6] the merit of the fathers,[7] the vicarious suffering of the righteous,[8] the death of innocent children,[9] the death of the High Priest,[10] the death of martyrs,[11] and others. There are recognized means of atonement for all sins and sinners, with *one specific exception*; it is given in Mek. Ex. 21.30. '*For the heathen nations there will be no redemption*, as it is said: "No man can redeem his brother, nor give to God a ransom for him; for the redemption of their soul is too costly" (Ps. 49.8f.)'. Why is there no redemption for the heathen? The Mekilta text continues: 'Beloved are the Israelites, for the Holy One has given the heathen nations of the world as a ransom for them, as it is said: "I have given Egypt as thy ransom" (Isa. 43.3).'[12] This conception is even read into Isa. 53: Targ. Isa. 53 renders v. 8: 'he will lay to their (the heathens') charge the sins of which my people were guilty'. For the nations there

---

[1] A. Büchler, *Studies in Sin and Atonement in the Rabbinic Literature of the First Century* (Jews' College Publications 11), London, 1928.

[2] According to b. Yoma 86a the author is R. Ishmael (c. AD 90).

[3] Büchler, *Studies*, 375–461.

[4] Ps. Sol. 3.8, etc.

[5] b. R. H. 17b (Bar.), etc.

[6] b. Zeb. 88b, etc.

[7] Billerbeck I, 117–20.

[8] Billerbeck II, 274–97.

[9] Billerbeck II, 281; IV, 564, 595, 768, 1109. Cf. E. Lohse, *Märtyrer und Gottesknecht* (FRLANT N.F. 46)[2], Göttingen, 1963, 92–94.

[10] Mak. 2.6, 8. Cf. Jeremias, *Jerusalem*[3], 168; Lohse, *op. cit.*, 64–66.

[11] IV Macc. 6.29. Cf. Lohse, *op. cit.*, 66–78.

[12] Cf. Siphre Deut. 333 on 32.43; Ex. R. 11.3 on 8.19. Cf. Jeremias, *Judaica* 3 (1947–8), 256f.

is no ransom—Jesus says that *also for the peoples of the world* there is a
means of atonement: his vicarious (ὑπέρ) death.

The oft-repeated assertion that it is inconceivable that Jesus should have
ascribed atoning power to his death, that such statements belong rather to
the 'dogmatic' of the Early Church or of the apostle Paul, is astonishing to
anyone who knows the Palestinian sources. Conceptions of the atoning
power of death play a large part in the thought of Jesus' contemporaries.
Every death has atoning power (see, e.g., p. 230 under (*d*))—even that of
a criminal if he dies penitent. An innocent death offered to God has
vicarious power of atonement for others.[1] The sources compel the conclusion that *it is inconceivable that Jesus should not have thought of the atoning
power of his death.*[2]

This is therefore what Jesus said at the Last Supper about the
meaning of his death: *his death is the vicarious death of the suffering servant,
which atones for the sins of the 'many', the peoples of the world, which ushers
in the beginning of the final salvation and which effects the new covenant with
God.*

(c) The gift

But the words of Jesus are not only parable and instruction. They
are probably more than that, for he says them over the unleavened
bread and the wine at the very time[3] *when he offers them, both the bread
and the wine*, to be taken by the disciples. Or should we suppose that
it is only a coincidence that Jesus says both the bread-word and the
cup-word immediately after the grace (Mark 14.22, 'having said the
blessing'; 14.23, 'having given thanks') and so associates them with
the distribution of the bread and of the wine? We cannot make any
such supposition, for the reason that the appointed and proper place
for Jesus' words of interpretation was the passover *haggadah*, in the
course of which an interpretation of the various elements of the meal
was prescribed, as we have seen.[4] When Jesus, contrary to all

[1] For examples see above, previous notes. Cf. Lohse, *op. cit.*, 9–110 ('The
Atoning Death in Late Judaism').
[2] Jeremias, *Judaica* 3 (1947–8), 249–64.
[3] Cf. Mark 14.22, 'take'. Mark 14.23 has 'and they all drank of it' before the
word of interpretation, but this is anticipation, cf. the correction in Matt. 26.27,
'drink of it, all of you'. This can be the more confidently stated because 'this phrase
(*sc.* Mark 14.23, "and they all drank of it"), the Greek of which has a strong
Hebrew flavour, can signify simultaneous as well as successive action' (J. Rivière,
Le dogme de la Rédemption. Essai d'étude historique[2], in *Études d'histoire des dogmes et
d'ancienne littérature ecclésiastique*, Paris, 1905, 82).
[4] See above, p. 56.

expectation, repeated the interpretation he had already given during the passover *haggadah* at the distribution of the bread and the wine, then he must have done this with a definite purpose.[1] Can we discover what this purpose was? It is naturally not possible, 1,900 years later, to determine with absolute certainty in every single instance what the purpose of Jesus was in an action reported in our sources, nor can we say how the disciples understood it. None the less, it is by no means hopeless to try to see whether we can feel our way to the purpose which led Jesus to associate the words of interpretation with the distribution. Essential to any such attempt is a recapitulation of the ideas which Jesus' contemporaries associated with the breaking of bread and the blessing of the cup.

It is an ancient oriental idea that a common meal binds the table companions into a table fellowship. This table fellowship is religious, and therein rest its obligations: its violation is a particularly heinous crime (Ps. 41.10), and hence the deep grief felt by Jesus, Mark 14.20 par. Above all, the passover table fellowship is religious; this is seen most clearly in the fact that the membership of every *ḥaburah* had to be determined before the lamb was killed and its blood sprinkled on the altar of burnt-offerings. At every common meal *the constitution of the table fellowship* is accomplished by the rite of the breaking of bread.[2] The breaking of the bread is 'l'atto di comunione'.[3] When at the daily meal the *paterfamilias* recites the blessing over the bread—which the members of the household make their own by the 'Amen'—and breaks it and hands a piece to each member to eat, the meaning of the action is that each of the members *is made a recipient of the blessing by this eating*; the common 'Amen' and the common eating of the bread of benediction unite the members into a table fellowship. The same is true of the 'cup of blessing', which is the cup of wine over which grace has been spoken, when it is in circulation among the members:[4] *drinking from it mediates a share in the blessing.* This, it

---

[1] It should not be forgotten that Jesus said *more* at the Last Supper than has been transmitted in the concisely formulated accounts of it in what are, after all, cultic texts.

[2] Dalman, *Jesus-Jeshua*, 137; Zolli, *Il Nazareno*, 236. Therefore not by the taking of one's place at the common meal (so Fiebig, *Neues Sächsisches Kirchenblatt* 42 [1935], col. 375, who erroneously adduces Tos. Ber.—probably referring to 4.8 [9.8]).

[3] Zolli, *Il Nazareno*, 236. He rightly stresses, pp. 216–24, that the sacral character of the Last Supper consists in the table fellowship.

[4] This was probably the earlier rite which was common at the time of Jesus (see above, p. 69).

must be remembered, is true of every meal and was therefore a familiar and self-evident idea to the disciples from their earliest childhood: the eating of the broken bread and the drinking of the wine from the 'cup of blessing' gives—be it said once more: at *every* common meal—a share in the blessing which was spoken over the bread or the wine before the distribution.

Jesus, however, not only pronounced the blessing over the bread and wine, but also added the words which referred the broken bread and the red wine to his atoning death for 'many'. When immediately afterwards he gives this same bread and wine to his disciples to eat and drink, the meaning is *that by eating and drinking he gives them a share in the atoning power of his death.*

We can state this all the more confidently when we remember that to orientals the idea *that divine gifts are communicated by eating and drinking* is very familiar.[1] Reference may be made to *the symbolic language of eschatology.* In apocalyptic and Talmudic literature[2] as well as in the New Testament there are innumerable variations on the theme of the bread of life which satisfies all hunger;[3] the tree of life, the fruit of which cures the sick;[4] the heavenly manna, which will be the food of the redeemed in the world to come;[5] the water of life—'for he that hath mercy on them shall lead them, even by the springs of water shall he guide them' (Isa. 49.10, cf. Rev. 7.17) —which is given freely and quenches all thirst for ever;[6] the wine of the world to come which is kept for the children of the kingdom;[7] the feast of salvation in the last days, which imparts salvation and life.[8] 'Those who

[1] Cf. Jeremias, *Weltvollender*, 46–53, 74–79; *Golgotha* (Angelos-Beiheft 1), Leipzig–Göttingen, 1926, 60–64, 80–84.

[2] Billerbeck IV, 1146f., 1154–65.

[3] Jeremias, *Weltvollender*, 74–79. From the rich evidence we may quote Matt. 5.6: 'Blessed are they who hunger and thirst after righteousness, for God will satisfy them (the passive χορτασθήσονται is circumscription for the divine name)' (par. Luke 6.21); John 6.35, 50. Cf. also *laḥma šel ʿolam habba* (below, p. 234 n. 1).

[4] Ezek. 47.12; I Enoch 24.4–25.7; Test. Levi 18.11; Rev. 22.2, 14,19.

[5] Syr. Bar. 29.8; Sib. Orac. 7.149; b. Ḥag. 12b; Midr. Ḳoh. 28 on 1.9; Midr. Ruth 5.6 on 2.14. This concept also plays a large part in the NT. Jesus is expected to repeat the miracle of the manna (Matt. 4.3 par.; John 6.30f.). The 'hidden manna' will be the food of the redeemed: Rev. 2.17. The fourth petition in the Lord's Prayer is also to be understood in this sense: as a prayer that God may give today the 'bread of the morrow' (i.e. the bread of the time of salvation).

[6] John 4.13f.; 6.35; 7.37–39; Rev. 21.6; 22.1, 17. The expectation that the miracle of Mount Horeb (Ex. 17.6; Num. 20.11) would be repeated in the Messianic age is found, e.g., in Gen. R. 48.10 on 18.4. Further, see Billerbeck II, 436, 481, 492; Jeremias, *Golgotha*, 82f.; *Weltvollender*, 49–52.

[7] Schlatter, *Matthäus*, 745; Billerbeck I, 992; b. Pes. 119b, etc.

[8] Isa. 25.6f.; 65.13f.; I Enoch 62.14f.; Syr. Bar. 29.3–8. Many sources in Billerbeck I, 603, 684, 992; II, 551, 720; III, 22, 33, 823; IV, 840, 1146f., 1154–65.

serve God unto death, will eat of the bread of the world to come in plenty.'[1]
'Blessed is he that shall eat bread in the kingdom of God' (Luke 14.15).
'Blessed are they which are called unto the marriage supper of the Lamb'
(Rev. 19.9). The righteous will 'be filled with the glory of the Šekinah'.[2] It is
well known that in the New Testament the idea of the feast of salvation
which imparts the gifts of redemption is very common. Matt. 5.6; 8.11
par.; 22.1–14 (par. Luke 14.15–24); 25.10, 21, 23 ($\chi\alpha\rho\acute{a}$ means 'meal of
joy');[3] Luke 22.15–18 (par. Mark 14.25); 22.29f.; Rev. 3.20; 19.7, 9 may
be mentioned here.[4] I am indebted to my colleague Rudolf Hermann for
pointing out to me that even the story of the Canaanite woman (Mark
7.24–30 par.) becomes fully understandable only in this connection: Jesus'
saying about the bread which is meant for the children and not for the
dogs refers to the eschatological meal, and the great faith of the woman
consists in this, that, by her word about the crumbs which are eaten by
the dogs, she acknowledges Jesus as the giver of the bread of life. The
passages in the Fourth Gospel where Jesus calls himself the bread of life
(John 6.33, 35, 41, 48, 50, 51) and his Gospel bread (6.35; cf. Mark 7.27
par.)[5] and water (John 4.10, 14; 6.35; 7.37f.), are to be understood
similarly in an eschatological sense. Mark, too, may know of the comparison of Jesus with the bread of life, if the 'one loaf' which the disciples
had in the boat during the crossing (Mark 8.14) is meant to be Jesus, the
bread of life. Jesus is the giver of the water of life in I Cor. 10.4; I Peter
2.4f.[6] In whatever way the metaphor is presented, the meaning is always
that divine gifts are imparted in eating and drinking.

These eschatological metaphors of the bread and water of life are closely
connected with the widespread allegorical interpretation of bread and
water which is at home particularly in the Wisdom literature. Already
Amos speaks in forceful words about hungering and thirsting after the
Word of God (8.11–14); Jeremiah calls God's commands his food (15.16);
Deutero-Isaiah (55.1–3) calls the promises of God water and bread which
are given freely; the Psalmist even says that Yahweh is 'the portion of my
cup' (16.5);[7] in the Book of Proverbs (3.18) Wisdom is called 'tree of life',
and Wisdom herself exhorts, 'come eat ye of my bread and drink of the
wine which I have mingled' (9.5; cf. 9.2). Ecclesiasticus speaks of the
'bread of understanding',[8] which Wisdom offers to her disciples (Ecclus

[1] Gen. R. 82.8 on 35.17.
[2] Midr. Ps. 45 § 3.
[3] Dalman, *Words*, 117f.
[4] Jeremias, *Weltvollender*, 46–53, 74–79. Cf. I Enoch 62.14: 'and with that Son
of Man they will eat'.
[5] Jesus is at the same time the giver and the gift.
[6] The 'living stone' is the rock which gives forth the water of life, cf. Jeremias,
Golgotha, 84f.
[7] Cf. on this Otto, *Kingdom of God and Son of Man*, 281f.
[8] *leḥem da'at*.

15.3), and makes her say: 'they that eat me shall yet be hungry; and they that drink me shall yet be thirsty' (24.21). Lastly, in the rabbinical literature comparisons of the Torah with bread and water[1] or bread and wine[2] are frequent.[3] Jesus himself used this metaphor calling the word of God his bread of life (Matt. 4.4 par.), and the will of God his daily food (John 4.32, 34).[4] All these examples show how familiar was the metaphor of bread and water (or wine) which gave the true life, and that it was by no means limited to the eschatological sphere.

The idea that eating and drinking imparts divine gifts is also expressed in the *interpretation of history*. From Ps. 78.25; Wisd. 16.20, we know that the manna was regarded as the food of the angels,[5] an idea which is fancifully said in the midrash to mean that manna adapted itself to everyone's taste and 'tempered itself to every man's liking' (Wisd. 16.21).[6] Paul had a more profound conception of the idea, when he spoke of the spiritual food and drink which were offered to the wandering Israelites by the miracles of the manna and of the water at Mount Horeb (I Cor. 10.3f.). It follows both from the description of Christ, 'that spiritual rock that followed them' (I Cor. 10.4), as the giver, and from the parallel drawn with the Eucharist of the Christian Church, that he is thinking of actual spiritual gifts here. A second example from a much earlier period may be found in Ex. 24.11, where it is said of Moses and the elders when they ascended Mount Sinai: 'and upon the nobles of the children of Israel he (God) laid not his hand; and they beheld God and did eat and drink (before him)'. In these last words the thought is of a covenant meal: the fact that God grants to the envoys the fellowship of his table is the pledge of the covenant.

There is, furthermore, the *cultic* aspect to be considered: 'Behold Israel after the flesh: have not they which eat the sacrifices communion with the altar?' (I Cor. 10. 18), says Paul; and the subsequent verses show that he intends to say that the eating of sacrificial meat brings the priests and participants in sacrificial meals into a very close relationship to God. Especially instructive is a passage *which positively ascribes an atoning effect to the cultic meal*: 'Where (is it said) that the eating of the sacred sacrifices

---

[1] Billerbeck II, 433ff., 483f., 485, 492, 752.

[2] Billerbeck II, 482c, 484, 614.

[3] On the comparison between the Torah, wisdom, insight and righteousness with 'living water', cf. the comprehensive collection of the material by H. Odeberg, *The Fourth Gospel*, Uppsala–Stockholm, 1929, 152–69. On the comparison of the Torah, etc. with the bread of life, cf. *ibid.*, 238–50.

[4] Cf. I Enoch 69.24, saying of God's creatures: 'their food consists of incessant thanksgiving'.

[5] Cf. Ex. 16.4; Ps. 78.24; 105.40; Neh. 9.15; Wisd. 16.20; 19.21; John 6.31–33: bread of heaven; b. Yoma 75b: the manna is 'the bread eaten by the ministering angels'.

[6] Rabbinical sources in Billerbeck II, 481f.

brings atonement to Israel? The Scripture teaches: "And He (Yahweh) hath given it (the sin-offering) to you to bear the iniquity of the congregation, to make atonement for them before the Lord" (Lev. 10.17). How so? The priests eat, and for the masters (who provide the sacrifice) atonement is made'.[1]

Even in everyday life there was to be found something like realized apocalyptic. 'If one partakes of a meal at which a scholar is present, it is as if he feasted on the effulgence of the *Šekinah*.'[2]

As a last instance of the idea that eating and drinking impart 'spiritual' gifts, we may quote a passage from the Slavonic book of Enoch, to which R. Otto has drawn attention.[3] It is particularly instructive, because it contemplates a situation similar to the Last Supper. It concerns the *farewell meal* which Enoch's sons intend to hold with their father before he leaves this world. 'Mefusailom answered his father Enoch: "What food (*sc.* meal) is agreeable to thy eyes, father, that we may make before thy face, that thou mayst bless our dwellings and thy sons, and all thy household, and glorify thy people, and thus after that depart?" '[4] *The last common meal is intended to impart to those who are left behind, at their request,[5] the blessing of the departing one. This blessing would be irrevocable.[6]*

Jesus' actions at his farewell meal belong to this circle of ideas. When he surprisingly repeated, at the distribution of the bread and the wine after the two blessings at table, the interpretations he had previously given during the passover *haggadah*, the intention was *to make clear to the disciples their participation in the gift*. The eating of the bread and the drinking from the cup that had been blessed is meant to give them not only a share in the blessing pronounced by Jesus as the *paterfamilias* but also, beyond that, a share in the redemptive work of Jesus as the saviour. This is Jesus' last and greatest gift. The forgiveness of sins is the gift of the time of salvation. A greater gift than a share in the redeeming power of his death Jesus could not give.

Through the appropriation of the forgiveness of sins the disciples become the redeemed community of the End time. This is what resolves the remarkable contrast between the universalistic emphasis of the 'for many' and the restricted nature of the small group to which

---

[1] Siphra Lev. on 10.17 (ed. princ., Venice, 1545, 24d.38–40).

[2] b. Ber. 64a.

[3] Otto, *Kingdom of God and Son of Man*, 308f.

[4] Slav. Enoch 56.1 (Charles, *APOT* II, 463), B text. The longer text A is little different.

[5] Enoch, however, refuses to partake of earthly food, Slav. Enoch 56.2.

[6] In the same way the dying Abraham blesses his descendants at a farewell meal, Jub. 22.1–30.

Jesus offered his gift. As recipients of Jesus' gift the disciples are *representatives of the new people of God*. However, according to Luke there is one restriction in connection with Jesus' gift. The adversative 'but behold' (Luke 22.21) which introduces the announcement of the betrayal imposes a limitation on the preceding 'for you':[1] the betrayer has excluded himself (22.22) from a share in the redeeming power of Jesus' death and from membership in the new people of God.

The fact that *Paul*, the earliest commentator, also understood the meaning of the Eucharist in this way is an important confirmation of our exegesis. In I Cor. 10.16 he describes the gift received in the Eucharist as 'a participation in the blood of Christ' and 'a participation in the body of Christ'. Verse 17 makes it clear that Paul uses 'the body of Christ' in his characteristic way, signifying the Church. Correspondingly, he will also have understood 'the blood of Christ' in its frequently repeated, specifically Pauline sense (Rom. 3.25; 5.9; Eph. 1.7; 2.13, cf. Col. 1.20) of the saving death of Christ. *To share in the atoning death of Jesus and to become part of the redeemed community—that is, according to Paul, the gift of the Eucharist.* This interpretation tallies with our exegesis even in detail.

'. . . THAT GOD MAY REMEMBER ME'

According to the Pauline report Jesus added to each of the words of interpretation a command for repetition: 'Do this (v. 25 adds "as often as you drink it") in remembrance of me' (I Cor. 11.24, 25). Luke also has this, although only after the word of interpretation of the bread (22.19).

Now, the early community, apparently from the very beginning, met regularly for common meals and so continued the daily table fellowship of Jesus with his disciples.[2] The question naturally arises as to whether in this the Church was obeying the command of Jesus to repeat the rite, or whether it is not much more likely that the mealtimes themselves gave rise to the command, which was then read back on to the lips of Jesus.

The first point that can be made against the authenticity of the command for repetition is that it is found only in some of the witnesses, namely in the Pauline-Lukan branch of the tradition. It is

[1] H. Schürmann, 'Lk 22, 19b–20 als ursprüngliche Textüberlieferung [I]', *Biblica* 32 (1951), 386f.
[2] See above, p. 66.

true that on linguistic and stylistic grounds it must be regarded as
pre-Pauline,[1] but, as we have seen,[2] it does not belong to the earliest
form of the Lord's Supper narrative. In itself this would not make it
unhistorical, because the command to repeat the rite is not necessarily
a part of the liturgical formula, since the celebration itself was its
fulfilment. '*On ne récite pas une rubrique, on l'exécute.*'[3] It could be that
we are dealing with an early, special tradition which found a place
only in the Antiochene branch of the tradition.[4] After all, Jesus said
more at the Last Supper than the few words preserved in the liturgical formulae.[5]

A fact which tells more heavily against the historicity of this
commandment is that its wording has affinities with the formulae
used for the foundation of ancient ceremonies of commemoration of
the dead. What is the position here?

(a) A formula as used in the institution of the ancient commemorative meals for the dead?

In 1903 in the third fascicle of F. Cabrol's great *Dictionnaire
d'archéologie chrétienne et de liturgie*, vol. I, H. Leclercq expressed the
opinion that the early Christian meal celebration was 'un véritable
banquet funèbre'.[6] This insight was taken up four years later, in 1907,
by H. Lietzmann, who used it on the sources by arguing, in the
first edition of his commentary on I Corinthians, that 'Do this in
remembrance of me' has 'its parallels'[7] in the hellenistic world,
namely in the 'records of the foundation of ancient cultic fellowships'.[8] Since these fellowships also celebrated commemorative feasts
for the dead, meals in remembrance of the dead person that were
'held regularly on the anniversary of the death or oftener' (so at any
rate Lietzmann assumed in the beginning), he drew the conclusion
that the use of the formula 'in remembrance of me' was evidence for
the fact that the Lord's Supper was 'shaped on the analogy of these
memorial meals' in hellenistic Christian circles.[9] Later, in 1926, he

[1] See above, p. 104; cf. also p. 188 no. 4.
[2] See above, p. 168.
[3] P. Benoit, 'Le récit de la Cène dans Lc. XXII, 15–20', *RB* 48 (1939), 386.
[4] See above, p. 189.
[5] See above, pp. 219, 222.
[6] H. Leclercq, 'Agape', *Dictionnaire d'archéologie chrétienne et de liturgie* I (1907),
col. 786.
[7] Lietzmann, *An die Korinther I*[1], Tübingen, 1907, 132.
[8] *Ibid.*, 131.
[9] *Ibid.*

formulated the matter more precisely: by the use of the formula 'this do in remembrance of me' the Lord's Supper 'assumes the character of a "meal of remembrance" for one departed, and thereby ranks distinctly as a type of the religious meals that were customary everywhere in the Graeco-Roman world'.[1] Still later, in 1931, he took a last step and suggested: when Paul introduces the Lord's Supper narrative by saying that he has received what follows 'of the Lord' (which Lietzmann interprets in terms of a personal revelation of the risen Lord to Paul),[2] he is thinking of this new understanding of the Lord's Supper; the risen Lord has taught him to understand this meal as a memorial of his death.[3] So the formula 'in remembrance of me' would be an indication that the Lord's Supper, under hellenistic influences, was completely transformed: from the daily repeated table fellowship with Jesus (ancient Palestinian form of the Lord's Supper) it became, under the influence of hellenistic meals in memory of the dead, the festival in commemoration of the dead (Pauline form of the Lord's Supper). Three things may be said in criticism of this view.

1. The analogy between the wording of the commandment to repetition and the ancient records of the institution of commemorative meals for the dead is indeed, at first sight, surprising and impressive, and it is understandable that Lietzmann's reference to this analogy should have been widely taken up.[4]

The clearest example of the analogy is to be found in the Testament of the philosopher Epicurus[5] (d. 271/70 BC) drawn up at the beginning of the third century BC. Epicurus left his whole estate to the philosophical school he had founded with the following conditions: the garden and its appurtenances as well as the house in Melite should be at the disposal of the school; the heirs of the estate should make arrangements (1) that sacrifices should be made for Epicurus' 'father, mother, brothers and us'; (2) that from the income of the estate each year on the 10th Gamelion the usual birthday celebration should be held, and (3) that each month on the

[1] Lietzmann, *Mass and Lord's Supper*, 182.
[2] Against this above, pp. 101, 202f.
[3] Lietzmann, *An die Korinther I. II*[3], Tübingen, 1931, 58,
[4] J. Weiss, *Earliest Christianity* II, New York, 1959, 645 n. 52; C. Clemen, *Religionsgeschichtliche Erklärung*, 179; H. Windisch, *Paulus und Christus* (UNT 24), Leipzig, 1934, 53; Finegan, *Überlieferung*, 66; A. Fridrichsen, 'Église et Sacrement dans le Nouveau Testament', *RHPhR* 17 (1937), 353; Benoit, *op. cit.*, 386 n. 2, and others.
[5] In Diogenes Laertius, 10.16 (ed. H. Usener, *Epicurea*, Leipzig, 1887, 165–8).

twentieth day a meeting of his students should take place. This last-named
meeting of the students on the twentieth of each month should be held
εἰς τὴν ἡμῶν τε καὶ Μητροδώρου ⟨μνήμην⟩ 'in our memory and that of
Metrodorus'.[1] The decisive word μνήμην is not actually in the text, but
has been supplied; since, however, Cicero in his translation of this text has
the word *memoria*, the conjecture μνήμην would seem to be valid.[2] Here
therefore we have an institution εἰς τὴν μνήμην, the institution of a meeting
of philosophers. True, there is no express mention of a meal, but one would
have been a feature of such a meeting.

If one turns to the comprehensive two-volume work by B. Laum,
Stiftungen in der griechischen und römischen Antike, Leipzig–Berlin, 1914, for
further analogies with the command for repetition,[3] then one finds a
second example in an inscription from Nicomedia. It runs . . . [δίδωμι
δὲ κ]αὶ κατα[λ]ε[ί]πω τῇ κώμῃ ['Ρ]ακήλων [ἀργ]υ[ρ]ίου (δηνάρια) ⟨there
follows a break which contained the number⟩ [ἐπὶ τῷ] ποιεῖν αὐτοὺς
ἀνά[μ]νη[σ]ίν μου, [ἣν] ποιήσουσιν [ἐν τῇ συγγ]ενε[ίᾳ] Δραδιζανῶν, '. . . with
the condition that they celebrate my ἀνάμνησις, which they should do in the
family circle of Dradizane'.[4] Again there is here no explicit mention of a
memorial meal, but the fact that the participation of the whole family
group seems to be presupposed led Laum[5] to the conclusion that a meal
was involved. But the text itself puts serious difficulties in the way of this
conclusion. The end of the inscription is damaged: of the conjectured
word συγγένεια (family group) only the three letters ενε are preserved,
and these could represent a quite different word, perhaps a place name.
So it is not absolutely certain that this Nicomedian inscription is concerned with a memorial meal of the relatives. None the less the giving of
the purpose of the bequest ἐπὶ τῷ ποιεῖν αὐτοὺς ἀνάμνησίν μου is interest-
ing enough, although we must remember that we do not have, as in I Cor.
11.24, 25, the construction εἰς ἀνάμνησιν, but that here ἀνάμνησις is a
technical designation of a memorial celebration.

Finally, the construction εἰς μνήμην occurs in isolated instances—so
far as I can see twice—in the endowment inscriptions. At Sillyon in
Pamphylia at the time of the Roman Empire a mother gives εἰς μνήμην
καὶ τειμὴν τοῦ υἱοῦ, 300,000 *denarii*, for the education of children.[6] And
an inscription from Magnesia in Asia Minor (second century AD) speaks of
mystery cult initiates who have left monies εἰς μνήμην,[7] the interest from

---

1 Usener, *op. cit.*, 166.9f.
2 Usener, *op. cit.*, 166.
3 Laum discusses the foundation of memorial ceremonies in vol. I, 74–81.
Vol. II has the texts.
4 Laum, II, 141 no. 203.
5 Laum, I, 74.
6 Laum, I, 42.
7 Laum, II, 117 no. 126.

which is intended to guarantee the presentation of sacrifices for the dead. In this last instance it is possible to conceive of banquets being held on the occasion of the sacrifices, but nothing is said about this and the interest from the noticeably small amount of money left for the purpose would scarcely suffice for an expenditure considerably greater than that of presenting the sacrifices. For the sake of completeness the related construction μνήμης χάριν should be noted: it is to be found on two tomb inscriptions from the time of the Roman Empire which concern the establishment of an annual decoration with roses[1] or an annual burning of roses,[2] and on a very late honorific inscription from Palmyra (AD 451) which was erected τειμῆς καὶ [μ]νήμης χάριν for one who had founded sacrifices and votive offerings for Moloch.[3]

All this should not lead us in any way to underrate the extraordinary role which the μνήμη-motive plays in the numerous foundations of antiquity, especially in the agonal and social foundations;[4] its increasing importance after the third century BC is due to the fact that the original religious motives for these foundations are being replaced by more worldly ones, especially that of a desire for personal or family standing.[5] But, although the μνήμη-motive is unquestionably widespread, *we must note in connection with our particular problem that the construction εἰς ἀνάμνησιν is completely absent* and that in not one of the five instances of an endowment εἰς μνήμην or μνήμης χάριν is a memorial meal explicitly mentioned: in the case of the large fund for the education of children a meal cannot be intended, and in the case of that for grave decoration more probably not. So lies the matter as far as Greek language inscriptions are concerned. It is only in the *Latin* inscriptions that we find repeatedly in connection with the institution of memorial meals the construction *in memoriam, ad memoriam, ob memoriam* of the actual person or another.[6]

---

[1] Laum, II, 141 no. 200 (Bithynia).

[2] Laum, II, 41 no. 38 (Philippi).

[3] Laum, II, 153 no. 211.

[4] Laum, I, 42-44, 74-81.

[5] Laum, I, 42.

[6] Laum, II, 164 no. 6 (distribution of gratuities *ob memoriam*); 180 no. 61 (a meal in honour of the dead *in memoriam eorum*); 181 no. 68 (a meal in honour of the dead *in memoriam sui*); 184 no. 86 (a meal in honour of the dead *ad [memoriam cole]ndam*); 195 no. 125 (*ob memoriam . . . fratris sui*). Meals in memory of the dead in Asia Minor: II, 88 no. 75; 97 no. 91; 135 no. 175; 136f. no. 178; 141 no. 203 (see above, p. 240 n. 4). In Christian literature we find εἰς ἀνάμνησιν, *Const. Apost.* 8.42.5 (F. X. Funk, *Didascalia et Constitutiones Apostolorum* I, Paderborn, 1905, 554.2f.). This is, however, not concerned with a foundation but with an annual distribution of alms.

2. More important than this first observation, that the construction εἰς ἀνάμνησιν is not to be found in the records of ancient endowments, is in my opinion a second one. As was mentioned at the beginning of this section, Lietzmann originally (1907) assumed that the commemorative meals held in honour of a dead person by their family, slaves or friends took place 'regularly on the *anniversary of the death* or oftener',[1] and it was on the basis of this assumption, among other things, that he explained the transformation of the Lord's Supper into a meal commemorating the death of Jesus. In the later editions of his commentary on the Corinthian Epistles, however, Lietzmann omitted the words 'regularly on the anniversary of the death or oftener'. With good reason! For the commemorative meals, strangely enough, were not held on the anniversary of the death of the founder. Sometimes the date for the meal was determined by the general days for commemoration of the dead (the *dies violarum* [day of violets] on March 22, the *dies rosarum* [day of roses] on May 11 or the *Parentalia*), mostly, however, by the *birthday of the founder* or of the member of the family whose memory was commemorated.[2] Not infrequently the wording of an endowment will presuppose several memorial celebrations in a year (as many as six), but then in honour of different deceased persons or heroes on the birthday of each one;[3] for the most part, however, the memorial meal seems to have been held *once* a year, and that, as already said, on the birthday of the founder or his son or brother (according to the purpose of the endowment).[4] This circumstance, that the commemorative meals of these cultic fellowships were as a rule *annual birthday memorial celebrations*, is an indication that we find ourselves here in a sphere quite different from that of the early Christian Lord's Supper; and this difference becomes still clearer when we look briefly at the development of these ancient meals in commemoration of the dead.

3. The ancient foundations begin sporadically in the fifth century BC, show a temporary falling off around 100 BC, reach a sudden high point about AD 200, and then dwindle away, disappearing towards the end of the fifth century AD.[5] They are, so far as they are connected with the cult of the dead, a product of secularization, the

---

[1] Lietzmann, *An die Korinther I*[1], 131. My italics.
[2] Laum, I, 75f.
[3] So Laum, II, 164f. no. 6.
[4] Cf. the table given by Laum, I, 77.
[5] See the table in Laum, I, 9.

growing influence of which is reflected in their development. In ancient times the strength of the cult of the dead was due to the fear of the vengeful souls of the departed and to the sense of family unity.[1] The growth of religious indifference and the loosening of the sense of family unity led to a neglect of the cult of the dead. This in turn led to the endowment of cults for the dead; they developed out of the fear that the descendants would neglect the cult of the dead and the up-keep of their graves.[2] Family groups or cultic fellowships were founded which were committed to caring for the grave as well as to making sacrifices to the family gods on behalf of the dead. The opportunity was taken—especially during the time of the Roman Empire—to unite with the sacrifices a memorial celebration with a banquet and the distribution of gratuities. Apparently the endowment of the cultic meal was intended to increase the incentive to take part and to guarantee that the sacrifice for the dead would not be neglected. For the most part it was a matter of a small group which held a memorial celebration once or more in a year, at which celebration wine and food was served, candles were burnt and gifts distributed;[3] 'the concern was more for the celebrants than for the dead'[4] and they became more and more—especially in the Roman world—purely *pleasurable affairs*.[5] The increasing worldliness of these celebrations was brought about, as A. M. Schneider pointed out to me, by the political situation. The Roman authorities were extremely suspicious of clubs: in Rome itself a *senatus consultum* absolutely forbade the founding of any new ones.[6] So the meals commemorating the dead held by artisans' corporations and funeral guilds were a welcome opportunity for irreproachable assemblies.

If due consideration is given to these facts—(1) the absence of the construction εἰς ἀνάμνησιν, (2) that it is never a matter of daily or weekly meals, as with the early Christian Eucharist, but usually of an annual birthday celebration in honour of the dead, and finally (3) the increasing worldliness of the memorial feasts—then it is scarcely conceivable that the command for repetition should be considered as having any connection with the institution of ancient meals for the dead.

[1] Laum, I, 41.
[2] *Ibid.*
[3] Laum, I, 247f.
[4] Laum, I, 248.
[5] Laum, I, 251.
[6] Laum, I, 249.

(b) Palestinian memorial formulae

Quite a different picture is to be seen when we turn to the realm of Palestinian Judaism.

1. In Palestine *memorial formulae* are very common in religious language.

We find them first in connection with the *cult*. That part of the cereal offering which was burnt is called already in the Old Testament *azkarah*, LXX, μνημόσυνον ('memorial [portion]', Lev. 2.2, 9, 16 etc.); the frankincense which is put with the shewbread is said to serve *leazkarah*, LXX, εἰς ἀνάμνησιν ('as a memorial [portion]', Lev. 24.7); the blowing of the trumpets by the priests over the burnt-offerings and the peace-offerings is to serve *lezikkaron liphne elohekem*, LXX, ἀνάμνησις ἔναντι τοῦ θεοῦ ὑμῶν ('for remembrance before your God', Num. 10.10), i.e. to insure that God remembers mercifully the givers of the sacrifices. God's merciful remembrance is similarly insured by the stones set in Aaron's breastplate, which bear the names of the twelve tribes *lezikkaron* ('for [continual] remembrance', Ex. 28.12, 29; 39.7), and by the atonement money which brings the people *lezikkaron liphne Yhwh* ('to remembrance before the Lord', 30.16). The twelve precious stones which Jael will put above the cherubim, *erunt in conspectu meo* (God's) *in memoria* (A: *in memoriam*) *domui* (A: *domus*) *Israel*.[1] Examples of the use of the construction εἰς μνημόσυνον in relation to the cult (bells and precious stones in Aaron's breastplate, incense, the sound of trumpets) are to be found in Ecclesiasticus (45.9, 11, 16; 50.16) and will be discussed below.[2]

Related to the temple and synogogue cult are the *donation formulae*, which are also concerned with remembrance.[3] The oldest is to be found in Zech. 6.14, where it is said that a crown should be deposited in the temple of Jahweh to the merciful remembrance (*lehen . . . lezikkaron*) of certain individuals,[4] i.e. to ensure God's merciful remembrance. Numerous later examples have been found in synagogue donors' inscriptions, which mostly begin with the phrase *dkyr ltb* in which the passive is circumlocution of the divine name, therefore: 'God remember so and so

---

[1] Ps.-Philo, *Ant. bibl.* 26.12 (G. Kisch, *Pseudo-Philo's Liber Antiquitatum Biblicarum* [Publications in Mediaeval Studies. The University of Notre Dame 10], Notre Dame, Indiana, 1949, 187).

[2] See below, p. 247.

[3] K. Galling, 'Königliche und nichtkönigliche Stifter beim Tempel von Jerusalem', *ZDPV* 68 (1946–51), 134–42.

[4] For the text (*lhn*) cf. O. Procksch in R. Kittel, *Biblica Hebraica*[3], Stuttgart, 1937, *ad loc.*; F. Horst in T. H. Robinson–F. Horst, *Die Zwölf Kleinen Propheten*[2], Tübingen, 1954, 236; Galling, *op. cit.*, 138.

mercifully'.[1] In the donor's inscription in the synagogue at Jericho this phrase is explicated by the additional sentence: 'He who knows their names and (the names) of their children and (the names) of the people of their households, shall write them in the Book of Life (together with) the Just.'[2] E. R. Goodenough has shown that the conclusion to be drawn from this is that the donor's inscription is eschatologically oriented; the prayer is that God's remembrance may be realized through the acceptance of the donor in the Book of Life.[3]

Next, memorial formulae are to be found in the *liturgy and in prayers*. Among the special prayers (*musaph* prayers) of the New Year festival are the *malkiyyot*, *zikronot* and *šopharot*. The *zikronot*[4] are prayers which enclose biblical passages concerned with 'remembrance', exclusively with God's merciful remembrance of his covenant promises in the past and in the future. The closing prayer of the *zikronot* ends with the doxology: 'Praised be thou, O Lord, that rememberest the covenant (*zoker habberit*).' Already in the Old Testament it is said that the passover is to be celebrated *lezikkaron* (Ex. 12.14; Targ. Jer. I, Onḳ. *ldwkrn'*). In the blessings for Sabbath, festivals and the new moon God is praised as the one who has given Sabbaths, festivals and new moons *lezikkaron* (b. Ber. 49a). It is said explicitly of prayers that they are raised εἰς μνημόσυνον (I Enoch 99.3), that they, together with alms, have ascended 'as a memorial before God' (Acts 10.4), that they are *lzkrwn* (1QS 10.5). An especially important example of an ancient prayer for God's remembrance is the liturgical prayer quoted below, p. 252.

Further, the memorial formula is to be found in *ritual language*. The pharisaic custom of wearing prayer phylacteries on the head, which can be traced back to pre-Christian times in Palestine,[5] is dependent upon the (literally interpreted) commandment Ex. 13.9: 'And it shall be to you . . . *lezikkaron* (Targ. Jer. I, Onḳ. *ldwkrn*) between your eyes.'

Finally, there are the Jewish *tomb inscriptions* in which is to be found both in Hebrew[6] and Greek[7]—with many variations—the formula from

---

[1] S. Klein, *Jüdisch-palästinisches Corpus Inscriptionum*, Vienna–Berlin, 1920, 69f. no. 3 (*'Ain ed-Dōq*), 75 no. 4 (*Kafr Kenna*), 77 no. 5 (*Sepphoris*), 82 no. 12 (*Khirbet Kanef*); E. L. Sukenik, *Ancient Synagogues in Palestine and Greece*, London, 1934, 72 (*Beit Djibrin*), 73 (*'Ain ed-Dōq*), 75, 76 (*Na'aran*), cf. 76 (*Beit Alpha*: μνησθῶσιν). Rabbinical examples in J. Jeremias, 'Mc 14, 9', *ZNW* 44 (1952–3), 106 n. 21, and in E. Bammel, 'Zum jüdischen Märtyrerkult', *ThLZ* 78 (1953), col. 124 n. 50.

[2] English translation by M. Avi-Yonah in D. C. Baramki–M. Avi-Yonah, *Quarterly of the Department of Antiquities in Palestine* 6 (1936–7), 76 n. 2, quoted by E. R. Goodenough, *Jewish Symbols in the Greco-Roman Period* (Bollingen Series 37) I, New York, 1952, 261; II, 1952, 129.

[3] *Ibid.*

[4] Text, e.g., in P. Fiebig, *Rosch ha-schana* (*Neujahr*), Giessen, 1914, 53–58.

[5] Billerbeck IV, 251.

[6] Klein, *op. cit.*, 39 no. 114; J.-B. Frey, *Corpus Inscriptionum Iudaicarum* (Sussidi

Prov. 10.7, 'the memory of the righteous is a blessing'. This biblical text
was differently understood in hellenistic and Palestinian Judaism. In
hellenistic Judaism it was interpreted, as the multilingual tomb inscriptions show, as referring to the good memories which the deceased left
behind among his contemporaries. In Palestinian Judaism, on the other
hand, it was understood as a wish ('may the memory of the righteous be a
blessing') relating to the merciful remembrance of God. We can see that
from, among other things, the formula of blessing to be used of a father
who had been dead for more than a year: *zkrwnw lbrkh lhyy h'wlm hb'*, 'His
memory be for a blessing, (namely) for the life of the world to come'.[1] In
this context also we find the εἰς-formula: LXX, Ps. 111 (112).6, εἰς
μνημόσυνον αἰώνιον ἔσται δίκαιος, 'the righteous will be for eternal remembrance'; Targ. Ps. 112.6, *ldkrn 'lm yhy zky*.

2. For our question it is especially important to notice that the
command for repetition εἰς ἀνάμνησιν, which we sought in vain in
the hellenistic records of the institution of commemorative meals, is
not only to be found in the language usage of Greek-speaking Judaism
but is also—when we consider the parallel phrases εἰς μνημόσυνον
and *in memoriam* as well as the Hebrew[2] and Aramaic[3] equivalents—
to be found with what may be described as extraordinary frequency
in late Judaism as a whole. The review which we have just given
shows that the formula is found several times already in the Old
Testament and that it is used frequently in the Judaism of New
Testament times. We find it in Ecclesiasticus, in the Wisdom of
Solomon, in I Enoch, in the Essene literature, in Pseudo-Philo and
in the rabbinical literature.

In the LXX we notice immediately a significant fact: whereas
εἰς ἀνάμνησιν is used in the Wisdom of Solomon, a book composed
in Greek, of *men* remembering the commandments of God (16.6), in
Lev. 24.7 LXX it is used meaning 'that *God* may mercifully remember'.[4] It has the same meaning in the remaining two places in which
it is found in the LXX: Ps. 69(70).1f., τῷ Δαυιδ. Εἰς ἀνάμνησιν, εἰς τὸ

allo studio delle antichità cristiane 1), Vatican City–Rome–Paris, 1936, 446 no. 625,
447f. no. 629, 453f. no. 635, 474f. no. 661. Cf. Ecclus 45.1 (of Moses): *zkrw lṭwbh*.
    [7] Frey, *op. cit.*, 60 no. 86, 140f. no. 201 (268f. no. 343), 287f. no. 270, cf. 361f.
no. 496: simply μνησθῇ.

    [1] b. Ḳid. 31b.
    [2] *lzkrwn, l'zkrh, lzkr.*
    [3] *ldkrn, ldwkrn'.*
    [4] See above, p. 244.

σῶσαί με κύριον (note the explanatory addition of the infinitive), and similarly Ps. 37(38).1. The same is true of the parallel εἰς μνημόσυνον. Occasionally it is used in the LXX of human remembering, although almost only in the more profane context of things being written down in a book εἰς μνημόσυνον (so several times in the book of Esther).[1] In religious or cultic contexts, on the other hand, εἰς μνημόσυνον regularly[2] has God as the subject. Such is the case throughout Ecclesiasticus. We read that Aaron had bells on his garments εἰς μνημόσυνον υἱοῖς λαοῦ αὐτοῦ, 'that God might remember mercifully the children of his people' (45.9), the stones on his garment were inscribed εἰς μνημόσυνον (45.11), he offered incense and fragrance εἰς μνημόσυνον (45.16), and the priests sounded the trumpets εἰς μνημόσυνον ἔναντι ὑψίστου (50.16). Further examples of the use of εἰς μνημόσυνον in New Testament times have been found in the fragments of the Greek text of I Enoch.[3] Following a series of woes over sinners it says: 'Then make ready, you righteous, and offer your prayers εἰς μνημόσυνον; place them as a testimony before the angels, that they may bring the sins of the unrighteous before the most high God εἰς μνημόσυνον' (99.3); again it is the merciful and punishing remembrance of God that is meant by εἰς μνημόσυνον, and μνημόσυνον has the same meaning in the two other places at which it is to be found in these fragments (97.7; 103.4).

To summarize: the formula εἰς ἀνάμνησιν and its variations were not infrequently used in Judaism in Jesus' time with reference to human remembering, but the occasions are for the most part (a) in texts originally written in Greek such as the Wisdom of Solomon (εἰς ἀνάμνησιν), IV Macc. 17.8 (εἰς μνείαν) and twice in Philo (εἰς μνήμην),[4] or (b) translations of such Old Testament texts as speak of human remembrance. By far the more frequent practice of Judaism at the time of Jesus, however, is to use εἰς ἀνάμνησιν and its equivalents of God's remembrance. The reader who will take the trouble to check the references to Old Testament and Jewish remembrance formulae gathered together on pp. 244–6 from the viewpoint as to

[1] But each time (1.1p; 2.23; 9.32; 10.2) without an equivalent in the Hebrew text.
[2] LXX, Ps. 111(112).6, εἰς μνημόσυνον αἰώνιον ἔσται δίκαιος, 'the righteous will be for eternal remembrance', is to be judged according to what has been said on Prov. 10.7 above, p. 246.
[3] Ed. C. Bonner, *The Last Chapters of Enoch in Greek* (Studies and Documents 8), London, 1937.
[4] Philo, *Quis rer. div. heres sit* 170; *De vita Mos.* 1.186.

whether they are concerned with human or divine remembrance will see at once that for the most part they speak of God's remembrance.[1]

3. Where, however, εἰς ἀνάμνησιν and its equivalents mean 'that God may remember', this has a twofold significance. In the first place it means *that something is brought before God*.[2] So, for example, when a bequest is deposited in the temple *lezikkaron* (Zech. 6.14), when of the shewbread it is said that it is laid before the eyes of the Lord εἰς ἀνάμνησιν (LXX, Lev. 24.7), when the priests sound the trumpets at a sacrifice to effect μνημοσύνη (Ecclus 50.16), when the prayers of the righteous and their complaints against the sinners are brought before God εἰς μνημόσυνον (Enoch 99.3, Gr.), when prayers and alms ascend 'as a memorial before God' (Acts 10.4)—always it is not simply a matter of God being reminded of a person or thing, but of something being *brought before God*. This is conceived quite realistically. When in Num. 5.15 it says of the offering brought on the occasion of a complaint of adultery that it is a *zkrwn*-offering, a θυσία μνημοσύνου ἀναμιμνήσκουσα ἁμαρτίαν (LXX), this means that the sin itself is 're-called' before God by means of the offering, is re-presented before him,[3] the past thus becoming present before God. 'Have you come to bring my sin to remembrance (before God?'), cries the widow from Zarepheth to Elijah after the death of her son (I Kings 17.18). The meaning could be similar when the Epistle to the Hebrews says of the Old Testament Day of Atonement sacrifices, that the blood of bulls and goats only effects ἀνάμνησις ἁμαρτιῶν (10.3) —it can bring the sins to life before God, but it cannot blot them out.[4] In all of these places ἀνάμνησις denotes *representation before God*.

This is, however, only one side of that which is said in the phrase εἰς ἀνάμνησιν when this is used of God. This calling into the presence of God, this bringing to life before God, this recalling of the past, this is, on the other side, effective. It has a purpose, it is intended to effect something: *that God may remember*—mercifully or punishingly. God's remembrance is, namely (this is an important fact to which O. Michel called attention), never a simple remembering of something, but

---

[1] That additions such as Acts 10.4 (ἔμπροσθεν τοῦ θεοῦ), Ecclus 50.16 (ἔναντι ὑψίστου), I Enoch 99.3 (ἐνώπιον τοῦ ὑψίστου θεοῦ) are found only occasionally is to be explained by the fact that the formulae are firmly established.
[2] R. Stählin, 'Herrenmahl und Heilsgeschichte', *Evangelisch-lutherische Kirchenzeitung* 2 (1948), 153b.
[3] Dix, *Liturgy*, 161.
[4] *Ibid.*

always and without exception 'an effecting and creating event'.[1] When Luke 1.72 says that God remembers his covenant, this means that he is now fulfilling the eschatological covenant promise. When God remembers the iniquities of Babylon the Great (Rev. 18.5), this means that he is now releasing the eschatological judgment. When the sinner 'is not to be remembered' at the resurrection, this means that he will have no part in it (Ps. Sol. 3.11). And when God no longer remembers sin, when he forgets it (Jer. 31.34; Heb. 8.12; 10.17), this means that he forgives it.[2] God's remembrance is always an action in mercy or judgment.

This is therefore the result of our investigation of the use of the construction εἰς ἀνάμνησιν and its variants in Palestinian linguistic usage: (1) εἰς ἀνάμνησιν is said *for the most part in reference to God* and (2) it then designates, always and without exception, *a presentation before God intended to induce God to act.*

(c) Τοῦτο ποιεῖτε εἰς τὴν ἐμὴν ἀνάμνησιν ('*This do in remembrance of me*')

It is clear that these conclusions are important to an understanding of the command for repetition. We recall, before we turn to the exegesis of this command, that it is given twice by Paul, both after the word over the bread and after the word over the cup (I Cor. 11.24, 25), by Luke on the other hand only after the word over the bread (22.19). Since Luke (alone) gives the 'for you' twice, it is not very likely that he is himself responsible for the omission of the second command for repetition. In giving the command *only in connection with the bread word* he is more probably reflecting an earlier stage of the tradition.[3]

We consider first the command τοῦτο ποιεῖτε ('this do') and then the purpose given εἰς τὴν ἐμὴν ἀνάμνησιν ('in remembrance of me'). Τοῦτο ποιεῖτε is, as can be seen from comparison with Ex. 29.35; Num. 15.11–13; Deut. 25.9; Jeb. 12.3,[4] an established expression for the

---

[1] O. Michel, μιμνῄσκομαι κτλ., *TWNT* IV (1942), 678.26f.

[2] Heb. 10.18: therefore there is no further need from that moment for any sin-offerings. The meaning of the cry of the penitent thief in Luke 23.42 is similar: with the words 'Jesus, remember me when you come as king' (ἐν τῇ βασιλείᾳ [ℵ C ℜ Θ pl Th] σου = bemalkutak, 'when you become king', i.e. at the Parousia) he asks that Jesus speak for him at the final judgment.

[3] Schürmann, *Einsetzungsbericht*, 70.

[4] All of these texts have kakah (LXX, οὕτως) with a jussive form of ʿasah (LXX, ποιεῖν).

repetition of a rite. This usage lives on in the Qumran texts.[1] 1QS
2.19 commands the annual repetition of the covenant renewal with
the words *kkh y'šw*, and in 1 QSa 2.21 a depiction of the ritual beginning of a meal in the Messianic time is followed by ordaining that this
rite be observed, using the phrase *wkhwk hzh y'š(w)*.[2] If the command
for repetition uses τοῦτο in reference to a rite, then the question is which
rite is intended. It cannot refer to the simple recital of the words of
interpretation (that is ruled out by ποιεῖτε which contemplates action);
nor can it mean the whole meal (that is ruled out by the repetition
with the cup and the limiting 'as often as you drink', I Cor. 11.25);
there remains only the possibility that τοῦτο refers to the *rite of breaking
the bread*, i.e. the rite of grace at table. To be exact, it is scarcely
possible that the reference is to the normal table prayer—that would
need no special instruction—it is rather to the special grace by means
of which the table fellowship of the Messianic community was established, which extolled the salvation activity of God and prayed for
its consummation,[3] a prayer which Jesus himself may have used
during his lifetime.[4] As we saw, 1QSa 2.21 uses an analogous formula
to organize a specific form of the beginning of the meal and of the
constitution of the table fellowship. Paul also refers the τοῦτο to the
rite of grace at table; this can be seen from I Cor. 10.16, 'The cup of
blessing which we bless. . . . The bread which we break': 'we bless'
and 'we break' refer to the carrying out of the command τοῦτο ποιεῖτε,
which he has in a doubled form.[5] There is, finally, one further argument, and a strong one, in support of this interpretation of the τοῦτο
ποιεῖτε as referring to the rite of grace at table. We have seen that
very early, presumably even before the writing of I Corinthians, the
normal meal and the Eucharist were separated from one another.[6]
That such a separation should have become desirable is understandable when we realize that in the beginning the non-baptized took
part in the meal.[7] But how did it come about that the particular,
and somewhat strange, solution to the problem was chosen, of giving

[1] This was pointed out to me by my son, Gert Jeremias.
[2] On this text see above, p. 35.
[3] Cf. Did. 9.1–10.5.
[4] On this possibility see above, p. 109 n.8 and p. 120 n. 3 under 2a.
[5] Cf. also I Cor. 11.26, where the words 'as often as you eat this bread and
drink the cup' also describe the carrying out of the doubled τοῦτο ποιεῖτε-com-
mand (see below, pp. 252f.).
[6] See above, p. 121.
[7] See above, p. 133.

an independent existence to the rite of breaking the bread and repeating it together with the rite of blessing the cup at the end of the meal? This question allows of scarcely any other answer than this: even before the separation of the Eucharist from the meal proper the rite of breaking the bread (Luke 22.19) and, as a consequence, the rite of blessing the cup (I Cor. 11.25) already possessed an importance by themselves. This intrinsic importance of the breaking of the bread, which is also expressed in the use of 'the breaking of bread', 'to break bread' as technical terms,[1] is probably due to the command for repetition.

The breaking of bread by the disciples (τοῦτο) shall be done (ποιεῖτε) εἰς τὴν ἐμὴν ἀνάμνησιν ('in remembrance of me'). The expression is ambiguous. It is clear that ἐμήν[2] represents an objective genitive.[3] The phrase therefore means: 'that I be remembered', 'in rememberance of me' (RSV). The only question is: Who should remember Jesus? The usual interpretation, according to which it is the disciples who should remember, is strange. Was Jesus afraid that his disciples would forget him? But this is not the only possible interpretation, indeed it is not even the most obvious. In the New Testament we find a parallel construction εἰς μνημόσυνον at two places: Mark 14.9 (par. Matt. 26.13) and Acts 10.4, 'as a memorial before God'. Acts 10.4 specifically names God as the subject of the remembering[4] and similarly Mark 14.9 par., 'in memory of her', in all probability relates to the merciful remembrance of God: 'that God may (mercifully) remember her (at the last judgment)'.[5] This is in agreement with what we saw above, pp. 246-9, that in the Old Testament and Palestinian memorial formulae it is almost always

---

[1] On these see above, p. 120f.

[2] The emphatic position of the possessive pronoun before the noun has led many to see a contrast between the remembrance of Jesus and the remembrance of the Passover (e.g. O. Procksch, 'Passa und Abendmahl', in H. Sasse, Vom Sakrament des Altars, 23). But it is most questionable whether in Aramaic the pronoun was especially emphasized (by dili).

[3] An objective genitive with ἀνάμνησις, μνημόσυνον is the established usage, cf. Mark 14.9; Wisd. 16.6; Ecclus 10.17; 23.26; 38.23; 39.9; 41.1; 44.9; 45.1; 46.11; 49.1, 13; LXX, Esth. 8.12 u; I Macc. 3.7, 35; 8.22; 12.53; II Macc. 6.31.

[4] Cf. Num. 10.10, LXX, ἔσται ὑμῖν ἀνάμνησις ἔναντι τοῦ θεοῦ ὑμῶν.

[5] I have attempted to give the linguistic arguments in support of the eschatological interpretation of Mark 14.9 ('Amen, I say to you, when [God's angel] proclaims the [triumphant] message in all the world, then will what she has done be told [before God], so that he may [mercifully] remember her') in 'Mc 14, 9', ZNW 44 (1952-3), 103-7. Cf. also Jeremias, Promise, 22f.

God who remembers. In accordance with this the command for repetition may be translated: 'This do, *that God may remember me.*'

How is this to be understood? Here an old passover prayer is illuminating. On passover evening a prayer (*y'lh wyb'*) is inserted into the third benediction of the grace after the meal, a prayer which asks God *to remember the Messiah.*[1] The wording of this prayer has been transmitted with unusual accuracy (it is practically the same in all the rites)[2] and it may go back in essence to the time of Jesus.[3] It runs: 'Our God and God of our fathers, may there arise, and come, and come unto, be seen, accepted, heard, recollected and remembered, the remembrance of us and the recollection of us, and the remembrance of our fathers, and the *remembrance of the Messiah, son of David, thy servant* (*zikron mašiaḥ ben Dawid 'abdeka*), and the remembrance of Jerusalem thy holy city, and the remembrance of all thy people, the house of Israel. May their remembrance come before thee, for rescue, goodness. . . .'[4] In this very common prayer, which is also used on other festival days,[5] God is petitioned at every passover concerning 'the remembrance of the Messiah', i.e. concerning the appearance of the Messiah, which means the bringing about of the *parousia.* We shall see[6] how very strongly this petition that God may 'remember' the Messiah has influenced and even determined the whole passover festival: every passover celebration concluded with the jubilant antiphonal choir which one day would greet the Messiah at his entry into Jerusalem. Consequently the command for repetition may be understood as: 'This do, that God may remember me': *God remembers the Messiah in that he causes the kingdom to break in by the parousia.*

It is in this way that Paul already understood the ἀνάμνησις commandment, and his words have special weight in that they represent the oldest interpretation of the commandment which we possess. After quoting the liturgical formula, I Cor. 11.23–25, Paul continues:

[1] The prayer is to be found in all the countless editions of the passover *haggadah.* In the Schocken Books edition, New York, 1953, it is on pp. 63f.

[2] Elbogen, *Gottesdienst*, 125.

[3] Elbogen, *Gottesdienst*, 125: 'since the days of the first Tannaites'. Elbogen gives the evidence for this on p. 533.

[4] Quoted from *The Passover Haggadah*, Schocken Books, New York, 1953, 63.

[5] S. R. Hirsch, *Siddur tephillot Yiśrael. Israels Gebete*[3], Frankfurt a. M., 1921, 146, 274, 330, 396, 598, 624, 657, 684. Cf. H. Kosmala, 'Das tut zu meinem Gedächtnis', *Novum Testamentum* 4 (1960), 85.

[6] See below, pp. 256ff.

'For as often as you eat this bread and drink this cup, you proclaim the Lord's death until he comes' (v. 26). We must first clarify the relationship between v. 26 and the liturgical formula. Both the resumptive 'as often as' (ὁσάκις) and above all the 'for' (γάρ) show that v. 26 is directly related to the preceding sentence, i.e. to the ἀνάμνησις-commandment. 'The Lord has commanded the repetition εἰς ἀνάμνησιν and you are indeed fulfilling this command;[1] for at every celebration of the Lord's supper you proclaim his death.' *The ἀνάμνησις commandment is therefore fulfilled by the proclamation of the death of Jesus at the Lord's supper.* So everything depends upon how the 'proclamation of the Lord's death' is to be understood. That it is a verbal proclamation, and what the probable form of this proclamation was, we saw above, pp. 106ff. The content of the 'proclamation of the Lord's death' has to be deduced from the subordinate clause 'until he comes' (ἄχρι οὗ ἔλθῃ).[2] This clause is not a simple time reference, but ἔλθῃ is a prospective subjunctive which, as appears from the omission of ἄν, has a certain affinity with the final clause[3] and may therefore be freely translated 'until (matters have developed to the point at which) he comes', 'until (the goal is reached, that) he comes'. Actually, in the New Testament ἄχρι οὗ with the aorist subjunctive without ἄν regularly introduces a reference to reaching the eschatological goal, Rom. 11.25; I Cor. 15.25; Luke 21.24. 'Until he comes' apparently alludes to the *maranatha* of the liturgy[4] with which the community prays for the eschatological coming of the Lord. This means that the death of the Lord is not proclaimed at every celebration of the meal as a past event but as an eschatological event, as the beginning of the New Covenant.[5] The proclamation of the death of Jesus is not therefore intended to call to the remembrance of the community the event of the Passion; rather this proclamation expresses the vicarious death of Jesus as the beginning of the salvation time and prays for the coming of the consummation. *As often as the death of the Lord is proclaimed at the Lord's supper, and the maranatha rises upwards, God is reminded of the unfulfilled climax of the work of salvation* 'until (the goal is reached, that) he comes'. Paul has therefore under-

---

[1] In view of the preceding γάρ, καταγγέλλετε must be taken as indicative; before the γάρ we must therefore again (cf. p. 211 n. 4) supply the thought which is to be supported by it.

[2] Cf. *'d bw'* 1QS 9.11, and *'d 'mwd* CD 12.23; 20.1.

[3] Blass-Debrunner, §383.2.

[4] J. Schniewind, ἀγγελία κτλ., *TWNT* I (1933), 70 n. 25.

[5] Schlatter, *Paulus*, 325.

stood the ἀνάμνησις as the eschatological remembrance of God that is to be realized in the *parousia*.

Paul does not stand alone in this eschatological understanding of the ἀνάμνησις-commandment; it is supported by all the other texts to which we have access. In this connection we must first consider the meal prayers of the Didache. It is significant that the grace after the ordinary meal leads up to a prayer for the eschatological remembrance of God: 'Remember, Lord, thy Church to deliver it from all evil and to perfect it in thy love; and gather it together from the four winds, (even the Church) that has been sanctified, into thy kingdom which thou hast prepared for her' (10.5). The community celebrating the meal petitions God that he may 'remember' his Church, in that he grants her the consummation and gathers her into the kingdom which he has prepared for her. Still more important is the fact that the prayer calls immediately following, which lead up to the celebration of the Eucharist, are absolutely and completely directed towards the *parousia*:

'May the Lord (Coptic) come and this world pass away.
Amen.
Hosanna to the house (Coptic) of David.[1]
If any man is holy, let him come; if any man is not, let him repent.
Maranatha.
Amen (10.6).'

At every celebration of the Eucharist therefore the community prays for the coming of the Lord, indeed it anticipates the blessed hour by greeting the returning Lord with the jubilant Hosanna, the cry of salvation at the *parousia*.[2] With a similar intent, Luke speaks of the 'gladness' (ἀγαλλίασις), the eschatological jubilation, which ruled the mealtimes of the earliest community (Acts 2.46).

To summarize my argument: it seems to me certain that the command for repetition may no longer be interpreted on the basis of hellenistic presuppositions, but must be interpreted against a Palestinian background. 'In remembrance of me' can then scarcely mean

---

[1] 'The house of David' is not, as Audet, *La Didachè*, 422, erroneously supposes, the temple, which is never called 'the house of David', but the ruling house. 'Hosanna to the house of David' therefore means 'Hosanna to (the descendant of) the ruling house!', 'Hosanna to the Messiah!'

[2] See below, pp. 258ff. For the history of the hosanna greeting and the change of its significance from a cry for help to an acclamation, see below, p. 260 n. 4.

'that *you* may remember me', but most probably 'that *God* may remember me'.[1] This means that the command to repeat the rite is not a summons to the disciples to preserve the memory of Jesus and be vigilant ('repeat the breaking of bread so that you may not forget me'), but it is an eschatologically oriented instruction: 'Keep joining yourselves together as the redeemed community by the table rite, that in this way God may be daily implored to bring about the consummation in the *parousia*.' *By coming together daily for table fellowship in the short period of time before the* parousia *and by confessing in this way Jesus as their Lord*, the disciples *represent the initiated salvation work before God and they pray for its consummation*.[2]

If this is correct, then the question of authenticity must be raised anew. In any case a reference to the *parousia* is much nearer to Jesus than would be a hellenistic foundation formula. But we can say more than this. We shall see in the next section that the liturgical anticipation of the *parousia* was a regular part of the passover ritual. The anticipation of the antiphonal choir at the *parousia*, with which the passover celebration ended, is an illustration of the way in which God could be petitioned, in a liturgical rite, to remember the Messiah. What Israel did annually at the passover meal the disciples should do daily. This close relationship between the command for repetition and the passover ritual makes it very probable that the command goes back to Jesus himself, and this is supported by the considerations mentioned above, pp. 250f.

THE ACTS OF PRAISE

(a) *The 'Hallel'*

The saying of grace after the meal was followed immediately by the singing of the *hallel*, Pss. 114[3]–118 (Mark 14.26 par.). It was sung antiphonally: one member of the table fellowship recited the text,

---

[1] Cf. LXX, Ps. 131(132).1: μνήσθητι, κύριε, τοῦ Δαυιδ, 'Lord, remember David'.

[2] A. D. Müller, Leipzig, remarks on this: 'The objective theological content of the Lord's supper celebration and the activity of the community are not mutually exclusive, but rather one demands the other. Precisely because God himself is the acting subject of the service in the vicarious death of the servant of God for the "many", the world's people, the community is included in the sacramental accomplishment not only as object but also as subject with full responsibility.' (Letter dated May 13, 1950.)

[3] See above, p. 55 n. 1.

the others responded after each half-verse with Hallelujah.[1] Jesus'
great knowledge of the Bible warrants the assumption that he himself
sang the *hallel*.[2] However that may be, whether he recited it or only
joined in the prayers and responses, we know the prayers with which
Jesus concluded the Last Supper. *They are all prayers of thanksgiving.*
They praise him who delivered Israel from the Egyptians, before
whose presence the earth trembles (Ps. 114). They praise him as the
one living God, in whom the people of God put their trust; and who
blesses those who fear him, and who will be blessed for evermore
(Ps. 115). They promise to the merciful redeemer, who has delivered
the living from death, sacrifices of thanksgiving and the payment of
vows in the presence of all his people (Ps. 116). They call upon the
heathen to join in praise (Ps. 117). And they conclude with a prayer
expressing the thanksgiving and jubilation of the festal congregation:
'O give thanks to the Lord, for he is good; his steadfast love endures
for ever' (Ps. 118.1). 'Out of my distress has the Lord heard me' (v.
5). Now the songs of jubilation resound: 'I shall not die, but I shall
live, and recount the deeds of the Lord' (v. 17). 'The rejected stone
has become the chief cornerstone through God's marvellous doing'
(vv. 22f.). 'Blessed be in the name of the Lord he who comes' (v. 26).
To thee will I give thanks: 'Give thanks to the Lord, for he is good;
yea, his steadfast love endures for ever' (v. 29). *These were the words*
in which Jesus prayed.

(b) The antiphonal choir at the 'parousia'

From numerous individual witnesses we learn that the exegesis
of the *hallel* in late Judaism was predominantly eschatological-
Messianic.[3] The closing section of the *hallel* in particular was given a

---

[1] Suk. 3.10, cf. Soṭ. 5.4; j. Soṭ. 5.20c.9ff.; b. Soṭ. 30b; b. Suk. 38b. According
to j. Shab. 16.15c.39, this resulted in a 123-fold Hallelujah. The response with
Hallelujah seems to be the oldest (Elbogen, *Gottesdienst*, 496). In the synagogue
service the *hallel* was at some places recited in such a way that the congregation
repeated the beginning of the verses (Tos. Soṭ. 6.3 [303.19]; b. Suk. 38b). Tos. Pes.
10.7 (172.22) (repetition of the last words of each line) is applicable only in the case
of children reciting.

[2] It often happened that no member of the table fellowship was able to recite
the *hallel*, Tos. Pes. 10.8 (172.24).

[3] Ps. 113.2 — The praise of God in the world to come (Midr. Ps. 113, §4).
113.9 — Zion in the End time (Pesiḳ. 141a).
115.1 — The suffering of the Messianic times (b. Pes. 118a); war against Gog and Magog (*ibid.*).
116.1 — The days of the Messiah (j. Ber. 2.4d.48f.).
116.1f. — Israel's prayer for redemption (b. Pes. 118b).

Messianic interpretation. It is worthwhile to look more closely at the interpretation given to this part of the *hallel*, as this interpretation has been preserved in the Midrash on the Psalms.[1]

Midr. Ps. 118, § 22, interprets Ps. 118.24 ('This is the day which the Lord hath made') as referring to the day of redemption which ends all enslavement for ever, i.e. to the Messianic redemption. This eschatological interpretation of 'the day which the Lord hath made' (v. 24) is the point of departure for the exposition of the remaining verses of the Psalm (25–29) in the Midrash: they depict the high point of the events which will take place on the day of redemption.

'From inside the walls, the men of Jerusalem will say,
   "We beseech Thee, O Lord, save now!" (v. 25a).
And from outside, the men of Judah will say,
   "We beseech Thee, O Lord, make us now to prosper!" (v. 25b).

From inside, the men of Jerusalem will say,
   "Blessed be he that cometh IN the name of the Lord!" (v. 26a).
And from outside, the men of Judah will say,
   "We bless you OUT of the house of the Lord!" (v. 26b).

From inside, the men of Jerusalem will say,
   "The Lord is God and hath given us light" (v. 27a).
And from outside, the men of Judah will say,
   "Order the festival procession with boughs, even unto the horns of the altar!" (v. 27b).

116.4	Saving of the souls of the pious from Gehenna (b. Pes. 118a).
116.9	Resurrection of the dead (b. Pes. 118a); the eschatological meal (Ex. R. 25.10 on 16.4).
116.13	David's table-blessing after the meal of the salvation time (b. Pes. 119b; Ex. R. 25.10 on 16.4).
118.7	The last judgment (Midr. Ps. 118, § 10).
118.10–12	War against Gog and Magog (Midr. Ps. 118, § 12).
118.15	Beginning of the Messianic times (Pesiḳ. 132a).
118.24	The Messianic redemption (Midr. Ps. 118, § 22).
118.25–29	The antiphonal choir at the Parousia (*ibid.*, see above, pp. 257f.).
118.27a	God the light of salvation time (Midr. Ps. 36, § 6).
118.27b	The days of Gog and Magog (j. Ber. 2.4d.49).
118.28	The future world (j. Ber. 2.4d.50).

[1] [The English version by W. G. Braude, *The Midrash on Psalms* (Yale Judaica Series 13), 2 vols., New Haven, Conn., 1959, has been utilized in the translation. Transl.]

EWJ–R

From inside, the men of Jerusalem will say,
   "Thou art my God, and I will give thanks unto Thee!" (v. 28a).
And from outside, the men of Judah will say,
   "Thou art my God, I will exalt Thee" (v. 28b).

Then the men of Jerusalem and the men of Judah, together, opening their mouths in praise of the Holy One, blessed be He, will say:

   "O give thanks unto the Lord, for He is good, for His mercy endureth for ever" (v. 29).'[1]

The Midrash depicts for us a vivid and moving scene. In the eschatological hour the inhabitants of Jerusalem are standing on the pinnacles of the holy city, with the temple priests, and descending from the Mount of Olives the Messianic King draws near at the head of the pilgrim caravan from Judea. The Jerusalemites and the arriving pilgrims greet one another by singing *a hymn as an antiphonal choir*, using the words from Ps. 118.25–28, until at the climax both groups unite in the praise of God in v. 29.

This eschatological exegesis of Ps. 118.24–29 which we find in the Midrash on Psalms is not dated. But the New Testament shows that it certainly *goes back to the days of Jesus*, and that it was the common property of the people. For when the evangelists report that at his entry into Jerusalem Jesus was greeted with Ps. 118.25f., this not only presupposes that these verses were eschatologically interpreted, as in the Midrash, but also that they were understood as acclamations to hail the entering Messiah. Indeed, it is possible that the interpretation given to Ps. 118.24–29 in the Midrash has influenced the accounts of the Triumphal Entry even down to details. Thus it is noticeable that Mark 11.9; Matt. 21.9; John 12.13 agree in quoting the Psalm with the omission of v. 25b ('Hosanna' [v. 25a] is followed immediately by 'Blessed be he who comes' [26a]), and this could be due to the fact that the Midrash ascribes the two quoted acclamations (vv. 25a, 26a) to the choir of Jerusalemites and the omitted half-verse 25b, on the other hand, to the choir of those accompanying the Messiah. True, Mark 11.9; Matt. 21.9 ascribe both to 'those who went before and those who followed', but according to John 12.12f.

---

[1] Midr. Ps. 118, § 22 (ET II, 245).

it is the crowd coming out of Jerusalem to meet Jesus which calls them out, just as according to Matt. 23.39 (Luke 13.35) it is the Jerusalemites who will call 'Blessed be he who comes. . . .' But quite apart from this, the account of the Triumphal Entry shows that the interpretation of Ps. 118.25–29 in terms of the choirs at the entry of the Messiah into Jerusalem is pre-New Testament.[1]

The evangelists further report that *Jesus himself* was very much concerned with Ps. 118 and that he also interpreted it Messianically. In the saying concerning the rejected building stone which God makes the key stone (Ps. 118.22) he is said to have seen a prophecy of his own death and exaltation (Mark 8.31 par., cf. 12.10f. par.; Luke 17.25). That Jesus indeed found in Ps. 118 how God would guide his Messiah through suffering to glory, through chastisement to the opened door of salvation, and at the same time the ceaseless praise of God at the time of the consummation, is made probable by the fact that according to Matt. 23.39 (par. Luke 13.35b) he knew the dynamic interpretation given to Ps. 118.24–29 in the Midrash quoted above. When we read Matt. 23.39 (par. Luke 13.35b): 'For I tell you, you will not see me again, until you say, "Blessed be he who comes in the name of the Lord" ', not only here, as in the Midrash, is Ps. 118.26a understood by Jesus as a Messianic acclamation in the eschatological hour, but also the half-line is put by Jesus, as in the Midrash, into the mouths of the inhabitants of Jerusalem. This observation throws new light upon the context. Matt. 23.37–39 par. Luke 13.34f. constitutes a unity: the verses are held together by the address to Jerusalem. They are in *Ḳina* rhythm (3 + 2 stresses) as far as the final verse we just quoted, the metre of which is determined by the scriptural quote (4 stresses).[2] The change of rhythm corresponds to a significant change in content. Jesus' woe over the city which murders the prophets is drowned out by the choral acclamation at the *parousia*: 'Blessed be in the name of the Lord he who comes.' Jesus is certain that the promise of God will be fulfilled and that

---

[1] Targ. Ps. 118.23–29 and b. Pes. 119a (R. Jonathan, c. 220) both show that the division of half-verses at the end of Ps. 118 into calls and responses which we find in Midr. Ps. 118, § 22, on vv. 25ff., was an established exegetical tradition. Both of these two witnesses relate the antiphonal calling to the historical situation of the anointing of David as king (I Sam. 16.13), but this could be a secondary reinterpretation arising out of anti-Christian polemic. The fact that it is none the less related to David shows the influence of the older Messianic interpretation.

[2] C. F. Burney, *The Poetry of our Lord*, Oxford, 1925, 146.

even in the blind and obdurate city God will arouse a remnant which will greet the coming one, the returning one[1] in the name of God.[2]

We can see from Did. 10.6 that the *earliest community* also understood the Hosanna acclamation (Ps. 118.25) in terms of the jubilation at the *parousia*. The cry 'Hosanna to the house[3] of David' is part of the ancient liturgical acclamation which introduced the Eucharist, with which the celebrating community anticipated the return of its Lord.[4] How natural it was to link the Hosanna acclamation with the *parousia* can be seen from the report of Hegesippus concerning the stoning of James, the Lord's brother, despite its legendary character. This says that at the passover when James, from the pinnacle of the temple, made a public confession to Jesus as the Son of Man who would come, many from the crowd enthusiastically responded with the cry: 'Hosanna to the son of David.'[5]

The results of this investigation are: the interpretation of Ps. 118. 25–29 in terms of the antiphonal choir at the *parousia* as in the Midrash goes back to the time of Jesus, it was common property, and Jesus also understood these verses of the Psalm in this way. All this is of direct significance for our understanding of the reports of Jesus' last meal. The ritual of the passover meal closed with Ps. 118. Thus the end of the Psalm was given a special liturgical emphasis, either by the leader repeating vv. 21–29[6] or by the members of the fellowship (who up to that point had responded 'Hallelujah' to each half-verse[7]) repeating vv. 1a, 25a, 25b, and replying to the first part of v. 26a with the second part of that half-

---

[1] Compound verbs are unknown in Semite languages. In the gospels Heb. *ba*, Aram. *ata*, Greek ἔρχεσθαι mean both 'to come' and 'to come again' (e.g. Matt. 9.1, ἦλθεν, 'he came again'; John 9.7, ἦλθεν, 'he came back').

[2] 'In the name of the Lord' probably is to be taken with 'blessed be', not with 'he who comes'; so LXX, Ps. 128(129).8; Ecclus 45.15; cf. Gen. 27.7.

[3] So the Coptic version. See above, p. 254.

[4] On 'Hosanna' as jubilant acclamation see J. Jeremias, 'Die Muttersprache des Evangelisten Matthäus', ZNW 50 (1959), 270–4. The change of the word from a cry for help to an acclamation becomes understandable when one realizes that the liturgical exclamation 'Hosanna' was a strange word to the majority of people in Jesus' day, because the root *yšʿ*, 'help', is completely unknown in Aramaic.

[5] Hegesippus, quoted by Eusebius, *Hist. Eccl.* 2.23.14. Further evidence from the ancient Church is given by E. Werner, ' "Hosanna" in the Gospels', *JBL* 45 (1946), 97–112, especially 116 n. 47; 117 n. 50.

[6] As today in all passover rituals. The custom is old: Tos. Pes. 10.9 (172.26). Cf. Elbogen, *Gottesdienst*, 496.

[7] See above, pp. 255f. and 256 n. 1.

verse.[1] Already from the liturgical emphasis upon the end of Ps. 118 the conclusion can be drawn that this was the high point of the *hallel*, indeed of the whole passover ritual: These verses were an anticipation of the antiphonal choir with which the Messiah would be greeted and accompanied by his community on the day when he would come. This anticipation shows, as does no other piece of evidence, that at the time of Jesus the Passover was in no way celebrated only as a memorial meal but at the same time, indeed primarily, as a representation of the hour of redemption.

Jesus also, with his disciples, ended the passover meal with the second part of the *hallel* (Mark 14.26 par. Matt. 26.30, 'when they had sung a hymn') in accordance with the ritual. The end of Ps. 118 forms the last prayer that he prayed before he began his journey to Gethsemane. The establishment of this point, that he ended the last meal with his disciples by anticipating the jubilation of the antiphonal choir which would greet him at his return, opens the way to understanding the deepest meaning of this hour and with it of the Lord's supper altogether: *it is an anticipatory gift of the consummation.*

In this way the manifold ideas combine into a very simple unity. This Messianic meal is distinguished from the series of Messianic meals which began with Peter's confession[2] by the fact that it is the passover meal, and at the same time the last, the farewell meal. The Messiah will die and his death will be the opening act of the eschatological πειρασμός, the great time of temptation which will come over all the earth (Mark 14.38). In this situation all that Jesus says and does is directed towards one purpose, to assure the disciples of their possession of salvation. *Everything is embraced in this one purpose of assurance.* When he impresses upon his disciples the imminence of the Kingdom of God by means of his intercessory fasting for Israel; when he lays upon their hearts the effective prayer for the consummation in the command for repetition; when he, in anticipation of the consummation, makes them partakers of the atoning power of his death by their eating and drinking, and in this way includes them already in the victory of the rule of God—all this is a pledge and an assurance, a summons to thanksgiving for the gifts of God. *As surely as they eat the bread* which Jesus breaks for them *and drink the wine* over which he spoke the word referring to his outpoured blood, *so surely the 'for many'*

---

[1] b. Suk. 38b.
[2] See above, p. 205.

of his dying and the 'with you' of the future eucharistic fellowship on a trans-formed earth is valid also for them.

To put it quite simply: table fellowship with Jesus is an anticipatory gift of the final consummation. Even now God's lost children may come home and sit down at their Father's table.

INDEXES

INDEX OF MODERN AUTHORS

INDEX OF REFERENCES

OLD TESTAMENT

NEW TESTAMENT